T0375251

BLOOD
SACRIFICES

Front Cover Image: Santa Muerte Shrine by the roadside in Acuña, Coahuila, Mexico. Most of Coahuila was initially controlled by the Cartel del Golfo (CDG) and after Los Zetas split off from the CDG in February 2010 this shrine and many others like it appeared in major cities throughout Coahuila marking Los Zetas territory. It was subsequently demolished by Mexican authorities in June 2013. Photo courtesy of Chivis Martinez, *Borderland Beat*.

BLOOD SACRIFICES

*Violent Non-State Actors and
Dark Magico-Religious Activities*

EDITED BY ROBERT J. BUNKER

A Terrorism Research Center Book

BLOOD SACRIFICES
Violent Non-State Actors and Dark Magico-Religious Activities
—A Terrorism Research Center Book

iUniverse books may be ordered through booksellers or by contacting:

iUniverse
1663 Liberty Drive
Bloomington, IN 47403
www.iuniverse.com
1-800-Authors (1-800-288-4677)

ISBN: 978-1-4917-9196-7 (sc)
ISBN: 978-1-4917-9197-4 (e)

Print information available on the last page.

iUniverse rev. date: 07/08/2016

About the Terrorism Research Center

The Terrorism Research Center (TRC) is non-profit think tank focused on investigating and researching global terrorism issues through multi-disciplinary collaboration amongst a group of international experts. Originally founded as a commercial entity in 1996, the TRC was an independent institute dedicated to the research of terrorism, information warfare and security, critical infrastructure protection, homeland security, and other issues of low-intensity political violence and gray-area phenomena. Over the course of 15 years, the TRC has conducted research, analysis, and training on a wide range of counterterrorism and homeland security issues.

* * * * *

First established on April 19, 1996, the year anniversary of the Oklahoma City terrorist bombing, the TRC operated for 15 years as a commercial entity providing research, analysis, and training on issues of terrorism and international security. The three original co-founders, Matthew Devost, Brian Houghton, and Neal Pollard, are reconstituting a new board of directors, comprised of researchers, first responders, and academic and professional experts. "The TRC had an incredible legacy as a commercial company," says Matthew Devost. "We believe there is still a strong need to continue the research and collaboration on such critical topics in the public's best interest."

From 1996 through 2010, the TRC contributed to international counterterrorism and homeland security initiatives such as Project Responder and the Responder Knowledge Base, Terrorism Early Warning Groups, Project Pediatric Preparedness, Global Fusion Center, and the "Mirror Image" training program. These long-standing programs leveraged an international network of specialists from government, industry, and academia. Reconstituting TRC as a non-profit will help establish the next generation of programs, research, and training to combat the emerging international security issues.

"Thousands of researchers utilized the TRC knowledge base on a daily basis, says Brian Houghton, "Our intent is to open the dialogue, provide valuable counterterrorism resources, and advance the latest thinking in counterterrorism for the public good."

"We want to put the 15-year legacy and goodwill of TRC to continuing benefit for the public, rather than focus on a specific business model," says Neal Pollard. "TRC was founded in the wake of the 1995 Oklahoma City bombing and made its most significant contributions to the nation and the world after the attacks of September 11, 2001. Now that the War on Terrorism has evolved and the United States is entering a new era of transnational threats, the TRC will maintain its familiar role as the vanguard of next-generation research into these emerging threats."

For more information visit www.terrorism.org

The views expressed in this anthology are those of the author(s) and do not necessarily reflect the official policy or position of the Department of the Army, the Department of Defense, the Federal Bureau of Investigation, the Department of Justice, or the U.S. Government, or any other U.S. armed service, intelligence or law enforcement agency, or local or state government.

Contents

Acronyms

AQ	Al Qaeda
AQIM	Al Qaeda in the Islamic Maghreb
AQLIM	Al Qaeda in the Land of the Islamic Maghreb
ARUF	Armed Forces Revolutionary Council
BBC	British Broadcasting Corporation
BC	Before Christ
BLO	Beltrán Leyva Organization
BRIU	Behavioral Research and Instruction Unit
BSU	Behavioral Science Unit
CA	California
CAR	Central African Republic
CBS	Columbia Broadcasting System
CD	Compac Disc
CDF	Civil Defense Forces
CDG	Cartel del Golfo
CE	Christian Era
CGI	Computer Generated Imagery
CIDA	Contras Independientes de Acapulco
CJNG	Cartel de Jalisco Nueva Generation
CR	Community of the Resurrection
CVNSA	Criminally Violent Non-State Actor
DoD	Department of Defense
DRC	Democratic Republic of the Congo
DTO	Drug Trafficking Organization
ECOMOG	Economic Community of West African States Monitoring Group

ETA	Euskadi Ta Askatasuna

FARC	Fuerzas Armadas Revolucionarias de Colombia
FBI	Federal Bureau of Investigation
Fr.	Friar
Frelimo	Frente de Libertaçâo de Moçambique

HAMAS	Harakat al-Muqāwama al-Islāmiyya
HSM	Holy Spirit Movement

ICC	International Criminal Court
IHL	International Humanitarian Law
IRA	Irish Republican Army
IS	Islamic State
ISI	Islamic State in Iraq
ISIS	Islamic State of Iraq and Syria

JTJ	Jam'at al-Tawhid wal-Jihad

LFM	La Familia Michoacana
LRA	Lord's Resistance Army
LSD	Lysergic Acid Diethylamide
Lt.	Lieutenant
Lt. Col.	Lieutenant Colonel
LTTE	Liberation Tigers of Tamil Eelam

NAFTA	North American Free Trade Agreement
NFPL	National Patriotic Front of Liberia
NGO	Non-Governmental Organization
NRM/A	National Resistance Movement/Army

OPFOR	Opposing Force

PAN	Partido Acción Nacional
Ph.D.	Philosophiae Doctor (Doctor of Philosophy)
PKK	Partiya Karkerên Kurdistanê

POB   Predictability of Behavior
PRI   Partido Revolucionario Institucional
PSI   Praeger Security International

Renamo   Resistência Nacional Moçambicana
RUF   Revolutionary United Front
RULES   Ritualistic Understanding for Law Enforcement
           Agencies

SA   Special Agent
SAS   Special Air Service
SEAL   Sea, Air, Land
SLA   Sierra Leone Army
SME   Subject Matter Expert
SUR 13   Surenos Thirteen
SWAY   Survey of War Affected Youth

TCOs   Transnational Criminal Organizations
TTP   Tactics, Techniques, and Procedures

UK   United Kingdom
UN   United Nations
UNCHR   United Nations High Commissioner for Refugees
U.S.   United States

VNSA   Violent Non-State Actor
VSA   Violent State Actor

ybp   Years Before Present

ZANLA   Zimbabwe African National Liberation Army

Acknowledgments

The initial formulation of this research project began in March 2013 and continued to grow with the addition of more and more contributors as the need to fulfill the recognized research gaps in this endeavor became apparent. For the initial contributors to the project—Marc W.D. Tyrrell, Paul Rexton Kan, Pamela Ligouri Bunker, Andrew Bringuel, II, and José de Arimatéia da Cruz—the *Blood Sacrifices* book has been a roughly three year intellectual saga. I would like to deeply thank them for sticking by me through thick and thin during this exploratory research endeavor into violent non-state actors (VNSAs) and their interrelationship with dark magico-religious activity and the supporting themes related to radicalism, from a terrorist and insurgent analytical perspective, and illicit narcotics utilization. For the second and third wave of contributors—Lisa J. Campbell, Mark Safranski, Charles Cameron, Dawn Perlmutter, Tony M. Kail, Pauletta Otis, and Alma Keshavarz—I wish to thank them for pitching in to support the initial contributor team and myself and also accepting their exposure to the potential disapproval of the mainstream Western intellectual academy. For, as noted by Dawn Perlmutter in the Preface, even attempting to acknowledge the existence of blood sacrifice, particularly human sacrifice, in contemporary scholarly research is itself a Herculean feat given the dominance of secular, utilitarian, and behaviorist biases.

The Terrorism Research Center (TRC), under whose auspices this book is being published, is also acknowledged for its support of this research endeavor. Its three founders, Matthew Devost, Brian Houghton, and Neal Pollard, who have reconstituted this group into a non-profit entity, have had a long history of supporting US counterterrorism and early warning efforts. Their legacy projects include the Terrorism Early Warning Group Expansion Project, which predated the intelligence fusion centers established throughout the US post-9/11, and Mirror Image Training, which provided an immersive Jihadi terrorist training camp experience. It is my honor to have this work be my 4ᵗʰ TRC book published.

I would also like to thank my wife Pamela Ligouri Bunker, also a contributor to this book, for providing her considerable editing skills to keep me honest concerning my edits of the numerous contributions contained within it. Further, I'd like to single out Chivis Martinez over at *Borderland Beat* for providing the Santa Muerte shrine photo utilized on the cover of the book as well as a number of the images used within the supporting virtual image gallery. Chivis and her blog's contributors living in Mexico are under constant threat of certain torture and death if their true identities are ever discovered by the drug gangs and cartels that are waging a criminal—if not spiritual insurgency—against our southern neighbor. They imperil themselves with the knowledge that standing up for Mexico's future is worth the daily risk they have accepted for themselves and their loved ones.

Dr. Robert J. Bunker
March 2016
Claremont, CA

Preface

ANALYZING SACRIFICIAL VIOLENCE

Dawn Perlmutter

"The great thinkers who have defined man as an *animal rationale* were not empiricists, nor did they ever intend to give an empirical account of human nature. By this definition they were expressing rather a fundamental moral imperative. Reason is a very inadequate term with which to comprehend the forms of man's cultural life in all their richness and variety. But all these forms are symbolic forms. Hence, instead of defining man as an *animal rationale*, we should define him as *animal symbolicum*." (p. 145)

—Ernst Cassirer, *An Essay on Man*

"Aside from deaths from automobile accidents and murders committed in the course of robberies and other predatory crimes, the modal criminal homicide is an impassioned attempt to perform a sacrifice to embody one or another version of the "Good." (p. 12)

—Jack Katz, *Seductions of Crime*

Blood sacrifice has been a widespread and complex phenomenon throughout history and across cultures. Sacrificial practices involving the killing of humans and animals and/or the use of the flesh, blood, or bones of their bodies for ritual purposes dates back at least twenty thousand years. The concept of blood sacrifice and magico-religious activities has traditionally been studied as a historical inquiry in the academic disciplines of anthropology, religion, philosophy and sociology. This book is unique in several significant aspects. First, the concept of human sacrifice is acknowledged as an active contemporary phenomenon. Second, blood sacrifice is not studied as a theoretical endeavor. Significantly, the authors are conducting applied research with real life implications, specifically the study of sacrifice as it pertains to violent non-state actors. Finally, the authors utilize a variety of unique symbolic and anthropological methodologies that analyze violent crime in the context of culture, symbol systems, religious experience, ritual, mythology, magical thinking and other atypical approaches to criminology. The result is a collection of important essays that demonstrate that research into historical acts of sacrifice is remarkably pertinent to brutal acts committed by violent non-state actors.

The acknowledgment that blood sacrifice, particularly human sacrifice, actively occurs in the 21st century is a pivotal triumph in scholarly research. Twenty years ago, this book could not have been published. In most universities, think tanks, and government research facilities, characterizing any type of murder as sacrificial was viewed at best as a secondary motive and at worst as junk science. Many colleges and other prominent institutions still hold this view. Incidents involving beheadings, cannibalism, dismemberment, mutilation, torture, and a variety of other blood rituals are typically interpreted as either a form of psychological warfare, satanic panic, war crime, drug induced mania, or some specific form of sociopathy or psychopathy. The resistance to interpreting violence as a form of blood sacrifice is based on the Western philosophical tradition of rational scientific inquiry. Subsequently, the methodological foundations of criminology, sociology, and behavioral science are predicated on a logical, rational psychological worldview. Since the principle underlying theories of criminology and behavioral science are primarily responsible for the current accepted classifications and categories of violent crime, investigation and analysis has an inherent Western bias. Whereas alternative theories of violence, such as blood sacrifice, are predicated on magical religious worldviews. These philosophical differences in interpretation have substantial implications for research, intelligence analysis, homicide investigations, military strategies, and anti-drug trafficking approaches.

In conventional behavioral research, the analysis of violent crime, particularly murder, has been studied, categorized, and classified into types of psychopathology based on classifications of agreed upon designations of deviant behavior. These methods have attempted to identify the characteristics that predispose offenders to violence such as specific personality disorders, childhood abuse, in addition to social, economic, and other factors. The established criteria for deviant behavior and its corresponding typologies are often applied in criminal investigations regardless of an offender's culture, belief system, ideology, or stated intention. This is due to the fact that violence is interpreted from the viewpoint of the observer. In cultural anthropology, there are two types of research referred to as 'etic' and 'emic'. An etic analysis is an extrinsic approach that views cultures or subcultures from the perspective of the observer, an outsider attempting to be culturally neutral. The problem with an etic approach is that, when researchers interpret the meaning of violent incidents in an unfamiliar culture or subculture, they view the phenomenon in terms of universals; interpretations are based on the premise that all people have certain beliefs in common. An emic analysis is an intrinsic approach that views cultures and subcultures from the perspective of the subject, from the natives' point of view. In an emic approach, when researchers interpret the meaning of violent incidents in an unfamiliar culture or subculture, they view the phenomenon in terms of particulars: interpretations are based on the premise that beliefs are particular to that culture, and hence may seem incomprehensible to an outsider. Emic methodologies that take into consideration cross cultural, subcultural and magical religious concepts as the basis for their analytical criteria provide unique insights into seemingly inexplicable acts of violent crime.

A classic example of an emic approach to homicide investigation was one of the few acknowledged contemporary cases of human sacrifice in a Western country. On September 21, 2001, the torso of a six year old black child was pulled out of the River Thames next to the Globe Theatre in London. The body was dismembered, decapitated, exsanguinated, and dressed in bright orange shorts. A detailed analysis of his lower intestine revealed a highly unusual mix of plant extracts, traces of the toxic calabar bean, and tiny clay pellets containing small particles of pure gold. Scotland Yard detectives used pioneering scientific forensic techniques to determine that the boy, dubbed Adam, was from a specific area in Nigeria. Radioactive isotopes in the boy's bones matched rocks in his native Nigeria and the unusual plant extracts found in Adam's intestine were identified as growing only in the area around Benin City, capital of Edo. Further tests on the food in Adam's stomach and pollen in his lungs revealed that he had only been in Britain for a few days before he was murdered. It was determined that the orange shorts, the only clothing on his body, was exclusively sold in Woolworths in Germany and Austria. There were several forensic indicators that this was a ritual murder: 1) the severe trauma to the boys neck 2) the dismemberment of his head and limbs 3) the complete lack of blood in the boys body 4) the skilled precision of the incisions used to dismember the body 5) the disposal of his torso in a natural body of flowing water and 6) the unusual contents of his stomach. The forensic evidence established that Adam was ritually murdered and had recently arrived from Nigeria through Germany or Austria.

In an unprecedented effort, the Metropolitan Police conducted a cross cultural investigation that led them to Nigerian magico-religious beliefs, specifically African witchcraft traditions that involve the trafficking and ritual murder of children. This immediately resulted in more culturally specific interpretations of the forensic evidence. They discovered that the calabar bean is a West African poison often used in black magic rituals. They further discovered that Muti murder [Medicine murder] which is common in sub-Saharan Africa, involves the use of body parts for magical purposes as ingredients in rituals, concoctions, and magical potions and that the function of Muti Murder, which is used by Sangomas [traditional healers] in witchcraft, is to bring prosperity, protection, or power to the user. They learned that children, particularly African albino children, are targeted due to beliefs that their body parts are sacred and can transmit magical powers. Most disturbingly, they discovered that body parts taken from live victims are considered more potent and powerful. This explained the calabar poison in Adam's system. Calabar is a paralyzing agent, not an anesthetic, indicating that Adam would have been paralyzed but conscious when his throat was cut, increasing the efficacy of the sacrificial ritual. Just as different ingredients in a recipe are used for different purposes, certain body parts, plants, and other natural elements are used for particular goals. The traces of pure gold in Adam's stomach could have been used to attract wealth. Victims of Muti murder are often killed near or disposed of in rivers and other bodies of flowing water which functions both ritually, most likely as a form of purification, and as a counter forensic measure to hinder identification.

In March 2011, Adam was identified as 6-year old Ikpomwosa by Joyce Osagiede a Nigerian woman who said she cared for him in Germany prior to him being trafficked to London. In February 2013, she changed her story and claimed that Adam's real name was Patrick Erhabor and not Ikpomwosa. In 2002, Joyce Osagiede was living in Glasgow and was a person of interest in the case but, due to lack of evidence, was not arrested and deported back to Nigeria. An associate of hers, Kingsley Ojo, was arrested in London in 2002 by officers investigating the Adam case. In 2004, Ojo was sentenced to four and a half years in prison for human trafficking but there was no DNA evidence, linking him to the murder. After he served his sentence, Ojo was deported back to Nigeria. The 2001 ritual murder case remains unsolved but the investigation led to significant new investigative approaches to links between cold case homicides, human trafficking, and African magical traditions. Recognizing magico-religious motivations for the murder led to the re-examining of several homicide investigations in Europe and for acknowledging the possibility of sacrificial and other ritual violence from sub-Saharan Africa. Significantly, the Metropolitan Police applied emic anthropological methods that established that Adam's murder was not the result of a serial killer, sexual sadist, or psychopath but the result of magical ideologies that immigrated to London along with other local traditions. Similar to interpreting murder as a form of psychopathology, many scholars attribute the root causes of terrorism to societal issues such as poverty, oppression, alienation, and unresolved grievances. This is also the result of Western rational scientific methodologies that presume there are universal values; specifically, that all people share the same basic desires, particularly the love of life, pursuit of happiness, freedom, and democracy. A relevant example of how an emic analysis provides insights into seemingly inexplicable crimes is the case of Syed Rizwan Farook and his wife Tashfeen Malik who murdered fourteen people and seriously injured twenty-two on December 2, 2015 in San Bernardino, California. One of the most difficult aspects of the crime for the general public and many analysts to comprehend was how a young mother could be radicalized to commit mass murder and leave behind a six month old baby. A cultural analysis of the motivations for the San Bernardino mass murder from the subjects worldview must begin with the basic premise that the offenders were Islamist true believers. Additionally, analysts must abstain from any politically correct agendas or assumptions that would interfere with an objective analysis. From this ideological perspective, the killers would consider themselves to be good and righteous Muslims who were obligated to murder infidels (dis-believers). As Islamist true believers, the violence is justified as holy war (jihad) against evil. As martyrs, they believed they would go immediately to a higher level of paradise where they would be protected from the torments of the grave and, significantly, could intercede on behalf of the infant they left behind to join them in Paradise. The concept of intercession in Islamic martyrdom, which allows martyrs to intercede in Paradise for 70 relatives, is crucial in comprehending the sacrificial nature of the incident. In the context of their belief in Islamic martyrdom, Tashfeen Malik would be considered a good mother, one that sacrificed her life for her child. Farook would be considered a good father and son who gave up his life to intercede for his mother, daughter, and other family members in Paradise. They sacrificed their lives with the belief their family would be together again for eternity not just their temporary time on earth. Symbolic analysis of the San Bernardino massacre interprets the killings as a sacrificial ritual in the cause of Jihad (holy war), specifically a purification ritual that absolves prior sins, restores dignity, honor, and respect, and alleviates any feelings of humiliation and shame. The victims would be viewed as sacrificial animals and the killing as cleansing Islam of impurities. When murder or mass shootings are committed in the cause of Jihad, violence is transformed into a sacred ritual and sacred violence is always justified. The San Bernardino mass murder functioned to restore honor, serve vengeance, attain purity, save face, and achieve everlasting life in paradise. These beliefs do not meet any of the criteria for psychopathy, in fact a cultural emic analysis establishes that the killings were rational choices based on their religious worldview. Western methodologies habitually underestimate the ideological influence of belief systems that sanction murder and martyrdom as a form of worship. Hence, the denial of the significance of blood sacrifices as a root cause of violent crime and terrorism.

Theories that interpret crime as contemporary sacrificial violence have been challenged for several reasons: 1) behavioral science dominates the research as the accepted method of inquiry 2) resistance to acknowledging the existence of dark-magico religious activities, particularly as a motivation for crime and 3) little to no empirical evidence. Alternative theories of violence have been difficult to establish since evidence that magical and religious ideologies are the motivations for violent crime has been limited to rare emic interpretations of the crime and individual criminal's confessions that they committed murder as a blood sacrifice in the name of a specific ideology. This author can verify the difficulties encountered when applying alternative research methodologies to criminal cases. For the past 25 years, I have developed and applied interpretive symbolic anthropological methodologies to the investigation, analysis, and study of ritualistic crimes, including ritual homicides, many of which I have testified on as an expert witness. Murder cases have involved magico-religious ideologies that entailed torture, cannibalism, dismemberment, use of blood and body parts, flaying of skin, gouging out eyes, castration, exsanguination, and other violent acts in magical rites. Even with witness statements, physical evidence, and offender declarations, the denial of sacrifice as a motive for ritual murder has persisted throughout my career. Fortunately, advances in technology have changed the entire future scope of research into contemporary sacrificial violence. Cell phone and video camera images of thousands of ritual murders have supplied the missing empirical evidence substantiating the existence of contemporary blood sacrifice supporting magico-religious interpretations of murder, terrorism, and the root causes of violent crime.

Deplorably, many Western scholars still remain in denial that such barbaric savage violence occurs in the 21st century. Some have gone to great lengths to invalidate this new empirical evidence. In 2004, when Abu Musab al-Zarqawi leader of Al Qaeda in Iraq, the predecessor group to the Islamic State, began distributing beheading videos on the internet, their authenticity was immediately questioned, particularly the 2004 beheading video of Nicholas Evan Berg. Medical and forensic experts argued that the apparent lack of massive arterial bleeding, the lack of blood on the perpetrator's clothes, and lack of autonomic nervous system reactions demonstrated Berg was already dead prior to the beheading. Conspiracy theories and allegations of government cover-ups were rampant, claiming that Nick Berg's screams were the voice of a woman that were dubbed in, questioning the low quality of the videotape, the lapses in the timestamp of the video, and numerous other so called anomalies. In the subsequent ten years, visual documentation of violence became so prevalent it became unreasonable to doubt the authenticity of beheading videos. In fact, the technological quality of Islamic State beheading videos rival documentary films providing an enormous amount of forensic and geographic evidence. Furthermore, the violence has escalated to include multiple victims simultaneously beheaded by multiple offenders during synchronized ceremonial executions, clearly demonstrating the sacrificial ritual aspect of the killings.

Unfortunately, the next level of inexplicable violence provoked the next level of denial and conspiracy accusations. On February 3, 2015, the Islamic State released a video showing Jordanian pilot, Lt. Muath al-Kaseasbeh, 26, being burned alive while locked in a metal cage. The murder is part of a professionally produced 22 minute documentary film depicting Lt. Al-Kasasbeh alive while engulfed in flames for over 90 seconds before he collapses to the floor. The new wave of conspiracy theories involved claims that the flames were computer-generated imagery (CGI) with specific allegations that his hair would have caught fire quicker, that his body took too long to burn, and that the burning was too controlled and too highly choreographed. Critics failed to understand that burning people alive is a common method of ritual murder in Iraq and other countries, particularly in honor killings and the murder of Christians. The significant difference is that the Islamic State media filmed the execution using sophisticated editing and highly choreographed techniques turning the killing into what appeared to some as similar to a scripted reality show, their Western frame of reference. An emic cultural analysis makes it clear that this was not a simulated immolation murder on the video. Hundreds of women in the Muslim world have been murdered by fire in honor killings. In the first six months of 2007, in Iraqi Kurdistan, 255 women were killed, three-quarters of them by burning. An earlier report cited 366 cases of women who were the victims of so called fire accidents in Dohuk in 2006, up from 289 the year before. In Irbil, there were 576 burn cases since 2003, resulting in 358 deaths. In 2006 in Sulaimaniyah, Iraq, there were 400 cases of women burned. In Tunisia in May 2014, a father burned his 13 year old daughter to death for walking home with a boy. In October 2013, a 15 year old Yemeni girl was burned to death by her father for communicating with her fiancé. In March

2009, a sixteen year old Muslim girl suspected of having a relationship with a boy was burned to death by four male neighbors in her village in Ghaziabad, North India. In April 2011, three men were set on fire in Iraq for being gay. A video of that incident is easily accessible online. In June 2008, the Taliban burned three truck drivers of the Turi tribe alive for supplying the Pakistan Armed Forces. There have been numerous reports of Christians burned alive by Islamist jihadists. In November 2014, a Christian couple in Pakistan, Sajjad Maseeh, 27, and his wife Shama Bibi, 24, were burned alive in a brick furnace after it was rumored that they had burned verses from the Quran. These incidents are rarely reported by the mainstream media and were difficult for most people to comprehend as real until ISIS started producing propaganda documentaries that involved death rituals.

A symbolic analysis of the murder of Lt. Al-Kasasbeh reveals that fire signifies the destruction of evil. Symbolically, people who are burned alive are human sacrifices that are expiating evil from the community. Tainted victims are purified through fire because it is considered a powerful transformer of the negative to the positive. Because of such properties, fire is commonly found in purification rites throughout the world. In some cultural traditions, polluted persons may be required to walk around, jump over, or jump through fire. Historically, burning a person to death was reserved for the most threating evil, such as heresy or witchcraft, and considered an extreme form of purification. A cultural analysis interprets the immolation murder of Lt. Muath al-Kaseasbeh as an Islamic purification ritual that serves vengeance and restores honor and purity to the community of believers. Islamist jihadists from different movements, countries, sects, and factions all emphasize the need to cleanse Islam of its impurities. Al Qaeda's ideological belief is the purification of Islam through violent struggle. Bin Laden and Al-Zawahiri have continually called on supporters to purify Muslim holy lands of infidels, un-Islamic beliefs, and practices. The Islamic State cleanses Islam of its impurities while protecting its territory using brutal tactics that are justified as vengeance.

The amount of visual documents disseminated by the Islamic State and al Qaeda networks and eyewitness reports of survivors has ended most questioning of the authenticity of ritual murders. However, while some scholars will acknowledge the existence of brutal savage violence, they refuse to accept the root cause of the violence as magical religious ideologies, particularly Islamic beliefs. They attribute brutality, murder, and terrorist acts to economic deprivation, social injustice, and lack of education that cause people to adopt extreme views and turn to violence. They maintain these positions even though there has been an abundance of statistical and case study evidence demonstrating that many terrorists are educated, wealthy, and have social status. Theories of violence that attribute the root causes to magical and religious ideologies has been further complicated by political agendas that have actively stifled authentic objective cross cultural approaches to counterterrorism with allegations of Islamophobia or weaponizing anthropology. Fortunately, the authors in this book have not been dissuaded by prevailing restrictive political and academic surroundings that continue to suppress nonpolitical authentic inquiry into unfamiliar religious practices.

Beheading videos, images of ritual killings, and martyrdom operations are irrefutable primary sources that prove that sacrificial violence is not relegated to a few delusional individuals. Even more compelling is that contemporary blood sacrifice is not limited to one anomalous culture. Dark magico-religious activities involving beheadings, displaying dead bodies, blood offerings, flaying, mutilation, and dismemberment occur in countries around the world regardless of their economic and developmental status. Videotaped beheadings have become a cross cultural phenomenon among Jihadist terrorist groups and Mexican drug trafficking organizations. Globally, there have been hundreds of documented beheadings and thousands of victims. This visual documentation not only proves the existence of contemporary human sacrifice, it represents a full blown sacrificial crisis. From Asia and Africa to South America to Europe, North America, and Australia, patterns of culture are emerging. Instead of devolution, ritual violence is evolving. We are witnessing a new era in sacrificial violence whose documented number of victims far exceeds those of any other time in human history. The analysis of violent crime in this book goes beyond traditional behavioral science, criminology, and sociological methodologies to apply historical theories of sacrifice and emic interpretative methods to the criminal activities of violent non-state actors. The result is a book destined to become a classic foundational work for future research and innovative antidrug trafficking and counter-terrorism strategies.

Introduction

BLOOD SACRIFICES

Robert J. Bunker

"In this century, the Battle of Manizkert is more relevant than the Battle of Midway, and the overarching struggle will be about interpreting God's will." (p. 5)

—Ralph Peters, *Wars of Blood and Faith*

The *Blood Sacrifices* book project is focused on investigating the relationship between violent non-state actors (VNSAs) and dark magico-religious activities. It is set within the context of an increasingly globalized and high tech world in which, at the same time, barbarism and human sacrifice are making a resurgence.[1] The works presented within this anthology very much can be considered an exploratory research endeavor into a relatively unexplored area of contemporary interdisciplinary study. This is primarily due to the fact many of the disciplines involved do not normally interact with one another. These areas of research include:

- Violent non-state actors (VNSAs)
- The promotion of radical change by means of social movements and insurgency
- Magico-religious activities including offerings and human sacrifice
- Cults and apocalyptic (end of days) groups
- The use and distribution of illicit, and misused legitimate, narcotics, drugs, medicines, and pharmaceuticals

The diagram provided in Figure 1—*VNSAs Practicing Dark Magico-Religious Activities*—portrays the conceptual model drawn upon to provide a framework to both understand and analyze this subject matter. The diagram illustrates an exclusionary process of smaller and smaller population subsets of violent non-state actors. First, we have the general population of VNSAs. These include gangs, organized crime, cartels, terrorists, insurgents, pirates, mercenary bands, and warlords. Second, we have a smaller grouping of VNSAs who are promoting radical change. Not all VNSAs promote such change. Take, for instance, traditional organized crime. Such groups seek a symbiotic relationship with society much like a parasite in relationship to a host. However, politically focused VNSAs, and increasingly commercially (criminal) focused ones, can and do seek radical change. Spiritually focused armed non-state groups are also now thought to be capable of potentially seeking radical change within a society or state.

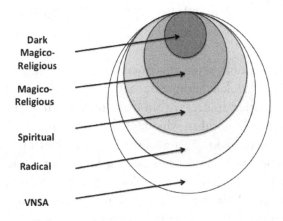

Figure. 1 VNSAs Practicing Dark Magico-Religious Activities

Third, such radical change promoting VNSAs are required to have a spiritual component to them. The group thus operates beyond the secular and openly acknowledges supernatural activity and phenomena.[2] As a result, its members will accept a belief system and recognize one or more gods, animism, or some other underlying metaphysical 'reality' from which to draw upon. Fourth, the VNSA must engage in magico-religious activity. Either petitions to one or more deities takes place for individual or collective gain or manna (spiritual energy) is recognized to exist in human beings and is utilized in spells and charms.[3] Fifth, and finally, the magico-religious activity that the VNSA is engaging in must fit the criteria of 'dark' as operationalized in this schema—that is, it is criminal in nature and involves morally reprehensible acts directed at other human beings. More on this overall process follows in the subsequent sections of this introduction.

Radicalism and Violent Non-State Actors

Radical VNSAs seeking a sudden transformation of policy, governance, state composition, or social organization are now viewed as generally having one or more observable orientations. These orientations draw upon the emerging insurgency literature on armed 21st century non-state groups[4] and are as follows:

- *Political Orientation:* This has been the dominant form from which insurgencies develop—especially for much of the 20th century—and is conceptually linked to Maoist and People's War thinking. Over time, it evolved from rural to urban operations and has merged with Socialist doctrines and perceptions. Rural peasants have given way to urban guerillas that have, in turn, given way to terrorists as the broader form of political insurgency has evolved. Typically, the revolutionary party conducting an insurgency creates shadow governmental structures in parallel to legitimate governmental structures that, in time, they replace as part of the political displacement process.[5]
- *Commercial (Criminal) Orientation:* A focus on commercially based radicalism, rather than the politically based radicalism, was first articulated in 1993. The projection of commercial insurgency emerging was derived from the "quasi-political distortion of materialism" found "when the discontented define personal meaning by material possessions rather than psychic fulfillment."[6] One of the two derivatives of this form of insurgency—criminal insurgency—was identified in 2008 as it applied to the narco conflict in Mexico and later Central America.[7] It was later said of this insurgency form derivative, "Though they target the state, gangs and cartels are not after

revolution. In these evolving 'criminal insurgencies' criminal organizations are acting in a neo-feudal manner challenging the legitimacy of the state and creating autonomous zones outside of state control."[8]

- *Spiritual Orientation:* This form of insurgency is viewed as the evolutionary descendant of traditional revolution and was also projected in 1993 by the same scholar that developed the commercial insurgency construct. This orientation is anomie focused, and concerns the search for meaning and the ensuing religious renaissance in the underdeveloped world as a visceral reaction to Western development programs promoting secularization. It is said, "The essence of spiritual insurgency is rejection of a regime and, more broadly, of the social, economic, and political system associated with that regime."[9] This construct has been further refined by other authors who contend that this VNSA orientation is not simply a secular-political construct but linked to violent new movements—identified as 'Blood Cultist'—that seek social transformation through divinely-sanctioned violence.[10]

These orientations readily exist in various overlapping combinations with anyone VNSA exhibiting a singular orientation, two such orientations, or even three of them.[11] Islamist radicals, for instance—born in a tradition devoid of the separation of mosque (the spiritual) and state (the political)—cannot be considered akin to traditional Maoist insurgents only following a political and secular orientation. A criminal organization, on the other hand, which has gained 'impunity' from governmental authority to the point that it *de facto* controls a town or region of a country, has become politicized, even if this was not the intent of its initial actions, because it has taken on the role of the sovereign. If that same criminal organization also has a strong spiritual component, as exists within some of the cartels in Mexico, then all three orientations may be present.

What makes determining the above orientations problematic is that amongst VNSAs—such as criminals, gangs, organized crime, cartels, terrorists, and insurgents—we are observing increasing evolution, devolution, and convergence of these actors as a byproduct of the unintended effects of globalization.[12] The world has become a massive 'petri dish' where, in many instances, these entities are becoming more sophisticated and deadlier organizational forms vis-à-vis states—that is, they are challenging legitimate states with their radical world views to the point that an apparent shift in the international system is increasingly being recognized.[13] Some of these state challengers, in turn, adhere to magico-religious perspectives very alien to traditionalist state forms, whose populations are grounded in the more mainstream spiritualism of the centrist interpretations held by dominant religions such as Judaism, Christianity, Islam, Hinduism, and Buddhism.

Magico-Religious vs. Dark Magico-Religious Activities

To engage in dark magico-religious activities[14], some sort of spiritual orientation is required on the part of a VNSA to begin with. All because a VNSA has some form of spiritual component does not mean it will engage in such activities. In fact, its members may not engage in any form of magico-religious petitions at all and instead only engage in normal prayer.[15] Further, if the members of a violent non-state actor do engage in such activities, these may still be benign in nature. For example a Sinaloa cartel gunman placing beer, beef, tobacco, and even money in the chapel of a Jesus Malverde tomb shrine in the narco cemetery (*Cementerio de Narcos*)[16] in Culiacán would be considered a benign act. With this in mind, the moral criteria used to determine the difference between 'benign' and 'dark' will be based on that of the offering (sacrifice) or action utilized in a magico-religious activity. Hence, well-established traditional practices can be perverted or misappropriated by VNSAs for dark and cult-like purposes. Related to such activity, three types of offerings will be said to exist:[17]

    a. An inanimate object
    b. One's self (the individual, part of him or her, or something done to him or her)
    c. Another living thing (the thing itself, part of it, or something done to it)

What distinguishes a benign versus a dark offering/action will be said to be *that of the undertaking of a severe and grievous act that is criminal in nature principally upon another living (or formerly living) thing—in this instance, a human being. Such an act must either be physically and/or psychologically damaging to another individual and be conducted in pursuit of magico-religious benefit by the perpetrator(s).* The operationalization is somewhat akin to that of the concept of 'evil' as articulated by James Waller who defines "…human evil as the deliberate harming of humans by other humans" however, by necessity, it is far more limited in scope and, rather than being concerned with secular or interactive human behaviors, focuses on the metaphysical.[18]

Further, the reason the term 'action' has been included, in addition to offering (sacrifice), in this operationalization is that not all magico-religious rituals are petition based—rather, in many African traditions, both human sacrificial and non-human sacrificial events take place:

> In Africa, the motives for human sacrifice and non-sacrificial killings are not the same. On the one hand, people have been sacrificed as a means to propitiate the deities. Thus a sacrificial victim is killed as an offer to a deity in exchange for some divine/supernatural favor. On the other hand, in non-sacrificial killings, the so-called "medicine murders" people have been killed in order to access and use their "vital force" or "energy" which, it is believed, every human being embodies. The body parts cut off the victim are used in "medicine" to "strengthen" another person, to enhance their luck, or for protection.[19]

Of course, based on this purposefully restrictive operationalization, a very large gray area exists along the offering continuum from benign to dark. For instance, conducting an animal sacrifice to gain magical powers would be excluded from this operationalization even if that sacrifice includes the torture killing of an animal. This operationalization also excludes self-sacrifice to gain God's favor (e.g. sacrifice *for* God) in the afterlife as may be the case related to the motivation of an Islamist suicide (martyrdom) bomber—though, if the intended targets of such an attack were in fact considered offerings as part of a larger blood sacrifice *to* God—then the action would be considered a dark magico-religious event.[20]

Secular torture, torture killing, and desecration of the dead form the preponderance of such activity—as opposed to more finite instances of ritualized magico-religious behavior—and is, of course, also excluded from this operationalization.[21] Going back to the Culiacán narco cemetery shrine example provided earlier, another example, in this case a specific incident in January 2010, would be more along the lines of a probable magico-religious event. In the case of that incident, a severed head with a flower behind an ear was carefully placed at the new tomb of the cartel boss Arturo Beltran Leyva. It was likely left by one of his former retainers and may be considered an offering with spiritual significance—especially given the fact Santa Muerte items had been found in his hideout at the time of his death by Mexican marines and such offerings have been linked to some of its followers.

The Role of Illicit Narcotics

While not part of the initial Figure 1 model related to VNSA and dark magico-religious activities, it is relatively clear to those steeped in the subject matter that illicit narcotics—and of course otherwise legitimate, yet misused, medicines, drugs, and pharmaceuticals—are strongly linked to the activities of these actors. Illicit (and misused legal) narcotics provide revenues to armed non-state groups and also provide numerous benefits to the actors themselves and their members. Narcotics, for instance, can be used to both enhance combat performance and as a reward to be given for recreational use after a mission has been conducted or a battle has been fought. Islamic State (IS) fighters are so hooked on Captagon for instance that they and other belligerents in Syria are going through millions of these tablets which provide cheap highs and keep combatants awake for long periods of time.[22] Such substances can also be utilized for the re-socialization and psychological conditioning of VNSA members. From a magico-religious perspective, the mind altering and hallucinogenic properties of such drugs open avenues into the spiritual world and are thus incorporated into some ritualized practices.[23] When criminal magic and blood sacrifices are involved, illicit (and misused legitimate) narcotics are commonly present in many instances—either to deaden the senses of the victim, make the perpetrator(s) of the heinous act uninhibited, increase the spiritual significance of the event, or similar uses. For this reason, the non-medical use of narcotics—with the Hassashins representing the classic cult—will be both focused upon and incorporated into the essays comprising this anthology as applicable.

Three Violent Non State Actor Examples

Derived from the narrowing down process highlighted in Figure 1, three violent non-state actor clusters appear to fit our criteria which is to:

- Promote radical change and social movements
- Have a spiritual component
- Engage in dark magico-religious activities—that is, engage in offerings or actions that involve severe and grievous acts that are criminal in nature and directed at human beings to provide magico-religious benefit to the perpetrator(s)

These three identifiable VNSA clusters follows. It should be noted, however, that not all VNSAs found in these clusters engage in dark magico-religious behaviors. In fact, in most of these instances, definitely as it relates to the Mexican cartels, such behavior may be more the exception than the rule:

The Mexican Cartels. Such offerings and activities have been tied to Santa Muerte worshipers belonging to Los Zetas and Cartel del Golfo (CDG) and the Beltran Leyva Organization (BLO) and to the pseudo-Christian cult-like behavior of La Familia Michoacana/Los Caballeros Templarios. Incidents related to these activities have included human sacrifices, ritual cannibalism, and the desecration of Catholic religious shrines.[24] Death magic and rituals have also been noted along with protective spell use as well as wide spread incidents of extreme forms of torture-killings taking place with both secular and magico-religious overtures.

Islamist Terrorists & Insurgents. Some of the Al Qaeda affiliated groups have moved beyond self-martyrdom and have engaged in redemptive rituals focused on 'blood and souls,' as in the case of Abu Musab al-Zarqawi's group who beheaded Nicholas Berg in Iraq in 2004.[25] Additional works on Al Qaeda 'beheading signatures' suggest that such blood sacrifices are more prevalent than typically recognized—even crucifixions have now been noted in Yemen as a component of spiritual warfare.[26] Such dark rituals are not limited to Al Qaeda members and have recently taken place in Syria with an anti-Assad commander symbolically eating either part of a heart or lung of a dead government fighter on camera.[27] More recently Islamic State (IS) insurgents have also gone down the path of crucifixions, beheadings, and other blood rituals as a component of the holy war that they are waging.[28] Further, Boko Haram having recently pledged allegiance to IS may as a result be increasing its dark-magico religious activities.

Central & West African Rebels & Organized Crime. The Lord's Resistance Army (LRA) in Central Africa, fighters belonging to various *Poro* secret societies in Sierra Leone—like members of the *Kamajors* and the Revolutionary United Front (RUF)—who ingested the hearts and livers of enemy prisoners,[29] and Nigerian and Ghanan human traffickers who engage in criminal witchcraft are but a few examples of VNSAs involved in this activity in these regions.[30] The horrors surrounding the Okija shrine, discovered in Nigeria in 2004, with its numerous corpses and magical symbolism provides yet another incident highlighting these types of activities—in this case, tied in to clandestine political systems.[31]

The above VNSAs will, in some instances, be focused upon in the essays contained in this book project and, at other times, only marginally addressed. While they will all be touched upon at one point or another in parts of this work—given the exploratory nature of this research—the various writings will also address attributes belonging to the rungs farther out such as the broader magico-religious, spiritual, and radical and related themes such as human sacrifice and narcotics use only.

Book Project Overview

The *Blood Sacrifices* anthology is composed of a preface, this introduction, five topical essays, a research note, a review essay, four book reviews, and a postscript. It also contains an upfront section discussing the Terrorism Research Center, an acronyms listing, acknowledgments, selected references related to the various anthology contributions, and a biographies section highlighting the credentials of the participating authors involved in this book project. Additionally, a virtual image gallery supporting the work provides a visual confirmation of the ritualistic behaviors and blood sacrifices chronicled within it. This gallery can be accessed at http://bloodsacrifices.oodaloop.com which is a site linked to an organization associated with the Terrorism Research Center (TRC).

The preface by Dawn Perlmutter, Director of the Symbol Intelligence Group, provides both an analysis of sacrificial violence and places it in context vis-à-vis conventional behavioral research that attempts to marginalize it. This maginalization is derived from designating such dark spiritual practioneers as psyschopaths, deviants, and homicidal criminals. Our inherent Western bias (e.g. etic based), derived from a rationalistic, secular, and utilitarian philosophical tradition, does not allow for non— and pre/post—Western cultures (e.g. emic based) to intrinsically manifest blood and human sacrificial practices as coherent magical ideologies. Her recognition that "barbaric savage violence occurs in the 21st century" helps to underscore the themes developed and explored in this multi-year scholarly research endeavor.

The lead essay is a theoretical contribution provided by Marc W.D. Tyrrell, a recognized expert of symbolism and symbol systems and a past Senior Research Fellow, the Canadian Centre of Intelligence and Security Studies, Carleton University, on the subject of radical magic applied to criminal ends by armed and radicalized groups. The essay provides an excellent overview of "magic" within symbology and consciousness—linked together in sense making systems—and illustrates this through implications drawn from Laughlin's *The Cycle of Meaning*. The work then goes on to identify two primary forms of criminal magic systems—"socially criminal" ones and ones that can be considered 'evil' within their own broader system. Meta-systems of magic, and the analytical dangers of examining them, are then looked at followed by a conclusion focusing upon the social environment of the second type of criminal magic that includes Satanism and some of the darker forms of Mexican cartel spirituality.

The second essay written by Paul Rexton Kan, Professor of National Security Studies at the U.S. Army War College, addresses drug use by violent non-state actors which is one of his areas of research expertise. This is a very important topic given the role of illicit substances in relationship to our thematic focus. His essay is divided into sections on drug demand, drug supply, concepts of 'set and setting' (sociological reasons to use drugs), the complications and challenges that this represents, and ultimately how law enforcement and the military contend with intoxicated VNSAs. Radicalized non-state belligerents have benefited from these substances on the battlefield with confirmed incidents in which jihadi fighters have suffered life threatening wounds but—like something out of a zombie movie—have continued engaging in combat long after they should have fallen down dead. Dark magico-religious acts and drug use are also highlighted in this article that links these groups—primarily in Africa but also in the Middle East—to the spiritual and the divine.

The third essay, by this author (Robert Bunker, the project editor), a past Minerva Chair at the Strategic Studies Institute, U.S. Army War College, focuses on narcocultura and spirituality in Mexico as they relate to the gangs and cartels—two forms of violent non-state actors heavily invested in illicit narcotics trafficking and numerous other types of criminality including kidnapping, extortion, murder-for-hire, street taxation, and human trafficking including, in some instances, even the body parts trade. While a focus on the death saint—Santa Muerte—will get a good deal of attention as will San Nazario, other sanctioned and unsanctioned saints and metaphysical realities will be touched upon as they relate to the book project themes. As will be seen in this article, individual Mexican gangs and cartels fall into many of the circles composing Figure 1. with some of the groups and sub-groups actively engaging in dark magico-religious activities—most notably Los Zetas and quite possibly La Familia Michoacána (and the Los Caballeros Templarios successor) depending on how one views their cultish activities.

Lisa Campbell, Lt. Col. California Air National Guard, is an intelligence specialist with years of radical Islamist research specialization that includes projects related to extremist ideology, jihadi beheadings, al Qaeda order of battle, and suicide bombing analysis. She provides us with the fourth essay that delves into case studies of al Qaeda, Islamic State, and Boko Haram ritual killings and their relationship to dark magico-religious activities. This detailed work initially addresses Islamist spirituality and religious doctrine and Islamist views on forms of sacrifice. Such killings readily fall into the caliphate narrative of end of days eschatology promoted by jihadists.[32] Important components of this work include drawing upon comparisons between traditional animal sacrifice and the ritual killings of humans and how they relate to both the physical and spiritual worlds and the identifiable differences that exist related *to* God and *for* God sacrifices. Additionally, the use of narcotics related to ritual killings is discussed and a proposed Islamic State place hierarchy that spans the temporal through the spiritual worlds is presented.

The chapter by Tony M. Kail, an esoteric religions and security threats SME and author of the new book *Narco-Cults* (CRC Press, 2015), contains the fifth thematic essay contributed to the book project. It provides research insights and analysis into the cultural appropriation by narco traffickers of Afro-Caribbean religious traditions, specifically 'Las Reglas de Kongo,' derived from the author's field and consulting work. The Palo Mayombe form of spirituality is highlighted in the essay due to its allure to narcos stemming from its perceived powerful magical properties. Additionally, three case studies related to police investigations of narco trafficking incidents in which magical cauldrons (ngangas) are evident are discussed and analyzed. The essay concludes with a warning concerning the further emergence of hybrid spirituality among drug traffickers who utilize cross-cultural religious artifacts and practices much of which is based on skulls, serpents, and other forms of spiritual aggression and power iconography.

The research note by Pamela Ligouri Bunker, a former Senior Analyst with the Counter-OPFOR Corporation and present Associate with *Small Wars Journal—El Centro*, focuses on three new works looking at the Lord's Resistance Army (LRA) in Central Africa in terms of their relation to dark magico-religious activities. She provides a cautionary tale concerning the early reporting on the LRA as they relate to dark spiritualty—as opposed to instrumental violence origins—and how over time the nature and activities of a VNSA may change, stemming from both internal dynamics and external pressures influencing it. What is apparent from this essay is that the LRA is far less magico-religious based than it once was. This is due to the fact that this group is constantly on the run in order to survive and, as a result, has dispensed with the luxury of such time consuming activities as group prayer, spirit possessions, and other forms of expressed spirituality.

The review essay by Charles Cameron focuses on the significance of sacramental analysis—what he calls the 'Dark Sacred.' Cameron who has a research specialization in apocalyptic violence is a former Associate at the Center for Millennial Studies, Boston University. Sacramental analysis follows the "'...assumption that 'outward and visible signs' correspond in believers' hearts to 'inward and spiritual graces'" and that groups such as the Islamic State are not purely dominated by political ideology considerations. In supporting his analysis he draws principally upon Zulaika's work on Basque violence along with works focusing on the Rwandan genocide and the erasure of the sacramental vision itself derived from the Chilean experience under Pinochet's despotic rule. His work reinforces the fact "...that behind every act of terror or resistance there may be a sacramental or purely symbolic motive..." associated with it.

The initial, and interpretive, book review by Andrew Bringuel, II, until recently a Supervisory Special Agent with the Behavioral Research and Instruction Unit (BRIU)—formerly the famed Behavioral Science Unit (BSU)—housed at the FBI Academy, focuses on the links between sacrifice and radicalism. He explores Jan Bremmer's edited work on human sacrifice and compares the case studies of violent state actors (VSAs) juxtaposed with violent non-state actor (VNSA) examples utilizing a four-prong typology of political, social, economic, and personal motives. Blood sacrifices, and even instances of cannibalism, are some of the dark practices highlighted in his analysis. Of note is how his VNSA examples gravitate toward the Islamist terrorist and insurgent cluster identified in this introductory essay. Further, his insight of how historical VSAs have used human sacrifice for status quo reinforcing, rather than radical change eliciting, purposes was an unexpected but important conclusion. This, of course, then begs the unanswered question if a VNSA facilitates radical political change and evolves in to a VSA, will human sacrifice be discontinued or will it then become a mechanism for insuring the status quo based on new normative behaviors.

The second, more classic, book review by José de Arimatéia da Cruz, a past Distinguished Visiting Research Professor with the Strategic Studies Institute, U.S. Army War College, explores Jeffrey Carter's edited work on religious sacrifice. The work reviewed contains twenty-five influential essays on various elements of religious sacrifice written between 1871 and 1993. Not only do a diversity of theories related to religious sacrifice exist—e.g. gift, fear, communication, magic—but so do a diversity of author emphases on the various aspects and understandings that emerge. A number of the essays provided in this reader are of interest to this special issue theme including Jame Frazer's *The Golden Bough* (1890) that helps to explain sacrificial phenomena by means of magic theory and Maurice Block's *Prey into Hunter* (1992) which links sacrifice to violence theory in order to maintain the social order. Of note is how the act of sacrifice can have either a status quo reinforcing or a radical change-promoting element to it.

Mark Safranski, a Senior Analyst at Wikistrat and the Publisher of zenpundit.com, provides the third review. He analyzes Moshe Halbertal's work that looks at "...the role of sacrifice in six thousand years of religious and temporal affairs, including an explanatory model of political violence, that is rooted in an understanding of the *Torah* and classical works of Western political philosophy." The work is divided into "Sacrificing to" and "Sacrificing for" distinctions which cross both the sacred and secular realms. An examination of early animal sacrifice and its substitution is provided as well as a discourse on the relationship between sacrifice and violence. The tensions between sacrifice as a primordial ritual and the modern secular state—with its capacity for industrial scale killing—are also highlighted with atonement giving way to a "vengeful eruption of political violence." Safranski's analysis in some ways begs the question if the Islamic State is not some new fusion of pre-modern ritual and post-modern state based political-religious violence.

The fourth and final book review concerns Nathalie Wlodarczyk's work *Magic and Warfare*. The review, written by Alma Keshavarz, a Ph.D. student at Claremont Graduate University with expertise related to VNSAs such as Hezbollah and associated entities, discusses the book's focus on the use of magic in warfare in traditional West and

Central African socities with a specific case study emphasis on the Kamajor society of Sierra Leone. The origins of this society and their rituals are highlighted in this short review as well as a mention of the special Yamorto Squad which engaged in instances of cannibalism and ritual killing that were said to transfer the strength of captured opposing warriors (e.g strong men) to squad members that ingested their body parts. Further, a discussion of fighter 'spiritual armor' worn on the battlefield—derived from magical oinments, markings, and charms— to provide invulnerability against bullets is touched upon.

The postscript, provided by Pauletta Otis, former Professor of Security Studies at the Marine Corps University Command and Staff College and who has expertise in religious factors in violence, provides a deft summation of the work. Her closing essay is divided into sections discussing the work's basic queries and assumptions, cases and comparative analysis, the basic theoretical connections between religion, war, and blood sacrifice, and explanations for these dark spiritual phenomena. She notes that various explanations for violent non-state actor blood sacrifice acvitivity exists derived from episodic social/ political violence, nativism, poverty/underclass effect, and powerful leader explanations as well as that there may be no explanation at all. Additionally, she notes that blood sacrifice, both *for* and *to* God, is a global phenomenon and most scholars and practioneers would rather ignore this reality than face up to the facts as the authors of this work have courageously done.

Notes

[1] Hans Magnus Enzensberger, "The Resurgence of Human Sacrifice." *Society* 39. March-April 2002: 75-77. For a review essay related to this topic, see Julian Bourg, "On Terrorism as Human Sacrifice." *Humanity* 1. Fall 2010: 137-154.

[2] The secular, rational, and cost-benefit based Western mind has great difficulty in accepting the importance of narratives, alternate— metaphysical—worlds, and the spiritual in VNSA activities. As an example "…SMT [Social Movement Theory]—and social science more generally—has been unable to conceptualise and study the role of the spiritual in social movement dynamics." Jeroen Gunning, "Social movement theory and the study of terrorism" in Richard English et.al.,

Eds., *Critical Terrorism Studies: A new research agenda.* New York: Routledge, 2009: 174. Referencing Kristin Wolff, "New Orientalism: Political Islam and Social Movement Theory" in Ahmad Moussalli, Ed., *Islamic Fundamentalism: Myths & Realities.* Reading: Ithaca, 1998: 63.

[3]   Marc Tyrrell has provided the following insight that "...this is the crucial differentiator between a "spiritually" (or metaphysically) centered group and a magico-religious oriented group; the use of magico-religious technology. The first may or may not have a magico-religious technology that "works", while the second does and uses it. It is also the marker point between "political insurgencies" and "spiritual insurgencies", and the adoption of a magico-religious technology system may be a potential hallmark of a commercial insurgency as a means of gaining transcendent justification for their actions." See the following section for VNSA orientations.

[4]   See the author's forthcoming manuscript *Old and New Insurgency Forms.* Carlisle: Strategic Studies Institute, U.S. Army War College, 2016.

[5]   See, for instance, Mao Tse-Tung (Mao Zedong) *On Guerilla Warfare* originally written in Chinese in 1937 and later translated into English. A number of translations existed including the one by Samuel Griffith. New York: Praeger, 1961; and Vo Nguyen Giap, *People's War People's Army: The Viet Cong Insurrection Manual for Underdeveloped Countries.* New York: Praeger, 1962.

[6]   Steven Metz, *The Future of Insurgency.* Carlisle: Strategic Studies Institute, U.S. Army War College, December 1993: 15-16.

[7]   John P. Sullivan and Adam Elkus, "State of Siege: Mexico's Criminal Insurgency," *Small Wars Journal.* 19 August 2008, http://smallwarsjournal. com/jrnl/art/state-of-siege-mexicos-criminal-insurgency.

[8]   John P. Sullivan and Adam Elkus, "Mexican Gangs and Cartels: Evolving Criminal Insurgencies." *Mexidata.* 30 August 2010, http:// mexidata.info/id2783.html.

[9]   Steven Metz, *The Future of Insurgency*: 13.

[10] Matthew A. Lauder, *Religion and Resistance: Examining the Role of Religion in Irregular Warfare,* Technical Note 2009-049. Toronto: Defence R&D, March 2009: 9. For an overview of both of these new insurgency constructs and how they have developed over time, see John P. Sullivan and Robert J. Bunker, "Rethinking insurgency: criminality,

spirituality, and societal warfare in the Americas." Robert J. Bunker, Ed., *Criminal Insurgencies in Mexico and the Americas: The Gangs and Cartels Wage War*. London: Routledge, 2013: 29-50. For a discussion of the emerging 'Blood Cultist' insurgency form see *Old and New Insurgency Forms*, forthcoming.

[11] Some debate surrounds Metz's contention that only a spiritual insurgency orientation can exist within a VNSA. Such a singular orientation would be devoid of political and the economic elements.

[12] Michael Miklaucic and Jacqueline Brewer, Eds., *Convergence: Illicit Networks and National Security in the Age of Globalization*. Washington, D.C.: National Defense University Press, 2013 and Jennifer L. Hesterman, *The Terrorist-Criminal Nexus*. Boca Raton: CRC Press, 2013. See also Robert J. Bunker and John P. Sullivan, *Studies in Gangs and Cartels*. London: Routledge, 2013: especially 186-194.

[13] Robert Mandel, *Global Security Upheaval: Armed Nonstate Groups Usurping State Stability Functions*. Stanford: Stanford University Press, 2013. This emerging threat to the state based international system has long been recognized. See Martin van Creveld, *The Transformation of War*. New York: The Free Press, 1991.

[14] These 'rituals of magic and sorcery' can in some ways be considered the VNSA equivalent of advanced Western "virtual warfare" technologies. See Neil L. Whitehead and Sverker Finnström, Eds., *Virtual War and Magical Death: Technologies and Imaginaries for Terror and Killing*. Durham: Duke University Press, 2013.

[15] While simple prayer is the most basic form of supernatural petition—which includes asking for favors and forgiveness from a god or its intermediaries or representatives—it will only be considered spiritual, not magico-religious, in nature because the activity is devoid of offerings (sacrifices) and actions.

[16] "MEXICO: El ostentoso narco-cementerio de Culiacán," *Reportero 24*. 17 May 2012, http://www.reportero24.com/2012/05/mexico-el-ostentoso-narco-cementerio-de-culiacan/.

[17] A gray area between basic spirituality and magico-religious activities of course exists. A Catholic worshiper who fasts (does not eat certain foods), takes communion; the symbolic 'blood and flesh of Christ', lights a candle to better focus prayer energy, and wears the charm of a patron saint would exist somewhere in this continuum.

[18]   James Waller, *Becoming Evil.* Oxford: Oxford University Press, Second Edition, 2007: 13. The author goes on to develop the construct of 'extraordinary evil'— "...the malevolent human evil perpetrated in times of collective social unrest, war, mass killings, and genocide.... inflicted against a defenseless and helpless group targeted by a political, social or religious authority—human evil *in extremis*": 13-14. The focus of his work is thus more conducive to genocide studies then radicalism, spirituality, and dark magico-religious practices.

[19]   Lawrence E. Y. Mbogoni, *Human Sacrifice and the Supernatural in African History.* Dar es Salaam: Mkuki na Nyota Publishers Ltd., 2013: vii.

[20]   Islamist suicide (martyrdom) bombings are conducted for numerous reasons in addition to martyrdom and, in many instances, are revenge or rational actor based and have no religious component to them. Influential works are Robert A. Pape, *Dying to Win: The Strategic Logic of Suicide Bombing.* New York: Random House, 2005 and Mia Bloom, *Dying to Kill: Allure of Suicide Terror.* New York: Columbia University Press, 2007.

[21]   In Mexico, for instance, narco (cartel and drug gang) violence is predominately secularly based even though numerous instances of violence related to magico-religious activity has taken place. See Pamela L. Bunker, Lisa J. Campbell, and Robert J. Bunker, "Torture, beheadings, and narcocultos." *Small Wars & Insurgencies* 21. 2010: 145-178.

[22]   Michaela Whitton, "Captagon: The Jihadist's Drug." *Antimedia.* 27 November 2015, http://theantimedia.org/captagon-the-jihadists-drug/. See also "Pharmaceutical Drugs and the Syrian War." *OE Watch.* Fort Leavenworth: Foreign Military Studies Office, December 2015: 11-12.

[23]   For the religious uses of narcotics see, for example, Robert W. Fuller, *Stairways To Heaven: Drugs In American Religious History.* Boulder: Westview Press, 2000.

[24]   The Mexican cartels and their dark magico-religious activities will be focused on by the author in a later essay in this book project.

[25]   Ronald H. Jones, *Terrorist Beheadings: Cultural and Strategic Implications.* Carlisle: Strategic Studies Institute, U.S. Army War College, June 2005: 6-7 and Joel Roberts, "American Beheaded in Iraq." *CBS News.* 12 May 2004, http://www.cbsnews.com/news/american-beheaded-in-iraq/.

[26] Dawn Perlmutter, "Mujahideen Blood Rituals: The Religious and Forensic Symbolism of Al Qaeda Beheading." *Anthropoetics* 11. Fall 2005 / Winter 2006, http://www.anthropoetics.ucla.edu/ap1102/muja. htm; and Lisa J. Campbell, "The Use of Beheadings by Fundamentalist Islam." *Global Crime* 7. August-November 2006: 583-614. One of these crucifixions has been posted online; https://www.youtube.com/watch?v=bJy6KGyIAkM.

[27] Ian Black and Martin Chulov, "Syria mutilation footage sparks doubts over wisdom of backing rebels." *The Guardian.* 14 May 2013, http://www.theguardian.com/world/2013/may/14/syria-mutilation-footage-rebels-eat.

[28] This includes organ harvesting from living 'apostates'—an activity that has been sanctioned by fatwa. See "ISIS sanctions organ harvesting from living 'apostates'...even if it kills them." *Russia Today.* 25 December 2015, https://www.rt.com/news/327078-isis-captives-organs-harvesting/.

[29] Mbogoni, *Human Sacrifice and the Supernatural in African History*: 65-67. For additional thinking on spirituality in African conflict see Nathalie Wlodarczyk, *Magic and Warfare: Appearance and Reality in Contemporary African Conflict and Beyond.* New York: Palgrave Macmillan, 2009.

[30] See Elizabeth Willmott Harrop, "Africa: A Bewitching Economy—Witchcraft and Human Trafficking." *ThinkAfricaPress.* 17 September 2012, http://thinkafricapress.com/society/african-witchcraft-contemporary-slavery-human-trafficking-nigeria; and Tom Porter, "Rotting Corpses and Chained Kidnap Victims Found in Nigeria's 'House of Horrors.'" *International Business Times.* 23 March 2014, http://www.ibtimes.co.uk/rotting-corpses-chained-kidnap-victims-found-nigerias-house-horrors-1441494.

[31] Stephen Ellis, "The Okija Shrine: Death and Life in Nigerian Politics." *The Journal of African History* 49. 2008: 445-466.

[32] Hakim Hazim and Robert J. Bunker, "Perpetual Jihad: Striving for a Caliphate." *Global Crime* 7. 2006: 428-445.

Chapter 1

WARRIORS OF THE LEFT HAND PATH: RADICAL MAGIC APPLIED TO CRIMINAL ENDS

Marc W.D. Tyrrell

"Our tendency is to emphasize technologically-produced solutions to what are inherently political challenges that can only be resolved in the minds and will of the social community that is challenged."

—Frank Hoffman and Michael C. Davies,
Small Wars Journal[1]

"Any sufficiently advanced technology is indistinguishable from magic."

—Arthur C. Clarke, *Profiles of The Future*

Introduction

At first glance, it might appear to be far fetched to introduce the concept, and topic, of "magic" into the empirical discourses surrounding criminality and radicalization. What possible benefit could be gained by introducing a discussion of rank "superstition" into a serious, scientific discourse? After all, we "know" that people who attempt to divine the future, cast spells and talk with spirits are, at best, superstitious and, more probably, delusional. Or are they?

Attempts to divine the future appear to be alive and well in the secular world, although we now call them "data mining," "futures modelling" and "threat assessments."[2] How about the casting of spells? Again, alive and well if by "spell casting," we mean the ritualized repetition of actions designed to produce specific results and/or reduce uncertainty in future events.[3] And, as far as "talking with spirits" is concerned, I would merely suggest that the reader discuss this with their priest, minister, rabbi, imam, or local shaman.

So, what possible benefit can be gained by introducing the topic of "magic" into the empirical discourses surrounding criminality and radicalization? The answer to this question lies in two main areas: a) the functional properties of the technologies and techniques that make up what, collectively, is know as "magic" and b) the evolved psychological need states of human populations for certain forms of symbolic answers.

In the case of functional properties, these technologies of "magic" are designed to reshape perceptions of reality at both the individual and group levels in such a manner that their product is perceived as both "real" and "true." At the individual and small group level, we might consider the case of Adolpho Constanzo (the Godfather of Matamoros).[4] For larger groups, the Solar Temple cult[5] and the People's Temple (the Jonestown Massacre)[6] come to mind, as does the Takfirism of Ayman al Zawahiri. At the national level, we see the same processes and, often, technologies operating in cult-like political groups such as the Bolsheviks of 1917, the Nazi's of the early 1930's, the Khmer Rouge of the 1970's and the Kim family regime in North Korea.

In the case of population level evolved need states, we see patterns in the production of meaning systems such that certain specific emotional needs are met. In particular, the needs most commonly addressed are the basic philosophical questions of meaning: "Where do I come from?," "Where am I going?," "How does the world operate?," "What does the future bring?" and "What should I be doing?" In other words, these need states are the ones dealing with the production and maintenance of identity, religion and ideology.[7]

The scholarly empirical study of the processes, technologies, and techniques that, collectively, comprise "magic" takes place at the intersection of numerous disciplines—Epistemology, Symbolic Anthropology, Comparative Religion, Folklore, Evolutionary Psychology, and Neuroscience to name just a few. The centre of this study, however, lies in two areas: a) the use of symbols to constrain and manipulate perceptions, actions, and consciousness and b) the use of empirical knowledge to produce perceptible effects.[8]

This paper starts by placing "magic" within the broader subject of symbology and consciousness, and how the two are linked together in sense making systems. It then goes on to argue that there are two primary forms of magic that may be considered as "criminal:" systems that are socially "criminal" (e.g. Christianity in 1st century CE Rome), and systems that are "criminal" within their own broader system (e.g. Satanism within Christianity). This leads into a broader discussion of the meta-structures of magic systems, and some of the analytic dangers associated with examining them. The final sections of the paper deal with the social environment of magic and the social settings in which the second type of criminal magic is most likely to appear.

Systems of Symbols as a Part of Consciousness

Let me start with a simple statement: we, as a species, do not perceive objective reality but, rather, a series of limited, mediated, and interlinked symbolic schemas that we, as individuals, assume to be "reality." In philosophy, this is sometimes referred to as the "Map-Territory Problem" and goes back to Alfred Korzybski's famous observation that "the map is not the territory."[9] Korzybski's observation, as later expanded on by Gregory Bateson,[10] highlights one of the central paradoxes of how humans think: we assume that the map <u>is</u> the territory, even while knowing at some level that the map <u>is not</u> the territory. In effect, humans think and operate using limited symbol systems—abstractions of the "territory"—both to interpret objective reality and to decide how we will operate within it.[11]

These symbolic abstractions of various territories are, in turn, linked together to produce emergent symbol systems that act as a group's symbolic interface with objective reality; its culture in one meaning of that term.[12] In its earliest form, these emergent symbol systems appear as religions, dating back at least 50,000 ybp (years before present) and, quite possibly, much earlier.

The term "religion", however, is somewhat misleading for many readers who may assume that "religion" implies certain structures and beliefs. In cultural phylogenetic terms, the earliest "religions" were

3

forms of animism, totemism, and shamanism.[13] It is only in relatively recent times, ~12,000 ybp, when we find the beginnings of horticulture, stratified societies, and the emergence of cities, do we really find the emergence of pantheons of recognizable deities.

This understanding of how humans think and how religions emerge and change over time is at the core of Clifford Geertz's definition of religion. For Geertz, religion is:

(1) a system of symbols (2) which acts to establish powerful, pervasive and long-lasting moods and motivations in men (3) by formulating conceptions of a general order of existence and (4) clothing these conceptions with such an aura of factuality that (5) the moods and motivations seem uniquely realistic.[14]

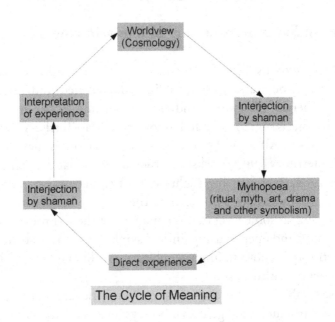

The Cycle of Meaning

While Geertz's model appears static, it is, in fact, based on a continual, low level process of what might be termed "affirmation by experience." This process is described in some detail in Charles Laughlin's work *The Cycle of Meaning*.[15] Laughlin, drawing on extensive fieldwork and theoretical modelling, lays out how humans interact with each other, symbol systems, and experiences to produce systems of meaning (cf Figure 1).

The cycle of meaning operates in a very simple manner starting with a worldview or cosmology—a "system of meaning". Some part of this system is taken by a "shaman" or "ritual specialist" and used to produce an act of "mythopoea"; a ritual, myth, piece of art, architecture, music, etc. This mythopoeaic product is then experienced by an individual, and that experience is interpreted by the shaman in such a manner as to reinforce the overall worldview.

Despite the scholarly precision and particularity of the language in Laughlin's model, the process he describes should be familiar to anyone who has raised a child, taught a student, or mentored a junior colleague. This familiarity should not be a surprise since we, as a species (including our species pre-cursors), have used the basic process for millions of years, and it has merely been exapted into the service of religions and other institutions.[16]

While the process should be familiar, some of the implications may be less so. For example, the model as presented tends to be interpreted as always reinforcing a particular worldview, but this is not the actual case under certain conditions.

First of all, individual shaman may disagree with components of the dominant worldview and produce mythopoeaic experiences that reinforce that different interpretation. Martin Luther's restructuring of Catholicism is a classic example of this, but there are many others.

Second, individuals may experience a mythopoeaic act in a manner that cannot be adequately interpreted by a shaman. In effect, the shaman's interpretation in support of the given worldview does not "ring true" to the person experiencing the act, producing a negative feedback loop in respect to the individual accepting the worldview. At the individual level, this often leads to people "opting out" of a meaning system, while at the group level it often leads to a crisis of legitimacy.

The third condition is when there is a "crisis of faith" in a worldview brought on by external events that openly challenge a core component of the worldview. The classic study of this situation is Eric Hoffer's *The True Believer*.[17]

Fourth, individuals operating in a high communications density situation with multiple, competing mythopoea have an increased likelihood of developing syncretic worldviews that challenge the dominant one(s). Some classic Western examples of this are the rise of multiple cults and sects during the Roman Empire (including the various Christian ones), the plethora of "protestant" sects following the introduction of the Gutenberg Press, and the rise of New Religious Movements in the 1960's.

Criminal Magic

These examples bring us to the first, and for our purposes least important, form of criminal magic: the mythopoeaic acts of a worldview that opposes the socially dominant one. For example, Christianity was both derided and criminalized in the first century in the Roman Empire; Protestant sects were, likewise, illegal in most Catholic areas, and certain political ideologies have also been criminalized at various times.

In and of itself, the process whereby a dominant worldview manages to have a challenging worldview declared as "illegal" and "criminal" is important solely at the level of the rhetorical political process; it says nothing about the content of that worldview or its mythopoeaic acts.

Indeed, we find a commonality of accusations aimed by the dominant world-view against the challenging one. In the case of religious worldviews, these accusations usually centre around accusations of child-stealing, ritual murder and cannibalism, and the worship of "evil."[18] In the case of political worldviews, the accusations usually centre around disruption/overthrow of the social order, a desecration of "tradition" or "history", and the overthrow of social morality.[19]

Why do I state that this is the least important form of criminal magic? The answer to that is simple: at the level of longue durée, the types of conflict engendered by such opposing worldviews is a simple form of Darwinian selection[20] that tends to work itself out over time to suit the socio-technical environment. Contra Herbert Spencer, this working out is not a "survival of the fittest," with all of the implications of teleological progress; it is a "survival of the survivors," which is a totally different matter.

The more important, and dangerous, form of criminal magic is that which inverts core components of its own worldview with the specific aim of gaining dominance and power via fear and terror through the use of techniques and technologies that are proscribed by the symbol system. In effect, the individual practising this type of magic suffers from an idée fixe where the means used to achieve an end either become irrelevant—the ends justify the means—or become the ends themselves. Such forms of criminal magic are more dangerous, and hence important, simply because they degrade the symbol system from within as opposed to challenging it. This type two criminal magic is referred to by many occultists as the Left Hand Path.[21]

This degradation takes place in three main forms. First, it degrades the individual who uses it through objectifying other members of their society by constructing them as pawns to be manipulated, used, and thrown away. In effect, it acts to encourage the practitioner to become a de facto sociopath; a trait shared with a number of serial killers. Second, it degrades the group in which the practitioner operates by eroding the social trust necessary within complex societies.[22] Third, if unchecked, it endangers the survival of the entire society and its worldview by a) eroding general popular trust in that worldview and b) by focusing social energies and resources on containing and dealing with the priorities of these practitioners.

This third form may sound somewhat far-fetched. There are, however, several secular, political illustrations of the process that are fairly well known. For example, consider the actions of Senator Joseph McCarthy through his control of the Senate Permanent Subcommittee on Investigations, of which Senators Susan Collins and Carl Levin wrote:

> Senator McCarthy's zeal to uncover subversion and espionage led to disturbing excesses. His browbeating tactics destroyed careers of people who were not involved in the infiltration of our government. His freewheeling style caused both the Senate and the Subcommittee to revise the rules governing future investigations, and prompted the courts to act to protect the Constitutional rights of witnesses at Congressional hearings.[23]

Other, secular, political examples of the process include the agrarian redistribution of the population in Kampuchea under Pol Pot, and the maintenance of the Kim Family Regime in North Korea. Both are good examples of where the original symbol system, Communism, was subverted from within and the ends justify any means to achieve them, regardless of the social cost.

The Meta-Structures of Magic: Narrative, Ritual and Moral Effect

Few of the examples I have used so far would, to the general public, be seen as "magic." This situation exists for one simple reason: most people in the Western world have a very inaccurate idea of what "magic" actually is and how it operates. At best, some people will recognize that "magic" is one or more symbol systems tied in with a "religion" and quite possibly dangerous while, at worst, they view it either as rank superstition and, hence, irrelevant to modern life or as something out of a Disney movie where someone waves a magic wand and changes reality.

So, what is "magic?" According to one of the best known Western occultists, Dion Fortune, "Magic is the Art and Science of causing changes in Consciousness in accordance with Will." As with most specialist definitions, it is accurate to the limits of the contextual linguistic precision of the reader. In this particular instance, there are four key terms that need to be drawn out so that their precise meanings will be understood, namely Art, Science, Consciousness and Will.

Within Fortune's universe of discourse, and that of many modern occultists and magicians drawing on the same traditions, the term "Art" refers to both the construction of a specific mythopoeaic event and its linking to a specific emotional state or a sequence of states. In a similar manner, the term "Science" is used to refer to specific techniques and technologies derived from associated "theories" ("Cosmology/Worldview" in Laughlin's model) that can be used to evoke emotional and perceptual states. "Art" differs from "Science" in this usage in that "Art" is applied to the tailoring of a technique to a specific, unique situation or event.

I have already discussed consciousness and its relationship to symbol systems above. The part that is missing from the Geertz and Laughlin model of consciousness lies in the narratives contained in the Cosmology/Worldviews of different systems. In effect, each different system acts to manipulate individual consciousness in order to construct a desired form of "Consciousness" that is bounded by the desired end states and narrative pathways of its Cosmology. Thus, for example, one narrative may hold that "speaking with spirits" is a crucial skill, while another may hold that "speaking with spirits" is extremely dangerous and either to be avoided or strictly controlled.[24]

The final term, "Will," refers to several different concepts: will power, emotional resilience and flexibility/adaptability. Will power, the sheer ability to focus on working within a system, is crucial to becoming an active user of any magical system since, without it, no individual can learn enough of the symbol system and associated techniques and technologies to apply them systematically. Emotional resilience is considered a component of Will simply because all these systems operate on the emotions of individual practitioners. Flexibility or adaptability is also considered to be part of Will in most magical systems because anyone employing them as an active user will inevitably have experiences that do not match or follow the generic narratives of that systems' cosmology.[25]

For the majority of people, magic is perceived as operating only within certain specific settings, namely specific types of rituals and their aftermaths. These settings encapsulate and incarnate specific components of narratives from the larger cosmology. Consider, by way of example, the various forms of the Christian Mass. Drawing on a single narrative component, they operate to retell the story of the Last Supper, drawing the participants into the "story" such that they experience it and, through that experience, become bound into the larger cosmology of sacrifice and redemption.

When conducted properly, the participants' consciousness is shifted to reflect the values and perceptions inherent in that narrative that are highlighted by the ritual. In effect, the participants perceive their experience to be, as Geertz terms it, "uniquely realistic" and clothed in an aura of factuality based on the experiential knowledge gained during the ritual. The perceptual effects, the changes in "moods and motivations," shift how individuals perceive and act within day-to-day reality and further serve to reinforce the cosmology of the religion.

Rituals, of course, may also be conducted "improperly." They may be "sterile," mere ritualized actions—a "going through the motions"—with no belief or investment of emotional energy and, hence, no shifts in perceptions, moods and motivations. Gradually, the symbol system embedded within these rituals loses its power to motivate and change people, eventually producing a legitimacy crisis within the population as people look outside the system to find structures of meaning that "work" for them.[26]

In a similar manner, ritualized behaviour may "invert" from its proper use. Instead of acting as a means of maintaining a cosmology and transforming individuals, ritualized behaviour may induce a compulsive neurosis, binding the emotional force of the ritual to the individual though a fear compulsion lacking in any survival value.[27] In its mildest form, one might see behaviour such as avoiding stepping on the "cracks" between sidewalk segments or slavishly following the reports of daily horoscopes. In more intense forms, one might see people exhibiting Obsessive Compulsive Disorder-like symptoms such as excessive self-mortification for perceived sins or the "signatures" of serial killers.

The "inversion" of ritual behaviour from its socially accepted and formally legitimate "normal" values is not enough to make a ritual practice in and of itself "evil" (i.e. Type Two criminal magic). Indeed, ritualized inversion is a common phenomenon in all religions that have formalized systems and stems, in part, from how that system acts as a buffer and mediator with the real world. It is inherent, one might argue as Max Weber did, in the process of routinizing charisma.[28]

One of the best known, Western, examples of this is the Reformation which, amongst other points, argued that the Roman Catholic Church had inverted the "True" meanings of many rituals.[29] And, while the Roman Catholic Church did argue that the Protestant sects were "Evil" (and vice versa), that stemmed more from a fight for power than from any moral failings of either group.[30] The Reformation and Counter-Reformation were instances of Type One criminal magic mentioned earlier.

Where Left Hand Path, Type Two criminal magic, in the sense of total inversions of the symbol systems leading to contra-survival situations at the population level, showed up was in the religious cleansings conducted by and upon many groups and, ultimately, in the Thirty Years War that threatened to destroy the belief in any system.

In order for this to happen, it was necessary to produce an abstraction of a coherent "anti-cosmology" and a series of rituals to bring that anti-cosmology into "reality" (i.e. Geertz's "to establish powerful, pervasive and long-lasting moods and motivations in men (3) by formulating conceptions of a general order of existence and (4) clothing these conceptions with such an aura of factuality...").

10

Such an abstracted anti-cosmology was produced between 1400 and 1650 through the construction of Satanism, the application of that construct to Witchcraft and surviving pagan beliefs, and the production of institutions whose role was to level charges as they saw fit, thereby creating a reign of terror.[31] Indeed, much of that constructed anti-cosmology is still around today, as are the associated rituals such as the Satanic Black Mass.[32]

Analytic Dangers

"Magic," as Randall Garret notes, "is a matter of symbolism and intent;"[33] a situation which makes it all too easy for analysts to concentrate on the "simple" part—the symbolism—and assume the intent.[34] In part, this tendency arises from the basic fact that all people have inherited certain forms of symbolism to which they react unconsciously.

Thus, for example, if someone raised in a nominally Christian society entered a room and saw a skull with a lit black candle on either side of it, an emotional reaction of shock, fear, and revulsion would be quite normal. If, in addition to the skull and black candles, one also saw a bowl filled with what appeared to be blood in front of the skull with symbols drawn on the skull in blood and smelled burning incense that left the taste of blood in the back of their throats, that fear/shock/revulsion response could easily lead to screaming, fainting or being violently ill. These are all perfectly natural and reasonable responses for someone encountering what appear to be symbols of a cosmology antithetical to what they have internalized.

The example quoted above, however, comes from my own fieldwork, and refers to a specific ritual derived from the Celtic Cult of the Head as a means of divination. The intent behind it was beneficent, and the symbols made perfect, logical sense within the symbol system of the group who conducted it. That said, the exact same symbols could also be used by a group whose intention was maleficent, and they would also make perfectly logical sense within the symbol system of that group.

The danger operating in this type of situation is that people will, understandably, substitute their emotional reactions for an analysis of the intent that lies behind the use of those symbols in that configuration and by that group. In addition to "feeling right," it is also extremely easy to "sell" such an "analysis" to others who are symbolically primed with similar reactions, but this is a temptation that must be contained lest a social "panic" reaction start.[35]

An additional analytic pitfall is that symbolism and intentions, in and of themselves, are not sufficient to understand whether or not an individual or group is engaging in Left Hand Path, Type Two criminal magic. In order to make such a determination, we must look at the moral effects of such practice on both the practitioners and the general population in which they operate. Unfortunately, such an analysis cannot rely on the use of dominant moral or ethical codes, since that is much more likely to identify Type One criminal magic, i.e. that which opposes and/or is different from the dominant symbol system, while being unable to identify certain forms of Type Two criminal magic.[36]

Before getting into specifics, let us return to the definition of Left Hand Path, Type Two criminal magic I gave earlier. It is the inversion of core components of its own worldview with the specific aim of gaining dominance and power via fear and terror through the use of techniques and technologies that are proscribed by the symbol system. Again, as I noted earlier, the effects of this type of criminal magic appear as forms of degradation on the personal, group, and social levels.

As I pointed out in a previous example, the Reformation and Counter-Reformation offer us some very good examples of effects. While the general conflict centred over power, within each area controlled by one or the other group (Roman Catholics and Lutherans[37]) there was no noticeable difference in moral effects. The same, however, cannot be said of the "border areas" (part Catholic, part Lutheran), where witchcraft trials flourished[38] as they also did during the post-Peace of Augsburg period in areas of "religious cleansing."[39]

Did active, intentional Left Hand Path, Type Two criminal magical practitioners, exist? It is almost certain that they did throughout much of Europe. The evidence for this comes from a number of trials for sorcery, and involves the rise of a form of magic designed to control both Angels and Demons, which was a close relative of the construction of the Satanic anti-cosmology.[40]

The moral effects of intentional Left Hand Path practitioners, however, appears to have been less damaging than that of the unintentional practitioners; their investigators.[41] In terms of cultural genetics, there were two central moral effects of these trials and the general conflict.[42] First, the sheer hypocrisy of the trial system reduced the level of trust in both ecclesiastical and civil court systems, undermining the utility of the legal system, and thereby destabilizing the legitimacy of state (and religious) organizations as guarantors of predictability. Second, the publications and trials both created and spread the anti-cosmology along with certain ritual practices thereby making these readily available for use by anyone while, at the same time, providing them with a form of legitimacy.

This second effect is, in many ways, more important than the first since it produced effects that were much more long lasting. At a subtle level, the existence and spread of this anti-cosmology and associated ritual practices produced a symbolic susceptibility within European derived cultures that is still alive and well today as was clearly shown by the Satanic Ritual Abuse panic of 1985-1990.[43]

The Social Environment of Magic

Carl Jung once noted that:

Rationalism and superstition are complementary. It is a psychological rule that the brighter the light, the blacker the shadow; in other words, the more rationalistic we are in our conscious minds, the more alive becomes the spectral world of the unconscious.[44]

Jung's observation highlights an interesting phenomenon: an over reliance on conscious rationality, however that may be culturally defined, increases the susceptibility of individuals to the influence of unconscious, emotionally-driven, irrationality. In effect, the more "rational" an individual is, the more emotionally "brittle" they are.

"Rationality," however, is culturally bounded. In cultures where the cycle of meaning operates well, this "brittleness" is contained and moderated by that symbol system's mythopoeaic events; what we might, following Kuhn, term as "normal magic." In effect, the mythopoeaic events provide structures, settings, justifications and pathways for "the spectral world of the unconscious", acting as the cathartic outlets for emotionally-driven irrationality that all societies and cultures need to survive.

What, however, happens when a cycle of meaning fails, and the mythopoeaic events contained in it are no longer able to provide meaning to individuals? Or, in other words, what happens when "rationality" no longer produces predictable results that are desirable? The example of the Reformation—Counter-Reformation period gives us some critical insight into what can happen during a symbolic legitimation crisis and the failure of normal magic.

Initially, we see that the cosmology is often elaborated in an attempt to explain the failures. This elaboration, however, also produces an abstracted, recognized, and legitimated anti-cosmology.[45] The anti-cosmology becomes the symbolically licenced form and shape of utter rebellion against the core components of the cosmology. The rituals associated with the anti-cosmology (the mythopoeaic events) are generally inversions or mirror images of the original cosmology. Thus, for example, in the anti-cosmology of the Reformation-Counter-Reformation we see an elaboration over time of the Hierarchy of Hell and, by the time of John Dee, the development of an exact mirror image between Angels and Demons and elaborate rituals for summoning and commanding both groups.

Second, we see the emergence of alternative interpretations of the basic cosmology that retain certain key components, but reject other parts. The alternate interpretations, many of which are what Wallace refers to as "Revitalization Movements", serve to move the original organization from being "universal" to being merely one amongst many legitimate interpretations of the now abstracted key components.[46]

Third, and as a consequence of the second point, the entire field of inquiry contained within the original cosmology is opened up for non-controlled examination to the limits of the generally accepted core components.[47] Thus, in the case of the early modern period, we see the rise of empirical science moving into areas that had previously been the province of the Roman Catholic church (in the case of physics) and of "folk magicians" in the case of medicine.[48]

This pathway of resolving a symbolic legitimation crisis is, however, not the only way in which such a resolution can happen. For example, a cosmology may be conquered and suppressed: the early conquests of Islam followed this pattern as did the Reconquista in the Iberian Peninsula, and the conquests of Central and South America. A variant of this is the "peaceful conquest" model that happened in the 5th to 11th centuries in England, the Germanies, and Scandanavia where Christian missionaries produced symbolically syncretic, local versions to draw in and convert the local populations. In such cases of symbolic conquest, either "peaceful" or forced, remnants of the previous mythopoeaic structures frequently remain under a thinly veiled gloss of the new cosmology, creating a localized, syncretic cosmology.[49]

We also see other situations were syncretic cosmologies are appearing. First, in cases of forced population movement, such as the importation of West African slaves into the Caribbean and North and South America, we often find core mythopoeaic events from the original cosmology being retained and used as a way of maintaining some type of identity (e.g. the mixtures of Vodun and Christianity such as Voodoo [Haiti, Dominican Republic], Candomblé Jejé [Brazil], Winti [Surinam], Palo [Cuba], etc.). In this case, the syncretic cosmology has a tendency to contain strong, anti-dominant cosmology elements.

A second situation which encourages syncretic cosmologies appears when there is fairly peaceful contact between different cosmologies, either a loose social control over cosmologies or a general symbolic legitimation crisis, and a fairly high communications density. The three best Western examples are the 1st through 3rd centuries in the Roman Empire, the 16th-18th centuries during the Reformation-Counter-Reformation, and the later half of the 1960's with the rise of many New Religious Movements.[50]

Enter the Warriors of the Left Hand Path

So, under what conditions are we most likely to see Left Hand Path, Type Two criminal magic appear? We see it appearing when specific, legitimated anti-cosmologies exist. In the case of the construction of Satanism, it usually only produces Type Two criminal magicians in small numbers or during times when the dominant cosmology is losing sway. Thus, for example, we find that actual Satanic activity is quite rare before, say, 1580, and we only really find organized, group based Satanic activity in the late 19th century and during the late 20th century.[51]

We also find Type Two criminal magic appearing in situations where it is integrated and institutionalized within the overall cosmology. For example, the Thugees of India appear to have ritualized murder for gain as part of their worship of Kali, something that is noticeably absent from most forms of Kali worship.

One clear example of Left Hand Path magic, at least in terms of documentation, is evident in Haiti in the case of the Tonton Macoutes. Initially created in 1959 as a paramilitary force to support the dictatorship of Papa Doc Duvalier, the Tonton Macoutes used systematic symbolic inversions of Voodoo to increase their capability of producing terror in the population.

In particular, the example of Luckner Cambronne, who ran the Tonton Macoutes until 1971, clearly shows all of the elements of a Left Hand Path magician, i.e. someone out for personal gain through violence and terror and using illegal techniques and technologies to achieve his results. In Cambronne's case, and that of the Tonton Macoutes in general, they were clearly using specific mythopoeaic events to achieve these ends as a force multiplier for their overt function as a secret police.[52]

A second clear example of Left Hand Path, Type Two criminal magic appears in the case of Adolfo Constanzo, The Godfather of Matamoros. Constanzo started to practice Palo Mayombe, a syncretic religion mixing African roots with Christianity, as a teenager and later turned his knowledge of rituals into a profitable business in Mexico City. Constanzo's rituals drew in a crowd of drug dealers and, by 1988, had already established human sacrifice as one of the key components of both his cult and his drug dealing business. In 1989, Constanzo's henchmen kidnapped an American citizen, Mark Kilroy, and sacrificed him, leading to an investigation of the cult and, ultimately, Constanzo's death. [53]

Constanzo was, quite clearly, a Left Hand Path, Type Two criminal magician. He was also involved with several figures from the world of Mexican cartels who, apparently, enjoyed the violence of his rituals.[54] Constanzo was able to use a syncretic cosmology that was attractive to both his followers and, also, to certain members of the cartels; probably because it ritualized, rationalized, and promoted the violence they were involved with. Perhaps more importantly, Constanzo illustrated how to construct rituals—mythopoeaic events—that would convey meaning and ground lived experience in situations were extreme violence can be normal.

Conclusions

With these examples in mind, what happens when we look at modern (2016) situations? First, as Peter Berger argued rather persuasively, the key components of Christianity have disappeared from civil discourse and been replaced by a sacralization of the democratic process and "civil religion", at least in the United States.[55] While not new or unique— the communists under Lenin enforced an absence of "religion" from public discourse replacing it with their own "sacred cannon" (i.e. Marx, Engels & Lenin)—the forcible displacement of Christianity as a moral arbiter from public discourse and its replacement with a civil religion that is increasingly dominated by politically correct fad-du jour issues, has created a dangerous, symbolic situation.

I call this situation "dangerous" for one simple reason: if the state will not or can not give its backing to any particular overarching cosmology, where is meaning to be derived for individuals? It is quite possible to have multiple cosmologies operating in a society providing a variety of cycles of meaning to people, but there needs to be a larger, "meta-cosmology" that can serve to link them together.[56] Within the Anglosphere, this meta-cosmology has tended to be centred around the volk moot and its successors, but these are in some danger of losing their unifying power.

From the 1960's onwards, we can see that increasing numbers of people have been searching for meaning. While most apparent in the rise of the New Religious Movements of the 1960's and 70's, it is also seen in the increase in Revitalization Movements such as the Moral Majority, the Militia Movements, and the diasporic radicalization of Muslims to name only a few. Such a "fragmentation" can be linked together, but it requires both a strong national meta-cosmology and, at the same time, effective local action.[57]

While the civil societies of many Western nations may be subject to an increase in revitalization movements, the real danger is in those areas that are both symbolically ungoverned and, at the same time, suffering from increased violence and the breakdown of social order. This type of susceptibility was certainly apparent in the case of Uganda and the Lord's Resistance Army under Joseph Kony, but may be even more apparent in the rather rapid emergence and spread of the Santa

Muerte cult in Mexico, especially given the already prevalent cult/ magical activities tied in with the cartels.

La Familia Michoacana and its founder, Nazario Moreno González, make an interesting case in point. Founded in the 1980's as a vigilante, self-protection organization, it rapidly shifted into becoming both a full fledged drug cartel and cult. La Familia Michoacana appears to have codified violence into a series of ritualized acts, complete with shamanic interpretations.[58] While González appears to have produced a somewhat coherent cycle of meaning, it was both extremely limited in its scope and rather poor in its construction of rituals.[59]

The initial success of La Familia, and the current success of their descendants, Los Caballeros Templarios, points toward the potential effects of mixing a coherent cycle of meaning that matches and explains lived reality with a criminal organization focused on increasingly violent "messaging". One has to wonder how long it will be before one of these cartels finds an equivalent of Adolfo Constanzo who, unlike González, at least had training in constructing rituals?[60]

The rise of Santa Muerte, especially in its narcocultura form, is quite disturbing since, unlike the concern that, say, Los Caballeros Templarios might acquire a competent ritual specialist, the Santa Muerte cosmology crosses most cartels and many non-cartel members. In other words, it has a relatively wide reach covering large areas of Mexico, Central America, parts of the United States, and some intrusions into Canada and Europe.[61] When this reach is added to the rapid shifts in the economic and social environment covered by the area, I would argue that the potential for a competent ritual specialist—a "prophet"—to emerge is increasingly likely.[62]

The emergence of such a prophet, however, is unlikely to do anything to counter the cartels, especially given their habit of killing off priests who oppose them.[63] A more plausible scenario would involve a prophet who supported the broad anti-government context of the cartels, proceeded to ritualize both inter-cartel and extra-cartel violence and, at the same time, managed to provide basic services to the members of the Santa Muerte cult.

Human consciousness operates in the same patterns, regardless of situation. Throughout our evolution as a species, we have learned and passed on many techniques of manipulating and changing consciousness, and regardless of what we call that collection of techniques—marketing, psychology, politics or magic—collectively, they form the art and science of causing changes in consciousness in accordance with will.

As with all human technologies, some will use them for the greater good, most for getting by, and some for purely personal gain regardless of the cost to anyone else. No society can be resilient and able to survive shocks either by meekly succumbing to the depredations of sociopaths or by being so rigid that it enforces absolute conformity.

Notes

[1]   Frank Hoffman and Michael C. Davies, "Joint Force 2020 and the Human Domain: Time for a New Conceptual Framework?" *Small Wars Journal.* 10 June 2013, http://smallwarsjournal.com/jrnl/art/joint-force-2020-and-the-human-domain-time-for-a-new-conceptual-framework. dl: 15 August 2013.

[2]   Consult Stanislav Andrevski, *Social Science as Sorcery.* New York: St. Martin's Press, 1972 for the classic analysis of social science as a form of divination.

[3]   Consult Bronislaw Malinowski, *Magic, Science and Religion.* New York: Anchor Books, 1954 [1916] and, in particular, his discussion of how "magic" becomes "technology."

[4]   See Peter Applebome, "Drugs, Death and the Occult Meet In Grisly Inquiry at Mexico Border." *The New York Times.* 13 April 1989, http://www.nytimes.com/1989/04/13/us/drugs-death-and-the-occult-meet-in-grisly-inquiry-at-mexico-border.html. dl: 15 October 2013.

[5]   See James R. Lewis. Ed., *The Order of the Solar Temple: The Temple of Death.* Burlington: Ashgate Publishing Company, 2006 and CBC Digital Archives, "Solar Temple: A cult gone wrong," http://www.cbc.ca/archives/categories/society/crime-justice/solar-temple-a-cult-gone-wrong/the-madness-begins.html. dl: 15 October 2013.

[6]   See Tim Reiterman and John Jacobs, *Raven: The Untold Story of Rev. Jim Jones and His People.* New York: Dutton, 1982.

[7]   While not immediately obvious, individual identity derives from roles within larger narratives which, in turn, are produced and maintained by the symbol systems (meta-narratives) that comprise religions and ideologies.

[8]   One central point made by many practitioners of magic is that every spell has both a symbolic and a material component. Often, the material

component produces the effect, while the symbolic component situates the effect within a symbolic universe. In some cases, however, the symbolic component produces the effect, while the material component has no actual effect at all (e.g. It uses the "Placebo Effect").

[9]   Alfred Korzybski, "A Non-Aristotelian System and its Necessity for Rigour in Mathematics and Physics", paper presented at the American Mathematical Society, New Orleans, Louisiana, 28 December 1931. Reprinted in Alfred Zorzybski, *Science and Sanity*, 5th Edition. Englewood: Institute of General Semantics, 1933: 747–761.

[10]   Gregory Bateson and Mary Catherine Bateson, *Angel's Fear*. New York: Bantam, 1988.

[11]   In intelligence circles, this is often cast as the problem of mirror imaging. Consult U.S. Government, *A Tradecraft Primer: Structured Analytic Techniques for Improving Intelligence Analysis*. Washington, DC: 2009, https://www.cia.gov/library/center-for-the-study-of-intelligence/csi-publications/books-and-monographs/Tradecraft%20Primer-apr09.pdf.

[12]   See Bronislaw Malinowski, *A Scientific Theory of Culture*. New York: Oxford University Press, 1960 [1944] for one model of emergence.

[13]   Consult Mircea Eliade, *Shamanism: Archaic Techniques of Ecstasy*. Princeton: Princeton University Press, 1964 [1951].

[14]   Clifford Geertz, *The Interpretation of Culture*. New York: Basic Books, 1973: 90.

[15]   Charles D. Laughlin, "The Cycle of Meaning" in Stephen Glazier, Ed, *Anthropology of Religion: Handbook of Theory and Method*. Westport: Greenwood Press, 1997: 471-488, http://www.biogeneticstructuralism.com/articles.htm. dl: August 20th, 2013. The graphic was produced by the author based on Laughlin's original article.

[16]   Both Geertz's discussion of the overall model and Laughlin's examination of the specific process are generally embedded within the discourse of Cultural Anthropology and, more particularly, the Anthropology of Religion and Symbolic Anthropology. As such, they tend to be used as ways of examining cultural processes that already exist such as rites of passage (e.g. births, marriages, deaths, etc.), rituals of maintenance (e.g. standardized or emergent ritual behaviour within a culture) or the emergence of "cults."

[17]   Eric Hoffer, *The True Believer*. New York: Time, 1963.

[18]   See David G. Bromley, Joel Best and James R. Richardson, Eds., *The Satanism Scare*. New York: De Gruyter, 1991.

[19] While generally "secular" in tone, these political rhetorical attacks are actually based on attacks against a competing metaphysical perception of the zeitgeist of the society as expressed through its secular "sacred canopy". See Peter L. Berger, *The Sacred Canopy.* New York: Doubleday, 1967.

[20] See William H. Calvin, "The Six Essentials? Minimal Requirements for the Darwinian Bootstrapping of Quality" *Journal of Memetics— Evolutionary Models of Information Transmission* 1. 1997, http://www.williamcalvin.com/1990s/1997JMemetics.htm. dl: 25 October 2013.

[21] While the exact origins of the term Left Hand Path are lost, there are two different meanings. First, there is the idea of a direct opposition of Light and Dark (absolute order vs. chaos), seen in Manichean Cosmology. Second, there is the idea of paired opposition of limited (vs. absolute) order and chaos, seen in the Horus—Set myth cycles. Most modern occultists, such as Dion Fortune (e.g. *The Training and Work of an Initiate.* Wellingborough: The Aquarian Press, 1982 [1930]) and Franz Bardon (*Initiation Into Hermetics.* Wuppertal: Dieter Rüggerberg, 1987 [1956]) tend to default to the first understanding, but also use and recognize the more limited, oppositional form.

[22] On this form of social trust, see Emile Durkheim, *The Division of Labor in Society.* W.D. Halls Trans., New York: The Free Press, 1984 and Mary Douglas, *How Institutions Think.* Syracuse: Syracuse University Press, 1986.

[23] Susan Collins and Carl Levin, "Preface" in Executive Sessions of the Senate Permanent Subcommittee On Investigations. Washington, DC: U.S. Government Printing Office, 2003: XI. dl: 30 October 2013. This is clearly an example of an "ends justifies the means" form of degradation.

[24] On the first, see Eliade, *Shamanism.* The second is a common element in most Christian traditions, although some will develop it but hedged round with numerous symbolic safe guards. As a note, the skill itself appears to lie in developing the ability of an individual to project abductive reasoning about a problem or concern on to an external "hallucination".

[25] Note well: The inclusion of flexibility / adaptability in the concept of Will is one of the primary differences between how occultists and magicians understand magic and how most academics understand magic. In much of the academic literature examining magic, there is a distinction between "sorcery"—rituals that must be followed exactly with predictable outcomes and where the practitioner does not have to

be able to perceive their operations—and "witchcraft"—rituals where the ability to perceive and directly influence "power" is necessary (see, for example, E.E. Evans-Pritchard *Witchcraft, Oracles and Magic among the Azande,* abridged version, Eva Giles. Ed., Oxford: Clarendon Press, 1976). The vast majority of modern magicians hold that the ability to perceive and manipulate "power" is crucial.

[26] See Peter Berger, *The Sacred Canopy.*

[27] Many behavioural neuroses rooted in fear actually contain positive survival characteristics, and are often implanted in children at an early age. For example, having children wandering around in the woods of medieval Europe was a good way for them to end up dead, often killed by wolves, hence stories such as Little Red Riding Hood.

[28] Consult Max Weber, *The Sociology of Religion,* Trans. Ephraim Fischoff. Boston: Beacon Press, 1963 [1922].

[29] Probably the best known of the inversions was the movement of praying for the souls of the dead to lessen their time in Purgatory had shifted to the outright purchase of Indulgences where one could literally buy, for cash, time off. A more important, but less consciously discussed, reason behind the Reformation was that as a ritual system, the Roman Catholic Church was not providing a good symbolic interface to understand and operate within the changing socio-technical system of the early modern period. See Max Weber's *The Protestant Ethic and the Spirit of Capitalism.* T. Parsons, Ed., New York: The Free Press, 1958 [1905] for an analysis along these lines.

[30] In this instance, "moral failings" refers not to any published standard of morality from the time but, rather, to the survival effects of using one or other religious system for a population.

[31] These institutions were originally bound up in the various Inquisitorial orders, such as the Dominicans, The Spanish Inquisition, etc. On the construction of the anti-cosmology of Satanism, see Jeffrey Burton Russell's "Witchcraft and the Demonization of Heresy." with Mark Wyndham. *Medievalia* 2. 1976: 1-21. Reprinted in Brian Levack, Ed., *Witchcraft, Magic, and Demonology.* New York: Garland, 1992; *Satan: The Early Christian Tradition.* Ithaca: Cornell, 1981; *Lucifer: The Devil in the Middle Ages.* Ithaca: Cornell, 1984; and *Mephistopheles: The Devil in the Modern World.* Ithaca: Cornell, 1986. On the construction of rituals supporting this anti-cosmology, see the Malleus Mallifacrum as the classic "manual". On the process of applying this anti-cosmology to

groups during the period, see Carlo Ginsburg's *The Night Battles*. New York: Penguin, 1985 [1966]. On the production of a "reign of terror," see Gustav Henningsen, *The Witches' Advocate: Basque Witchcraft and the Spanish Inquisition (1609–1619)*. Reno: University of Nevada Press, 1980.

[32] Within the Satanic Black Mass, inversions are quite simple to see. For example, while a cross is still used, it is upside down. On the most recent, general outbreak of the application of this anti-cosmology to groups, see David G. Bromley et.al., *The Satanism Scare*.

[33] See Randall Garrett, *Lord Darcy*. Wake Forest: Baen Books, 2002. While a collection of fictional tales in the fantasy/alternate history genre, Garrett's work draws on both occult literature and academic studies of magic, and many of his observations are quite astute. It should also be noted that the use of fiction by occultists and other practitioners of magic is quite common, including, but by no means limited to, Apuleius, Dion Fortune, Gerald Gardner (the "Father" of modern Witchcraft), and many others.

[34] This is an exact parallel with the operation of intelligence analysis where most agencies concentrate on analyzing capabilities rather than intentions.

[35] The case of the Jamestown Satanic Panic is a good example of what can happen; see Jeffrey S. Victor, *Satanic Panic: The Creation of a Contemporary Legend*. Chicago: Open Court Publishing Company, 1993.

[36] The main form of Left Hand Path magic such an analysis is unable to detect is that which hides in plain sight. For example, a person who for all intents and purposes appears to be supporting and upholding the dominant cosmology while, at the same time, twisting the operational rules for their own ends with no concern for their effects on the overall system. A religious example would be that of Savonarola in Florence, while a political example would be Senator Joseph McCarthy, both of whom placed their vision of the ends justifying the means, used current techniques and technologies to support that choice, and ended up damaging the system in which they operated. Please note that there is absolutely no indication whatsoever that either of these individuals consciously practised what they thought of as "magic" to achieve their ends, merely that what they did practice—"religion" and "politics,"

respectively—are both symbol systems embedded in cosmologies which were negatively effected by their practice.

[37] The Reformed Churches, especially the Calvinists, are specifically excluded simply because they were not included in the original Peace of Augsburg (1555) which gave the Lutheran Confession a legal standing within the Holy Roman Empire and, at the same time, established the principle of *cuius regio, eius religio* ("who rules, his religion"). The Calvinists, and other Reformed churches, did not have any legal standing until the Treaty of Westphalia (1648), a situation that appears to have been the proximate cause of the Thirty Years War.

[38] For a contemporary analysis of witchcraft trials, see Friedrich Spee von Langenfeld, *Cautio Criminalis, or a Book on Witch Trials*. Trans. Marcus Hellyer. Charlottesville: University of Virginia Press, 2003 [1631].

[39] It is important to note that this possibility of "religious cleansing" was actually addressed <u>for Lutherans and Catholics only</u> in article 24 of the peace of Augsburg that allowed for the free resettlement of members of the two main confessions into areas of the same confession. One of the most egregious examples of religious cleansing took place in Bavaria between 1579 and 1597 under Duke William V, a period also noted for witch hunts.

[40] The exact relationship between the two is tricky since the magical systems themselves claim derivation from a number of sources including the Corpus Hermeticum (via the de Medici Academy). The form, as opposed to the content, is actually a Greco-Roman form of talismans, usually made out of lead, and inscribed with specific names and sigils. The content—names, sigils, etc.—deals with angels and demons that, according to the anti-cosmology, have power over different areas of reality and daily life. In England, the best known practitioner of this type of magic was Dr. John Dee, court astrologer to Elizabeth I. On the French versions of this type, see also Maurice Bouisson, *Magic: It's History and Practice*. Trans. G. Almayrac. New York: Dutton & Co, 1961 [1958], Chapter 7, and Robert Lionel Séguin, *La sorcellerie au Québec du XVIIe au XIXe siècle*. Montréal: Leméac, 1978.

[41] In *Cautio Criminalis*, Friedrich Spee von Langenfeld makes several powerful arguments that the true evil in the witchcraft and sorcery trials he was involved with was practised by the judges and lawyers rather than the accused. See also Ginzburg's *Night Battles*.

[42] On the use of cultural genetics to analyze conflicts, see Marc Tyrrell, "The Use of Evolutionary Theory in Modeling Culture and Cultural Conflict" in Thomas H. Johnson and Barry Scott Zellen, Eds., *Culture, Conflict and Counterinsurgency*. Redwood City: Stanford University Press, 2014.

[43] See Bromley et.al., *The Satanism Scare*.

[44] Carl Gustav Jung, *Collected Works*, Vol. 18, Bollingen Series XX, Trans. R.F.C. Hull, Princeton: Princeton University Press, 1976, #759: 318.

[45] As an effect, this appears to be a human universal where every act of "good" has an opposite act of "evil". In the legal terminology of Rome, this was the distinction between malleficium and beneficium. In medicine, this is often talked about as those who can cure can kill. It is really a recognition that any type of knowledge that can be applied to observable effect contains its moral antithesis. Symbolically, Claude Levi-Strauss discusses this in his concept of Binary Opposition; see *Structural Anthropology*. New York: Basic Books, 1974.

[46] Al Qaeda and, especially, Zawahiri's doctrine of takfirism, is an example of an abstracted revitalization movement. On revitalization movements in general, see Anthony F. C. Wallace, "Revitalization Movements." *American Anthropologist* New Series 58. April 1956: 264-281.

[47] As organizations expand their control over areas of knowledge, fields of inquiry in those areas become limited to members of the organization. As their social monopoly over an area of knowledge lessons, the area becomes more open to alternative forms of knowledge and practice (consult Andrew Abbot, *The System of the Professions*. Chicago: University of Chicago Press, 1988).

[48] In the first instance, the Roman Catholic Church had reserved the monopoly over acceptance of physics that had an implied effect on Christian cosmology. This monopoly was weakened during the 16th and 17th centuries, allowing for the development of empirical science. In the second instance, most medical practice had been the province of midwives and "wise women", many of whom were caught up in the witch hunts. The emergence of modern medicine, however, did not come under the control of any of the Churches operating, instead, across confessions and, in many cases, outside of confessional controls.

[49] It is interesting to note that in at least one case, Iceland, the older religion survived intact and as an officially licenced alternative to Christianity. In almost every other case, the older religions were originally suppressed

through peer pressure, ridicule, and expulsion (consult the Canon Episcopi of the 11th century). Sir J.G. Fraser noted hundreds of these remnants, which he termed "artifacts", in his 12 volume work *The Golden Bough*. A few modern examples of this are Mexico's Day of the Dead (Día de Muertos) with roots in the worship of Mictecacihuatl and also from Spain, the Anglosphere's Halloween with its old Celtic roots in Samhain, and the Christmas Tree with its roots in Donar's Oak. For more European examples, see, also, Carlo Ginzburg, *The Night Battles and Ecstasies: Deciphering the Witch's Sabbath*. New York: Pantheon Books, 1991.

[50] See Sharon Kelly Heyob, *The Cult of Isis among the Women of the Greco-Roman World*. Leiden: Leiden Brill, 1975 for one examination of how syncretic mystery cults spread. The Reformation-Counter-Reformation period, in addition to producing some rather strange syncretic versions of Christianity (consult Carlo Ginzburg, *The Cheese and the Worms*. Trans. John Tedesci and Anne C. Tedesci, Baltimore: Johns Hopkins University Press, 1992), this period also saw the rise of a number of "secret societies" and "occult fraternities". For a rather biased, albeit fairly comprehensive, account, see Lady Queensborough, *Occult Theocrasy*. Hawethorne: The Christian Book Club of America, 1933. For a good introduction to the more modern New Religious Movements, see Jacob Needleman and George Baker, Eds., *Understanding the New Religions*. New York: The Seabury Press, 1981.

[51] One of the few, and probably the most notorious, early Satanists who was clearly a Left Hand Path practitioner was Giles de Rais (d. 1440) whose use of both blood and sex magic is fairly well documented, at least in terms of the children he kidnapped, tortured and killed. For Satanism in 1880's France, see Joris-Karl Huysmans, *Là-Bas*. Trans. Terry Hale, New York: Penguin Classics, 2002. Modern public Satanism started with the Church of Satan founded by Anton LaVey in 1966, although there are precursor, semi-public groups.

[52] For an excellent, pre-Duvalier, examination of Haitian Voodoo, see Alfred Métraux *Voodoo in Haiti*. Trans. Hugo Charteris, London: Andre Deutsch, 1959. For a modern examination of Voodoo and its use surrounding violence, see Bettina E. Schmidt, "Anthropological Reflections on Religion and Violence" in Andrew R. Murphy, Ed., *The Blackwell Companion to Religion and Violence*. Oxford: Wiley-Blackwell, 2011. A similar example of attempts to use mythopoeaic

events and displays of magic, although much less successful, lies in Joseph Kony and the Lord's Resistance Army.

[53]   See Applebome, "Drugs, Death and the Occult."

[54]   See Charlotte Greig, *Evil Serial Killers: In the Minds of Monsters*. New York: Barnes & Noble, 2005.

[55]   Consult Peter Berger, *The Sacred Canopy* and, also, Robert N. Bellah and Phillip E. Hammond, *Varieties of Civil Religion*. New York: Harper and Row, 1980. Similar arguments can be made for such a process in most Western democracies; see, for example, Reginald Bibby, *Fragmented Gods: The Poverty and Potential of Religion in Canada*. Toronto: Stoddard Press, 1990 and *Restless Gods: The Renaissance of Religion in Canada*. Ottawa: Novalis Press, 2004.

[56]   Hinduism has such a meta-cosmology built into it at a core philosophical level. The Romans, being a much more "pragmatic" people, used the office of Pontifex Maximus (Great Bridge Builder) to provide that link, and within Chinese (and Japanese) history, the linkage is provided by an extremely functionalist approach.

[57]   This is discussed in some detail in Marc Tyrrell and Tom Quiggan, "Fear and (In)Security theatre," *Broken Mirrors* podcast. October 2013, http://www.brokenmirrors.ca/?p=339 and http://warontherocks.com/2013/10/broken-mirrors-episode-3-fear-insecurity-theatre/. What can serve as such a unifying meta-cosmology is, unfortunately, not apparent at the present time.

[58]   In a 6 September 2006 incident, Familia operatives tossed five severed heads onto a night club dance floor in Uruapan, Michoacan. The message they left behind is a clear shamanic interpretation—"The family doesn't kill for money. It doesn't kill women. It doesn't kill innocent people, only those who deserve to die. Know that this is divine justice." George W. Grayson, *La Familia: Another Deadly Mexican Syndicate*. Washington, DC: Foreign Policy Research Institute, February 2009, http://www.fpri.org/enotes/200901.grayson.lafamilia.html. dl: 23 November 2013.

[59]   The poverty of its rituals is in comparison with the rituals used by the Tonton Macoutes, who drew on hundreds of years of ritual history, symbology, and mythopoeaic events, and the Nazi-party's use of grand rituals such as the Nuremberg Rallies which showed an extremely sophisticated understanding of ritual processes. In comparison, La

Familia's rituals or, rather, what we can determine of them, were quite poor.

[60] As a note, constructing and running effective rituals—mythopoeaic events—that link together within a cosmology is much harder than constructing semi-coherent cosmologies. This relates back to the Art and Science components of the definition of magic discussed earlier, and is one of the reasons why training and experience in ritual construction and operation is so useful in producing effective rituals. Unfortunately, the spread of published books and, later, the Internet makes a plethora of rituals and ritual components available to budding cult leaders.

[61] See Robert J. Bunker, "Santa Muerte: Inspired and Ritualistic Killings." *FBI Law Enforcement Bulletin.* February 2013 in three parts available, http://www.fbi.gov/stats-services/publications/law-enforcement-bulletin/2013/february/santa-muerte-inspired-and-ritualistic-killings-part-1-of-3 for a good, quick overview.

[62] It appears that there have already been human sacrifice killings associated with the Santa Muerte cult (see "Mexico arrests over La Santa Muerte cult killings," *BBC Online.* 31 March, 2012, http://www.bbc.co.uk/news/world-latin-america-17570199. dl: 25 November 2013), although this may be a "standard" witch killing. Witch killing, in its standard form, is the identification of an individual and their ritual killing to stop the spell; see, for example, E. E. Evans-Pritchard, *Witchcraft, Oracles and Magic among the Azande.*

[63] This is especially so since the Roman Catholic Church appears to have declared war against Santa Muerte. See Vladimir Hernandez, "The country where exorcisms are on the rise," *BBC Mundo.* 25 November 2013, http://www.bbc.co.uk/news/magazine-25032305. dl: 26 November 2013.

Chapter 2

CONFLICT IN THE VEINS: DRUG USE BY VIOLENT NON-STATE ACTORS

Paul Rexton Kan

The non-medical use of drugs by combatants has a long history. Drugs used for medical and recuperative reasons have been commonplace on the battlefield, but the consumption of mind-altering substances before, during, and after combat has also been a regular feature of war. Before armed clashes with British, French and American colonial armies, warriors from various Native American tribes used peyote. The Zulu warriors of Isandlwana cooked a cannabis broth, emboldening them and making them unpredictable as they faced British troops in 1879. The use of opium took its toll on the forces of the Chinese emperor during the time of the Opium Wars; many of the Chinese soldiers fighting to defend the empire from British forces were addicted. During World War I, prior to a particularly severe attack in Gallipoli, Australian pharmacists were ordered to distribute their cocaine supplies to troops. During World War II, amphetamines were widely used among all sides to keep fighting men alert. Methamphetamine was synthesized in an injectable form by the Japanese in 1919 and was widely used by Imperial Japanese forces in World War II.[1]

The use of drugs continues in contemporary wars among a number of radical violent non-state actors, be they insurgents, terrorists, militia members, maritime pirates, or criminal gangs. The use of drugs by belligerents is part of what appears to be a universal human drive to seek intoxication, whether during peacetime or during war.[2] Indeed the many reasons people use drugs in times of peace are the same as the reasons for using them in an atmosphere of organized violence: to numb the body, recreation, to join a social group, for social functioning, for mind expansion, to connect with the divine, to improve performance, to change the body, and for self-medication.[3]

The reasons people choose to use drugs reveals what sociologists have labeled the "set and setting". What a person believes the drug will do to him or her is known as "set" while the physical and social environment in which the drug is taken is considered the "setting".[4] Placed together in the context of today's wars, set is the desired effects of consuming a drug by a violent non-state actor and the setting is irregular conflicts that undermine the structures of national government. Law enforcement has broken down as have societal norms that would have inhibited the ingesting of illegal narcotics. In such an atmosphere, atrocities that defy an ordinary sense of logic and morality are commonplace. By understanding set and setting along with the twin forces of combatant supply and demand, we can draw a fuller connection between the role of drug intoxication and acts of violent non-state actors.

Drug Demand Among Violent Non-State Actors

For violent non-state actors, the setting for drug use is an atmosphere of organized violence, where hostile acts are perpetrated by them against others as well as perpetrated against them by others. In various contexts, they battle professional security forces like militaries and law enforcement; in different contexts they face other violent non-state actors. No matter the context, war is an environment that is fraught with danger and risk of personal injury or death. Taking mind-altering substances may seem like an additional risk for an individual fighter who must be not only aware of danger but competent enough to defend himself, his comrades and equipment. Maintaining a clear mind would seem to be more advantageous than being intoxicated or strung out. However, much like drug use by ordinary citizens in peacetime, "gains generally loom larger than risks [because] gains tend to be immediate" while jeopardy, danger and consequence are more remote.[5] An individual's fears and concerns are often mitigated by the atmosphere of organized violence—the gain of cheating death outweighs the possibility of impairment, illness or injury in the minds of many combatants who consume drugs. Also, the types of equipment used by irregular forces do not require a great degree of skill. The lack of sophisticated weaponry facilitates the ease of their use; shooting a gun, planting a mine and aiming a mortar do not require a combatant to be clean and sober to do so. In contrast to the high tech weapons of professional Western militaries and the integrated way they fight, easy to use weapons provide very little restraint on drug use and intoxication by irregular or untrained forces.

Moreover, a heavy proportion of violent non-state actors are in weak and failing states where government institutions and civil society are heavily compromised, fragile or extinct. In these countries, external pressures that constrain an individual's desire to use drugs in peacetime are often lacking. Social norms, legal controls, expense, and availability along with individual fears of addiction, toxicity, and concerns about the lack of knowledge about a drug and supervision of its use are highly diminished or gone altogether. These constraints are often vitiated by the nature of contemporary wars because belligerents focus their attacks on the state's institutions, and people who promulgate them. The prime example is Somalia where the breakdown of the state and ongoing internal violence has created the conditions for widespread drug use by combatants. One study revealed that "self-reported khat use was more frequent and excessive among male ex-combatants (60%) than among adult male civilian war survivors (28%) and males without war experience (18%)."[6]

As constraints begin to erode in war, the appeals of setting that lead an individual to abuse drugs during peacetime are heightened. Peer pressure and "turning on" a friend to a drug are more acutely felt in wartime when an individual fighter must demonstrate his bravery and honor. Small group cohesion occurs when individuals experience and survive danger with their fellow comrades. Drug use allows an individual to "prove himself" to his comrades and eases his transition into a battlefield context.

Additionally, unlike drug use by conventional forces, violent non-state actors are neither prescribed and administered drugs by a centralized government bureaucracy nor do medical professionals closely monitor their use. Violent non-state groups are mainly comprised of civilians who are not trained to handle combat stress nor equipped with sophisticated weapons like their professional military counterparts. Without sophisticated weaponry, individual fighters engage in close combat encounters and experience the extreme tension of hand-to-hand combat. Drugs provide a means to cope with the physical stress and mental anxiety that are a part of such violent encounters. In essence, drugs can compensate for the lack of training and mental discipline that are part of the composition of professional military forces and are a resource that can increase the probability of winning for militarily weaker groups. Professional soldiers diagnosed with post-traumatic stress disorder are routinely put on a drug regimen to treat their symptoms. Irregular fighters, by contrast, who experience the post-traumatic stress disorder do not have the same access to medical professionals or dispensaries; they will self-medicate with whatever drug might be available. Marijuana is particularly helpful because as a cannabinoid, it not only eases physical pain, but dulls memory formation and emotion.[7] This is one reason that marijuana use is present in nearly every contemporary conflict.

While drugs can compensate for the lack of formal training that members of professional militaries receive, drug consumption can also empower the ways irregular fighters engage in violence. Since traditional societies do not have standing armies, they rely on men of fighting age who display courage, honor and valor in battle.[8] The consumption of drugs aids in the display of these qualities. Drug use also helps a violent non-state group enhance its reputation. Conventional militaries have established reputations that come with years of experience and tradition. Violence is often meant to send a message; "a primary goal of communication, namely to modify people's beliefs about a situation or a person, is often better achieved by deeds than by words. Actions send signals and are often meant to."[9] In Mexico, horrific acts like decapitations in discos, displaying heads in soccer fields, and sewing a rival's face to a soccer ball, all serve as signals to rivals and to the government.[10] They are a cartel's version of "shock and awe".[11] As Jorge Chabat puts it, "this is psychological warfare. These beheadings serve to stun. They cut them off *to show us what they are capable of.*"[12] The effect is to gain a reputation for ruthlessness that will make a cartel more credible, perhaps forestalling the future need to use violence and to achieve a level of security to continue its operations. In Mexico, many low level cartel and gang members are intoxicated on drugs; it easier to commit gruesome killings while intoxicated. Videos on YouTube and Facebook show members taking drugs and celebrating their recent actions against rivals and police. "[The gruesome murders] occur while they are consuming their product. They are not sober. They are operating in a group, they are drugged up, and they are operating with a sense of absolute impunity."[13]

In some conflicts, the widespread presence of civilians on the battlefield is also made worse if a violent non-state group relies on the drug trade for financing. With the growing wartime significance of drug crops and smuggling routes to the financing of warring groups, civilians who cultivate drug crops, inhabit valuable agricultural space, or live near transportation routes, therefore come to be seen as legitimate targets by opposing groups. Actions taken against these civilians by non-professional and poorly equipped troops also cause the same type of combat stress that individual fighters seek to lessen by using narcotics.

In a war setting, individual fighters use drugs for four main reasons related to "set"—stimulation, reward, relaxation, and pursuit of the sacred. Drugs can stimulate a person's will to fight and to ignore the possibilities of injury and death. The notion of "liquid courage" is not just applicable to the use of alcohol, but to the use of other drugs in situations of organized violence. Afghan soldiers who worked with Soviet forces in the 1980s against the mujahedin were provided hashish in their rations; "when you get high on hashish, you become completely revolutionary and attack the enemy—fear simply disappears."[14] Drugs are often used to fend off the boredom that accompanies being a part of a group that, when not fighting, is waiting to fight, hiding or carrying on the mundane duties that are required to keep a combatant group effective. Drugs have been offered as rewards for conducting hazardous or unpalatable operations against civilians. John Mueller describes the phenomenon as "carnival" whereby warring groups take a territory and celebrate by looting medical buildings for drugs and then following up with orgies of rape, torture and murder of local residents.[15]

The consumption of drugs for sacred purposes occupies a special category of drug use by violent non-state actors because it is another setting within and surrounding the setting of war. In states that are weak and failing, where formal institutions of social control are contested and broken, and where informal levers of civil society are fragile, violent non-state actors will fill the vacuum by creating new norms for intragroup bonding, to gain recruits, and to generate legitimacy among the populace. These new norms are often based on religious practices that exist in the culture of a weak or failing state, but are perverted for dubious ends. Violent non-state actors commit religious misappropriation. For example,

> Since ancient times, drugs have probably been part of the "conditioning" of African warriors in very strict ritual settings. Even today, although the social control exercised through the activity by the shamans, witches and other initiates over the use of psychoactive substances has, in many instances, disappeared, these substances are still in widespread use, as was observed, for example, during the conflicts in Liberia and Sierra Leone. Like the grigri, the power to make warriors invisible, leave them unaffected by bullets and so on is attributed to certain substances.[16]

Violent non-state actors will often call on the divine to give them an advantage in battle against their enemies. Connections to the mystical are seen as ways to fight honorably or to become impervious to injury and death in combat. This may also have a long history. The word "assassin" is widely believed to be derived from "hashish" which was said to be ingested by a radical sect of Shia Muslims fighters in the 11th century.[17] As in the past, when fighters ingest drugs for mystical reasons, they believe they are given protection from harm and are imbued with not only courage but also a sense of righteousness. Drug intoxication enables them to commit violent acts to achieve religiously inspired goals; drug use helps an individual combatant engage in violence in the name of the divine. For them, drug use is not immoral, but sacred because it helps an individual link the earthly with the divine.

Dark magico-religious activities by violent non-state actors are enabled and complimented by sacred drug use. This is clear in the case of Mexican drug cartels and gangs who participate in the Santa Muerte cult. Described in this book's other essays, the Santa Muerte cult can be summarized as a set of ritual practices offered on behalf a supernatural personification of death who is feminine and, to believers, exists within the context of Catholic theology, comparable to one of the archangels.[18] The "dark" portion of the Santa Muerte cult is the focus on doing harm to others through veneration and ritual. Over half of the prayers directed at her include petitions to harm other people via curses and death magic.[19] A sizeable minority of worshipers follows the fully criminalized variant of Santa Muerte worship steeped in the narco culture that exists in areas of Mexican society. The imminent mortality facing adherents in cartels and gangs makes the worship of Santa Muerte a comfortable fit.

In dark magico-religious instances, a portion of the rewards must be shared with the diety that granted them. Once again, by connecting with the divine, the individual must show gratitude by providing a blood offering or a sacrifice from the enemy that is made easier by the ingestion of drugs. The death of someone's enemies, protection from harm, cultivation of a dangerous reputation, and ability to enjoy the benefits of fabulous riches are rewards for criminal adherents. "With the stakes so high, the sacrifices and offerings to Santa Muerte have become primeval and barbaric. Rather than plates of food, beer, and tobacco, in some instances, the heads of victims (and presumably their souls) have served as offerings to invoke powerful petitions for divine intervention."[20]

The complimentary nature of dark magico-religious groups and sacred drug use is also evident in the actions of jihadi terror groups. Some assume that Islam's theological proscription against intoxication prevents the consumption of narcotics by jihadists who are committed to a "purer" form of Islam. As such, some believe that these groups limit their participation to merely trafficking narcotics as part of their cause to undermine their enemies: "Just as 'puritanical' communists of decades past were willing to traffic in narcotics even if they would never allow their legal sale and use, modern self-proclaimed 'jihadis' are proving willing to be traffickers—*just not users*."[21] However, this assumption is incorrect. Religion, in some cases, is actually more likely to promote drug use if it supports a group's long-term struggle to undermine an infidel's society. Members of jihadist groups from West Africa to the Hindu Kush have consumed a wide range of narcotics as a way to conduct violent operations like suicide bombings. The brief sin of intoxication can be washed away by martyrdom. Jihadi suicide bombers are also known to consume drugs as varied as heroin, meth, and Ritalin as a way to steady themselves before detonating their devices.[22]

Drug Supply in Contemporary Conflicts

The demand for drugs by combatants must also be juxtaposed with the availability of drugs to combatants. A supply of drugs must somehow be accessible and attained in order for set and setting to have any analytical value. In areas of widespread or intense violence, finding narcotics is easy. Typically, the supply for drugs in today's wars falls into at least one of four categories: transshipped, looted, manufactured, and traditional. These categories are not mutually exclusive to a single conflict since combatants often find access to drugs from a number of differing sources.

Some drugs are consumed because they are available due to the presence of a transit route through the territory where a conflict is occurring. Globalization has been a significant factor because it has made a variety of drugs available to new markets where there are both conflicts and valuable transshipment points. Coca, for example, is not grown in Africa, yet belligerents routinely use cocaine because they are "paid" with it by traffickers who seek to move the drug to the European market. Such bartering for securing routes is not uncommon. Before committing their atrocities, RUF fighters in Sierra Leone regularly consumed crack cocaine and "brown-brown" (heroin) that were transshipped through their territories.[23]

Violent non-state actors can also attain drugs by looting them from pharmacies, clinics, and hospitals. These drugs are prescription drugs manufactured by pharmaceutical companies for ailments unrelated to combat. Nonetheless, they can alter the consciousness of a fighter for the four reasons related to set. Drugs looted from pharmacies were used as rewards and motivators for those Hutus who committed atrocities against Tutsis during the Rwanda genocide in 1994.[24] During the Iraq War in the immediate aftermath of the fall of the Hussein regime, several violent non-state actors abused numerous pharmaceutical drugs like Captagon (stimulant), Benzhexol (relaxant), Benzodizeapines (a stimulant when abused), and Valium which were looted from clinics, pharmacies, and hospitals in the chaos that ensued.[25]

Groups linked to dark magico-religious acts also ingest traditional drugs because their use is part of the longstanding cultural practices of the society shared by the violent non-state group and are readily available in the territory where the conflict takes place. For example, the drug *khat* is part of the social landscape of east African societies and combatants in Somalia and Sudan incorporate its use. As mentioned previously, these drugs can be sacred because they link the fighter to the traditions of the past and connect fighters to the divine. This was commonplace in Liberia's civil wars where warfare had an added spiritual dimension. The belligerents believed that bullets were destined to kill specific people. As a way to defend against this, violent non-state actors fortified themselves with marijuana and palm wine and donned dresses and wigs to alter their appearance and their spirit, believing that bullets would be confused and misidentify their true targets. In Sierra Leone, animist based beliefs contributed to unorthodox warfighting. Some fighters believed in *juju* spirits which could be strengthened in an individual by ingesting drugs. One ritual consisted of having a naked woman walk backwards and look in a mirror (which made her invisible), allowing her to bury charms near the opposing group's position, thus improving the fighters' chances of victory.[26]

Manufactured drugs like methamphetamine have been part of sacred drug use, most notably among jihadi fighters. In Iraq, evidence of methamphetamine production was found in insurgent hideouts linked to Al Qaeda in Iraq. Numerous returning military field commanders have substantiated claims of drugged insurgent fighters from Abu Mussab al-Zarqawi's group; hideouts used by Zarqawi's fighters were frequently found littered with drug paraphernalia like pipes and needles.[27] A Marine in Ramadi reported that random autopsies of insurgents discovered high levels of narcotics use.[28] In another instance, the terrorists that attack hotels in Mumbai were also high on at least one type of manufactured drug. "'Injections containing traces of cocaine and LSD [were] left behind by the terrorists and [we] later found drugs in their blood,' said one official....This explains why they managed to battle the commandos for over 50 hours with no food or sleep....One terrorist used the drugs to keep on fighting despite suffering a life-threatening injury."[29]

It is evident that groups linked to dark magico-religious activities are pragmatic when it comes to using drugs; they will use whatever happens to be available as a means to commit acts that connect them with the divine. In Mali, jihadi fighters have taken advantage of cocaine being trafficked through their territory. Not only do they earn profits from "taxing" shipments as they transit through areas they control, they have also used the drug. Witnesses watched the rebels who had captured their town regularly use cocaine. "We saw them sniffing it, smoking it. Some were injecting it."[30] Once again, the theological proscription against intoxication can be absolved by hewing oneself to the larger cause.

Complications and Challenges of Set and Setting

There is very little that conventional militaries or law enforcement can do to significantly alter set and setting of drug consumption by violent non-state groups. The increasing number of civilians comprising belligerent groups when combined with the types and availability of drugs means that the presence of intoxicated combatants and criminals is likely to be an abiding feature of conflict in the near term. While drug use by individuals in conflict occurs for a variety of reasons linked to set and setting, the effects are more far reaching in an era of globalization. Members of violent non-state groups under the influence of drugs have been known to commit massive human rights abuses against rival groups, creating immense human suffering that affects regional stability. For example, "carnival" activities in Yugoslavia sent waves of refugees throughout Europe and eventually led to a Western military response to the immense humanitarian catastrophe unfolding in the heart of Europe.[31] Narco-refugees from Mexico who are fleeing the drug violence continue to increase in number every year and can be found not only across the border in the United States, but in Canada, Spain, and as far away as Australia.

More significantly, as globalization draws more actors together for purposes that range from development projects to security and law enforcement operations, from peacekeeping to humanitarian missions, they are more likely to come into contact with intoxicated combatants. It is likely that militaries and law enforcement will continue to deal with the effects of the presence of drugs in a variety of circumstances. Over time, this will likely pressure governments to reconsider their current approaches. With patterns of conflicts composed of mostly internal violence fought by non-professional armed groups with less sophisticated weaponry, few violent non-state actors will wage a conventional, high tech war because doing so presents enormous training, logistical and resource requirements that few groups can produce.[32] Criminals take on insurgent style tactics against police forces and thus ratchet up the levels of violence in society. Drug use, with its effects on combatant behavior, can narrow the gap by exploiting the legal and ethical regimes under which troops and police forces must operate. Violent non-state actors may consider the humanitarian sensitivity to casualties as an advantage: they "may purposely put their own people in jeopardy if doing so complicates or adversely affects the West's use of its military power."[33] Increasingly, violent non-state actors have sought to present militaries and law enforcement with moral and ethical quandaries. Drug use by violent non-state actors makes such quandaries more acute.

These quandaries are revealed by the British experience in Sierra Leone in 2000. In September of that year, a British patrol was conducting training exercises in Sierra Leone when it was confronted by a rebel force. The patrol was captured and taken hostage when the patrol leader refused to fire on the enemy force which was comprised of drugged boys, of whom the oldest was fifteen and the youngest seven. In response, the British sent paratroopers and the Special Air Service (SAS) to rescue the captured patrol. The response by the British military was in this instance was starkly different—the patrol was successfully recovered with the loss of one British soldier, but estimates on enemy dead vary from 25 to 150 child soldiers.[34]

Another quandary emerged, not when violent non-state actors were intoxicated, but when they were experiencing physical symptoms brought on by a lack of drugs. When drug supplies run low, drug users among fighting forces can suffer withdrawal symptoms which can still lead to the outbreak of violence. For example, forensic evidence shows that some of the militants who seized over one thousand hostages in a southern Russian school in 2004 were long time heroin addicts who were in a state of withdrawal shortly before the violent outcome which claimed more than 300 lives.[35] Withdrawal can last from a few days in the cases of cocaine and heroin to a few months in the case of methamphetamine, thus varying the length and severity of unpredictable behavior. This was the case in April 2009 when the U.S. Navy had to deal with Somali pirates who had taken an American hostage. As negotiations were occurring, the teenage pirates were experiencing withdrawal after days without khat. "'[The pirates] were realizing they were in a no-win situation,' said a senior U.S.

military official. 'They were floating around in rough waters, they were tired.... These guys didn't have their chew with them.'"[36] Drugged fighters may operate in unfamiliar and seemingly irrational ways to members of professional conventional forces, yet the standard response to engaging any fighter whether he is sober or intoxicated is the same—a threat is dealt with by lethal force. This tactic is problematic since the battlefield and combat are no longer the only contexts where professional militaries are deployed and operate. In the years since the end of the Cold War, Western militaries have engaged in peacekeeping, stability and security missions, nation-building activities, and counter-insurgency.

As a generally accepted part of many of these types of operations, ceasefires and the decommissioning of violent non-state groups are required to set a foundation for greater political stability and personal security. However, decommissioning intoxicated combatants can be perilous due to the effects of intoxication, long term abuse, or withdrawals.[37] Efforts to disarm Liberia's warring factions have been fraught with danger due to the widespread abuse of drugs by the fighters who used a variety of traditional, transshipped, and looted drugs.[38] UN peacekeepers in the eastern Democratic Republic of the Congo (DRC) demolished four camps belonging to armed rebel militias and seized drugs, uniforms, and women's clothing used for disguises.[39] These problems are exacerbated by the already loose nature of the command structure of many of these forces and commanders often have little means to limit the amount and type of drugs that their fighters consume.

In law enforcement situations, drug use for dark magico-religious reasons by criminals has presented enormous challenges. The savagery of homicides in Mexico has created a type of anomic cycle of violence. Anomic violence is "the degradation of norms and inhibitions, as the use of violence is an end in itself."[40] Such anomic violence leads a society to being inured by violent scenes and less likely to report crimes to police who are seen as less powerful than non-state actors who are purveyors of dark magico-religious violence. To the detriment of law and order in Mexico, the prevalence of Santa Muerte rituals and depictions intimidates police officers.

Coping with Set and Setting

Although militaries and law enforcement are beginning to recognize the strategic and tactical effects of drugged members of violent non-state groups, little has changed in the way military and police forces have conceptualized the role of illegal narcotics and internal conflicts. Leaders of professional militaries are beginning to recognize the characteristics and effects of drugged combatants to explain their battlefield behavior. For example, United States Pacific Command describes the Abu Sayyaf Group in the Philippines as one that employs "ad hoc strategies and activities that are determined by the mood swings of individual leaders, many with eccentric nicknames reflecting bizarre bandit camaraderie. Discipline is haphazard, and some are addicted to drugs."[41]

Law enforcement agencies, as a matter of routine, send bulletins to officers in various departments that include intelligence on how gangs and cartels use drugs and religious symbolism. In some US police jurisdictions, the possession of certain Mexican narco iconography is enough probable cause for officers to detain an individual. At one stage, Mexican authorities did act to destroy certain Santa Muerte shrines, but by doing so, alienated citizens who were unaffiliated with drug trafficking. The Mexican military and law enforcement have since ceased the practice.

Nonetheless, more is needed to deal with drug intoxicated non-state actors; militaries and law enforcement are tools of policy makers. Although little can be done to eliminate set and setting, there are approaches that can ameliorate them. One step is greater interagency cooperation among agencies of the Department of Defense (DoD), Department of Justice, Department of Treasury, and the Department of Homeland Security to monitor and assess the ways drugs are being used by violent non-state actors so that new strategies can be added to the plans of conventional forces who may intervene in such operational environments. Joint coordination among military and civilian agencies like the Federal Bureau of Investigation, the Drug Enforcement Administration, and Customs is not unusual. Military and civilian cooperation routinely happens with counternarcotics operations; an example is the Joint Interagency Task Force-East, headquartered in Key West, Florida. More techniques from law enforcement to track and trace combatant supply and demand would be valuable. This can help prepare militaries and law enforcement for encounters with drug intoxicated violent non-state actors by developing early warning signals in order to adjust their tactics in particular contexts. Empowering intelligence agencies is pivotal to supporting long-term strategies to bring drug trafficking under control and to build a foundation for a sustainable peace in internal conflicts. Knowing who among the population is involved in the drug trade and the methods used to transport the product can contribute to tactics designed to sap the economic and social base of a violent non-state group. Practices like community mapping, used by big city police forces like Boston to chart who is dealing and consuming drugs, should be integrated into military operations that occur in environments where drugged combatants are known to be active.

Although militaries have resisted participating in counternarcotics operations, dealing with drugged combatants is separate from interdiction and eradication programs. Nesting operations targeted at reducing drug use in campaign plans from the beginning, while including new training to reconsider the military objectives in these types of conflicts, will lessen institutional apprehension of the military over time. Smuggling routes through transshipment countries need to be thought of by military planners as crucial lines of support for the enemy. Such routes are not just for weapons, but are critical to the operations of many violent non-state actors. Hospitals, clinics, and pharmacies should be added to campaign lists as objectives that need to be secured in any military intervention. These facilities are also now a warmaking resource for combatant groups and their looting has contributed to human rights abuses and combatant unpredictability. Attaching as much importance to these facilities as to weapons depots, ammunition dumps, and campaign headquarters will lead to a decrease in the overall violence in the conflict. Additional institutional measures should be put in place before the next intervention in environments that include drug intoxicated non-state actors.

In situations where nation-building and stability operations are mandated, the main goal of governments in responding to conflicts where there is widespread drug use by combatants should be to reduce the level of violence through a reduction of the use of drugs. By lowering the demand for drug use, command and control can be strengthened among irregular forces, thus increasing the likelihood of adherence to the parameters of any possible peace accord. Reducing drug use also limits the potential for further atrocities. By focusing on reduced drug use, peace initiatives have a greater chance to flourish and thereby lessen the setting of intense violence that led many fighters to take up the drug habit. Therefore, detoxification programs should be integrated into demobilization efforts, no matter the degree or types of drugs used by combatants. While militaries may have their medical corps undertake such detoxification programs, merely providing security for NGOs who do so may be enough. These programs should not be thought of as separate from demobilization to be run in its aftermath; they should happen concomitantly and include members of society who form the basis of informal social controls on drug use. Village elders, mayors and the displaced must be empowered again—detoxification programs under traditional social norms offer that chance.

Outside agencies, NGOs, and the UN Office of the High Commissioner for Refugees (UNHCR) should begin to put such considerations within their existing activities in war torn countries. In many cases, this is not possible, given the duration and magnitude of the conflicts. In such instances, members of diaspora communities may be able to assist in reconstructing the rough outlines of these informal social controls. Once again, these programs need to become part of existing military doctrine on counterinsurgency, peacekeeping, and stability operations.

In the case of dark magico-religious use of drugs, policies and strategies should be aimed at "delegitimizing and deprograming" members. As previously mentioned, drug use by members of these groups is an enabling element for their ritualistic killings. Treatment for drug use should be part of a larger effort to sway individuals away from these groups. Again, traditional, legitimate religious authorities can be useful in designing ways to bring members out of dark magico religious groups and back into mainstream life.

Drug use by violent non-state actors for intoxication purposes will be an abiding part of the landscape of internal conflicts. After all, the non-medical use of drugs has been part of the history of war and violence. Little will change with set and setting within these contexts. However, without awareness and a dedication by governments to design policies and strategies to lessen the effects of drug intoxicated non-state actors means surrendering to a grimmer future.

Notes

[1]   This liquid form allowed the body to more quickly absorb the drug than amphetamine pills, but was more highly addictive. The addictive quality of the drug was felt particularly acutely in Japan when returning soldiers arrived home and methamphetamine supplies stored for military use became available to the public at the conclusion of the war.

[2]   Mary Midgley, *Beast and Man: The Roots of Human Nature*. Ithaca: Cornell University Press, 1978; Thomas Stephen Szasz, *Ceremonial Chemistry*. New York: Anchor Press, 1974.

[3]   Paul Galinger, *Illegal Drugs: A Complete Guide to their History, Chemistry, Use and Abuse*. New York: Plume Books, 2004: 102-103.

[4]   Andrew Weil, *The Natural Mind*. Boston: Houghton Miflin, 1972: 29. See also, Norman Zinberg, *Drug, Set and Setting*. New Haven: Yale, 1984.

[5]   Robert MacCoun and Peter Reuter, *Drug War Heresies: Learning from Other Vices, Times and Places*. New York: Cambridge University Press, 2001: 85.

[6]   Michael Odenwald, Harald Hinkel, et. al., "The Consumption of Khat and Other Drugs in Somali Combatants: A Cross-Sectional Study." *PLOS Medicine*. 2007: 1960, http://www.plosmedicine.org/article/fetchObject.action?uri=info%3Adoi%2F10.1371%2Fjournal.pmed.0040341&representation=PDF.

[7]   See, for example Michael Pollan's chapter, "Marijuana" in *The Botany of Desire*. New York: Random House, 2001: 154-155.

[8]   Richard H. Shultz, Jr. and Andrea Dew, *Insurgents, Terrorists and Militias*. New York: Columbia University Press, 2006: 262.

[9]   Diego Gambetta, *Codes of the Underworld*. Princeton: Princeton University Press, 2009: ix.

[10] "Drug Cartel in Mexico Killing Street Dealers," azcentral.com. 18 June 2009, http://www.azcentral.com/news/articles/2009/06/18/2009 0618DrugWarMexico.html; "Cartel Stitches Victim's Face on Soccer Ball," msnbc.com. 8 January 2010, http://www.msnbc.msn.com/id/34774234/ns/world_news-americas/.

[11] William Booth, "Mexican Cartels Send Messages of Death," msnbc.com. 4 December 2008, www.msnbc.com/id/2804515/print/1/display mode/1098.

[12] Ibid. (emphasis added)

[13] Tony Payan as quoted in Booth, "Mexican Cartels Send Messages of Death."

[14] "Afghan Soldiers Report Getting Hashish Rations," *St. Louis Dispatch.* 25 May 1989: 18A.

[15] John Mueller, *Remnants of War*. Ithaca: Cornell University Press, 2004: 92-93. Using drugs as a reward is not exclusively a part of irregular forces. Some government forces have also turned to narcotics to reward troops who conducted unpalatable missions. It was widely reported that Zimbabwean army commandos had smoked a special grade of marijuana for the special mission which included the arrest and torture of government opposition members. See "Police Witness Details of Brutal Assault," *The Zimbabwe Times.* 15 March 2007, http://www.thezimbabwetimes.com/ index.php?option=com_content&task=view&id=627&Itemid=44.

[16] Parliament of Canada, "Sub-Saharan Africa Facing the Problems of Drugs." April 2001, http://www.parl.gc.ca/37/1/parlbus/commbus/ senate/com-e/ille-e/presentation-e/labrousse1-e.htm.

[17] The debate over the etymological roots of the words and whether the assassins actually committed their acts while high on hashish continues to rage today. Scholarship remains divided over the issues.

[18] Kevin Freese, *Death Cult of the Drug Lords*. Fort Leavenworth: Foreign Military Studies Office, 2006, http://fmso.leavenworth.army.mil/ documents/Santa-Muerte/santa-muerte.htm.

[19] Alfredo Ortega-Trillo, "The Cult of Santa Muerte in Tijuana." *San Diego News Notes.* June 2006.

[20] Robert J. Bunker, "Santa Muerte: Inspired and Ritualistic Killings." *FBI Law Enforcement Bulletin.* February 2013, http://www.fbi.gov/ stats-services/publications/law-enforcement-bulletin/2013/february/ santa-muerte-inspired-and-ritualistic-killings-part-1-of-3.

[21] Chris Harmon, *Terrorism Today*. New York: Routledge, 2nd edition 2008: 77. Emphasis added.

[22] Iftikhar Fidous, "What Goes Into the Making of Suicide Bomber." *The Express Tribune.* 20 July 2010, http://tribune.com.pk/story/28976/ what-goes-into-the-making-of-a-suicide-bomber/.

[23] Martin Boas and Anne Hatloy, *Alcohol and Drug Consumption in Post War Sierra Leone—An Exploration*. Norway: Institute for Applied International Studies, 2005: 43-44.

[24] Mueller, 89-92.

[25] United Nations Office on Drugs and Crime, *Addressing Organized Crime and Drug Trafficking in Iraq: Report of the UNODC Fact Finding Mission.* New York, 2005: 13.

[26] Robert Kaplan, *The Coming Anarchy: Shattering the Dreams of the Post-Cold War World.* New York: Vintage, 2002: 6.

[27] Interviews conducted with the author at the U.S. Army War College 6 January 2006. Interviewees wish to remain anonymous.

[28] Anonymous Marine, "A Marine Reports from Iraq," *Washington Times.* 22 November 2005: 21. The production of methamphetamine does require certain chemicals with an essential ingredient, pseudophedrine, which is found in commercial decongestants like Sudafed. Obtaining the needed amounts of pseudophedrine to create methamphetamine requires access to pharmacies or other places where the drug is available, which in turn often necessitates burglary, robbery or looting. See also Robert Looney, "The Business of Insurgency: The Expansion of Iraq's Shadow Economy." *The National Interest,* Fall 2005.

[29] *The Daily Telegraph.* 3 December 2008.

[30] Alan Boswell, "In Mali, Diabaly Residents Helped Repel Islamist Militants." *McClatchy.* 24 January 2013, http://www.mcclatchydc.com/2013/01/24/180985/in-mali-diabaly-residents-helped.htmlS.

[31] Mats Berdal and David Malone, op cit.

[32] Charles Dunlap, Jr., "Preliminary Observations: Asymmetric Warfare and the Western Mindset," in *Challenging the US Symmetrically and Asymmetrically.* Carlisle Barracks: U.S. Army War College Strategic Studies Institute, July 1998: 5.

[33] Ibid., 8.

[34] P.W. Singer, "Caution: Children at War." *Parameters,* Winter 2001-2002: 40.

[35] Healthcare Customwire, "Beslan School Attackers Were Drug Addicts." 17 October 2004. In addition, one of the effects of heroin withdrawal is insomnia which may have contributed to stress and unpredictability of the Beslan hostage takers.

[36] *The Washington Post.* 14 April 2009.

[37] Another psychological effect of ceasing long term or intense drug use is anhedonia, or the inability to experience pleasure. People with anhedonia describe being emotionally empty. There has been little study of the effects of anhedonia on the recurrence of violence. Leaders of violent groups and their followers may be suffering from anhedonia

where violence becomes associated with the feelings caused by the drug. Committing acts of violence may be a way to remind the fighter of the positive effects of the drug they ceased using. See Chapter Three of Paul Rexton Kan, *Drugs and Contemporary Warfare*. Dulles: Potomac Books, 2009.

[38] Kim Gamel, "UN: Liberia Peacekeeping Mission on Track." The Associated Press. 14 December 2004.

[39] "DR Of Congo Violence Provides Work For UN Peacekeepers." *Europaworld*. 28 January 2005, http://www.europaworld.org/week209/drofcongo28105.htm.

[40] Phil Williams, "Mexican Organized Crime and Violence: A Comparative Perspective," forthcoming.

[41] United States Pacific Command, "Combating Terrorism in the Phillipines," http://www.pacom.mil/piupdates/abusayyafhist.shtml. nd, accessed on 16 July 2006.

Chapter 3

NARCOCULTURA AND SPIRITUALITY: NARCO SAINTS, SANTA MUERTE, AND OTHER ENTITIES

Robert J. Bunker

This essay focuses on the relationship of violent non-state actors (VNSAs) in Mexico, specifically the cartels and gangs, to the book project theme of radicalism and dark magico-religious activities. The work itself is divided into sections on narcocultura and social conflict and the major sanctioned and unsanctioned saints in Mexico along with the other metaphysical realities that exist. A dark magico-religious and radicalism analysis is then provided along with an organizing table listing the various Mexican saints and metaphysical realities. This table is organized by the specific saint/metaphysical reality, its orientation to the Catholic Church, basic narco magico-religious activity, more threatening dark magico-religious activity, and a listing of criminals and/or violent non-state actors involved.

Before looking at these essay themes, some context should first be provided. Mexico is presently in a multi-year narco war dating back to at least December 2006 when President Felipe Calderon came into power. Since that time, over 100,000 deaths and 20,000 disappearances have taken place with large swaths of that country falling under cartel and gang control.[1] This situation did not happen overnight and instead is a result of decades of increasing internal conflict. The coming of NAFTA (North American Free Trade Agreement) in January 1994 and true multiparty rule in 2000 with the election of the PAN (Partido Acción Nacional) presidential candidate Vincente Fox were the final sparks that ignited this conflict. These events can be considered both a blessing and a curse for Mexico. Prior to this time, Mexico was an autocratic state with an insular economy ruled by the PRI (Partido Revolucionario Institucional) since 1929. Under the PRI, narcotics traffickers were kept subordinate to the state whose elite greatly profited from this agreement with the drug smugglers.[2] Free trade and globalization upset this relationship—with the cartels and gangs increasing in power—along with the emergence of the plaza system of the late 1980s that unintentionally created illicit organizational competition between the newly formed cartels.[3] The 2000 election of a PAN president swept away any final chance of subordinating the cartels to the dictates of the federal government. In 2006, a de facto declaration of war was made when Calderon, also from PAN, deployed Army forces to regain sovereign territories lost to the cartels.[4]

As a result, with the coming of the free market and democracy to Mexico also came violent non-state actor empowerment. VNSAs became economically empowered due to free trade and globalization and politically empowered when no longer shackled by an autocratic regime which democracy had swept aside. These factors, combined with the new cartel system's creation of major trafficking factions, resulted in VNSA conflict with not only the government but also with each other. The ensuing clash between the values of an old and corrupt Mexico with the popular expectations of a new and more fairly governed one only added to the severity of this threat to national sovereignty. Not only were the institutions of the Mexican state now vulnerable but the domestic social fabric itself also became frayed.[5] A narcocultura fully entered into the gaps in Mexican society that emerged with narco and dark magico-religious activities soon following.

Narcocultura and Social Conflict

Narcocultura (illicit drug trafficking derived culture) in Mexico has been frequently compared to Gangsta Rap (lyrics related to urban African American drug gang violence) in the United States. This is an inaccurate comparison due to the fact that the influence of Gangsta Rap has remained relatively limited as a music, dress, and behavioral genre, and as a result, has only influenced limited segments of the broader society in which it emerged. On the other hand, narcocultura has become both a Mexican and U.S. cross border phenomena that is deeply influencing societies, predominately in Mexico, at multiple levels within the social fabric.[6]

One method of looking at narcocultura is as organizationally generated propaganda being created by the cartels to further their criminal objectives:

Mexican drug cartels have actively sought to transform the Mexican populace with their intense forms of propaganda as they use violence, introduced the "narco" concept, the narco-culture, narco-saints, intimidation tactics, and intent to control the media. Their use of propaganda is also intended to create immense fear among rivaling cartels and public/effected officials, defend their plazas, and provide a warning sign for those who dare cross their path.[7]

This view is illustrative of the rational actor 'areas of impunity' approach in which the cartels are simply looking to escape Mexican governmental interference with their drug trafficking and related illicit economic pursuits. While this approach is technically correct if the cartels and gangs are viewed only as organized crime, a much deeper social process can also be said to be taking place. From this perspective, traditional Mexican values and norms are being incrementally replaced by those steeped in illicit drug use, criminality, and violence. These alternative and radical life styles and norms of behavior represent a cultural challenge to the Mexican state over how people will live, work, and relate to one anther. The growing internal conflict in Mexico can thus be likened to social conflict—even societal warfare—between the values of a sovereign state and those of the violent non-state actors that are challenging its physical and moral authority.[8]

An early glimpse of these concerns, which went beyond the emergence of secular criminality and its insurgent attributes, was first seen expressed in a 2010 essay on the morally corrosive effect of the cartel TTP (tactics, techniques, and procedures) of offering the bribe or the bullet—criminal conversion at the barrel of a gun. Those accepting this Faustian bargain, rather than death, compromised their values and, in a sense, tainted their soul with the morally subversive effects of corruption.[9] Greater spirituality concerns vis-à-vis the ongoing assault by narcocultura were then highlighted in a 2011 essay in which it was viewed that:

> Traditional Mexican values and competing criminal value systems are engaged in a brutal contest over the 'hearts, minds, and souls' of its citizens in a street-by-street, block-by-block, and city-by-city war over the future social and political organization of Mexico. Environmental modification is taking place in some urban centers and rural outposts as deviant norms replace traditional ones and the younger generation fully accepts a criminal value system as their baseline of behavior because they have known no other. The continuing incidents of ever increasing barbarism—some would call this a manifestation of evil even if secularly motivated—and the growing popularity of a death cult are but two examples of this clash of values. Additionally, the early rise of what appears to be cartel holy warriors may now also be taking place.[10]

These consternations have also been echoed in Ioan Grillo's work *El Narco* which compares the cartels and drug gangs to a criminal cultural movement that draws upon insurgent behaviors.[11] In 2013, a visual representation of this process came to the big screen in the cross border documentary *Narco Cultura*. Set in Los Angeles, Ciudad Juárez, and Culiacán, it highlights a narcocorrido singer and this music industry in Los Angeles, the killing fields of the contested Juárez plaza, and the spiritual font of Culiacán that is the center of Sinaloa cartel power.[12]

The gradual criminal cultural siege in Mexico, with observable spillover both into the United States and even Central America, is replacing the bonds and relationships of Mexican society with criminal values. This, of course, is taking place in tandem with local political power structures being replaced in numerous villages and towns by cartel controlled ones. Recognizable attributes of narcocultura—essentially Mexican criminal and violent non-state actor culture—include:

- Anti-authoritarianism; rejection of the state, the legal system, and the formal economy
- Criminality; with an emphasis on illicit narcotics trafficking and use

- Machismo; especially men possessing guns, lots of money, and beautiful women, vehicles, and homes
- Heroic tales; underdogs who survive against the odds and do great deeds
- Violence; torture, beheadings, and an early death
- Disenfranchisement of women; distorted sex and family roles

In the case of the last example, the Sierra region of Sinaloa where 'El Chapo' Guzman head of the Sinaloa cartel grew up is illustrative of the dysfunctional family structures and values narcocultura is helping to propagate:

Domestic violence is rampant in the Sierra, as is child abuse. Young girls are sometimes raped by their fathers and uncles; women effectively have no rights. Mothers are revered by their sons, but once they marry, the cycle of abuse continues with their new wives. The majority of the Sierra's population is illiterate. Alcoholism is rampant. Life has no value. When they are young, locals snap the necks of chickens; when they grow older, some don't hesitate to snap the necks of their fellow men.[13]

Examples of narcocultura can be found in these components of Mexican society:[14]

- Language; new terminology used to explain this criminal cultural form[15]
- Literature; narcoliterature as a blend of fiction and investigative reporting[16]
- Music; narcocorridos which are the ballads of successful traffickers with themes of drugs, violence, wealth, women, betrayal, revenge, and death[17]
- Videos; low budget narcocinema, with titles such as El Pozolero (The Stew-Maker), sold via CD[18]
- Internet social media; websites, blogs, Facebook pages, Tumblr postings, and YouTube videos of all things narco[19]
- Clothing, fashion, and jewelry; typically manifested in cowboy dress but also in expensive suits, leisure polo wear, bling, and tactical military and police dress[20]

- Tattoos and body art; cartel and drug gang imagery is prevalent with members of these organizations, common criminals, and affinity groups. Some branding of cartel symbols onto their foot soldiers has taken place[21]
- Burial practices; palatial tombs and graves belonging to successful traffickers, their families, mistresses, and henchmen[22]

This divergent culture to traditional Mexican society is also directly attacking that society at the spiritual level. It initially utilized folk Catholicism, whose origins are with the marginalized and criminalized populations, to graft itself onto unsanctioned folk saint worship. It has now also penetrated into traditional and sanctioned Catholic saint veneration to some extent and has even created its own forms of distinct narco spirituality and religion.[23] The later and more evolved deviant spirituality, of course, dovetails with the dark magico-religious concerns of this work.

Catholic, Folk, and Narco Saints—and Beyond

This section provides an overview of the major Catholic, folk, and narco saints that exist which may be honored (if sanctioned by the Church) or worshipped (if unsanctioned by the Church).[24] Criminals and violent non-state actors honoring sanctioned saints, however, can cause incompatibilities with Church doctrines.[25] This section also provides an overview of some pre-modern and non-Catholic based metaphysical 'realities' that form the belief systems of disenfranchised and criminally orientated segments of the population. The approach utilized is to divide these saints and realities into three groupings based on their orientation to the Catholic Church—those sanctioned by the Church, those unsanctioned by the Church but still generally falling within its extended spiritual paradigm (e.g. a Juan Soldado follower who adheres to folk Catholicism), and the more extreme unsanctioned saints and realities that are considered blasphemies by the Church.

It should be noted that individuals engaging in illicit behaviors readily manifest many diverse and eclectic forms of spirituality. U.S. law enforcement officers regularly come across individuals hauling drug loads with all kinds of good luck charms and talismans in their vehicles. These artifacts include items related to Scarface (Al Pacino in his movie role), Tweety Bird (who always gets away), and Buddha (who is just lucky) along with more traditional icons of Jesus, the Virgin, and the various sanctioned and unsanctioned saints.

Sanctioned by the Church

Saints within the Catholic metaphysical reality represent "…holy men and women who, through extraordinary lives of virtue, have already entered Heaven."[26] This grouping of saints—'white zone' (good) saints—are sanctioned by the Catholic Church and considered legitimate spiritual beings that may be honored by the faithful. In honoring these saints through prayer, petitions can be made for their blessing, favor, and divine intercession that may result in miracles—that is 'beneficial physical reality outcomes' provided to the petitioner and his/her relatives and friends. The following four saints, because of the virtues that they express, have become the patrons of many within certain marginalized populations of Mexican society. This may be because they resonate well with the underlying Mexican Curanderismo (folk medicine based on a traditional Mexican healer or shaman) traditions.

San Judas Tadeo: The veneration of San Judas Tadeo (Saint Jude) is extremely strong—even challenging the popularity of the Virgin of Guadalupe (patron saint of Mexico)[27]—with a major shrine existing in San Hipolito Church in a poor neighborhood of Mexico City with masses held to honor him on the 28th of each month. This saint is the patron of those facing hopeless and desperate causes and can also be appealed to help locate lost objects. He was one of the original Twelve Apostles and a relative of Jesus who was martyred by decapitation with an axe. The saint is actively petitioned by the disenfranchised, working class citizens, and criminals alike since he is viewed as having a direct path to Jesus with many miracles attributed to his intercession. His image is that of bearded man with long hair wearing a white and green robe. He wears a large gold medallion of Christ (symbolizing his evangelism) around his neck, holds a staff in his right hand, and has a flame coming from his head with a holy disk behind it. One icon variant includes him holding a martyr's palm and axe. Both traditional/folk and narco strains honoring this saint exist with the later strain—partially tied into left hand path/criminal symbolism (he holds his staff in his left hand) due to the illegal copying of Italian prints[28]—becoming so pronounced that numerous street shrines to this saint now exist in marginalized urban areas of Mexico. Tattoos of him on addicts, criminals, and cartel members are not uncommon and his image has also been found on pistol grips belonging to gang and cartel members in addition to more traditional artifacts such as medallions, clothing, candles, figurines, and prayer cards.[29]

Santo Niño de Atocha: This saint dates back to 13th Century Spain under Moorish rule when the caliph had ordered that only children under 12 could bring food to the Christian prisoners of war. It was soon reported that a mysterious young boy dressed like a pilgrim would come to Atocha each night to bring food to the childless and starving Christians who were locally imprisoned. The origins of the mysterious boy could not be explained, nor could the fact that the shoes of the child Jesus in the local Church became worn out each time they were replaced, and as a result the miracle soon became attributed to the child Jesus. Out of this lore the 'child saint of Atocha' eventually developed within the Catholic Church with his becoming the patron of prisoners and travellers. Within this mythos, he is said to give nighttime aid to his patrons and to have even directly interceded to give aid to trapped miners in Fresnillo, Zacatecas where one of his primary shrines exists. His image is that of a child in a brown cloak and white lace collar over a blue robe bearing a cockleshell. He traditionally carries a basket, staff, and drinking gourd and many times is depicted seated in a chair. The image of this saint appears on medallions, bracelets, figurines, candles, and occasionally in tattoos. From a criminal spiritual perspective, he is honored by smugglers and prisoners who seek his protection.[30]

San Ramon Nonato: This 13th century Spanish saint long suffered at the hands of the Moors who are said to have created a hole through his lips with hot iron and then padlocked his mouth so he could no longer preach. Canonized in the 17th century by the Church, his image is associated with a red friar's hat, monstrance, and martyr's palm branch. Having 'not been born'—he was delivered via caesarean section from his mother who died in childbirth—he is the patron saint of childbirth, pregnant women, midwives, and children. Because of his piety and suffering due to his mouth being padlocked, he is also the patron saint of secrets and confession. An old ritual associated with this saint is openly placing a padlock at a Church altar on special days and then taking a seat in the main pew. He is associated with water blessing and candle magic as part of the Roman ritual and his image can be found on medallions, prayer cards, figurines, and candles. From a criminal perspective, his ability to keep his mouth shut has made him a favorite of some drug dealers who fear breaking while being interrogated and testifying in court. San Ramon is also prayed to by criminals so that witnesses to drug dealer activities and snitches and confidential informants will not speak out against them.[31]

San Toribio Romo: This Catholic priest was martyred in the Cistero War in 1928 when he was shot and killed by Mexican soldiers. Later canonized in 2000 by Pope John Paul II, he is viewed as the patron saint of immigrants and honored by many undocumented migrants crossing the border into the United States. A chapel to him—containing his coffin and blood stained clothing—exists in the primary church of Tequila, Jalisco and it has been said that his spirit has appeared in the desert to help some immigrants in distress. This saint is associated with food, water, safety, and finding, work in the U.S. Good luck medallions, cards, figurines, candles and a 'Migrants Prayer Book' bear his image. From a criminal spirituality perspective, this saint is honored by some smugglers who seek his guidance and protection while engaging in their illicit activities.[32]

Unsanctioned by the Church

The following three saints are derived from the folk religion of rural peoples and intertwined with criminal and anti-authoritarian symbolism. These 'narco saints' are unsanctioned by the Catholic Church and viewed as illegitimate. They can be considered 'gray zone' (neutral) spiritual entities, yet still relatively benign in their orientations. Those worshiping them—illegitimate saints may not be honored with the Church—still generally adhere to the Holy Trinity (e.g. the Father, the Son, and the Holy Spirit) and subordinate these saints within the broader Catholic religious traditions.

Jesus Malverde: This saint is derived from the social bandit archetype of Hobsbawm[33] and represents a 'Robin Hood' like figure for natives of Sinaloa, Mexico dating back to the late 19th and early 20th centuries. He is a mixture of folk-saint worship, rural anti-authoritarianism, and, increasingly, illicit narcotics based criminality all in one. It has been remarked by a Canadian scholar that his growing popularity—and that of Santa Muerte—can be seen as "…indicators of socio-economic uncertainty and stress, and of the human attempt to control these situations…" for disenfranchised and physically threatened groups in Mexico.[34] His image is reminiscent of the old Mexican matinee idol Pedro Infante of the 1940s and 1950s with his dark hair, mustache, neckerchief, and cowboy clothing. This 'Angel of the Poor' and 'Generous Bandit' is the de facto saint of Sinaloa cowboys (growers and traffickers) and has a new major shrine (La Capilla de Malverde) built in Culiacán, Sinaloa in 1979. The icons of other sanctioned and unsanctioned saints are also housed in this chapel such as Santo Niño de Atocha, San Juan Tadeo, and, even now, Santa Muerte along with the Virgin of Guadalupe.[35] Many other chapels and shrines to Malverde have been built in Mexico and the Western United States. While numerous non-narcotics affiliated devotees of this saint exist— mainly poor, destitute, and working class individuals— his spirituality is overwhelmingly linked to the cultural identity of the powerful Sinaloa cartel and most of its gunmen.[36] The image of this saint has appeared on amulets, candles, figurines, prayer cards, clothing, women's finger nails, tattoos, and many other items including pistol grips, belt buckles, and cowboy boots. Offerings to him may consist of flowers, cash, food, drink, alcohol, tobacco products, narcotics and other commodities. Criminals and traffickers actively seek his protection and blessing in their activities, however, no physical manifestations of this saint interceding in human affairs have been attributed to him.

Juan Soldado: This saint—actually considered more of a benevolent spirit— is derived from the execution of a young Army private in 1938 in Tijuana, Baja California by a firing squad. As the legend goes, he was unjustly accused of raping and murdering a small girl and sentenced to death by a military tribunal. In actuality, a senior officer was guilty of the crime and had 'Soldier John' framed as the guilty party. Juan was taken to a local cemetery and dug his own grave and then was given the opportunity to run for his freedom but was shot down in the process. A small chapel to him has existed in Panteón Jardín Número Uno in Tijuana since the early 1980s along with an earlier shrine. He has become the patron saint of illegal aliens coming to the U.S. (many of whom do not see themselves engaging in an act of criminality), fugitives, the unjustly accused, and people seeking safe passage. Many of his devotees view him as an innocent—like themselves—whose spirit has been welcomed into God's Kingdom and invested with the ability to engage in earthly miracles on behalf of his followers. His image appears on prayer cards (typically with him wearing a uniform and standing next to a crucifix on a table), candles, medallions, figurines, and clothing. Individual smugglers and traffickers, primarily in Baja California and Sonora, petition this saint for safe passage and not being arrested by law enforcement when entering the United States.[37]

San Simon: This folk saint is popular in Guatemala, and also has influence in Mexico, and is represented by the figure of a man with a black mustache wearing a black hat and suit while sitting in an old style chair. Herman Simon also has a cigar in his mouth, holds a baston (walking stick) in his hand, and has a bottle of alcohol (Aguardiente) and a bag of gold coins with him. Variants include the saint wearing bright clothing, sunglasses, and an ammo belt. His image can be found on candles, figurines, bath salts (synthetic drugs), and ritual oils.[38] Offerings to this saint, who is also known as Maximon, include alcohol, Coca-Cola, and cigarettes. Cocaine and other drugs can also be placed in the base of his figurines as a special offering. His origins are thought to be that of a pre-Colombian deity. He will give financial success to those that pray to him.[39] As a result, criminals and drug dealers will petition him for his divine blessing in their trafficking and other illicit endeavors.

Unsanctioned by the Church and 'Blasphemies'

The following five 'narco saints' and other spiritual entities and realities range from being unsanctioned by the Church through being considered religious blasphemies which directly threaten Catholicism and its adherents. They can be considered 'dark gray through black zone' (malevolent through evil) spiritual entities—though the older forms of Santa Muerte, and to much lesser extent peripheral San Nazario, worship can be considered somewhat benign (gray zone)—making this typology at times problematic. Further, different variants of witchcraft and Palo Mayombe, Santeria, and Voodoo traditions exist, with more mainstream forms not inherently 'evil' in their intent. Still, themes of blood sacrifice and ritual torture and killing now begin to appear within this grouping vis-a-vis the darker variants of some of these forms of spirituality.

San Nazario ("The Craziest One"): The narco cult of worship built around Nazario Moreno Gonzales, aka 'El Mas Loco' or the 'Craziest One' has become more and more extreme over time with the sequential creation of first La Familia Michoacana—LFM (The Family Michoacana) and then Los Caballeros Templarios (Knights Templars). This Christian cult is a fusion of biblical teachings melded with the writings of John Eldredge—a Christian author (*Wild at Heart*, 2001) and founder of Ransomed Heart Ministries—and the religious doctrines created by 'El Mas Loco.' Ties to the local New Jerusalem movement in Michoacana—an older apocalyptic Christian group—have also been alleged. This cult of worship is a fusion of religious fundamentalism and narcotics trafficking along with many other forms of criminality (e.g. extortion and illicit taxation, levees on citrus, iron one smuggling, organ harvesting, etc) that utilizes both extreme violence and corruption of public officials to further its criminal, social, and political agendas. In its current form, Nazario—killed by Mexican authorities in March 2014— has become a saint to be venerated. His image is that of a medieval Knights Templar clad in a gold robe with a red cross and a black and white cloak, holding a sword, and dressed in armor. His followers are viewed as the protectors of Michoacana and the bringers of 'divine justice' to those that threaten its citizens—be they common criminals, opposing drug cartels and gangs, vigilantes (local self defense forces) or the Mexican government. Divine—extrajudicial—justice has been meted out by means of throwing a cluster of heads onto a disco floor, torture killings, at least one crucifixion, and bridge and sign hangings along with full body dismemberments. While peripheral indoctrination into LFM and the Templarios—in venues such as in rehab centers— may be somewhat benign, once an inductee is confirmed as a San Nazario follower very dark and cultish behaviors immediately begin to take hold.[40] Symbols of this cult include a sword with wings on either side, a red cross on white background, medieval helmets, shields, and weapons, LFM graffiti, narcomantas (sheets with text and images), and knightly robes. Numerous small chapels to San Nazario exist in Michoacana and in roughly nine other Mexican states where this cult has spread. Typically, they contain his statue and that of a black or red cross inside of them and a shield on the outside of the chapel.

Santa Muerte (Folk and narco variants): This entity ranges from a saint to a deity in its own right and is more European in origin—as an amoral and non-judgmental embodiment of the Angel of Death—than Aztec influenced. The folk component of this spirituality is relatively benign and incorporates Santa Muerte very much like a saint-of-last-resort. Adherents consider themselves good Catholics and, for the most part, follow Church teachings but are drawn from the disenfranchised, marginalized, and, at times, petty criminalized rungs of Mexican society. Here Santa Muerte, a skeletal figure wearing a robe and holding a scythe, is more brightly and gaily dressed with offerings of a more traditional nature being given; foods, alcohol, tobacco, flowers, and candles. This variant offers good health and fortune, healing and protection, and help with legal troubles and other problems for its marginalized worshipers.[41] At the other extreme, and of interest to this analysis, is the narcocultura variant which is becoming a blood soaked deity worshiped by some cartel killers and assassins. Many of these devotees are Los Zetas based but a component of El Gulfo cartel, BLO (Beltrán Leyva Organization) fragments, and some independent kill team operators are also thought to pay homage to this deity. This version of Santa Muerte—because of the high stakes involved—is darker in character and requires greater sacrifices for the divine petitions focusing on the death and protective magic being sought. Such offerings are becoming associated with blood and human sacrifices, the smoking death ritual, and the removal of heads and hearts (and possibly the flaying of victims) as part of the ritual petition process.[42] Of course, these two variants are not a black and white proposition with a large light to dark gray continuum existing between them.[43] Shrines and chapels to this saint exist throughout numerous parts of Mexico and into the United States following known drug trafficking routes with a well known shrine in Mexico City. Santa Muerte imagery is found on all forms of items including altars, figurines, on tattoos and amulets belonging to deceased narcos, and on many pistol grips.

Aztec War God (Huitzilopochtli): Concerns related to this metaphysical reality are presently unknown to most academics and are only now being expressed by some gang investigators and specialists.[44] Activities related to Aztec war god spirituality can be seen with Southern California prison (e.g. Mexican Mafia/La Eme) and street (e.g. Sur 13) gangs and the Barrio Azteca street and prison gang which exists in both Southern Texas and on the Mexican side of the border in Ciudad Juarez. A few public distribution and law enforcement restricted (which have been leaked online) publications exist on this topic.[45] At this point in time, this spirituality is primarily ideological (secular) in nature rather than magico-religious, however, at least in one incident it appears that a ritual Aztec self-sacrifice attempt was made. It involved Juan Miguel Alvarez, a drug addict and thief, who in January 2005 reportedly parked his jeep on a Metro Link track, stabbed himself in the chest, and cut his wrists. He abandoned the Jeep but the resulting train wreck led to the death of 11 innocents.[46]

Brujería Negra (Black Witchcraft): The potentials for some Mexican cartel members engaging in black witchcraft (the left hand path) have been around since the Mark Kilroy ritual killing in Matamoros, Tamaulipas in 1989. Kilroy was a U.S. college student on spring break who was captured and sacrificed by a local drug gang led by Adolfo Constanzo. The drug gang killed at least a dozen rival traffickers and innocents and offered them up as sacrifices in exchange for magico-religious protection and power. Constanzo and his cult engaged in a mixture of brujería, Palo Mayombe, and a mixture of other syncretic forms of spirituality.[47] Evidence suggests that since this incident, however, self-identified 'witches' and 'Satanists'—what would be considered traditional followers of the anti-Christ—have had little to do with narco violence or ritual killings in Mexico. Rather, the activities and adherents of the narco form of Santa Muerte are being labeled as 'Satanic' as part of the blanket Christian perspective of the ongoing struggle between good vs evil. Elements of narcocultura in a sense may have bypassed our normal anti-Christ conventions. Still, from the perspective of the Church, Santa Muerte is without question a new manifestation of Satanic influences with exorcisms greatly on the rise in Mexico.[48] Further, its narco variant may quite possibly have already become a new variation of the left hand path.

Palo Mayombe, Santeria, and Voodoo: This is an ad hoc grouping of Palo and Kongo religions, practiced in Cuba, which have come out of African Bantu spirituality, Santeria derived from Yoruba West Africa and exported to the New World, and Voodoo brought to the New World by slaves coming from Benin, Africa. These African magico-religious traditions are built upon animist principals mixed in with the polytheistic worship of numerous deities. The nganga (a cauldron containing human bones linked to the spirits of the dead) of Palo Mayombe, the primitive shrines and animal sacrifices of Santeria, and the spiritual rites, shrines, priestly ceremonies, and zombies (both astral and physical) found in Voodoo practices make these religions *persona non grata* with Christianity.[49] While the Adolfo Constanzo group in Matamoros brought some of these magio-religious practices into its spirituality—especially the use of the ritual nganga—the influence of these traditions on the present Mexican cartels and gangs appears to be limited. Still, some drug dealers are known to personally petition these deities or seek the aid of priests to cast both protective spells on themselves and harmful spells on their rivals and antagonists.[50] Also, certain hit men and sicarios (assassins) may on their own stray into the fringe and darker aspects of both Santa Muerte and these traditions—such as the victim blood drinking and eyelid 'eye' tattoos of the two member Zetas kill team in Texas which may represent a syncretic blending of spirituality forms.[51]

Dark Magico-Religious and Radicalism Analysis

An analysis of the three groupings, with their distinct orientations to the Catholic Church, can be viewed in Appendix 1. Mexican Saints & Metaphysical Realities. The initial grouping composed of San Judas Tadeo, Santo Niño de Atocha, San Ramon Nonato, and San Toribio Romo represent sanctioned Catholic saints. Of note is that San Judas Tadeo is getting increasing narco magico-religious petitions due to his rising popularity in Mexico with the disenfranchised classes, a good percentage of whom have turned to petty narcotics trafficking and other forms of criminality to survive. The other three saints in this grouping only appear to be minor players in narco spiritualty—typically for individual traffickers and their small cliques.

No instances of 'dark offerings'—that is severe and grievous acts that are criminal in nature undertaken principally upon another human being (or formerly human being) in pursuit of magico-religious benefit—exist in this grouping. While these sanctioned saints may be improperly honored by those engaged in criminal behaviors, the divine benefits that they can bestow on those petitioning them still are limited by the conventions of the Catholic Church. A smuggler might ask one of these saints for a safe journey or possibly not being arrested by law enforcement, but would never dream of petitioning for death magic against a rival. The offering of illicit narcotics would also not be a way of venerating these saints though incredibly strange behaviors take place with traffickers—especially those taking their own product—all the time. Additionally, given the fact that these saints are sanctioned and the petitions sought are more focused on individual and basic criminal concerns, no radicalism component tied to magico-religious activity is evident.

The second grouping of saints—those unsanctioned by the Catholic Church, yet still relatively benign—are composed of Jesus Malverde, Juan Soldado, and San Simon. Jesus Malverde, a Robin Hood-like character, is the primary narco saint of the Sinaloa cartel. This saint is somewhat benign in the sense that spiritual petitions to him are for success in narcotics trafficking and protection from harm and arrest. His devotees do not make human sacrifices to him or ask for him to intervene in human affairs and strike down one's antagonists. While Sinaloa cartel gunmen and hitmen readily engage in secular torture and killing, including one incident in which the face of a victim was sewn onto a soccer ball, such acts do not have a spiritual component to them.[52] Juan Soldado and San Simon have relatively minor roles in narco magico-religious activities compared to Jesus Malverde. Their imagery is found with smaller time traffickers and criminals and may also be mixed in with a number of narco saint icons. The reason for the mixing of icons is for the trafficker to 'cover their bases' and pray to a number of saints in the hopes that at least one of them will come through for the petitioner. Of course, no record of dark offerings to these minor narco saints exist either. The spirit of an innocent young soldier and a jovial saint of drunks and gamblers are not dark entities that would require such sacrifices. Still, all three of these narco saints can be readily petitioned with cocaine, heroin, and other illicit drugs and many of their statuettes and figurines have spots for such substances to be placed.

Of these three saints, only Jesus Malverde can truly be said to be tied into those involved with behaviors that are radical change seeking. The reason for this is that his close association with the Sinaloa cartel, which is arguably the strongest cartel operating in Mexico with well over ten billion dollars in yearly revenues, has both an illicit commercial and growing political orientation. This cartel has become so successful in its quest for impunity from governmental authority that it has *de facto* taken over control of numerous towns and regions of not only Sinaloa but within other territories it controls in over a dozen states of Mexico.[53] The character of this cartel has evolved well beyond traditional forms of organized crime and it is engaging in its own criminal insurgency against the sovereign Mexican state.[54] Still, no evidence of a developed spiritual orientation exists for the Sinaloa cartel so, while it promotes Jesus Malverde worship, this unsanctioned saint still exists within the larger Catholic religious paradigm. Because the spiritualty of this cartel is somewhat benign compared to a couple of the other major cartels, it is viewed as less threatening to both the federal state and the Church. To add to this is the fact that the Sinaloa cartel is also recognized for its strategic decision making processes, and as a result, tends to keep violence and citizen exploitation levels low in the plazas and territories that it governs.

The third grouping of narco saints and realities is where the major dark magico-religious concerns are focused. Both San Nazario and the narco variant of Santa Muerte worship have very real dark components to their spirituality. In fact, both forms of spirituality have now been linked to ritual acts of cannibalism. A recent report of the U.S. Army's Foreign Military Studies Office cites that:

...As for the death itself, victims were killed quickly to avoid the release of adrenaline as this substance allegedly makes meat tough and gives it a bitter taste. Once the victim was killed, Los Zetas would cook the flesh and add it to pozole (a type of soup) or use it to stuff tamales. The gluteal and hamstring would also be utilized to produce cuts similar to steaks.[55]

"Today we are going to eat the heart of a human being." This statement was allegedly made on multiple occasions by Nazario Moreno Gonzalez, a leader with Los Caballeros Templarios operators, prior to initiation ceremonies of new members. These initiation ceremonies are said to be conducted on a hill known as La Cucha in Apatzingán. At the start of the ceremony, new members gather around in a circle. In the center of the circle, a human body is hung and the heart is removed with a dagger and passed around to be eaten. Authorities also indicated that detained Los Caballeros Templarios provided additional information indicating that the victims sacrificed during initiation rites include young children.[56]

In the past, the smoking-death ritual of the Zetas, in which the ashes of a victim are mixed in a pipe with tobacco and cocaine, and the La Familia Michoacana practice of forcing new recruits to kill, cook, and eat innocent victims have been discussed. Additionally, it has been said that Arturo Beltrán Leyva, the old leader of the BLO and a Santa Muerte follower, served unsuspecting dinner guests meat sliced from his victims.[57] This degeneration into cult behaviors is one reason why the violence levels in Mexico have become so pronounced and macabre—although, on balance, secular torture killings still far overshadow spirituality derived ones.

In the case of the cult of San Nazario La Familia Michoacán (LFM) and the successor Los Caballeros Templarios, the gunmen of these groups who have been fully indoctrinated view themselves as spiritual avatars even if in the process the excesses of this criminal organization are resulting in the victimization of the local residents. The situation has gotten so bad in Michoacán with the loss of state and federal authority that a popular uprising with vigilante (autodefense forces) composed of local farmers and townspeople, backed by expatriates who have come back from California and other U.S. states, has emerged.[58] The sequential and spectacular rise of these cartels since the mid-2000s have in a relatively short time resulted in a definite sudden transformation of Michoacán society and governance. Violence and corruption have escalated, with these organizations dictating daily routines to the citizenry including when citrus products can be planted and harvested and their inflated market pricing.[59] The Templarios have also taken over the major port of Lazaro Cardenas and are heavily involved in the exportation of illicitly mined iron ore to China and the importation of crystal meth precursor chemicals and military grade small arms.[60]

These activities, and others not highlighted, clearly suggest that the organizations tied to San Nazario veneration are involved in both criminal and spiritual insurgencies being directed against the Mexican state.[61] Not only are the sovereign prerogatives of the state being usurped but its Catholic traditions are being challenged by Christian cultist values in areas under cartel control. The Church response has so far been limited with these followers labeled as having contaminated souls.[62] Of further note are how pseudo-offerings—such as those individuals selected to die—are viewed by followers of San Nazario. No mana or spiritual power appears to be gained by doing God's will and bringing 'divine justice' to those deserving of it (e.g. social undesirables and enemies of the cartel). Rather, this is simply a duty of God's chosen—much like a Medieval Templar fighting against the enemies of the faith in the Holy Land. For this reason, the killing itself may or may not also involve rituals and torture. Why a quick and clean death of a cartel enemy is chosen rather than something more elaborate and drawn out may be determined more by circumstance and the personal whim of the leadership than cult doctrines. Still, inductee initiation ceremonies appear to have a blood sacrifice component in order for a new recruit to become a true San Nazario devotee. Since cult doctrine calls for 'blood in and out,' cult members who later reject the spiritual teachings of this group and seek to leave it are killed. Currently, over 10,000 San Nazario followers linked to the LFM and the Templarios are estimated to exist though the armed component is considered to be far smaller in number.[63]

With regard to Santa Muerte, a clear blending of armed non-state actors, radical change, narcotics, and dark spirituality has been occurring. Los Zetas have an economic strategy that has gone well beyond just drug trafficking and are likened to locusts in areas that they operate within. Due to their superior military organization, brutality, and later ability to franchise operations, they now have a presence in roughly twenty Mexican states. When the Zetas come to a new plaza, life for the local citizens dramatically changes. Other followers of Santa Muerte—Gulf Cartel splinter groups, Beltran Levya Organization (BLO) fragments, mercenary hit teams, and some street gangs—are also promoting social and political change, though not to the extent of the Zetas, in the areas that they operate in. The more these groups are able to act with impunity, the more radical the changes become with increasing numbers of traditional norms and values swept aside by this form of narcocultura. Torture, beheadings, and, in some instances, ritual killings to gain favor with Santa Muerte are an ongoing affair. From an analytical perspective, a clear criminal, and to a lesser extent spiritual, insurgency is taking place with the Los Zetas cartel. Zeta controlled territories—including swaths of the states of Coahuila, Nuevo Leon, and Tamaulipas—have been operating under an alternative form of governance for many years now.

Santa Muerte spirituality, due to the violent non-state actors it is now linked to, has become a great enough threat to the Mexican state for forty shrines of this cult to be bulldozed by the Army near the U.S. border in 2009. This has been an ongoing process with more shrines subsequently bulldozed and eradicated. More recently, the many Santa Muerte altars in Matamoros, a city long fought over by the El Gulfo and Los Zetas cartels—were destroyed by the local government.[64] Santa Muerte worship—with both the more benign and narco variants thrown together—is also viewed as threatening the Catholic Church and has now been labeled a blasphemy. The fact that Catholic priests may have been recently targeted by cartel operatives who worship Santa Muerte and that a holy war was said to be taking placed by a high priest of this sect in the past only serves to heighten tensions.[65] As a result, the antipathy expressed by the Catholic religion is understandable on multiple levels including the fact that the cult of this saint is rapidly expanding while the Church is losing members. The number of Santa Muerte followers is estimated now to be in the millions, with a range of two to ten million having been estimated. Well armed cartels and gangs linked to this narco saint likely have well over ten-thousand gunmen.

Other violent non-state actors—specifically gangs, criminals, mercenaries, and cartels operating out of Mexico—engaging in dark magico-religious activities, or having the potential to engage in such activity, could conceivably also draw upon aspects of the Aztec, Brujería Negra, and the Palo Mayombe, Santeria, and Voodoo traditions. In the case of Huitzilopochtli followers—essentially Mexican Mafia, Sureños 13, and Barrio Azteca members—some could be influenced by narco based Santa Muerte spirituality. This stems from Santa Muerte as "...generally identified with Aztec dual personification of Death, god Mictlantecuhtli and goddess Mictlantecihuatl."[66] Quite possibly up to a couple of thousand Barrio Azteca gang members have been employed as the foot soldiers of the Juarez Cartel, with many of them being trained by Los Zetas forces (allied to Juarez) in the conflict over that plaza with the Sinaloa cartel. As a result of this direct contact with Los Zetas personnel, some of the Barrio Azteca members have no doubt been influenced by Santa Muerte teachings.[67] On the West Coast, some Sur 13 members in social media have also been paying homage to Santa Muerte but the extent of such influences is probably still quite limited.[68]

Since on their own Mexican Brujería Negra and the African inspired Palo Mayombe, Santeria, and Voodoo traditions have very limited involvement in the narco wars, they only way they can conceivably have more spiritual impact is for their worshipers to fall under Santa Muerte and related narcocultura influences and mix with them. As an example, as early as 1993, the death metal band Brujeria released the album Matando Güeros which featured a cover with a severed head being held up. The album theme is directly related to the 1989 Matamoros ritual killings and has songs related to drug dealers, Satanism, sex, and death.[69] In another syncretic crossover, an image from the Matamoros homicide scene clearly shows a Santa Muerte statue as the icons and practices of these various traditions influence each other.[70] Over the last few years, flayed victims—with the skin removed from their heads and in some instances their entire bodies—have appeared in contested Mexican plazas along with the skins of their bodies hung by them.[71] The taking of human skins as trophies is very much an old Aztec ritual practice.

As would be expected no evidence exists that the followers of any of these five traditions have political, commercial (criminal), or spiritual orientations that could raise radicalism concerns. On their own, Aztec war god devotees are more ideological in nature and exhibit simple criminal behaviors while the other realities are minor players compared to the big three narco saints represented by Jesus Malverde, San Nazario, and Santa Muerte.

In summation, numerous attributes of the conceptual model (Fig 1.) discussed in the introduction to *Blood Sacrifices* are evident in regard to the primary three of the narco saints. In addition, drug trafficking and use is inexorably tied to the activities of the criminals and non-state actors involved with these unsanctioned saints. In the case of Jesus Malverde worship, it does not enter the dark-magico religious realm and the narcocultura that is being promoted by the Sinaloa cartel that is tied to it is less radical in its character than that promoted by the adherents of these two other narco saints. San Nazario worship on one level fulfills all levels of the VNSAs engaging in dark magico-religious activities and on another does not. While some ritual killing, even cannibalism, has taken place with the LFM and Templarios cartels associated with this worship, these actions have not been undertaken as sacrifices for magico-religious benefit. Rather, these activities are undertaken as God's will on earth and directed by the leadership of these cartels. As a result, if San Nazario followers can or cannot be technically tied to dark magico-religious activities is unclear—though many would regard their torture killings as immoral—even evil—at least in a cult-like sense. The change San Nazario followers are bringing to Michoacán and other cartel territories is definitely radical and pronounced in nature, with spiritual insurgency attributes quite clear. The narco variant of the final saint, Santa Muerte, fully fits all the criteria of dark-magico religious activity with its more extreme adherents engaging in human sacrificial and other heinous crimes. While these Santa Muerte adherents also are engaging in a criminal insurgency, the spiritual component of this insurgency is less evident than the cult crusader mentality of the San Nazario adherents. Still, an extreme form of narcocultura is being promoted in Los Zetas and affiliated territories that is bringing radical forms of social and political change to the Mexican citizens living under their criminal suzerainty.

Appendix 1. Mexican Saints & Metaphysical Realities

Saint/ Metaphysical 'Reality'	Orientation to the Catholic Church	Magico-Religious; Narco	Magico-Religious; Dark	VNSAs Involved
San Judas Tadeo	Sanctioned; patron saint of hopeless or desperate causes	Yes (moderate); spiritual appeals for protection of drug loads and criminals; lots of miracles attributed to him *(Major shrine in San Hipolito Church in Mexico City; Image has been found on narco related items)*	No	Smugglers, bandits, gang and cartel members
Santo Niño de Atocha	Sanctioned; the patron of prisoners and travelers	Yes (minor); spiritual appeals for protection while imprisoned and travelling; cases of divine intervention *(Major shrine in Fresnillo, Zacatecas)*	No	Smugglers, prisoners

San Ramon Nonato	Sanctioned; patron saint of midwives and of silence	Yes (minor); spiritual appeals for protection from prosecution/ testimony; illicit activity kept secret	No	Drug dealers
San Toribio Romo	Sanctioned; patron saints of immigrants	Yes (minor); spirit has appeared to some immigrants in need; spiritual appeals by some smugglers *(Main chapel/ tomb in Tequila, Jalisco)*	No	Some smugglers
Jesus Malverde	Unsanctioned; 'patron saint' of drug traffickers, bandits, and outlaws	Yes (major); spiritual appeals for protection and successful drug loads *(Major shrine in Culiacan, Sinaloa; Image found on numerous narco related items)*	No	Sinaloa Cartel

Juan Soldado	Unsanctioned; 'patron saint' of illegal aliens, fugitives, and people seeking safe passage	Yes (minor); spiritual appeals for immigration papers, lottery winnings, successful drug loads *(Small chapel in Tijuana, Baja California)*	No	Smugglers (via Western Mexico)
San Simon	Unsanctioned; 'patron saint' of drunkards and gamblers	Yes (minor); spiritual appeals for riches and successful drug loads	No	Individual criminals and drug traffickers
San Nazario ("The Craziest One")	Contaminated souls (de facto heresy); cult behaviors; protectors of Michoacán	Yes (major); petitions for divine favor and success in illicit activities *(Numerous shrines in controlled territories)*	Unclear; killing as divine justice; torture, ritual killing, some cannibalism *(Spiritual insurgency potentials)*	La Familia Michoacán cartel, Caballeros Templarios cartel

Santa Muerte (Folk and narco Variants)	Unsanctioned (folk) & Blasphemous (narco); large gray area between the extremes of worship	Yes (major for narco variant); all forms of spells *(Shrines along trafficking routes and in plazas; dozens of roadside shrines destroyed by Mexican army)*	Yes (narco variant); ritual killing, some taking of heads, hearts, and skins; some cannibalism *(Spiritual insurgency potentials)*	Los Zetas cartel, El Gulfo cartel factions, BLO fragments, some independent kill teams
Aztec War God (Huitzilopochtli)	Blasphemous; Raza warrior archetype— this appears to be more ideologically driven than spiritual	No; some instances of quasi-religious spirituality *(Use of Nahuatl— Aztec dialect, war shield & war god images)*	No *(Inadvertent incident with Juan Miguel Alvarez, 2005)*	Mexican Mafia (Eme), Sur 13, Barrio Azteca
Brujería Negra (Black Witchcraft)	Blasphemous; self identified followers of Satan	Yes (limited); petitions for protection and success; curses	No *(Historical incident with drug cult in Matamoros in 1989)*	Some individual traffickers; syncretic mixing
Palo Mayombe, Santeria, and Voodoo	Blasphemous; African animist and polytheistic derived spiritual traditions	Yes (limited); petitions for protection and success; curses	Limited *(Historical incident with drug cult in Matamoros in 1989)*	Some individual traffickers; syncretic mixing

Notes

[1]   Molly Molloy, "The Mexican Undead: Toward a New History of the "Drug War" Killing Fields." *Small Wars Journal.* 21 August 2013, http://smallwarsjournal.com/jrnl/art/the-mexican-undead-toward-a-new-history-of-the-"drug-war"-killing-fields.

[2]   For more on these earlier relationships, see for instance Terrence E. Poppa, *Drug Lord: A True Story: The Life and Death of a Mexican Kingpin.* El Paso: Cinco Puntos Press, 2010 and Benjamin T. Smith, "The Rise and Fall of Narcopopulism." *Journal for the Study of Radicalism* 7. 2013: 125-166.

[3]   The plaza system was created by El Padrino to decentralize drug trafficking in Mexico due to fall out from the torture killing of DEA agent Kiki Camerana in 1985. See Chapter 4: The Godfather in Malcolm Beith, *The Last Narco.* London: Penguin Group, 2010: 40-55.

[4]   This war began with soldiers being deployed initially to Michoacan days after Calderon took office. See *BBC News,* "Mexico troops sent to fight drugs." 12 December 2006, http://news.bbc.co.uk/2/hi/americas/6170981.stm. Soldiers were then deployed to Tijuana a few weeks later. See Lizbeth Diaz, "Mexico troops enter Tijuana in drug gang crackdown." *Washington Post.* 3 January 2007, http://www.washingtonpost.com/wp-dyn/content/article/2007/01/03/AR2007010301382.html. While earlier presidents had deployed some troops to combat traffickers they were nowhere near the scale of Calderon's deployments.

[5]   See the table on "Summary of the Evolution of Cooperation and Coordination at Upper- and Underworld Level" concerning the institutional effects on the Mexican state. Irina Chindea, "Coordination Failures Among Mexican Security Forces." *Small Wars Journal.* 16 June 2014, http://smallwarsjournal.com/jrnl/art/coordination-failures-among-mexican-security-forces.

[6]   For an early work on narcocultura, see Alma Guillermoprieto, "Days of the Dead: The new narcocultura." *The New Yorker.* 10 November 2008, http://www.newyorker.com/magazine/2008/11/10/days-of-the-dead-2?currentPage=all.

[7]   America Y. Guevara, "Propaganda in Mexico's Drug War." *Journal of Strategic Security* 6. Fall 2013: 133.

[8]   For early works on these theoretical concerns, see Martin van Creveld, *The Transformation of War*. New York: The Free Press, 1991 and Robert J. Bunker, "Epochal Change: War Over Social and Political Organization." *Parameters* 27. Summer 1997: 15-25.

[9]   Pamela L. Bunker and Robert J. Bunker, "The Spiritual Significance of ¿Plata O Plomo?" *Small Wars Journal*. 27 May 2010, http://smallwarsjournal.com/jrnl/art/the-spiritual-significance-of-¿plata-o-plomo.

[10]   Robert J. Bunker and John P. Sullivan, "Societal Warfare South of the Border?" *Small Wars Journal*. 22 May 2011, http://smallwarsjournal.com/jrnl/art/societal-warfare-south-of-the-border.

[11]   See Chapter 10: Culture, Chapter 11: Faith, and Chapter 12: Insurgency. Ioan Grillo, *El Narco: Inside Mexico's Criminal Insurgency*. New York: Bloomsbury Press, 2011.

[12]   See the review of this documentary. John P. Sullivan et al., "Film Review: Narco Cultura—a Tale of Three Cities," *Small Wars Journal*. 20 December 2013, http://smallwarsjournal.com/jrnl/art/film-review-narco-cultura---a-tale-of-three-cities.

[13]   Malcolm Beith, *The Last Narco*, 27.

[14]   For more on the impact of narcocultura on Mexican society, see Shaylih Muehlmann, *When I Wear My Alligator Boots: Narco-Culture in the U.S. Mexico Borderlands*. Berkeley: University of California Press, 2014 and National Geographic, *El Lujo De Los Narcos* (Narco Bling). 50 Minutes—2012, http://www.youtube.com/watch?v=i--12v evuk.

[15]   "Narco Terms." *Borderland Beat*. 3 April 2009, http://www.borderlandbeat.com/2009/04/narco-terms.html.

[16]   Gisela Orozco, "Narcoliterature explores the realities of Mexico's drug culture," *Chicago Tribune*. 30 May 2014, http://articles.chicagotribune.com/2014-05-30/features/chi-narcoliteratura-20140530 1 drug-trade-printers-row-lit-fest-panel-discussion.

[17]   Elijah Wald, *Narcocorrido: A Journey into the Music of Drug, Guns, and Guerrillas*. New York: Rayo, 2001.

[18]   Julian Miglierini, "Narcocinema: Mexico's alternative film industry." *BBC News*. 28 September 2010, http://www.bbc.com/news/world-latin-america-11425913.

[19]   Type in the term narco or the names of any of the major cartels into a search engine and a plethora of narcocultura social media will appear.

[20]   This fashion wear is also now even penetrating into New York society. See Zaira Cortés, "'Narco Fashion' Takes Hold in New York City." *Voices of New York*. 20 May 2014, http://www.voicesofny.org/2014/05/narco-fashion-takes-hold-new-york-city/. Translated by Carlos Rodríguez Martorell from *El Diario/La Presna*.

[21]   Some of the Zetas gunmen once they graduate basic training get branded with a Z on the breast.

[22]   See *El Velador* (The Night Watchman), 52 Minutes—HD—2011, http://www.altamurafilms.com/el_velador.html. See also http://www.youtube.com/watch?v=UbyoG9xAr7g.

[23]   Jules Suzdaltsev, "Narco-Saints Are Melding Catholicism with the Drug War in Latin America." *Vice News*. 6 April 2014, https://news.vice.com/article/narco-saints-are-melding-catholicism-with-the-drug-war-in-latin-america.

[24]   Numerous Mexican folk saints exist which are not covered in this essay. They include Teresita Urrea—La Santa de Cabora, Pancho Villa, Don Pedrito, and El Niño Fidencio. For more on these saints, see James S. Griffith, *Folk Saints of the Borderlands*. Tucson: Rio Nuevo Publishers, 2003.

[25]   Marshal Robert Almonte, a Mexican drug saints researcher who has been training U.S. law enforcement for two decades on this issue, makes a clear distinction between sanctioned saints which may be honored by Church members and narco saints which may not. A murky area exists when a sanctioned saint—San Judas Tadeo for instance—is being appealed to for divine intervention by a drug smuggler to facilitate their illicit activities. Since this is an illegitimate magico-religious petition, this becomes a corruption of the process of honoring the sanctioned saints. The Church in the past has proclaimed such activities incompatible with its teachings. See "Archdiocese of Mexico City issues clarification about St. Jude and the 'St. Death,'" *Catholic News Agency*. 3 November 2008, http://www.catholicnewsagency.com/news/archdiocese_of_mexico_city_issues_clarification_about_st._jude_and_the_st._death/. However, if a criminal appeals to a sanctioned saint for legitimate—non-criminal—purposes it would appear they would not be in violation of Church teachings.

[26]   Scott P. Richert, "What Is a Saint?" *About.com Catholicism*. 2014, http://catholicism.about.com/od/thesaints/f/What_Is_A_Saint.htm.

[27]   David G. Bromley and Elizabeth Phillips, "Saint Jude the Apostle," World Religions & Spirituality Project VCU (Virginia Commonwealth University). 26 May 2013, http://www.has.vcu.edu/wrs/profiles/StJude.htm.

[28]   Roberto Bustamante, "San Judas Tadeo ¿el santo preferido de los delincuentes?" *Univision.* 28 August 2013, http://noticias.univision.com/article/1651754/2013-08-28/mexico/noticias/san-judas-tadeo-santo-preferido-de-los-delincuentes.

[29]   All narco imagery analysis is derived by the author from years of study of Mexican narcocultura and gang and cartel social media. For an overview of this saint, see David G. Bromley and Elizabeth Phillips, "Saint Jude the Apostle."

[30]   "El Santo Niño de Atocha--History." Nd, http://www.ninoatocha.com/history.html (Excerpted from *The Holy Infant Jesus* by Ann Ball and Damian Hinojosa) and Juan Javier Pescador, *Crossing Borders with the Santo Niño de Atocha.* Albuquerque: University of New Mexico Press, 2009.

[31]   "St. Raymond Nonnatus," *The Catholic Encyclopedia.* Nd, http://www.newadvent.org/cathen/12671b.htm; Plinio Correa de Oliveira, "St. Raymond Nonnatus, August 31." *The Saint of the Day.* Nd, http://www.traditioninaction.org/SOD/j144sd_RaymondNonnatus_8-31.shtml; and information provided in specialized law enforcement training courses.

[32]   See Ginger Thompson, "Santa Ana de Guadalupe Journal; A Saint Who Guides Migrants to a Promised Land." *The New York Times.* 14 August 2002, http://www.nytimes.com/2002/08/14/world/santa-ana-de-guadalupe-journal-a-saint-who-guides-migrants-to-a-promised-land.html and Alfredo Corchado, "The Migrant's Saint: Toribio Romo is a Favorite of Mexicans Crossing the Border." *Dallas Morning News.* 22 July 2006. See http://www.banderasnews.com/0607/nr-migrantssaint.htm.

[33]   Eric Hobsbawm, *Bandits.* New York Press: New Press, 2000.

[34]   Miranda Dahlin-Morfoot, "Socio-Economic Indicators and Patron Saints of the Underrepresented: An Analysis of Santa Muerte and Jesus Malverde in Mexico." *Manitoba Anthropology* 29. 2011: 6-7.

[35]   James H. Creechan and Jorge de la Herrán Garcia, "Without God or Law: Narcoculture and belief in Jesús Malverde." *Religious Studies and Theology* 24. 2005: 8.

[36]   Numerous works exist on this narco saint including James H. Creechan and Jorge de la Herrán Garcia, "Without God or Law: Narcoculture and belief in Jesús Malverde," *Religious Studies and Theology* 24. 2005:

5-57 and Robert J. Botsch, "Focus on Officer Safety: Jesus Malverde's Significance to Mexican Drug Traffickers." *The FBI Law Enforcement Bulletin 77*. August 2008: 19-22.

[37] James S. Griffith, *Folk Saints of the Borderlands*, 20-41 and Patrick Maka, "After They Shot Juan." *San Diego Weekly Reader*. 4 December 1997, http://www.sandiegoreader.com/news/1997/dec/04/after-they-shot-juan/#. See also Paul J. Vanderwood, *Juan Soldado: Rapist, Murderer, Martyr, Saint*. Durham: Duke University Press, 2004.

[38] Synopsis created from social media and imagery, "'Angel of the Poor' smiles on Mexico's deadly drug trade." *CBC News*. 22 March 2010, http://www.cbc.ca/news/world/angel-of-the-poor-smiles-on-mexico-s-deadly-drug-trade-1.884413, and the tribute essay by Brujo Negro, "San Simon: Folkloric Saint of Guatemala." Nd, http://www.brujonegrobrujeria.com/page/page/3100370.htm.

[39] Tony M. Kail, *Magico-Religious Groups and Ritualistic Activities: A Guide for First Responders*. Boca Raton: CRC Press, 2008: 113 and "'Angel of the Poor' smiles on Mexico's deadly drug trade."

[40] See George W. Grayson, *La Familia Drug Cartel: Implications for U.S.-Mexico Security*. Carlisle: Strategic Studies Institute, U.S. Army War College, December 2010, http://www.strategicstudiesinstitute.army.mil/pubs/display.cfm?pubID=1033, Ioan Grillo, "Crusaders of Meth: Mexico's Deadly Knights Templar." *Time*. 23 June 2011, http://content.time.com/time/world/article/0,8599,2079430,00.html, and Dudley Althaus, "Are the Knights Templar Mexico's Third Most Powerful Cartel?" *Insight Crime*. 23 August 2013, http://www.insightcrime.org/news-analysis/knights-templar.

[41] The more benign variant is for the most part explored in R. Andrew Chesnut, *Devoted to Death: Santa Muerte, the Skeleton Saint*. Oxford: Oxford University Press, 2012. Of interest is how this saint is viewed in the courts re probable cause for traffic stops related to suspected drug trafficking. See Russell Contreras, "Drug convictions overturned thanks to Death Saint." *The Santa Fe New Mexican*. 3 July 2014, http://www.santafenewmexican.com/news/local_news/drug-convictions-overturned-thanks-to-death-saint/article_2677e7ed-973d-595f-bdb3-d85d96a91744.html.

[42] Essays on the narco variant can be found in Pamela L. Bunker et al., "Torture, beheadings, and narcocultos," Robert J. Bunker, Ed., *Narcos Over the Border*. London: Routledge, 2011: 145-178 and Robert J. Bunker, "Santa Muerte: Inspired and Ritualistic Killings." *FBI Law*

Enforcement Bulletin 82. February 2013: 3 part series, http://www. fbi.gov/stats-services/publications/law-enforcement-bulletin/2013/ february/santa-muerte-inspired-and-ritualistic-killings-part-1-of-3.

[43] For the basis of Santa Muerte spells, symbols, and more of a general overview, see Tony Kail, *Santa Muerte: Mexico's Mysterious Saint of Death*. La Vergne: Fringe Research Press, 2010.

[44] For background on this spirituality, see Lewis Spence, *The Magic and Mysteries of Mexico: The Arcane Secrets and Occult Lore of the Ancient Mexicans and Maya*. London: Rider, 1930.

[45] See Richard Valdemar, "Do You Speak Nahuatl?" *Police Magazine*. 18 January 2011, http://www.policemag.com/blog/gangs/story/2011/01/ do-you-speak-nahuatl.aspx; "Geronimo," "Mirror, Mirror on the Wall," *Police Magazine*. 21 October 2013, http://www.policemag.com/blog/ gangs/story/2013/10/mirror-mirror-on-the-wall.aspx; "Mexican Mafia" and "Sureños" sections of National Gang Intelligence Center (NGIC), *2010 Tattoo Handbook California Hispanic Gangs*. Unclassified/LES. Washington, DC: April 2010: 31-78. For an online copy see http:// cryptocomb.org/2011%20tattoo%20handbook%20for%20police.pdf; "The Aztec/Mexica Influence on Sureños and the Eme," Al Valdez and Rene Enriquez, *Urban Street Terrorism: The Mexican Mafia and the Sureños*. Santa Ana: Police and Fire Publishing, 2011: 72-73.

[46] Richard Valdemar, "Do You Speak Nahuatl?"

[47] See Gary Provost, *Across the Border: True Story of Satanic Cult Killings in Matamoros, Mexico*. New York: Pocket Books, 1989 and Edward Humes, *Buried Secrets: A True Story of Drug Running, Black Magic, and Human Sacrifice*. New York: Dutton Books, 1991.

[48] For instance, see Vladimir Hernandez, "The country where exorcisms are on the rise." *BBC Mundo*. 25 November 2013, http://www.bbc.com/ news/magazine-25032305 and Deborah Hastings, "Exorcism rituals on the rise as way to battle evil of Mexican cartels." *New York Daily News*. 17 January 2014, http://www.nydailynews.com/news/world/ exorcisms-battle-evil-mexican-drug-cartels-article-1.1581063.

[49] See the sections on three magico-religious traditions in Tony M. Kail, *Magico-Religious Groups and Ritualistic Activities: A Guide for First Responders*: 41-108.

[50] Shrines and practices belonging to these groups tied into criminal activity appear in the news from time to time. For instance, see Richard Winton, "Car dealer gets 12 years in house fraud." *Los Angeles Times*.

3 June 2010: AA3 and *Daily Mail*, "Voodoo practicing JFK baggage handler gets three life sentences for international drug smuggling ring." 17 October 2012, http://www.dailymail.co.uk/news/article-2218771/ Voodoo-practicing-JFK-baggage-handler-gets-3-life-sentences-global-drug-smuggling-ring.html. At the same time Mexican police are looking to these traditions and witchcraft for their own spiritual protection. See Lizbeth Diaz, "Mexican police ask spirits to guard them in drug war." *Reuters.* 19 March 2010, http://www.reuters.com/article/2010/03/19/us-mexico-drugs-idUSTRE62I3Z220100319.

[51] For more on these Zetas assassins, see James C. McKinley, Jr. "Mexican Cartels Lure American Teens as Killers." *New York Times.* 22 June 2009, http://www.nytimes.com/2009/06/23/us/23killers.html?pagewanted=all&_r=0 and Ed Lavandera, "The secret world of teen cartel hit men." *CNN News.* 6 August 2013, http://www.cnn.com/2013/08/06/justice/teen-cartel-killers/.

[52] Soraya Roberts, "Mexico man's face skinned and stitched onto a soccer ball in Sinaloa in threat to Juarez drug cartel." *New York Daily News.* 9 January 2010, http://www.nydailynews.com/news/world/mexico-man-face-skinned-stitched-soccer-ball-sinaloa-threat-juarez-drug-cartel-article-1.181143.

[53] Areas of impunity in Mexico—essentially under cartel and gang control—were estimated by the Secretaría de Seguridad Pública federal (SSP) to be 980 in 2009. This was said to be a drop from earlier figures but statistics can be raised and lowered for political purposes as needed. More current figures are not available but it would not be surprising if these areas have not increased. See *Milenio*, "En México ya son 980 zonas de impunidad." 2 Junio 2009, http://sipse.com/archivo/en-mexico-ya-son-980-zonas-de-impunidad-1880.html.

[54] For more on the ongoing criminal insurgencies in Mexico, see John P. Sullivan and Robert J. Bunker, *Mexico's Criminal Insurgency: A Small Wars Journal—El Centro Anthology.* Bloomington: iUniverse, 2012 and Robert J. Bunker, Ed., *Criminal Insurgencies in Mexico and the Americas.* London: Routledge, 2013.

[55] Foreign Military Studies Office, "Cannibalism and the Initiation Rites of Los Zetas and Los Caballeros Templarios." *OE Watch: Foreign News and Perspectives of the Operational Environment.* July 2014: 29, http://fmso.leavenworth.army.mil/OEWatch/Current/LatAm_03.html. Original source is "Los Zetas realizaban ritos con carne. *El*

Blog del Narco. Accessed on 16 May 2014, http://www.elblogdelnarco. info/2014/03/los-zetas-realizaban-ritos-con-carne.html.

[56]   Foreign Military Studies Office, "Cannibalism and the Initiation Rites of Los Zetas and Los Caballeros Templarios." Original source is "Con ritos de iniciación justificaban canibalismo." *El Economista.* Accessed on 16 May 2014, http://eleconomista.com.mx/sociedad/2014/03/23/ ritos-iniciacion-justificaban-canibalismo.

[57]   For example see, "En ese momento –y este dato lo confirma la Secretaría de Seguridad Pública federal– el grupo de sicarios le dice al cadáver en voz alta: "Tú sigues aquí, tú no te has ido; ahora formas parte de nosotros y nos vas a cuidar siempre." Colin Brayton, "El Talibán Invades America: Zetas at the Alpha Beta?" 3 March 2008, http:// cbrayton.wordpress.com/2008/03/03/el-taliban-invades-america-zetas-at-the-alpha-beta/. Original source "Informe de FBI Los Zetas bajo amparo official," *Proceso* 1635. 2008 and George W. Grayson and Sam Logan, *The Executioner's Men: Los Zetas, Rogue Soldiers, Criminal Entrepreneurs, and the Shadow State They Created.* New Brunswick: Transaction Publishers, 2012: 98-99.

[58]   For Mexican vigilante imagery, see *The Atlantic*, "Mexico's Vigilantes." 13 May 2014, http://www.theatlantic.com/infocus/2014/05/mexicos-vigilantes/100734/. For background, see Catherine E. Shoichet, "Mexican forces struggle to rein in armed vigilantes battling drug cartel." *CNN News.* 17 January 2014, http://www.cnn.com/2014/01/17/world/ americas/mexico-michoacan-vigilante-groups/ and George W. Grayson, *Threat Posed by Mounting Vigilantism in Mexico.* Carlisle: Strategic Studies Institute, U.S. Army War College, 15 September 2011, http:// www.strategicstudiesinstitute.army.mil/pubs/display.cfm?pubID=1082.

[59]   H. Nelson Goodson, "Ten Lemon Picking Workers Dead, 17 Injured After Leaving Labor Rally In Michoacan." *Hispanic News Network.* 13 April 2013, http://hispanicnewsnetwork.blogspot.com/2013/04/ten-lemon-picking-workers-dead-17.html and *Mexico Gulf Reporter*, "Michoacán lemons, very pretty - and expensive." 7 March 2014, http://www.mexicogulfreporter. com/2014/03/michoacan-lemons-very-pretty-and.html.

[60]   David Iaconangelo, "Knights Templar Drug Cartel Takes Over Control Of Iron Exports To China." *Latin Times.* 3 January 2014, http://www. latintimes.com/knights-templar-drug-cartel-takes-over-control-iron-exports-china-142298 and Mimi Yagoub, "Mexico's 76,000 Ton Iron Seizure Fraction of Knights Templar Exports." *Insight Crime.* 2 May

2014, http://www.insightcrime.org/news-briefs/mexicos-76000-ton-iron-seizure-just-fraction-of-knights-templar-exports.

[61] See John P. Sullivan and Robert J. Bunker, "Rethinking insurgency: criminality, spirituality, and societal warfare in the Americas," Robert J. Bunker, Ed., *Criminal Insurgencies in Mexico and the Americas*. London: Routledge, 2013: 29-50.

[62] Joshua Partlow, "Mexican bishop takes on cultish cartel in drug war battleground state." *The Washington Post*. 1 December 2013, http://www.washingtonpost.com/world/the_americas/mexican-bishop-takes-on-cultish-cartel-in-drug-war-battleground-state/2013/12/01/62eea6d4-508f-11e3-9ee6-2580086d8254_story.htm.

[63] By April 2009, Rafael "El Cede" Cedeño Hernández, who ran LFM indoctrination operations, claimed to have brought in 9,000 into the fold. George W. Grayson, *La Familia Drug Cartel: Implications for U.S.-Mexican Security*: 38. See end note 78 in Grayson for the primary Mexican sources. One estimate of the armed component is 600. See Dudley Althaus, "Are the Knights Templar Mexico's Third Most Powerful Cartel?" *Insight Crime*. 12 August 2013, http://www.insightcrime.org/news-analysis/knights-templar. This number, however, seems too low if this cartel is indeed present in more than 100 towns and cities of Michoacán alone.

[64] Jo Tuckman, "Mexican 'Saint Death' cult members protest at destruction of shrines." *The Guardian*. 10 April 2009, http://www.theguardian.com/world/2009/apr/10/santa-muerte-cult-mexico, News Staff, "Santa Muerte shrine destroyed by Mexican authorities." *Valley Central News*. 27 June 2013, http://www.valleycentral.com/news/story.aspx?id=915163#.U8gLmhaIxFI, and *KRGV News*, "Santa Muerte Altars Demolished in Matamoros." 16 January 2014, http://www.krgv.com/news/santa-muerte-altars-demolished-in-matamoros.

[65] See Robert J. Bunker and Pamela L. Bunker, "Recent Santa Muerte Spiritual Conflict Trends." *Small Wars Journal*. 16 January 2014, http://smallwarsjournal.com/jrnl/art/recent-santa-muerte-spiritual-conflict-trends and R. Andrew Chestnut, *Devoted to Death*: 45.

[66] Piotr Gnegon Michalik, "Death with a Bonus Pack: New Age Spirituality, Folk Catholicism, and the Cult of Santa Muerte." *Archives De Sciences Socalies De Religions* 153. Janvier-Mars 2011: 168.

[67] Michael Lohmuller, "Zetas Training US Gang Members in Mexico: Witness." *Insight Crime.* 5 February 2014, http://www.insightcrime. org/news-briefs/zetas-training-us-gang-members-in-mexico-witness.

[68] See, for instance, "Santa Muerte-Crazy Azteca," http://www.youtube.com/ watch?v=M23vD8fZlyM and http://www.youtube.com/watch?v=Tu-uVx64kRY. March 2014.

[69] For the Matando Güeros lyrics, see http://www.darklyrics.com/lyrics/ brujeria/matandogueros.html.

[70] Tony M. Kail, "Crime Scenes and Folk Saints." *Counter Cult Apologetics Journal* 1. 2006: 4.

[71] The author has viewed a number of these flayings posted on various social media and blog sites including *Borderland Beat* and *Blog Del Narco*. For instance see, *Borderland Beat*, "Terror in Tepic: Two Men Skinned Alive." 7 April 2011, http://www.borderlandbeat.com/2011/04/ terror-in-tepic-two-men-skinned-alive.html.

Chapter 4

ISLAMIST RITUAL KILLING: AL QAEDA, ISLAMIC STATE, AND BOKO HARAM CASE STUDIES

Lisa J. Campbell

This essay provides an exploratory analysis of how radicalized jihadist groups utilize fundamental Islamic principles and practices to achieve their immediate to long-term objectives. The essay contains three case studies that examine the radical words and practices of al Qaeda, the Islamic State (referred to as IS in this essay), and Boko Haram. This work is centered on relationships to God, martyrdom, sacrifice, and the jihadist view of the legality of their operations. Their ritual killings are magico-religious in nature, since the acts are imitations of Mohammad's practices from his time to the present; are often proclaimed to be a reflection of or direct result of Allah's will; and are performed to help members secure a place in the afterlife. The essay contains a number of tables, figures, and appendices that attempt to delineate various jihadist group acts and beliefs in a suggested dark magico-religious version of reality, including life on earth and in the afterlife. Finally, the essay also assesses the use or non-use of narcotics by the groups as a means to achieve or enhance their dark purpose.

Jihadist ritual killings fall into two distinct categories—killing of oneself for martyrdom, i.e., as a jihadist fighter or suicide attacker, and the killing of another human as a sacrifice or obligation under jihad, such as a beheading ritual. Killing of oneself *for God* and killing of others *to God* both have implications and benefits for the killer or martyr in the physical world as well as in the spiritual world. Jihadist groups utilize suicide attacks, beheadings, stoning, and other even more barbaric practices as types of ritual killings performed to please Allah and benefit spiritually, on earth and in the afterlife.

Islamist Spirituality and Religious Doctrine

Relationship Between God and Man

"Inflicting terror on the enemies of Allah moves you closer to Him."

—Shaykh Abu Mus'ab al-Awlaki[1]

The case studies in this essay of al Qaeda, IS, and Boko Haram examine both individual and collective relationships to God for jihadists who perform ritual killings and the "believer" community that supports them. A variety of information sources, from jihadist magazines to social media to group representative's statements in videos made public, lend some insight into the jihadist's perceived relationship to God. Each of the three jihadist groups has roots in Salafi and Wahhabi beliefs and practices.

Among members of al Qaeda, IS and Boko Haram, there is evidence of a wide range of religious backgrounds and levels of devoutness, particularly when taking into consideration new recruits who may be freshly radicalized, hard core criminals, and illiterates. There are also those who join the groups as fighters for other reasons: provide for families, to obtain a share of the spoils of war, or to avoid a death sentence if they would not take up arms. A significant portion of jihadists since 9/11 are self-taught or recent converts to Islam and are thus assessed to be religious novices.[2] Still, the groups themselves recruit by spotlighting ritual killings and battlefield victories conducted in the name of God and focus their messaging on religiously practicing members. Group members have the appearance of being unified within a belief system that assures them their sacrificial killings (of self or their enemies) draw them closer to God, grant them a special place in the afterlife, and even provide them with special powers if performed as a sacrificial act.

Members and recruits who are very young are especially prone to become true followers and fervent practitioners of jihad. Those indoctrinated at a very young age will perhaps be incapable of separating killing from the religion, believing that every act is accomplished for an all-knowing God and is orchestrated by Him. Furthermore, the growing appeal for members and recruits to become part of a caliphate and to participate in the end of days are significant factors in the magico-religious aspects of jihadist groups.[3]

Martyrdom and Paradise

"The subjective dimension of a readiness to die for the sake of Allah is deeply inscribed in the history of Islam, beginning with its origins."

—Farhad Khosrokhavar[4]

For Shi'ites and Sunnis alike, martyrs don't actually die; they are alive and benefitting from many aspects of divine bounty, as in this quote from the Quran:

"Think not of those who are killed in the Way of Allah as dead, Nay they are alive, with their Lord, and they have provision... They rejoice in what Allah has bestowed upon them of His Bounty,...."[5]

The martyr bypasses purgatory as it is described in traditional Islam, to include the first night in the tomb, the asking of questions by the angel of death, and the Day of Reckoning in a *Barsakh* (the equivalent of Christian purgatory). Normal deaths incur pain and uncertainty, whereas the Islamic martyr's experience is painless and certain.[6] The martyr is said to go immediately to Paradise.

There are many accounts in Islamic texts that indicate different levels of Paradise exist, that spaces within Paradise differ in size, and that there are higher rewards for some over others. For example:

He [Mohammad] said, "Paradise has one-hundred grades which Allah has reserved for the Mujahidin who fight in His Cause, and the distance between each of two grades is like the distance between the Heaven and the Earth. So, when you ask Allah (for something), ask for Al-firdaus which is the best and highest part of Paradise."

—Abu Huraira quoting what the Prophet[7]

The following hadith—Book 56, Hadith 14—indicates there is also a space between heaven and earth:

And if a houri [virgin] from Paradise appeared to the people of the earth, she would fill the space between Heaven and the Earth with light and pleasant scent and her head cover is better than the world and whatever is in it.[8]

Suicide Attackers and Martyrdom

For jihadist groups, martyrs are created when the fighter dies in battle, which includes those who conduct suicide bombings. Many radical Islamic scholars approve of suicide bombings, most notably Abu Muhammad al-Maqdisi and Ayman al-Zawahiri. Maqdisi believes they are heroic acts and, since one is acting in the path of Allah, suicide bombers qualify as martyrs. Conversely, many traditional theologians and even some modern advocates of violent jihad are opposed to suicide bombings and consider them either un-Islamic, a sin, or a reprehensible act for other reasons.[9]

For jihadist groups, suicide bombers are not committing suicide by its common definition, rather they are legitimate fighters engaging in self-sacrifice, and will obtain martyr status. The historical ideal form of the holy warrior (mujahid) not only dies in battle, but does so by engaging in an action called *inghimas,* or throwing oneself recklessly at the enemy even if he is one man against a thousand enemies.[10] In his time, Mohammad often sent out individual fighters as "military expeditions" in and of themselves.[11] By physically immersing oneself into enemy ranks, the jihadist performs not only a legal act, but an act of the highest valor and courage.[12] Thus the very act of killing oneself in order to harm non-Muslims is considered an act of deep piety, and the martyr who dies this way in battle goes on to reap their heavenly reward.

The physical body of the martyred jihadist serves a purpose that is conceptually related to the Prophet Mohammad's use of his body just prior to his death. At the time of his farewell Pilgrimage, the Prophet Mohammad sacrificed 100 camels,[13] followed by his distribution of his own hair and nails to a large number of people. Muhammad's body (hair and nails) was apportioned to his followers and subsequently distributed to centers of Islamic civilization;[14] later, his follower's martyred bodies also became markers of the spread of Islamic civilization.[15] Similarly, followers of Mohammad and historical Muslims have described martyrdom as the ritual use of their bodies to mark territory.[16] Many hadith[17] tell of martyrs seeking to deposit their bodies far into enemy territory, and Muslim jurists have defined as virtuous the use of one's body to defend and define the boundaries of Islam.[18] This concept becomes rather disturbing if now post-modern jihadist groups intend for their own martyrs to mark territory for their intended caliphate(s) and to spread Islam by attacking in other countries. If so, for example, then the 9/11 al Qaeda "martyrs" who died at the World Trade Center and the Pentagon and elsewhere in the U.S. may represent a ritualized expansion into the U.S.[19]

Sacrifice

Blood and Animal Sacrifice

The following seeks to provide context, both historical and theoretical, to help explain why terrorist groups such as al Qaeda, IS, and Boko Haram have increasingly been sacrificing humans in ritualistic ways, sometimes similar to how animals are slaughtered in ritual ceremonies, while continuing to attach religious meaning to their killings (See Table 1).

Table 1. Comparison: Traditional Animal Sacrifice and Islamist Ritual Killing of Humans

SACRIFICE	REALITY — Physical World	REALITY — Spiritual World
Traditional Sacrifice (Clean animals)	**Method:** Ritual slaughter using sharpened knife;[1] Saying of God's (Allah's) name at the time of sacrifice **Benefits:** Goodwill; charity; sustenance for poor/needy; display of humility /gratitude before God **Who:** Sunni and Shia Muslims, Jews/other religions	**Method:** Ritual Slaughter using sharpened knife; Saying of God's (Allah's) name at the time of sacrifice **Benefits:** God is pleased; God accepts sacrifice **Who:** Sunni and Shia Muslims, Jews/other religions
To God — **Islamist Ritual Killing (Unclean humans)**	**Method:** Beheading: Execution (gunshot to head); Immolation (IS only); suicide bomber (unwilling); Saying of Allah's name at time of sacrifice **Benefits:** Status; Acceptance; Rank; Recruiting **Narcotics:** *Victim:* Ease victim's suffering[2] ensure cooperation/ appearance of submission (i.e., for video production) *Killer:* For courage and/or to limit psychological effect (i.e., unseasoned warrior's first time beheading)	**Method:** Beheading: Execution (gunshot to head); Immolation (IS only); suicide bomber (unwilling); Saying of Allah's name at the time of sacrifice **Benefits:** Killer gains favor with God; God accepts sacrifice; believer's hearts/souls healed; progress is made toward end times[3] (w/increased killings) **Who:** AQ, IS, BH **Narcotics:** *Victim:* showing kindness toward victim by easing his/her pain may please God. *Killer:* None (use of narcotics is a sin)
For God — **Islamist Ritual Killing (Self)**	**Method:** Killed-in-action (Mujahedin); martyrdom operation (willing suicide bomber); execution (various) of Muslim as punishment for a crime; Saying of Allah's name prior to sacrifice **Benefits:** Status, acceptance, rank, restored dignity **Who:** AQ, IS, BH **Narcotics:** Fighter endurance; strength in battle; more victories, more enemies of Islam killed	**Method:** Killed-in-action (Mujahedin); martyrdom operation (willing suicide bomber); execution (various) of Muslim as punishment for a crime; Saying of Allah's name prior to sacrifice **Benefits:** Soul immediately sees Paradise; Allah permits martyr to intercede for 60+ relatives; Punished Muslim is forgiven by Allah, gains access to Paradise; progress made toward end times. **Who:** AQ, IS, BH **Narcotics:** If martyred, all sins (including drug use) are forgiven. More victories/enemies killed pleases God

[1] Animals for halal are supposed to be slaughtered humanely, following strict guidelines

[2] In some cases the victim may be spared excessive pain or suffering (i.e., when the purpose to send a political message in a public video exceeds the purpose of punishing the individual/group); Or, the killer may have sympathy for victims, i.e., fellow Sunni Muslims.

[3] Only after the Muslims are purged of unreliable elements and place their trust entirely in God will He personally intervene in battle, favor the Muslims and defeat the infidels. See David Cook, *Understanding Jihad* (Berkeley and Los Angeles: University of California Press, 2005) 159-160.

To put some historical perspective on Islamic animal sacrifice, at the time of his camel sacrifice Mohammad and his company put a piece from each of the 100 camels in a stew, and the meat and broth from the camels served as food and drink for his followers. This ritual ceremony has been discussed as a possible reflection of Jesus' offering of bread and wine at the Last Supper symbolizing his own flesh and blood.[20] Furthermore, where Jesus sacrificed himself as substitute for the traditional animal, Mohammad sacrificed animals (camels), and this act is thought to recall Abraham's substitution of an animal for his son, and possibly refers to a personal substitution, the camels sacrificed in lieu of his own self.[21]

In the sacrifice at the end of Eid,[22] Mohammad himself proclaimed:

"Whoever offers a sacrifice after the prayer has completed his rituals (of Eid) and has followed the way of the Muslims." [Narrated by al-Bukhari, 5545]… The Prophet (peace and blessings of Allah be upon him) offered sacrifices, as did his companions (may Allah be pleased with them). And he said that sacrifice is the way of the Muslims."[23]

According to Muslim authorities today, all meat eaten by Muslims must be halal, meaning the animal has been killed in a certain type of 'permissible' way, typically in a humane manner but not necessarily so, and by invoking the name of Allah.[24] The name of Allah must be pronounced before cutting. Pronouncing the name of God before slaying an animal is meant to emphasize the sanctity of life and the fact that all life belongs to God, as well as to induce feelings of tenderness and compassion, serving to prevent cruelty.[25]

There are explanations on how to sacrifice animals according to the Quran and Sunnah. Animals acceptable for sacrifice are *Udhiyah*, defined as an animal of the 'An'aam class (i.e., camel, cow, sheep or goat). These animals are slaughtered during the days of Eid al-Adha because of the Eid and as an act of worship, intending to draw one closer to Allah.[26] 'An'aam animals are considered "clean" and are of a higher order or status than "unclean" animals such as pigs, dogs, or monkeys. Classes of various animals are evident in the Quran and are even hierarchical.[27] Based on the explanations above, Eid rules for sacrificing clean animals should not be comparable then, to the butchering of an unclean animal, unfit for sacrifice.

Radical jihadist groups have a different perspective on sacrifice than mainstream Muslims. Controversial Islamic cleric Abu Hamza al-Mazri in 2006 in a verbal attack directed at Western leaders, discussed sacrifice for Allah. To his audience, he said that there was no liquid loved more by Allah "than the liquid of blood...Whether you do it by the lamb, or you do it by a Serb, you do it by a Jew, you do it by any enemies of Allah," and that drop of blood "is very dear."[28] The aim of slaughtering an animal as a sacrifice is to make blood flow for the sake of Allah; at the time the blood flows, the sacrifice is valid.[29]

When referring to their human enemies—most often non-Muslims—jihadist groups such as al Qaeda, IS, and Boko Haram call them pigs, dogs, or monkeys, thus unclean animals. If their enemies, the infidel humans, are the equivalent of an unclean animal unfit for sacrifice to Allah, then how do these jihadist groups validate performing sacrifices on them that are religious in nature? And how do they assess that these acts will allow them to draw closer to God?[30]

IS and Boko Haram are known to conduct ritual killings of children, increasingly by beheading them. While the Quran may not contain passages that justify or even condone the slaughter of children, verses that allow for the sacrifice of young animals could suffice if selectively interpreted by jihadists. Passages such as the following could provide groups like IS or Boko Haram with a grotesque justification for slaughtering children:

> Amir al-Juhani reported: Allah's Messenger (may peace be upon him) distributed sacrificial animals (amongst us for sacrificing them on 'Id al-Adha). So we sacrificed them. There fell to my lot a lamb of less than one year I said: Allah's Messenger, there has fallen to my lot a lamb (Jadha'a), whereupon he said: Sacrifice that.[31]

Beheadings as Sacrifice

Ritual killings in the form of beheadings are sacrificial acts, where human beings are offered to God. For jihadist groups, the act of beheading, if deemed to be an acceptable sacrifice to God, may provide them with perceived power and future success. Beheadings will almost always have immediate success when used as part of a tactical engagement in battle or when overtaking a town; the remaining opposition fighters often flee, and the populace is terrorized into submission. Jihadist groups may partially attribute tactical successes on the battlefield to God's acceptance of beheadings as human sacrifices. Such representation could serve to perpetuate the act of beheadings if perceived as acts that are pleasing to God.

Crucifixions

Jesus Christ's crucifixion is well documented by Roman, Jewish, and Greek historians. However, the Quran denies the crucifixion occurred.[32] There are three generalizations by Muslims about the Crucifixion: that Jesus survived it, or that God made someone else look like Jesus, or that the Crucifixion simply did not occur.[33] Even with overwhelming historical evidence that Jesus was indeed crucified, that Jesus' death is portrayed otherwise in the Quran is probably significant to Muslims, who view the Quran as their singular authority:

And [for] their saying, "Indeed, we have killed the Messiah, 'Isa, the son of Maryam, the messenger of Allah." And they did not kill him, nor did they crucify him; but [another] was made to resemble him to them. And indeed, those who differ over it are in doubt about it. They have no knowledge of it except the following of assumption. And they did not kill him, for certain. Rather, Allah raised him to Himself. And ever is Allah Exalted in Might and Wise.[34]

Today's crucifixions by IS may be more of a reflection of the modern punitive practices of Wahhabi-based Saudi Arabia or a reach back into the practices of early Islam,[35] rather than a mockery of Christianity. Saudi Arabia still practices crucifixion with a court-ordered post-execution public display of the body, along with the separated head if beheaded. Saudi crucifixions take place in a public square to allegedly act as a deterrent. The poles from which the bodies are hung are not necessarily in the shape of a cross; they are often in the shape of a "T."

Legality Perspective

Numerous passages in the Quran and in hadith sanction the acts of beheadings and crucifixions. Passages from the Bible also sanction these same acts, particularly in the Old Testament, which contains vivid descriptions of bloodshed "celebrated for its divine purpose."[36] Jihadist groups today, however, are using both legal- and religiously-based justifications to sanction their ritual killing practices, without questioning their increasingly brutal nature.

Debates among scholars, journalists and politicians, about Islamist ritual killings become more complicated when considering how jihadist groups justify their acts, in comparison to how the West perceives these justifications. Jihadists justify—and sanctify—their killings by quoting suras from the Quran, stories from hadith, or by issuing fatwas or edicts. Western analysts often argue that either the Islamic ritual killings are an Islamic problem, whereby the Quran and the acts of Mohammad offer permission for jihadists to slaughter their enemies in this manner; or, that the radical jihadists selectively choose quotes from the Quran or hadith, and even alter or tailor the verses to match their narrative.[37] Even Muslim clerics have accused al Qaeda and IS of "cherry-picking" Quranic passages to justify ritual killings and other brutal practices.

The jihadist perspective on justifying ritual killings may in part involve the term *abrogation*. Abrogation is a common validation used by Islamic scholars to justify current practices; it nullifies the argument of "cherry picking" suras (verses), and instead argues that later suras overrule earlier ones simply because they came later. For example, the sword verses in the Quran came about later in history than more conciliatory ones, so the sword verses became the new legal standard.[38] Furthermore, behind abrogation is the idea that divine revelation was given to Mohammad in stages; these stages are said to reflect the context in which Mohammad was building his empire and his religion.[39] The theory is that during the early time when Islam was emerging, Mohammad, as Allah's messenger, began as politically weak, but as he experienced his journey he evolved from a persuader to a conqueror. And as Mohammad is considered Allah's final Prophet, there is also the sense of his experience being the final word of Allah.

Abrogation is a convenient tool for jihadist groups to capitalize on, not only to justify ritual killing acts, but because it supports the belief that jihadists then and now consider all religions before Islam as obsolete. As such, prior religions must be eliminated and replaced with the Mohammedan religion.[40]

An alternative means for justifying punitive acts for ritual killings or other kinds of punishments for lesser crimes is by the drawing of a consensus. The consensus is drawn by qualified leaders or clerics to make a determination or ruling on, for example, the type of punishment to match a particular crime. The case studies in this essay provide examples of consensus determinations made by jihadist leaders relating to legal dilemmas on ritual killings and other punishments.

Legal issues in Islam concern any threat to the *tawhid* (attributing oneness to Allah) and the need to protect the concept. Modern Islamic reformers, including Abdullah Azzam, have taken it upon themselves to eliminate any threats to the *tawhid* especially any idea that there could be intercession between man and God. Intercession or *"Shafa'at"* refers to an interceder using his power, influence, or nearness with authorities in order to change their view of the guilty or criminal.[41] The religious meaning of intercession refers to an interceder making a distinctive transformation in the state of the guilty person, resulting in their transformation into a cleaned state in which he or she becomes eligible for intercession.[42] The Wahabbi view is that human intercession is not acceptable; hence the Wahabbi-Salafi based jihadist groups make intervention for a criminal very difficult (as only Allah can authorize intercession). This is a magico-religious aspect of legal matters for jihadist groups, and is especially apparent with IS. IS issues punishment excessively and on a large scale and does not appear to hold trials where a victim's advocate could attempt to intercede on a criminal's behalf.

Other types of intercession that are prohibited in Islam include veneration of saints, shaykhs, imams, and even of the Prophet Mohammad. Also condemned by some Sunni reformers are pilgrimages to shrines or the tombs of saints, the wearing of amulets, and most aspects of Shi'ite religious observances. Similarly, the Islamic power model excludes *ulama* (religious scholars) as an intermediary authority between God and a head of state—no authority, religious or secular, can subvert or circumvent principles of Islam.[43]

Use of Narcotics

The use of drugs in Islam is considered *haram* or forbidden. Thus jihadist groups will not broadcast any involvement with drugs other than their selective punishment of those who are caught using them. As a result, providing credible evidence of jihadist use of drugs is difficult to do. Yet there are enough observations of commingling of jihadists and the drug trade to conceptualize what magico-religious role they have in jihad. The involvement of Salafi-jihadist groups in the drug trade in parts of the Middle East and Africa is a source for economic benefit to the groups, not only well-arming them militarily, but serving as a way out of miserable environments of poverty and disease. In some regions, the Islamist-drug trafficking connection elevates the life of a jihadi to one of comparative luxury.[44] While embedding themselves within the drug trade, some jihadists, especially group leadership, may be drawn away from their religious beliefs or any piety they may have and into a life of sheer corruption. But they continue to practice the legal aspects of jihad by imposing Sharia law in areas under their control. Economic benefits from involvement in the drug trade, along with use of performance-enhancing drugs by jihadists on the battlefield, may even be serving to enhance religious fervor particularly in the more cult-like or apocalyptic-leaning groups such as IS or Boko Haram.

Numerous stories that have emerged from recent wars involving Islam (e.g., most recently in Afghanistan, Bosnia-Herzegovina, and Chechnya) have created myths about mujahedin. These battlefield myths not only elevate the spiritual prestige of the fighter/martyr, but help to reassure large Muslim audiences that God is supporting them.[45] Use of narcotics by today's jihadists could serve to produce or embellish a fighter's religious "visions" or stories of miraculous events in battle, convincing their comrades and supporters they are God-driven. For example, reports have surfaced that some IS fighters, as a result of drug use, have experienced hallucinations when in battle, have shown excessive and abnormal bravery against their adversaries, and have displayed heightened levels of brutality in ritual killings on and off the battlefield.

Summary

There are numerous elements that will influence the direction a jihadist group takes with regard to magico-religious activities, such as its leadership structure or its interaction with outside elements, e.g., transnational criminal organizations. Religion and perceived magical outcomes within jihadist environments may help drive the groups into very dark activities. Perceptions of Allah-driven victories in battle, or evidence of progress within a post-modern caliphate, may serve to propel members of these groups into next-level brutal activity. Members of a growing caliphate may think there is progress being made by the bounty they receive, and attribute it to Allah. This bounty may come in the form of better income, newly acquired weapons, or through fellowship among like-minded members. For IS, the situation is enhanced by their apocalyptic and millenarian leanings. For example, the large-scale purging of non-believers is believed to gain Allah's approval, drawing nearer the time when He personally intervenes in the end of days' battle. According to prophecy, at the end of days Allah will favor the Muslims and drive out all infidels.[46]

The following case studies of al Qaeda, IS, and Boko Haram attempt to explore the ritual killings and other dark magico-religious activities conducted by these groups in association with their Islamic thought-processes, beliefs, and political objectives. The injection of widely different perceptions from the Western viewpoint (academia or media), from moderate to radical Islamic scholars, or from the jihadist groups' own view of themselves, may distort or confuse these case studies somewhat; hence, they should be viewed theoretically, for the purpose of provoking thought or further study on the topic.

Case Study: Al Qaeda

This case study reviews the background of al Qaeda including key influences on the group that led to its use of magico-religious practices as an extension of its jihad. This study examines primarily the past ritual sacrificial killings of al Qaeda, religious or spiritual behavior, and doctrine, while seeking to recognize any tendencies toward darker magico-religious practices. Periodic states of relative dormancy or transition, evidenced by its lack of ritual killings, have occurred with this group. The study also discusses how early-stage al Qaeda was a precursor organization that ushered in the Islamic State (IS).

Group Background—Temporal and Spiritual

Several Islamic thinkers, whose often debated writings span across history, influenced the early leadership of al Qaeda. These scholars were Middle Eastern Arabs and included Sayyad Qutb, Ibn Taymiyyah[47], Abdel Salam Faraj, Abdullah Azzam, and Abu Muhammad al Maqdisi. Each in his own way either introduced or inspired some level of violent jihad in today's terrorist groups; moreover, each held some acquired level of magico-religious thought that influenced al Qaeda. The scholarly discussions of these men mostly concerned the present state-of-affairs with their Islamic governments, the wrongful global influence being perpetuated by the West, and the degradation of true Islam and the need to restore it. A wide open debate however, was on just *how* to restore Islam and establish Sharia law. Al Qaeda eventually opted to use ritualistic, sacrificial killings in their endeavors to rid the post-modern world of wrongful Muslims and all other infidels.

Sayyad Qutb, who particularly influenced Osama bin Laden,[48] argued convincingly in his writings that contemporary societies, both Islamic and non-Islamic, are in a state of *Jahiliyya*. In Islamic history *Jahiliyya* denotes pre-Islamic pagan beliefs and practices—also characterized by ignorance of God's Word as revealed through the Prophet Mohammad as well as polytheism and idolatry.[49] *Jahiliyya* is a strong term that implies apostasy from Islam has occurred, and apostasy is traditionally punishable by death. In essence, a determination that an entity is jahili, is sentencing that entity to death.[50] Qutb also held the conviction that religion ought to permeate all aspects of human existence.[51]

The teachings of bin Laden's own mentor Abdullah Azzam, considered by many to be the father of jihad, may have helped lead al Qaeda into the practice of self-sacrifice and martyrdom.[52] Azzam successfully persuaded jihadists everywhere in the significance of self-sacrifice and argued that those who die for the sake of God will be rewarded in paradise. Martyrdom, according to Azzam, would wash away the jihadist's sins and bestow glory upon him.[53] He also sought to make armed jihad obligatory for all Muslims as a means to wipe out sin:

"Jihad today is individually obligatory (fard`ayn), by self and wealth, on every Muslim, and the Islamic community remains sinful until the last piece of Islamic land is freed from the hands of the Disbelievers, nor are any absolved from the sin other than the Mujahideen."[54]

Azzam also wrote:

"History does not write its lines except with blood...indeed those who think that they can change reality, or change societies, without blood, sacrifices and invalids, without pure, innocent souls, then they do not understand the essence of this Din (religion)."[55]

Another significant Islamic scholar and modern day influencer was Abdel Salam Faraj. Faraj's writings incorporate some of his magical thinking that, combined with the necessity to fight and slay opponents, may have contributed to al Qaeda's dark methodology. In his famous work *The Neglected Duty*, Faraj explains, for example, that, when the kingdom of God is spreading and if Islamic (e.g. God's) law is applied harvests will be better and that community material needs will be solved.[56] With this thinking, Faraj also promoted the concept of abrogation, quoting Muhammad ibn Juzayy al-Kalbi, who said that commands to be at peace with the infidels and to forgive them, preceded the command to fight them; thus the former were fully abrogated by the latter with Allah's words: "Slay the polytheists wherever ye find them" (Quran 9.5) and "Fighting is prescribed for you" (Quran 2.216).[57]

Other influences on al Qaeda include the thought processes of those young clerics who arose in the Saudi opposition movement in the 1990s and, who sought to Islamize Saudi society in response to the perceived Western cultural attack on the Muslim world.[58] The approach of these scholars was most comparable to Salafism, a school of thought that developed in Egypt and called for a return to the origins of Islam. Similarly, Wahhabi belief originated with Muhammad Ibn Abd al-Wahhab (1703-91), who had concerned himself about the cult of saints and the idolatrous rituals at their tombs, which he believed attributed divinity to mere mortals.[59] He felt instead that men and women should concentrate on the study of the Quran and traditions of the hadith, about the customary practices of the Prophet and his companions. A combination of both Salafi and Wahhabi schools of thought [60] played a significant role in influencing al Qaeda's very rigid ideology that upheld its ritual killing practices.

While al Qaeda began to put into practice what many radical Islamic scholars had only preached or written about, it was abu Musab al-Zarqawi,[61] the head of al Qaeda in Iraq, who helped steer the group towards darker magico-religious activity. Zarqawi, an undereducated common criminal for most of his life, became a powerful battlefield coordinator of ritual beheadings and suicide bombings. He had determined the only way to save the *umma* (community) from itself was through purging it, believed in the end of days as a near-term event, and led his followers to willingly conduct ritual killings in the name of God. He became revered by many fighters on the battlefield and later as a martyr because he led by example, by taking direct action against the enemy. He was preferred over the more scholarly men who discussed the issues but did not personally engage in jihad much less prove themselves on the battlefield.

Magico-Religious Aspects of al Qaeda

The most detailed and revealing examples of the magico-religious thought processes of al Qaeda are in the instructional document provided to the 9/11 attackers presumably by the al Qaeda network just prior to their suicide attacks on the U.S. homeland. This document is discussed at length in Bruce Lincoln's book *Holy Terrors: Thinking about Religion after September 11.*[62] Some examples from the instructions that indicate a pervasive magico-religious philosophy by al Qaeda put to practice in ritual, sacrificial attacks are as follows:

> Purify your soul from all unclean things. Completely forget something called "this world" [or "this life"]. The time for play is over and the serious time is upon us. How much time have we wasted in our lives? Shouldn't we take advantage of these last hours to offer good deeds and obedience? (§9)

> Pray the morning prayer in a group and ponder the great rewards of that prayer. Make supplications afterwards, and do

not leave your apartment unless you have performed ablution before leaving, because the angels will ask for your forgiveness as long as you are in a state of ablution, and will pray for you. (§17)

Earlier in the 9/11 document are specific instructions for cleansing one's body prior to the attack and, in the later quote (§17) above, this cleansing is described as ablution: a ritual act of self-purification that helps secure salvation.[63] Angels, which are referenced here, are described by various sources as a part of the world of the "unseen." Angels in the Islamic world are described as follows: they are created from light; they have existed possibly prior to the creation of the world; they are of great size and number; and they follow precisely the commands they are given from Allah.[64]

For the next phase of the 9/11 operation—driving to the airport—the hijackers were instructed to "remember God constantly" (§18) and to thereafter offer a series of prophylactic prayers every time they enter new space or terrain. Time and again the instructions promised victory and paradise, effortlessly mixing Quranic allusions with reassurance of God's support:[65]

When the hour of reality approaches...wholeheartedly welcome death for the sake of God. Always be remembering God. Either end your life while praying, seconds before the target, or make your last words: "There is no God but God, Muhammad is His messenger." (§35)

The 9/11 hijackers were also instructed to recite a verse that is found in a Quranic passage about the Battle of Uhud, which tells of fearless Muslims going into battle while stating "God is enough for us: He is the best protector," and because of their faith no harm came to them and they returned with "grace and bounty from God." The hijackers were assured that if they repeated these words they would find matters straightened, God's protection would surround them, and that no power could penetrate that. Recitation would not only keep their fear at bay but overcome all physical obstacles as well, such as airport security gates, American technology, etc.[66] This type of magical thinking is echoed in many of the subsequent suicide bombing rituals involving al Qaeda and other similar groups.

Legal and Religious Premises for Ritual and Sacrificial Killings

Al Qaeda drew its legal justifications for ritual killings primarily from hadith. Ritual and sacrificial killings have been authorized and encouraged by al Qaeda leadership through fatwas, edicts, and calls to emulate Mohammad and early Mujahedin. Al Qaeda always gave full credit, however, to Allah, whom they considered the driving force that controls all action. Al-Zarqawi, in a religious decree at the height of his period of beheadings, stated: "Praise to Allah who honoured Islam with his support, humiliated the infidels with His power, controlled everything with His Command, and tricked the infidels."[67]

In order to ritually kill innocent civilians or non-combatants, al Qaeda had to first legally justify killing them at all. Historical mandates in Islam were such that you couldn't kill another Muslim even if he fought with the enemy. Al Qaeda may have used the words of Ibn Taymiyah, who had invalidated the argument, and later Faraj quoted Taymiyah in *The Neglected Duty* to justify the killing of innocent bystanders, including Muslims. Additionally, al Qaeda's own leadership invoked hadith to justify collateral damage. In the 2014 Spring issue of al Qaeda's online magazine *Inspire,* Sheikh Anwar Al-'Awlaki discusses the topic at length and makes the case for the 1400 years of war where collateral damage occurred of necessity.[68]

In the 9/11 instructions, al Qaeda provided the hijackers with permission to kill non-combatants. The instructions for the third phase of the attack explained the violence needed to seize the plane, and the ethical problems that would be posed by the bloody acts they would commit. This phase presented two arguments: to legally justify the killings, and to sanctify the shedding of blood as a sacrificial act.[69]

The first argument is based on the practices of the Prophet Mohammad's time, and it admonishes the hijackers several times to strike only for God's sake and not to seek revenge for oneself. It also instructs the attackers to take prisoners and kill them, "As Almighty God said: 'No prophet should have prisoners until he has soaked the land with blood...God wants the other world [for you], and God is all-powerful, all-wise.'"[70]

The second argument refers to the hijackers' first victims—the flight attendants—as sacrificial animals, whose throats were to be slit in ritual fashion.[71] Paragraph 15 of their instructions states:

"Check your weapon before you leave and long before you leave. (You must make your knife sharp and must not discomfort your animal during the slaughter)." The instructions further state that if God decrees that they are to slaughter, they should: "dedicate the slaughter to your fathers and [unclear], because you have obligations toward them."[72]

The humans on the aircraft represent two objects: they were obstructions to the mission that had to be eliminated (i.e. as collateral damage) and some of them became substitutions for animals for traditional ritual slaughter. The justified act of killing to accomplish the greater mission must be for God's sake. By killing an innocent for God and not for personal reasons, the controversial but necessary act is acceptable to God. The actual blood sacrifice of the human (as substitution for an animal) should be *to* God,[73] and if the instructions are interpreted literally, the sacrifice is to be further dedicated *to* their fathers or possibly other personal human connections.

Suicide attacks also required legal justification by al Qaeda as they increasingly used this kind of attack. Ayman Zawahiri, longtime senior leader of al Qaeda, presented an argument in his book *Knights Under the Prophet's Banner*, where he states "In our means, methods, and resources we must combine patience with infliction of mass casualties and the best method to do this is suicide attacks."…"This confrontation with Islam's enemies must be to the last drop of blood."[74]

Examples of Ritual and Sacrificial Activities

To God

Al Qaeda became well known for sacrificial ritual killings *to* God by their beheadings of humans. In the example of the 9/11 hijacking discussed earlier, was the possibility of having to slit the throat of a flight attendant as a sacrificial "animal" during the attack. Following the 9/11 attacks, al Qaeda practiced ritualized beheadings, adopted from historical examples. Zarqawi, initially with permission from Osama bin Laden, was responsible for countless ritualized beheadings in Iraq, many of which were made public through internet video postings. Each beheading act included the invoking of Allah's name, and was similar to how an animal is sacrificed in Islam. By including ritual characteristics with beheadings, al Qaeda was able to sanction them, which elevated the acts above common barbarism.[75] Zarqawi and other Islamists believed that God ordained them to use beheadings to obliterate their enemies.[76][77] With reference to the 9/11 instructions, beheaded humans were also possible substitutes for animals, as sacrificial offerings to God.

For God

Al Qaeda institutionalized suicide bombings within its organization in part by instilling a spirit of self-sacrifice in its fighters. In a cult-like following, thousands of Muslim youths developed a fascination with martyrdom under al Qaeda. Bin Laden and Zawahiri both spoke of self-sacrifice often when referring to martyrdom missions and their greater war on the West. Zawahiri argued that the suicide attacker (martyr) does not kill himself for personal reasons but sacrifices himself *for* God.[78] Bin Laden implored Muslim youths to sacrifice themselves when he first declared war on the United States in 1996, and recounted a number of sayings that described the rewards of the martyr in Paradise.

Ahmad al-Haznawi, one of the Flight 93 hijackers on 9/11, spoke of his pending sacrifice in this manner:

O Allah, revive an entire nation by our deaths. O Allah, I sacrifice myself for your sake, accept me as a martyr [repeated two more times]...

To the Garden of Eden, our first house. We shall meet in the eternal Paradise with the prophets, honest people, martyrs and righteous people. They are the best of companions. Praise be to Allah. Allah's peace, mercy and blessings be upon you.

Use of Narcotics in Rituals

There is little evidence to be found linking drug use by al Qaeda to its ritual killings past or present, but its affiliates are now heavily involved in both human and drug trafficking. Trafficking is a key source of funding for al Qaeda. An example of al Qaeda's connection with drug-trafficking and possible drug use occurs in Northern Mali, where al Qaeda in the Islamic Maghreb (AQIM) remains influential.[79] AQIM's leadership and "morality police" turn a blind eye to its own involvement in trafficking, serving as a protection racket and escort service; simultaneously, the group imposes Sharia law in areas under its control, banning drinking, smoking, and dancing. Claims exist that AQIM jihadis use cocaine as a stimulant when fighting; witnesses have reportedly seen fighters sniffing white powder.[80] Similarly, in 2004, U.S. soldiers reported finding needles and quantities of amphetamines in al Qaeda safe houses.

Currently, al Qaeda is present in several major drug-trafficking regions, including Mali, Yemen, Somalia and Afghanistan. The types of drugs being trafficked vary by location. Al Qaeda is contradictory in its approach to narcotics, which also varies by location. In northern Mali, for example, smuggling *is* the economy; it is "in people's blood" and not deemed to be a nefarious activity,[81] even by AQIM leadership. In Yemen, however, al Qaeda claims to have a war on drugs. They have been reported to have distributed leaflets in Yemen saying those who consume khat "will be held fully responsible under Shariah law." Violence is increasing in northern Mali as AQIM increases its weapons acquisitions and improves its economic situation—a direct result of its lucrative trafficking business.[82] The increase in violence could be a precursor to a return to large-scale ritual killings by al Qaeda.

Summary

At the time of this case study, al Qaeda is not making headlines with ritual killings and their future magico-religious leanings as an organization is undetermined. Al Qaeda has factionalized and essentially become a movement, hence many of its previous affiliates have joined IS or are considering the move. As the first radical jihadist group in post-modern times to perform large-scale ritual killings observable to the public, it is worth looking at how they dealt with ethical issues—where they drew lines or stopped short. By comparison, IS does not seem to engage in ethical discussions as al Qaeda did when deciding on how to kill their enemies.

Case Study: Islamic State

The Islamic State (IS) was born in the second Iraq war, having emerged from al Qaeda as a deadlier form of its originator, especially with regard to its dark magico-religious nature. Brutal acts of ritual killing by IS are revealed in the news media on an almost daily basis. For every public criticism of its acts, IS has a rebuttal that is equally made public whether via social media, its own publications, or by other forms of mass communication. Whereas al Qaeda has operationally slowed down, IS is still evolving and growing as an organization and as a declared caliphate. Its acceptance of large numbers of diverse recruits from all over the world, as well as its clear articulation of end of days, potentially lends itself to further emergence of previously unseen and even more strange, brutal, or foreboding ritualized dark magico-religious practices.

Group Background—Temporal and Spiritual

IS was founded by Abu Musab al-Zarqawi in 1999 as Jamaat al-Tawhid wa-I-Jihad (JTWJ), its first in a series of names changes. By some accounts, al Qaeda and IS are two distinctly different organizations that came together for a marriage of convenience beginning in 2004.[83] Following Zarqawi's death, his replacement, assigned by al Qaeda in Iraq, pledged *baya* (allegiance) to the newly appointed leader of the Islamic State in Iraq (ISI),[84] Abu Omar al-Baghdadi, and not to al Qaeda leadership. Later, the current leader of IS, Abu Bakr al-Baghdadi, openly rebuked bin Laden's successor to al Qaeda, Ayman al-Zawahiri, stating he had "chosen the command of my Lord over the command in the letter that contradicts it." Successive statements by IS and al Qaeda denouncing one another led to open warfare in Syria between the two that continues today.

IS is made up of al Qaeda remnants, former Ba'athists from Sadaam Hussein's regime [85], and others from the regime including probable Saddam Fedayeen and former soldiers from Saddam's army. Additionally, disenfranchised Sunni tribes, secularists among the populace who resent the status quo in Iraq, and foreign recruits from numerous countries, including many from the West have also joined the group. Key leadership of IS includes military commanders from Saddam's army. Saddam's men were known to engage in brutal, even sadistic, ritual acts against regime opponents and civilians. IS is also comprised of approximately 50% foreigners, including large numbers of Saudis, Libyans, Tunisians, and Jordanians. Additionally, many other Islamic jihadist groups formerly aligned with al Qaeda, such as Boko Haram and The Islamic Movement of Uzbekistan, have now pledged allegiance to IS.

IS draws on ancient influences as well as historically recent and post-modern ones. The group is staunchly opposed to Shiaism and embodies Salafi piety, while at the same time, similarly to al Qaeda, enacts Wahhabi practices in an extreme way.[86] IS demonstrates its alignment with original Wahabbi thought not only through ritual killings but by its physical destruction of historical architecture, artifacts, and symbols representing other religions or even other Islamic sects. IS borrows from another Wahhabi practice—it seeks to undermine Islam's traditional pluralism by rejecting all other forms of Islam. IS is attempting to kill or convert everyone who does not subscribe to its narrowly defined brand of Islam or abide by the laws of its caliphate.

IS resembles the historic Ikhwan, a devout group of archtraditionalist Bedouins who were instructed in the fundamentalist form of Islam as taught by al-Wahhab.[87] These Bedouin fighters became violent and extreme, covered their faces when fighting outsiders and used lances and swords because they disdained weaponry not used by the Prophet. They routinely massacred "apostate" unarmed villagers by the thousands. Despite religious training, some of the Ikhwan's fighting practices may have emerged simply from survivalist needs for food, women, etc. in the ghazu raids, which at the time people of all religions and backgrounds engaged in. The Ikhwan became extremely militant in enforcing very rigid Islamic rules within their *hijra* (settlement),[88] to include enjoining public prayer, mosque attendance, and gender segregation while condemning music, smoking, alcohol, and any technology unknown in the time of the Prophet. Although the Ikhwan were eventually quashed in the 1930's, their spirit and dream of territorial expansion were revived in the 1970's in Saudi Arabia. IS may now be further reviving and perpetuating the Ikhwan message. Present day successes by IS in killing and driving out Christians from the Levant may be serving to reinforce and increase its faith in jihad and belief in the primacy of Allah over all other religions. Such reinforcement may serve to advance or accelerate the dark magico-religious behavior of IS.

Like the Bedouin Ikhwan, IS recruits are a combination of religious zealots and those fighting alongside jihadists for other reasons. Many of them may not practice the faith regularly except when being forced to and/or they lack religious literacy. According to a captured IS fighter who was interviewed, emirs from all corners of the world are tasked by IS to teach the jihadists about Islam.[89] Furthermore, numerous reports suggest that many IS fighters are also under the influence of narcotics or have been found dead with evidence on them of either drug possession or usage.

Magico-Religious Aspects of IS

IS encompasses the magico-religious in almost all aspects of its existence. Examples range from very simple day-to-day activities by its members to a very complex, dark to end of days approach at the hands of God. Some examples are as follows:

- Cleanliness for IS has magico-religious properties and includes purification rituals. According to IS, a non-virgin slave-woman's "uterus" must first undergo purification prior to her master being allowed to have intercourse with her. While IS does not specify any procedure, it is likely that it means something as simple as a bath. Testimonies by Yazidi women who have escaped from IS recalled that they were aware that when IS men instructed them to go into the bathroom to clean themselves it was usually a prelude to being raped.[90] Islam requires both spiritual and physical cleanliness and cleanliness is rewarded by Allah; there is extensive information found on proclaimed Islamic websites regarding very specific procedures and rules for maintaining cleanliness, as issued by the Quran and by hadith.[91]
- The freeing of a [believer] slave has magical liberating properties as indicated by IS in a pamphlet they published on the topic of female slaves. In response to the question "What is the reward for freeing a slave girl?," IS quotes Allah from the Quran: "And what can make you know what is [breaking through] the difficult pass [hell]? It is the freeing of a slave." And [the prophet Muhammad] said: "Whoever frees a believer Allah frees every organ of his body from hellfire."[92] For IS, the term "freeing" is probably not

literal but likely means that with captivity, the slave who converts to Islam is thereby liberated from their former life of sin and expectation of an afterlife of hellfire. Furthermore, all Muslims including Mohammad and even Jesus, also a messenger of God, are referred to as "slaves of Allah" in the Quran and elsewhere in Islamic text.

- IS frequently uses the phrase "healing the hearts" in videos and online publications, often in conjunction with a ritual killing including a graphic display, such as a decapitated head, or the burning alive of Lieutenant al-Kasasbeh. Quran 9:14-15, which suggests Allah heals the hearts of the believers and removes rage from their hearts, was reinforced in hadith and may be driving IS to use the phrase in conjunction with its ritual killings. At least one hadith implies the healing of hearts accomplished by Allah arises from a jihadist's ritual killing of an enemy "infidel,"[93] and numerous IS postings reflect this position. Furthermore, IS implies oneness in the believer community by quoting al-Bukhari: "The example of the believers with regards to their love, mercy, and sympathy is like that of a single body, if a limb feels pain, the rest of the body responds to it with sleeplessness and fever."[94]
- Ritual beheadings performed by IS are unquestionably magico-religious in nature. According to radical jihadist cleric Hussein bin Mahmoud, Allah revived the tradition of beheading by means of the mujahid and Abu Mus'ab Al-Zarqawi. Mahmoud, reflecting the view of IS, also stated that "beheading a *harbi*[95] infidel (an infidel without an agreement for protection) is a blessed act for which a Muslim is rewarded.[96]

IS commonly gives credit to Allah as the orchestrator of each ritual killing and battlefield event, whereby jihadist fighters carry out each act in His name. In the video of the immolation of Lieutenant Muath al-Kaseasbeh, IS quotes from the Quran: "Fight them and Allah will punish them by your hands...". And in an IS article discussing its operations in Libya: "Allah facilitated the emergence of the Islamic State on the Libyan scene,..."[97] Numerous quotes like these may be found in IS publications, including frequent petitioning of Allah for his continued support, blessings, forgiveness, and acceptance of martyrs:

Allah's Messenger said, 'You will invade the Arabian Peninsula, and Allah will enable you to conquer it. You will then invade Persia, and Allah will enable you to conquer it. You will then invade Rome, and Allah will enable you to conquer it. Then you will fight the Dajjal, and Allah will enable you to conquer him.' [Sahih Muslim][98]

IS promotes a current reality for the end of days and may be using the allure of imminent apocalypse as both a recruitment tool and a wartime strategy. The magico-religious element of end of days is likely believed by a great number of IS members as well as potential recruits. End of days is considered an outcome of the sword, which, according to IS will continue to be drawn, raised, and swung until 'Īsā (Jesus) kills the Dajjāl (the Devil, or Antichrist) and abolishes the jizyah (tax). "Thereafter, kufr and its tyranny will be destroyed; Islam and its justice will prevail on the entire earth."[99] IS also proclaims the abundance of blessings from Allah that will occur on earth in the aftermath of the apocalypse, when Islam prevails. End of days events are all magical in nature, such as: "Milk will be blessed so much that...a young female cow will suffice a tribe of people...", and "There will be no rivalries, no envy, no hatred, to the point that a man will pass by a lion yet it won't harm him...", and many more.[100]

From IS publications and social media portrayals, accompanying the end times is a lot more fire. IS discusses fire with regard to the arrival of the Dajjāl:

'Dajjāl will emerge with a river and fire. Whosoever enters into his fire, his reward is incumbent and his sin will be cast away. And whosoever enters into his river, his punishment will be incumbent, and his reward will be cast away.' I said, 'Then what?' He said, 'Then will be the establishment of the Hour.'[101]

This seeming twist on the use of fire as a means of purification, or pardoning of sin, as brought to the end of times by the devil himself is worth further study.

The youth of IS—referred to as the "Lion Cubs"—are fully indoctrinated into the belief system of IS including paradise and end of days. Children as young as age eleven participate in ritual killings. The future of dark magico-religious acts of IS is highly subject to these children when they transition to adulthood; they will have known no other way of life, thus will not know normal human thought processes including remorse, personal reflection, tolerance, etc. They will most likely view themselves as Allah's chosen ones and as Mujahedin and will seek to obtain for themselves a lofty place in Paradise. Already well aware of their predestination, under Allah's instruction they are obligated to hate their enemies and kill them for assured rewards. The IS youth may emerge as a more fearless and brutal group than current older recruits due to their training and indoctrination—both military and spiritual.

IS' media company, Ajnad Media, frequently publishes an abundance of religious songs, or nasheeds. They serve a variety of purposes for IS including for morale and recruitment; and some are exceptionally graphic.[102] The following nasheed was used in the video of the execution of the 'Israeli spy,' and represents one of the darker nasheeds of IS:

We have come, we have come, we have come, as soldiers
for God.
We have marched, we have marched, we have marched, out of
love for God. [chorus]
We know religion, we live by it; we build an edifice, we ascend it.
We nullify humiliation we have experienced; we put an end to
idolatrous tyranny.
We polish a sword that we sold; it is given to drink from what
quenches its thirst.
The one nearest it bleats, the one furthest away from it shrieks.
We destroy the despicable and haughty, in monstrosity his
world has become agitated.
He is afraid, he is afraid, his legs stumble from it.
Blessed is the one who obeys, loving truth. His encounter
builds an edifice.
He is put to the test. He destroys injustice he has thwarted.[103]

Legal and Religious Premises for Ritual and Sacrificial Killings

After all this and after the sun of the Khilāfah radiated once again, and the winds of victory and consolidation blew, and the Islamic State, by the grace of its Lord alone, brought out the Islamic punishments and rulings of the Sharī'ah from the darkness of books and papers, and we truly lived them after they were buried for centuries...

—Umm Sumayyah Al-Muhajirah[104]

IS has consistently assured its audiences that Sharia law is inseparable from its religion, thus punishments for broken laws are decided on both religious and legal grounds. Similarly, IS often refers to retaliation, or eye-for-an-eye as the reason for its punitive ritual killings. Retribution is an acceptable practice according to IS, not only justified in Islam but a concept that, like Sharia law, is also inseparable from the religion. IS has published a list of crimes matched to specific punishments, and they continue to amend the list with new punishment-to-crime scenarios, or by mixing and matching the existing ones. By amending punishments via consensus determinations by the elites followed by issuance of new edicts or fatwas, IS is possibly engaging in their own form of post-modern abrogation, where the newer punishments trump the older ones, or cause the older ones to be forgotten. Within the IS infrastructure, there exists the potential for increasing brutality or darker practices that stray further from its Wahhabi roots or similarities with nation state Sharia laws.

The following is a list of punishments for respective crimes committed, as released by IS in December 2014:[105]

Blasphemy against Allah: Death
Blasphemy against the Prophet Muhammad: Death – even if the accused repents
Blasphemy against Islam: Death
Adultery: Stoning until death in case the adulterer was married and 100 lashes and exile if he or she were unmarried
Sodomy (homosexuality): Death for person committing the act, as well as for the one receiving it[106]

Theft: Cutting off the hand
Drinking alcohol: 80 lashes
Slandering: 80 lashes
Spying for the unbelievers: Death
Apostasy: Death
Banditry:
1. Murder and stealing: Death and crucifixion
2. Murder only: Death
3. Stealing (as part of banditry): Cutting off the right hand and the left leg
4. Terrorizing people: Exile

Also susceptible to death sentencing by IS are those *harbi* who enter into the land of the Caliphate. According to jihadist cleric Hussein bin Mahmoud, *all* scholars, without exception, agree that when a *harbi* enters the land of Islam without a legal pact (of protection), his property, life, and progeny are fair game. Furthermore, most of the scholars agree on the permissibility of killing him [the harbi] if he is taken prisoner.[107] Death sentences used by IS include shooting, stoning, beheading, immolation, and being thrown from buildings. Crucifixion serves as either a temporary punishment or a death sentence.[108]

IS also imposes death sentences on its own members for crimes listed in its penal codes:

And indeed the Islamic State will not compromise on this great attainment for whose sake it has offered hundreds of martyrs from its pious and pure sons, but rather it has established the law of God among its soldiers, and it has brought judgments even of death without exception among them.[109]

Among "the gravest of sins" is the escape of a slave from their master: the punishment is not specified under the "Shari'a of Allah," other than vaguely stated for females, who are to be reprimanded in a way that deters others like her from escaping (See Appendix 2). Males of age seem to be most often killed and not taken as slaves, as was the case in the 2014 IS attack on the Yazidis in Mt. Sinjar, Iraq.

The list released by IS shown above is found elsewhere in Islamic publications in accordance with Sharia law and thus it is not an innovation of IS. It is said to match almost exactly the Saudi state penal code.[110] How IS uses the penal code is where they depart from any similarity to state-sponsored Sharia law; IS has "punished" extremely large numbers of people, including children, and many of the punishments have been ritualized and made public. Non-public killings are rumored to be even more brutal and barbaric, and in some cases the increased harshness may be due to drug use by the killer(s).

Beheading, one of several means for executing a death sentence and a common one for public display, is authorized by IS for infidel Jews, Christians, Alawites, and apostate Shi'ites. IS and al Qaeda have been known to behead Sunni Muslims as well. According to Hussein bin Mahmoud,[111] striking of necks was a well-known matter that did not elicit any condemnation in the time of the Prophet, the rightly-guided Caliphs, and their successors. Accordingly, there shouldn't be condemnation of beheadings in the present day. Mahmoud further declared that beheading is an act whose permissibility the Muslim ummah (community) agrees on, and the only matter scholars disagree about is the question of transferring the head from one place to another, travelling with it, and carrying it around. IS increasingly beheads its captives, unlike some factions of al Qaeda which have chosen to refrain from continuing the practice, even calling it *un*-Islamic. For IS, a ruling on whether or not to behead a captive may simply be a matter of a consensus of qualified radical Muslim clerics whose opinions are acceptable to the group.

IS also presents an argument for the immolation of enemy human beings, a controversial practice that mainstream Muslims openly disapprove of. While the media portrayed the immolation of Lieutenant al-Kasasbeh as a first time atrocity, immolation is a common method of ritual killing in Islamic countries, including for honor killing and in the murder of Christians in Iraq, and elsewhere.[112] Women are especially singled out for this treatment in Pakistan, Iraq and elsewhere in the Muslim world. To justify the immolation of the Jordanian pilot, IS provided an earlier edict from Ibn Taymiyya, a top historical Islamic authority:

So if horror of commonly desecrating the body is a call for them [the infidels] to believe [in Islam], or to stop their aggression, it is

from here that we carry out the punishment and the allowance
for legal Jihad.[113]

IS presents further a lengthy justification of immolation of the
Jordanian pilot in *Dabiq* Magazine Issue No. 7, drawing on the legality of
retribution; "So whoever has assaulted you, then assault him in the same
way that he has assaulted you."[114] IS also draws its legal justification
from many examples from hadith where people were punished by fire
throughout history, including the hadith of the "Uranī men whose eyes
were gouged out by the Prophet...with heated iron."[115] In another
hadith as told by IS, a man found guilty of sodomy was burned alive
after Abū Bakr's advisors from his Caliphate consulted and agreed on
the punishment. In its magazine, IS essentially outlined its legal strategy
and future intent to add immolation as a death sentence for other
crimes, including potentially for acts of sodomy.

IS discusses slavery at length from a legal perspective in an attempt
to discredit any external criticism: "Saby (taking slaves through war) is a
great prophetic Sunnah containing many divine wisdoms and religious
benefits...".[116] When they raid and capture kāfirah women, driving
them "like sheep by the edge of the sword," the glory belongs to Allah,
to his Messenger and to the believers[117] (See Appendix 2). IS further
justifies slavery as a blessed and righteous practice, by tracing it all the
way back to Ibrahīm (Abraham), whose first son Ismail (Ishmael) was
born from his slave Hājar (Hagar). Because the Prophet Mohammad is
a descendant of Ismail, so it is that "Allah made the best of mankind,
Mohammad, from his progeny."[118] And the Prophet as well took a
slave Mariyah as a concubine who bore him a son whom he named
Ibrahīm. Several verses in the Quran assert that every human being is a
slave of Allah, including His messengers; this may lend some perspective
as to why IS views slaves and slavery in an alternative way.

Examples of Ritual and Sacrificial Activities

To God

According to IS theology, if a Muslim is punished for his sin(s) by being
slaughtered, he is sacrificed as a martyr, even if his sin is apostasy. A
Christian who receives the same punishment will end up in eternal

hellfire.[119] A Muslim man who was accused of apostasy and scheduled to be slaughtered by IS, was told by the IS prison official "Rejoice, you will be sacrificed," when, in want of closure, he asked what his destiny would be.[120] According to IS, his sin would have been pardoned by the death sentence, therefore, it was his best option and thus cause for rejoicing.

Lt. al-Kaseasbeh, upon being burned alive, was a human sacrifice *to* God. Attributed to this event were healing properties, as seen in the title of the video of the killing: "Healing of the Believer's Chests." Since the community of IS, as a declared caliphate, has no physical boundaries, this restorative "healing" effect expands further into the global community of believers. IS stated several reasons for burning Lt. al-Kaseasbeh alive, including for retribution and to terrorize and make examples of the "murtaddīn (one who consciously abandons Islam)." This ritual killing may also have represented through its symbolism other purposes or meanings relating specifically to fire.[121]

Beheadings by IS have greatly increased in number over those conducted by other terrorist groups or militias in the first decade of the millennium, and they increasingly incorporate sacrificial properties. Large numbers of Christians, Kurds, and others are being ceremoniously beheaded by IS in this manner. Like al Qaeda, IS often first performs a judicial sentencing of its victim(s) based on its own laws. In one example from a translated video from Syria, one of three men about to be executed is delayed due to uncertainty of his crime.[122] The IS narrator in the video states "Because mistake in blood is a big matter...there should be investigation...until right is clear."[123] This example of reserved judgment by IS indicates that not all ritual killing sentences are executed randomly or capriciously, but rather that IS has its own verification system that has to be followed, and a mistake regarding "blood" is a bad thing. While the Islamic State's approach cannot reasonably be called a moral or ethical one, it is possible its leadership is concerned that God will not accept their sacrifice(s) if done incorrectly.

In another example, IS ritually beheads a man while verbally offering him as a sacrifice *to* Allah.[124] The victim was a Muslim man who had converted to Christianity and refused to revert back to Islam. The following are translated subtitles in the beheading video:

His masters are the Americans, the worshippers of the Cross,
Infiltrating the blood of the Muslims and their dignity,
So today we carry out the law of ridda (defecting from the faith
of Islam) with the strike of the sword...
Allah is great, may the losers be humiliated,
The crowd is praying for the sacrificial offering,
Oh, Allah, [accept] your deed in this to be an offering for your
glorified fate.[125]

The practice of crucifixion by IS that emerged in early 2014 appears to have little in connection with sacrifice, since in most cases the victim is already dead. In some cases, the victims are strung up while alive on crosses as a temporary punishment and typically they survive the event, but again a connection to sacrifice to God cannot be determined. In mid-2015 in eastern Syria, dozens of men were tied to electricity poles along a major road with their arms stretched out and affixed to a crosspiece. The men were being punished for eating during Ramadan and signs were hung around some of their necks describing their crime.[126] Some crucifixions by IS have possible references to Christianity. At least one crucifixion depicts a nail through the palm of the victim's hand; several instances have occurred where IS commanded that the victim be displayed on a cross for three days in the village square; and in one case the victim was shot in the head three times just prior to his crucifixion. In April 2014, when pictures of crucifixions by IS began to circulate on the internet, a Jihadist Twitter account responded to one photo with a quip about the image of the murdered man, "lol become new false jesus."[127]

Gunshot executions by IS are increasingly performed in a ritualistic way. One video shows a mass execution of approximately 15 blindfolded, kneeling men and it is reportedly filmed in a possible IS slaughterhouse in Syria.[128] The following prayer is heard and subtitled (translated) in the video just before each man is shot one-by-one in a ritualistic style:

In defense of the Sunnis O Lord, O Lord, We bring these offerings to you, O Lord. Please accept this sacrificial offering, O Lord. O Lord, accept this from us, accept this from us. In the name of Allah. Bismillah (In the name of Allah). Allahu Akbar

117

This is a rare example of an Islamist ritual killing by means of gunshot that is also displayed as a sacrificial offering of humans to God.[129]

In October 2014, IS announced and then posted to the internet a video of the stoning to death of a woman as punishment for adultery. An IS member in charge tells the woman she should be satisfied with the ruling decreed by Allah, to which she nods her head in the affirmative. An IS member, while pleading with her father to forgive her, states that she'll be delivered to Allah anyway, and that he (her father) will be rewarded [by Allah] for forgiving her. Before the act of stoning her, the IS member also sends a public message to all married men, urging them to not leave their wives alone for 1-3 years or "Satan will toy with them as he pleases." The woman's head is then covered; she is tied up and then pelted to death with large stones by her father and the men surrounding her.[130]

For God

IS members sacrifice themselves or are sacrificed *for* God in three different ways: by sacrificing oneself in a suicide attack; by sacrificing oneself by dying in battle as a jihadist fighter or mujahdin (e.g., dying as a result of an airstrike); or by being sacrificed through a punishment under Sharia law for an alleged crime. In each of these scenarios, the individual gains martyr status. The type of sacrificial act in connection with the reward granted to the martyr in the afterlife appears to be hierarchical. The mujahedin who dies in battle is the most worthy and is rewarded the most; next, the suicide attacker—referred to as istishhādīyyin by IS—who may have a lesser place in Paradise than the Mujahedin; and last the Muslim criminal, who with his punishment becomes forgiven and stands a good chance of going to Paradise. Further study is needed to understand whether a martyr's reward in Paradise is in terms of vertical (hierarchical) levels, or by spatial allocation (i.e., size of his or her dwelling place in heaven) (See Figure 1.).

Figure 1. Proposed IS Hierarchy: From the Temporal World to the Spiritual[1]

Figure 1A: Paradise

Estimated IS hierarchy based on status and deserving; provision by Allah is by levels, allocations of space and type and size of rewards.[2] This table represents both the living and the already dead, current and projected place(s) in the hierarchy.

Mohammad	Angel presence / Houri presence	Highest level
Issa (Jesus), other Prophets of Allah		
Key martyred leaders: (i.e., Zarqawi, Bin Laden, leaders of past Caliphates, Sunni descendents of Mohammad)		
Mujahedin		
Istishhadyyin (martyrdom bombers)		
Murabitun (military volunteers) who serve their time in ribat (frontier posts). They have performed honorable duty even if they don't die as a martyr.		
Muslim members who are punished by "slaughter" (if repentant, they die as martyrs even if sin was apostasy)		
Non-fighting jihadis (tax collectors, takfiri, clerics, etc.)		

	IS members who are	
Believer community, "true" Muslims	punished for a crime or infraction (not killed)	Some Sunni Muslim opposition fighters obtain salvation upon their death sentence via judicial ruling (Allah is forgiving)

Slave girl. Female slaves can move up the hierarchy if they convert to Islam, marry jihadi fighters, produce offspring etc.

Converted Mushrikah (female polytheist, pagan or idolater)	Converted Mushrik (male polytheist, pagan or idolater)	Lowest level

1 This table represents a transitioning scenario for people until Allah seals the gates of Paradise and Hell, at which time everyone is in their permanent place for eternity. Information for this table was derived from Dabiq magazine and other online sources reflecting the Sunni view, in an attempt to portray how IS interprets the afterlife. IS mostly sources the Quran and the hadith, where there is in depth information on Paradise and Hell.

2 Paradise varies by degrees and levels, the highest level/best part of paradise is known as al-Firdaws, reserved for the most deserving. It also varies by an individual's status and position.

Figure 1B: Purgatory (Barzakh) and Earth

Purgatory (Barzakh)[3]

Everyone except martyrs goes to Barzakh for questioning by angels. The angels make a preliminary determination or intercession, on where one will end up.

Angel Presence

Earth

On earth people are either alive or dead in their graves, awaiting end-of-days. While on earth both Muslims and non-Muslims can attain material wealth (Allah indifference); however Allah gives peace of mind only to Muslims. Fame and honor are conferred upon Martyrs and their families.

Angel Presence[4] / Houri Presence[5]

Earth consists of:
Believer Muslims
The Grayzone[6]
Crusaders and all other people

3 The duration of purgatory is said to be from the moment of death up to the time when all will rise from their graves regaining life (there may be variations on this)
4 Stern-looking angels also watch over the people who are in hell
5 The *houris* are the women or "fruit" of Paradise—they are not human. They descend from Paradise to assist martyrs in battle. See David Cook, *Understanding Jihad* (Berkely and Los Angeles: University of California Press, 2005) 28-29
6 The "Grayzone" consists of independent and neutral Islamic parties that refuse to join the Khilafah (caliphate), as well as hypocrites, deviant innovators and abandoners of jihad.

Fig 1C: Hell (Eternal hellfire)

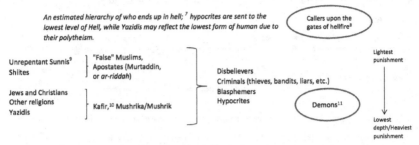

An estimated hierarchy of who ends up in hell;[7] hypocrites are sent to the lowest level of Hell, while Yazidis may reflect the lowest form of human due to their polytheism.

Callers upon the gates of hellfire[8]

Unrepentant Sunnis[9]
Shiites

"False" Muslims,
Apostates (Murtaddin,
or ar-riddah)

Jews and Christians
Other religions
Yazidis

Kafir,[10] Mushrika/Mushrik

Disbelievers
Criminals (thieves, bandits, liars, etc.)
Blasphemers
Hypocrites

Demons[11]

Lightest punishment

Lowest depth/Heaviest punishment

7 Levels of Hell may vary by the extent of its inhabitant's sins conducted while on earth
8 Whoever answers these callers will be thrown into hellfire by them
9 Some Muslims (possibly Shiites as well) will have the opportunity to get a second chance and gain a place in Paradise.
10 All non-Muslims are Kafir
11 Demons are present to torment those residing in hellfire

IS engages in coordinated suicide assaults using several suicide bombers (istishhadiyyin) at once, along with an assault team of mujahedin. The selected istishhad are often foreigners who have fought for an opposing side. One such operation in 2015 on an Iraqi military base, began after Fajr prayer. The soldiers of the Khalifa prayed, placed their trust and hope in Allah, and commenced the assault with the "istishhadi phase."[131] IS posted pictures of the suicide bombers (prior to their deaths) in *Dabiq* magazine and described their acts as heroic while implying they will attain shuhadā (martyrdom). In one example, an IS fighter had in previous years served with the German "crusader army" and was able to atone for his past that was "tainted with Muslim blood" by embracing Islam and carrying out a suicide bombing for IS. With Allah's permission and forgiveness—"through His grace and favor, Allah chose to guide him, replace his evil with good, and make him a warrior spilling his blood for this noble cause."[132]

Other IS Activities—Actual and Potential

Slaughterhouses. At least two slaughterhouses, reported to be in Syria, were revealed by an escaped hostage and subsequently posted to the internet. The slaughterhouses show extremely graphic video images of humans that have been butchered and even strung up very much like animals, reportedly by IS or a similar or precursor group to IS.[133]

Cannibalism. Cannibalism has been reported in at least one isolated case by an IS member and, in others by precursor or like groups, primarily by jihadist fighters, often following a killing in the heat of battle.[134] While not yet proven to be a common practice in post-modern times, historical Islamic examples and current edicts allowing for cannibalism may portend future activity in much the same way as beheadings and other dark practices have re-emerged today.[135] Current religious jurisprudence textbooks at a prominent Egyptian university teach students that Muslims are allowed to eat the dead flesh of Jews and Christians.[136] Edicts from various Islamic textbooks define what is and is not acceptable, even with some contradiction. Some examples include: Eating dead Jews and Christians is halal if it is a necessity, but non-Muslims are not allowed to eat dead Muslims, even out of necessity; Jews, Christians, and infidels should be eaten raw, not cooked or grilled; Muslims who don't pray can also be killed and eaten... [whomever] doesn't pray can be grilled and then eaten.[137]

Homosexual Group Rituals. Several interviews of former recruits of IS have reported being raped by IS leaders, while told "copulation" in this manner is permissible under halal in Islam. Torture and drugging are said to have accompanied some of these group rituals. The men who are raped as part of a group "marriage," which is recorded, then they are blackmailed into joining IS. In one video, an IS "prince" issues a fatwa allowing himself to rape the men, but they were not allowed to reciprocate.[138] In another earlier case, video-taped witnesses revealed that male captives were given a "marriage" number in addition to a "member" number they were issued upon capture or recruitment by IS. The men testified that they were "married" (raped) multiple times by men whose faces were covered.[139]

Use of Narcotics in Rituals. Several reports exist that assess that narcotics are distributed to fighters, and that some foreign recruits are drawn to IS by the appeal of obtaining free drugs. Drugs are also rumored to be given to captives to make them more compliant during filming of videos. A large bag of cocaine worth an estimated $5 million was discovered by Kurds at the home of an IS commander of approximately 30-40 troops. A possible use was for distribution to the fighters for endurance on the battlefield.[140] Drugs assessed to be used by IS fighters include amphetamines (primarily Captagon, a synthetic stimulant popular in the Middle East), "hallucinogenic pills," cocaine, heroin, hashish, and locally produced drugs such as Zolan, similar to Xanax. Khat, an "illegal" class C herbal stimulant is reportedly used by jihadis in Yemen and Somalia, and analysts have assessed Jihadi John to have possibly used khat when performing beheadings, based on his behavior and/or slurred speech.[141] In an interview, a captured IS member discussed his taking of Zolan, along with his comrades, just before battle which distorted the look of the battlefield—it changed the perception of what was going on there, and made them feel more empowered to kill.[142] Other effects of drug use by IS in battle include lack of empathy, fearlessness, and no feeling of pain as well as perceived superhuman strength.[143]

The reported use of drugs by IS fighters contributes to and perpetuates the dark magico-religious leanings of IS. Some of the extreme acts committed during and after ritual killings, such as reports of jihadists boiling decapitated heads in water, are similar to those used by Mexican drug trafficking organizations, members of which also employ the use of drugs. Prayer rituals conducted by fighters before and after battle as depicted in battlefield photos in IS online media—mixed with use of drugs—is a confusing and dangerous combination for their opposition—more often than not fellow Muslims—to contend with.

Summary

IS is traversing the increasingly dark magico-religious path increasingly enhanced by growth of the group and its caliphate, the influence of foreign fighters (and potentially the introduction of deviations from "true" Salafi-Wahhabi Islam), broad social media articulation of imminent end of days, the training and indoctrination of children/ youth as the future of IS, the creation of new "miracle stories and martyrologies"[144] of the mujahedin that strengthen morale and belief, and the likely drug use by fighters to enhance battlefield capabilities, success stories, and visions. IS will continue to spotlight its practicing true believers, both the martyred and living, successfully creating an illusion to many that IS is on the true Islamic path.

Case Study: Boko Haram

This case study assesses religious factors past and present that play a role in the ritualistic practices of Boko Haram. Boko Haram has had two key leaders (one the founder, the other the current leader), each having very different levels of intellect, education, interpretation of Islam, as well as methodologies for engaging in jihad. Boko Haram underwent significant transformational changes from one leader to the next. Boko Haram is well connected outside of Nigeria and has become a threat to neighboring countries; the group has had connections with al Qaeda, and most recently pledged allegiance to IS.

Group Background—Temporal and Spiritual

Boko Haram started as a movement in 2009 in Northern Nigeria and was founded by Muhammad Yūsuf. The actual name of the group is Jama'at Ahl us-Sunnah li'd-Da'wah wa'l-Jihād (The Group of the People of Sunnah for Preaching and Struggle).[145] Local Hausa peoples and the media re-named it Boko Haram, a name that is part Hausa and part Arabic, that in a literal sense means 'traversing the Western education system of education is harām' (forbidden).[146] Boko Haram evolved in part from a longstanding negative attitude toward Western education among Muslims in Northern Nigeria, and in part from Salafi-Wahhabi trends beginning in the late 1970's.[147] Not surprisingly, the rise of Boko Haram is often attributed to poor governance, misrule, and economic factors, while the salience of religious factors is largely ignored.[148]

In the 1980's, Mohammad Yūsuf, Boko Haram's eventual founder, along with many youth, joined the Muslim Brotherhood in Nigeria. The Ikhwān (brotherhood) movement was known for emotional rhetoric and enthusiasm in the name of Islam and against the Nigerian state. The group eventually fractured when some went towards Shi'ism, serving Iran's interests, while others, including Yusuf, chose to move towards Salafiyyah (following the way of the Prophet Mohammad).[149] Around 1999, approximately 12 states in Northern Nigeria began to institute Sharia law within their borders. In 2003, Yusuf and his group withdrew to the desert to set up a separatist community run on hard-line Islamic principles.

Boko Haram has perpetually had many links to other parts of Africa as well as other parts of the world. Many of its earliest recruits were young men who had travelled to Sudan for religious training and returned home.[150] Boko Haram forged ties with like-minded groups, including Al Qaeda in the Land of the Islamic Maghreb (AQLIM, or *AQIM*) based in Mali, and al Shabaab, based in Somalia. Many of Boko Haram's men are also said to have attended training in Afghanistan under the Taliban. The Taliban was a key driver of Boko Haram, having taught them many of their trade specialties including suicide attacks, bomb-making, and fighting as well as "advanced" weaponry.

Boko Haram's leaders were and still are inspired by the historical jihad led by Islamic scholar Usman Dan Fodio in 1804. Dan Fodio also established a caliphate that existed for one hundred years until the British arrived with colonial rule. Since then, the concept of a caliphate has resonated with Boko Haram and other Nigerian Islamist groups.[151]

Mohammad Yusuf based some of his preaching on Bakr ibn Abdullah Abū Zaid, a prominent Wahhabi scholar and author who held prestigious academic and religious positions in Saudi Arabia. Abū Zaid believed that the educational system introduced into Islamic societies was part of a vast conspiracy to maintain hegemony over Muslim societies, corrupt pure Islamic morals, and to undermine the solid Islamic individual and communal identities built on Salafi notions of piety and righteousness. Yusuf preached that it was imperative for Muslim religious leaders to wage unrelenting opposition to modern secular education by unmasking the hidden colonialist agenda. For Yusuf, it was haram for Muslims to acquire, accept, learn, or believe any aspect of subjects that contradicted the Quran and Sunna. These subjects included agriculture, biology, chemistry, engineering, geography, medicine, physics, and the English language—all subjects brought in by British colonial administrators. His arguments against these subjects were of a magico-religious nature, discussed later in this case study.

Yusuf's absolutist mentality and what one theorist refers to as his *will to power*[152], as derived from a higher power—from Allah, led him to violent confrontations with Nigerian security forces, eventually ending in his death. Following Yusuf's violent death by Nigerian police forces, his followers began a hit and run campaign against security forces. They also attacked military barracks, police stations, commercial banks, schools, and universities, Christians worshipping in their churches, local bars, and newspaper offices. These attacks were most often revenge based. A watershed moment in its history came in 2009 when Boko Haram launched previously unseen levels of violence and intensity in its attacks on Maiduguri, a city in the Northeast of Nigeria. Prior to that, Boko Haram was not considered a threat; it mostly resembled a religious commune whose members had periodic clashes with the police and army, and some undoubtedly performed criminal acts.[153]

Boko Haram's current leader, Mallam Abubakar Shekau, is considered a far more radical and violent leader than Yusuf was and has taken Boko Haram to heightened levels of violence and brutality. Shekau studied under an Islamic cleric and later attended the Borno State College of Legal and Islamic Studies. In August 2014, he announced the formation of a caliphate in the Northeast of Nigeria, and in each area captured, strict Sharia law is enforced. The following is excerpted from a video speech made by Abubakar Shekau, translated and posted to a website:

> I Pledge to Allah – Imam Abubakar Shekau
> My brethren in Islam, I am greeting you in the name of Allah like he instructed we should among Muslims. Allah is great and has given us privilege and temerity above all people. If we meet infidels, if we meet those that become infidels according to Allah, there is no any talk except hitting of the neck; I hope you chosen people of Allah are hearing. This is an instruction from Allah. It is not a distorted interpretation it is from Allah himself. This is from Allah on the need for us to break down infidels, practitioners of democracy, and constitutionalism, voodoo and those that are doing western education, in which they are practicing paganism.[154]

Magico-Religious Aspects of Boko Haram

Evidence of and insight into magico-religious aspects of Boko Haram are derived from the leadership perspectives of both Yusuf and Shekau, as well as from a number of testimonies of former Boko Haram fighters, hostages, and videos found on the internet.

Mohammad Yusuf during his time argued against the geographical concept of how rain occurs in that it contradicts Quran 23:18, where

Allah says: 'And We sent down water from the sky according to (due) measure, and We caused it to soak into the soil...' Another objection of Yusuf regarded the age of the earth, since the Quran 41:9 states that God created the earth in just two days, thus the time scales of the various deposits contributing to the earth's formation in four million years were wrong. Most geographical concepts contradict the Quran and hadith, therefore learning them is haram.

Yusuf had similar thoughts on evolution. Darwin's theory contradicted Quran 23:12 in which God created mankind out of clay. He argued that chemistry teaches that energy is not created and cannot be destroyed, but that to Islam only God is eternal and uncreated, and it contradicts Quran 55:26-27: "Everything/everyone on earth perishes. Only the face of your Lord of glory and honor endures."

Abubakar Shekau has announced publicly in videos that it is God who commands him and his followers to massacre hundreds of people, and insists publicly that more is on the way. "We are the ones who fought the people of Baga, and we have killed them with such a killing as he [God] commanded us in his book."[155]

A number of magico-religious practices by Boko Haram are indicative of a connection and use of the services of marabouts (e.g. Islamic shamans). Belief in consultation to a spiritual or occult master, the use of charms, and oath swearing is common to West Africa,[156] and marabouts are associated with some sects of Islam. Boko Haram, based on some evidence, most likely has brought in and has been consulting with marabouts for some time. Former Boko Haram member and Christian convert, Isiaku Nazir, said in interviews that they (Boko Haram fighters) received strange, weird-looking visitors to their camps, who "bore no resemblance to human beings."[157] Boko Haram leaders would have Nazir and other fighters recite passages from the Quran to these visitors. According to Nazir, the visitors fortified them with charms and prepared them to accomplish their task, asking them to be strong and fight.[158] Another former Boko Haram fighter named Hosea Bulus, when asked in an interview how he was initiated into the group, replied that he was given blood and charms, which he took inside food, after which time the urge to kill and destroy entered him.[159]

Charms have reportedly been found at Boko Haram hideouts after raids. The belief in the potency of charms may explain some militant's reported behavior of rushing forward in battles, even in direct line of fire of soldier's bullets.[160] Mohammed Yusuf was said to have been carrying several dozen charms all over his body when he was killed.[161]

A ritual practice of drinking human blood is discussed in at least two interviews with former Boko Haram fighters. One claimed that members often drank their victim's blood (human) as a spiritual remedy.[162] According to Nazir, they would shoot people in the legs, and then ask the victim if he agreed to become a Muslim. When he replied "no," they would "cut his throat like a goat."[163] After killing the infidel, they collected the blood in a small cup and drank. By doing this, the ghost of the slain person could not come back to haunt their dreams. This was told to them by their leader and, accordingly, Nazir said when they drank the blood they did not see it in their dreams. In another testimony, the fighters ritually drank blood as part of an oath-taking, whereby they were made to swear to Allah to do his bidding of fighting and killing the infidels. The tithe collectors (i.e. Pastors) were the most significant infidel target, as there was more reward from Allah for whoever kills a Pastor.[164]

Drinking of "spiritual water" was also revealed by former Boko Haram fighters. Spiritual water was a special type they drank as part of their training and prior to each operation. The fighters called it thus because it was "not ordinary water," and, taken prior to an operation, it made them very dangerous and allowed them to easily kill. The fighters were also convinced that this water protected them from bullets.[165]

Legal and Religious Premises for Ritual and Sacrificial Killings

"As for killing, we will kill because Allah says we should decapitate, we should amputate limbs, we should mutilate."

—Abubakar Shekau[166]

In the earlier days of Boko Haram, Yusuf authoritatively and vehemently condemned many things as religiously forbidden, often with very specific rulings. Participating in or being a fan of sports, for example, was forbidden because it could lead to developing affection for a non-Muslim. Watching movies was also haram, because movies typically cast Muslims in the role of hateful villain and non-Muslims in the role of lovable hero. According to Yusuf, employment in most governmental sectors was also forbidden because only God's law is valid.[167]

The current Islamic laws imposed by Boko Haram are not as well documented publicly as are those of IS. Killings by Boko Haram, ritual or otherwise, include suicide bombings, beheadings, burning people alive, stoning to death, mass slaughter, and burning of churches, schools, homes, and other infrastructure with or without people inside. Accusations and death sentences based on Sharia law often include spying, unwillingness to convert to Islam, unwillingness to fight alongside Boko Haram (males), or unwillingness to become a suicide bomber. Lesser punishments include 100 lashes, e.g., for sex outside of marriage,[168] (often a severe flogging with a whip); and amputations of hands for thievery.

Christians in Nigeria are the most affected by Boko Haram's laws. Men are beheaded for not converting to Islam, while women are often forced to convert and marry Boko Haram fighters. After bombing three Christian churches in June 2012, Boko Haram thanked Allah for giving them the victory in carrying out their task.[169] They reaffirmed that, for there to be peace, all Christians must convert to Islam. The statement claimed that Almighty Allah tasked all Muslims in Quran Chapter 9 v. 29 to launch attacks against Jews and Christians who refused to believe in him [and] his messenger Prophet Mohammed:

Fight those who do not believe in Allah or in the Last Day and who do not consider unlawful what Allah and His Messenger have made unlawful and who do not adopt the religion of truth from those who were given the Scripture – [fight] until they give the jizyah willingly while they are humbled. (Quran 9:29)

Both Christians and Muslims, especially women, are subject to enslavement. There are both legal and magical aspects to Boko Haram's policies with regard to slavery. Shekau is quoted as saying it is Allah's bidding: "I shall only but follow the Quran completely. In the Quran it says you should catch slaves, that's why I caught them…" and "I can't be someone that prays and [does] not catch slaves, it is impossible…" With the abduction of the 276 girls from Chobuk, Shekau said "God instructed me to sell them (the girls), they are his properties and I will carry out his instructions." The girls who did not escape were most likely forced to convert to Islam and marry jihadist fighters. Even if already Muslim, the women are still subject to enslavement and forced marriage.[170]

Examples of Ritual and Sacrificial Activities

Unlike the more media present al Qaeda or IS, it is more difficult to match ritual killings of Boko Haram with evidence of a will to sacrifice, either *to* God or *for* God. The video-taped beheading rituals released by Boko Haram, for example, do not contain many verses from the Quran or direct prayers. Instead, the ritual punishments are based on judicial outcomes, often with the victim's crime being announced, or with only a verbal confession from the victim. In the weeks leading up to announcing their alliance with IS, however, Boko Haram's videos began to appear very similar in production style to those of IS, even with the display of the IS flag.

To God

"I enjoy killing anyone that Allah commands me to kill the way I enjoy killing chickens and rams."

—A Boko Haram spokesman explaining his group's declared war on Nigerian Christians[171]

Former Boko Haram member Isiaku Nazir provided a confession and some insight into the group in 2013.[172] He discussed that sacrificial practices past and present are not limited to Boko Haram but involved the existence of many similar, linked organizations. Even the Islamic schools taught that "the more we kill Christians, the more we are likely to enter the paradise of God." [173] The schools Nazir attended urged him to get ready to fight the Christians, to "tighten their belts," and to always be armed with a knife or gun. According to Nazir, Boko Haram leaders read passages from the Quran to the fighters, such as "Oh you who believe, do not befriend your enemies" and this seemed to justify what he described as their own criminal actions—assassinating Christians. He referred to Boko Haram as a criminal cult.[174]

For God

Boko Haram increasingly uses suicide bombings in its operations, bearing the signature of al Qaeda.[175] Similar to IS, there is a range from very willing suicide bombers to those who are forced to conduct them under some threat. For the willing attackers, the bombings are probably a personal sacrifice *to* God. For unwilling bombers, in the absence of videos or propaganda on the subject, there is nothing to suggest the suicide bombings are anything other than part of a strategy to ensure successful operations for Boko Haram. Females and children as young as age 7 comprise an increasing percentage of suicide bombers for Boko Haram, and the young children may not even be aware of their mission.

Other Boko Haram Activities—Actual and Potential

There are indicators Boko Haram may be importing marabouts from Niger and Mali. The use of marabouts may be linked to using beheaded victims, or "those slain like goats" as objects of ritual. One claim is that the blood of those whose throats are slit are drained and taken to the marabouts.[176] Also possibly linked to marabouts are reports of harvesting and selling human organs by Boko Haram, for the purpose of generating income.

There are reports of Boko Haram resorting to cannibalism after being stranded in Nigerian forests without food or water. An escaped potential victim claimed that the group was slaughtering non-combatant members to provide food for the fighters.[177] There were no references to anything spiritual or religious in connection with this report. However, in another odd report, Shekau, when vividly describing an attack on a tank battalion in Bama, Nigeria, stated "Had Allah allowed us to eat them we would have eaten them but we are not cannibals. This is a victory from Allah."[178]

Use of Narcotics in Rituals

"It's religion we practice. Allah has forbidden us to drink beer. And it's not beer we give anyone or drugs."

—Abubakar Shekau

There is insufficient information to confirm any meaningful connection between narcotics and ritual or sacrificial killings by Boko Haram with regard to this study. Boko Haram fighters use narcotics for various reasons. Nazir mentioned that he no longer used drugs since his conversion to Christianity and removal from Boko Haram. It was not clear whether or not he had used them operationally as a fighter or recreationally or a combination of both.

Summary

Boko Haram has transformed itself over time and its ideology and strategies varied under Yusuf and Shekau. The group has continued to trend towards darker behavior, in a combination of the magico-religious and the purely criminal. Several factors indicate this trend will continue: its recent joining with IS, which has already strengthened and emboldened its movement within Nigeria; blending Islamic with indigenous practices such as its use of marabouts and their potent connections within and outside the group; the inability of the Nigerian army to suppress the group without the support of regional armies; its seeming ability to unabashedly conduct ritual killings under Sharia law mixed with other practices not sanctioned by Islam in any way—true Salafi-Wahhabi philosophy would not allow this blending to occur.

Conclusion

The analysis of the above case studies supports the notion that Islamist ritual killings and other ritual practices in recent times emerged as a result of historical precedent, particularly from Mohammad's time and beyond. Religious and philosophical disagreements that occurred amongst early to modern Islamic scholars, elites, and common thugs alike opened the way for the acceptability of ritual killings as the groups in this study took form. There are threads of similarities and differences among the three groups in how they operated, within the given timeframes of this article.

From the radical side of historical arguments emerged legal justifications for various ritual killing practices. Early AQ considered some ethical and legal issues that ritual killings presented prior to making decisions on whether or not to perform them. IS and Boko Haram, however, seemed less concerned with ethics, and publicly set forth religion-based justifications for ritual acts without hesitation, to include those acts for the purpose of retaliation; but they also gave pause to some ritual killings where there was a possibility the act would not be acceptable to Allah. Additionally, ritual killings were also allowable as a means of punishment i.e., within their respective caliphates, and these acts were based on the methods of capital punishment of some Middle Eastern nation states.

AQ and IS shared similar magico-religious philosophies, having emerged from the same origins. Some common themes were promises of paradise, grace, and bounty; that God intervenes during operations, enabling victory in battle; and that prayer is prophylactic in nature, ensuring protection from God. Bodily cleanliness and purification of oneself was also important for the two groups. IS took magico-religious concepts much further than AQ, however, by infusing an end-of-days, millenarian belief system into the daily activities of all of its members, not just those on the battlefield. Boko Haram differed from the other groups, beginning with the complex and detailed magico-religious beliefs embraced by its first leader Mohammad Yusuf, i.e., the rejection of scientific theories, to the very one dimensional ones of its current leader Abubakar Shekau, i.e., that he kills because Allah says he should kill. Additionally, there is evidence that Boko Haram mixes its proclaimed pure Islamic qualities with local African customs and traditions.

Regarding sacrifice, both AQ and IS appear to have regarded humans as substitutes for animals in some ritual killings, and that they are/were even sanctioned as sacrifices *to* God. Whether for the victim there is an expectation of a pardoning in Paradise or a lifetime in Hell in the hereafter, or that the victim dies as collateral damage, non-Muslims and Muslims alike were views as sacrifices. All three groups have many similarities with regard to sacrifice *for* God, especially via personal suicide bombings. IS took sacrifice *for* God a step further, to include sacrifice as punishment for a crime as a means to atone with God (i.e., the stoning to death of a Muslim woman). Furthermore, the promoting by IS of a more hierarchical afterlife in Paradise is based on various levels of personal sacrifice *for* God while on earth.

A number of factors will likely influence the future direction of ritual or sacrificial killings and other dark practices by these groups or later factions of them. One can get a glimpse of possible future trends by observing the recent ebb and flow of the similar but non-Islamic ritual killings by various transnational criminal organizations (TCOs) in Mexico. The staying power or growth of ritualistic killings of TCOs has depended on both internal and external factors that seek to break up or destroy them. While facing opposition by mostly external forces, IS, because of its global expansion and influence, still has the most freedom of the study groups to expand its ritual practices. IS and Boko Haram are both likely to continue to deviate from more traditional killing methods to highly inventive post-modern ones. In contrast, AQ has seemingly reverted to its earlier methods of warfare, i.e., suicide bombings and combined arms attacks, while its factions who disagree with this comparatively moderate tone have joined IS. Finally, all of the groups have the potential to become diluted by other cultural or religious influences as well as by the use of narcotics. For example, non-Islamic customs and traditions from other cultures may find a way of mixing into IS via Boko Haram or other groups, due to global recruiting efforts by IS that has brought unprecedented ethnic diversity to its ranks. Another potentially altering factor is the *un*-Islamic practice of using and selling narcotics, which serves both to enhance the brutality of ritual killings and to drive these jihadist groups towards becoming purely criminal and less religious entities.

Appendix 1. Religious Justification, Physical and Spiritual Significance of Jihadist Ritual Sacrificial Acts

ACTIVITY	EXAMPLE(S)	RELIGIOUS JUSTIFICATION	PHYSICAL SIGNIFICANCE	SPIRITUAL SIGNIFICANCE (*Magico-Religious*)	GROUPS
Beheading	Muslim convert to Christianity is beheaded by IS for refusing to convert back. Syria, March 28, 2015	IS is quoted in the video saying: "So today we carry out the law of ridda (defecting from the faith of Islam) with the strike of the sword"	Terrorize the enemy; warn the public against violating Sharia law; subdue the public; status / acceptance / rank for executioner	A blessed act that is rewarded. In this example, a sacrificial offering to God	Islamic State, Boko Haram, al Qaeda [179]
	A six-year-old Christian boy is beheaded by Boko Haram in an attack on a village as Sunday church services were beginning. June 1, 2014	Broader justification that Christianity stands in the way of Boko Haram's Islam. Boko Haram insurgents later tracked down the man who tried to save the boy, tied him to a tree and repeatedly tortured him while asking him if he would convert to Islam.	Terrorize the enemy; subdue the public (Christians); convert them or kill them	Beheading is allowed by Allah; hadith sets the example	

	Two civilian women and their husbands were beheaded by IS in Syria after being accused of sorcery and witchcraft. June 2015	Sharia law prohibits worship of any but Allah	Warn the public against violating Sharia law; subdue the public	Unknown	
Immolation	Jordanian pilot Lt al-Kaseasbeh is burned alive in Syria sometime after his plane went down December 24, 2014	"So whoever has assaulted you, then assault him in the same way that he has assaulted you." Quran 2: 194	Punish and terrorize the enemy; retaliation for like crimes	Allah's doing; healing/purifying the believer community—retribution—acceptable to God	Islamic State
Crucifixion	A 17-year-old boy was executed and crucified for "apostasy" his body left on display on a cross in Syria for three days. October 2014	Quran 5:33 "The punishment of those who wage war against Allah and His Messenger, and strive with might and main for mischief through the land is: execution, or crucifixion, or the cutting off of hands and feet from opposite sides, or exile from the land: that is their disgrace in this world, and a heavy punishment is theirs in the Hereafter"	Warning to public against committing various crimes.	Punishment acceptable to Allah. Possible allusion to Islamic disbelief in the Christian crucifixion.	Islamic State

Terrorism Research Center

	Eight men were strung up on crucifixes by IS while alive, for reportedly failing to fast during Ramadan. June 2015		Warning to public against committing various crimes.	Unknown	
Stoning	First woman publicly stoned by IS for adultery. Video of the event posted to the internet on October 21, 2014	IS spokesman at the event declares that the punishment was decreed by Allah, and that the woman will be delivered to Allah; implies she will be forgiven	Warning to public against committing adultery	Punishment decreed by/acceptable to Allah; communal ritual activity	Islamic State, Boko Haram
Slaughter-houses	Footage from two separate slaughterhouses in Syria shows bodies of men who were beheaded and disemboweled; some were hanging upside down similar to slaughtered sheep.[180]	IS Islamic theology that Muslims can be sacrificed as a martyr by being slaughtered for his sin.[181] The Christian's fate however, is still eternal hellfire.	De-humanize the enemy	Possible sacrificial element-human replaces animal in sacrifice to Allah; offer of a way out by means of atonement with Allah for captured Muslims who are fighting against IS.	Islamic State

Martyrdom (Bombing)	IS used seven suicide bombers in a coordinated attack in Iraq against the "Safawi army," or Shiites and Iraqi security forces, targeting militia bases and barracks near the Baiji oil refinery complex, on June 13, 2015.	Justification is jihad. IS refers to suicide bombers as "istishhadiyyin," or *martyrs*,[182] used in terms of war-time acts. The istishhadi brothers operate along with the mujahedin as a specific phase of an operation.[183]	Destruction of target/force multiplier; terrorize the enemy; meet tactical and strategic wartime objectives	A blessed act; instant martyrdom; rewards for family members. For foreign istishhadiyyin, it is a sacrificial act to atone for past wrongs, whereby Allah forgives and allows the fighter entry into Islam.[184]	Al Qaeda, Islamic State, Boko Haram
Taking of Female Slaves	Over 5,000 Yazidi women were taken captive by IS. IS men came periodically and chose up to three and four girls at a time to take home with them[185] Aug 2014	IS issued a pamphlet justifying its actions by citing the Quran, and authoritative Islamic scholars[186]	Allows growth of Caliphate (i.e. usefulness of slaves)	Taking/Sex With=Acceptable activity to Allah-growth of Caliphate; to deny or mock this practice is apostasy[187] Freeing slaves=freedom from hellfire	Islamic State, Boko Haram

137

Over 200 girls were abducted by Boko Haram. Most are assessed to have been forcibly married off to jihadi fighters or forced to become suicide bombers. 15 April 2014.	Boko Haram leader is following Allah's will and the Quran. Slavery is also mandated by hadith, which allows for selling of slaves even if they convert as Muslims.[188]	Brings more women into Boko Haram; usefulness as workers, child-bearers (to perpetuate the Caliphate) and/or suicide bombers. Recruitment message to girls around the world: "that Allah may guide them and show them the path that I follow now"[189]	Salvation for the girls as they convert to Islam.
A 12-year-old Yazidi girl is raped repeatedly by an IS fighter who explained to the girl that it was not a sin to rape her; he knelt and prayed by the bed both before and after the act.[190] 2014	According to the IS fighter, the Quran condoned, encouraged and gave him the right to rape her because she was an unbeliever who practiced a religion other than Islam. The fighter told her repeatedly that the act was "ibadah," (worship) as well as halal (allowed), and that raping her is his prayer to God.	The sex slave practice draws male recruits from deeply conservative Muslim societies where dating/casual sex are forbidden.	By raping the girl, the fighter is drawing closer to God.

Illicit Narcotics Fighter Use	An IS fighter taken captive by Kurds said in a CNN interview that IS provided "hallucinogenic pills" to the fighters	Narcotics use is a sin according to Islam, and is a punishable offence under Sharia Laws of IS (i.e., amputation) and Boko Haram. Neither group has attempted to publicly justify narcotics use by their fighters.	Endurance, courage, painkilling effect	Unknown if any spiritual significance – a fighter may be more able to commit dark religious –based acts/atrocities. The martyred fighter's sins are forgiven upon death—likely including the sin of drug usage.	Islamic State, Boko Haram
Illicit Narcotics Victim Use	Photos from Mosul show IS pumping drugs into a victim's hand prior to amputating his arm with a meat cleaver[191]	Certain drugs may be considered allowable if for medicinal purposes such as in this example.	Drugs probably used to lessen the pain for the amputee	No known spiritual significance	Islamic State

Appendix 2. Female Slaves of the Islamic State

IS publicly released a pamphlet in a question and answer format on the topic of female captives and slaves in late 2014.[192] In the document, IS defines *al-sabi* as a woman from among *ahl al-harb* (the people of war) who has been captured by Muslims and lists what is and is not permissible. Her unbelief is what makes a woman allowable for capture. Of no dispute among IS decision-makers is the enslavement of women from among the People of the Book (Jews and Christians) as well as polytheists.[193] Of dispute is the issue over enslavement of women who are apostates—IS leans toward accepting the consensus of forbidding it on these women.

Among permissible acts against female slaves in a very long list produced by IS are: having sexual intercourse with them; buying, selling or giving them as a gift; having intercourse with a female slave who has not reached puberty; beating them as discipline (but not for gratification or torture; and it is forbidden to hit the face). During the 2015 Ramadan, female slaves were offered as top prizes in a Quran reciting contest.[194]

Among non-permissible acts against female slaves: separating a mother from her prepubescent children through buying, selling, or giving away; having intercourse with a female if the master does not own her exclusively (the other owners must sell or give him their share first); selling a woman if she becomes pregnant; having intercourse with or kissing the female slave of his wife (because the slave is owned by someone else, also kissing involves pleasure, which is prohibited unless ownership is exclusive); marrying a Muslim or *kitabiyat* female slaves, except for those men who fear they will commit the sin of fornication.

Other rules regarding female enslavement include the following: if a man dies, the female captives are distributed as part of his estate; a female's private body parts must be concealed during prayer as well as outside of prayer, which includes all but the head, neck, hands and feet; a female may expose her head, neck, hands and feet to a foreign male so long as *fitna* (enticement) can be avoided.

Notes

[1]   Sheikh Anwar Al-Awlaki, "Q & A with Sheikh Anwar Al-'Awlaki." *Inspire* 12 (1435). Spring 2014: 17-18.

[2]   An example is the report of two jihadists heading for Syria having ordered *Islam for Dummies* from Amazon.com. See also Karen Armstrong, "Wahhabism to ISIS: how Saudi Arabia exported the main source of global terrorism." *New Statesman.* November 2014: 21-27, http://www.newstatesman.com/world-affairs/2014/11/wahhabism-isis-how-saudi-arabia-exported-main-source-global-terrorism.

[3]   IS is perpetuating and selling the concept of end times to its followers and potential recruits far more so than al Qaeda or Boko Haram. Both IS and Boko Haram have declared and/or established present day caliphates.

[4]   Farhad Khorsrokhavar, *Inside Jihadism.* Boulder: Paradigm Publishers, 2009: 41

[5]   Holy Quran, (Surah Aal Imran: Verse 169-170).

[6]   Farhad Khorsrokhavar, *Inside Jihadism.*

[7]   Sahih al-Bukhari, "Book of Fighting for the Cause of Allah (Jihad)," (2790), http://sunnah.com/bukhari/56.

[8]   Ibid.

[9]   Opponents of suicide bombings quote the Quran and other sayings to make their case, such as the following from a ninth century compiler of Sayings of the Prophet: "The Prophet says: he who kills himself for some reason in this world will endure the sufferings (of Hell) the Day of Judgement. See Farhad Khorsrokhavar, *Inside Jihadism.*

[10] Denis MacEoin, "Suicide Bombing as Worship—Dimensions of Jihad." *The Middle East Quarterly.* Fall 2009, http://www.meforum.org/2478/suicide-bombing-as-worship.

[11] Ibid.

[12] Abu Ayyub, a companion of Muhammad, viewed *inghimas* as 'life itself'. Ibid.

[13] Brannon Wheeler, "Collecting the Dead Body of the Prophet Muhammad" in Christiane J. Gruber, and Avinoam Shalem, Eds., *The Image of the Prophet between Ideal and Ideology.* Berlin: De Gruyter, 2014: 45-64. According to Wheeler, the prophet Muhammad sacrificed 100 Camels along with his son-in-law 'Ali b. Abi Talib. Other sources say the

prophet sacrificed 63 camels, each representing one year of his life. See: http://www.questionsonislam.com/content/eid-al-adha-approaches.

[14] The number of hairs distributed by Mohammad represents a sacrifice of an extremely large scale. Accompanying the distribution of his hair and as part of his farewell pilgrimage, Mohammad reportedly also sent messengers to the various Arab and non-Arab kings in different parts of the world. Abu Muhammad Abd al-Malik Ibn Hisham (d. 828), a biographer of the prophet Mohammad, compares this event explicitly to Jesus' sending of his disciples throughout the world following his death to spread Christianity. See Brannon Wheeler, "Gift of the Body in Islam: The Prophet Muhammad's Camel Sacrifice and Distribution of Hair and Nails at his Farewell Pilgrimage." Numen 57. Leiden 2010: 343.

[15] Brannon Wheeler, "Collecting the Dead Body of the Prophet Muhammad": 55.

[16] Brannon Wheeler, "Gift of the Body in Islam: The Prophet Muhammad's Camel Sacrifice and Distribution of Hair and Nails at his Farewell Pilgrimage": 341-388.

[17] The plural form of hadith is also written as *ahadith.*

[18] Brannon Wheeler, "Collecting the Dead Body of the Prophet Muhammad": 55.

[19] See also the public controversy regarding the "Ground Zero" mosque and discussions about its purpose as Islamic expansion.

[20] Brannon Wheeler, "Collecting the Dead Body of the Prophet Muhammad."

[21] Brannon Wheeler, "Gift of the Body in Islam: The Prophet Muhammad's Camel Sacrifice and Distribution of Hair and Nails at his Farewell Pilgrimage": 22.

[22] By definition, Eid is the feast marking the end of the fast of Ramadan, and the festival marking the culmination of the annual pilgrimage to Mecca and commemorating the sacrifice of Abraham.

[23] "Etiquette of Sacrifice." 2 Eids. n.d., http://www.2eids.com/etiquettes_of_sacrifice.php.

[24] *Telegram and Gazette,* "Muslim celebration today; 500 expected to attend sermon marking Abraham's 'sacrifice.'" Worcester: Gatehouse Media, Inc., Halifax Media Group. 22 June 1991.

[25] *Beautiful Islam,* "The Ritual Islamic Slaughter," n.d., http://www.beautifulislam.net/animals/ritual_islamic_slaughter.htm.

[26] Ibid.

[27] See Richard C. Foltz, *Animals in Islamic Tradition and Muslim Cultures*. Oxford: Oneworld Publications, 2006.

[28] *BBC News*, "Hamza attacked 'sugar daddy West.'" 6 January 2006, http://news.bbc.co.uk/2/hi/uk_news/4616968.stm.

[29] *Questions on Islam*, "As Eid-al-Adha Approaches…" 10 February 2014, http://www.questionsonislam.com/content/eid-al-adha-approaches%E2%80%A6.

[30] For other more complex interpretations of the meanings behind these acts, such as for cleansing of the impure for the sake of Islam and the believer community, see Dawn Perlmutter, "Mujahideen Blood Rituals: The Religion and Forensic Symbolism of Al Qaeda Beheading." *Anthropoetics* 11. Winter 2006, http://anthropoetics.ucla.edu/ap1102/muja.htm. Perlmutter associates these ritual slaughters with cleansing of impurities of humans. She states "…jihadists can commit unspeakable atrocities without remorse because they consider their deeds righteous slaughter in defense of the purity of Islam. Enemies are not people: They are unclean animals, pigs, monkeys or dogs that must be cleansed. And beheadings, throat slitting, body mutilation…are not atrocities but sacred blood rituals that restore purity and cleanse shame."

[31] "The Book of Sacrifices" (Kitab Al-Adahi); Translation of Sahih Muslim, Book 22: *University of Southern California, Center for Muslim-Jewish Engagement*. n.d., http://www.usc.edu/org/cmje/religious-texts/hadith/muslim/022-smt.php.

[32] *Answering Islam*, "Christ's Crucifixion." Silas, n.d., http://answering-islam.org/Silas/crucified.htm.

[33] Jon Sorensen, "Islam and the Crucifixion," *Catholic Answers*. 9 June 2014, http://www.catholic.com/blog/jon-sorensen/islam-and-the-crucifixion.

[34] The Quran, 4: 157-158.

[35] In the first caliphal dynasty of early Islam, the Umayyads employed crucifixion to punish brigands and heretics and to humiliate rebels and enemies. Like their Roman and Persian predecessors, the Umayyads wielded crucifixion, and thus the symbolism of violence against the body, to attest to their impunity as caliphs and the legitimacy of their rule. See Sean Anthony, "Crucifixion and Death as Spectacle: Umayyad Crucifixion in its Late Antique Context." *American Oriental Series* 96. 2014, http://www.eisenbrauns.com/item/ANTCRUCIF.

[36] Donald Holbrook, "Using the Quran to Justify Terrorist Violence: Analysing Selective Application of the Quran in English-Language Militant Islamist Discourse." *Terrorism Research Initiative*. 2010, http://www.terrorismanalysis.com/pt/index.php/pot/article/view/104/html. See also sections of Deuteronomy, Chapters 7:2, 5-6, and 20: 10-16.

[37] For example, al Qaeda leadership wrote of only the first part of the verse Sura At-Taubah (9):5 which urged Muslims to 'slay the idolaters' wherever they were found; they knowingly left out the second part of the verse, 'but if they repent and fulfill their devotional obligations and pay the zakat, then let them go their way, for God is forgiving and kind.' See Donald Holbrook, "Using the Quran to Justify Terrorist Violence: Analysing Selective Application of the Quran in English-Language Militant Islamist Discourse."

[38] See Dr. Sebastian Gorka, "Jihadist Ideology: The Core Texts" (transcript of a briefing given by Dr. Sebastian Gorka), *The Counter Jihad Report*. 5 October 2010, http://counterjihadreport.com/jihadist-ideology-the-core-texts/.

[39] Ibid.

[40] Frederick P. Isaac, "Indigenous Peoples Under the Rule of Islam," *Part II: The Rise and Spread of the Message (Al-Da'awa)*. Bloomington: Xlibris Corp, 2002: 1-3.

[41] Asad Raza, "Intercession: Meaning and Philosophy." *Islamic Insights*. 28 September 2010, http://www.islamicinsights.com/religion/intercession-meaning-and-philosophy.html.

[42] Ibid.

[43] Andrew McGregor, "'Jihad and the Rifle Alone:' 'Abdullah 'Azzam and the Islamist Revolution." *Journal of Conflict Studies* 23. Fall 2003: 1-14, https://journals.lib.unb.ca/index.php/jcs/article/view/219/377.

[44] The embedding of Salafi-jihadist groups in key areas or hubs of the drug trade is especially evident with al-Qaeda affiliated groups in Mali and Yemen, where AQIM and AQAP respectively, are centered in the midst of very lucrative drug trafficking. See Beatriz Mesa, "Mali Jihadists Mix Religion and Drugs." *AL Monitor*. 7 May 2013, http://www.al-monitor.com/pulse/security/2013/05/drug-trade-fuels-jihad-in-mali.html.

[45] David Cook, "Miracle Stories and Martyrologies" in *Understanding Jihad*. Berkeley: University of California Press, 2005: 153-157. See David Cook's six key categories of "miracle stories and martyrologies" and the significant role they play in globalist radical Islam.

[46]   Only after the Muslims are purged of unreliable elements and place their trust entirely in God will He personally intervene in battle, favor the Muslims and defeat the infidels. Ibid: 159-160.

[47]   Much has been written about Ibn-Taymiyyah, a professor of Islamic law born in 1269 in Syria, who argued for the requirements for jihad, including that it should be on the same level as the five pillars of Islam: prayer, pilgrimage, alms, the Declaration of Faith and the fast of Ramadan.

[48]   Usama Bin Laden had magical aspects about him that carry forth to this day, some of which may have derived from his simple message, his communication through poetry, or even from stories covering a decade of his evading capture by US and coalition forces. The Islamic State (IS) reveres him today as a martyr of very high standing, as in this quote from *Dabiq* 7 (1436 Rabi' Al-Akhir): "Amongst them was the shahīd of Islam – as we consider him – the imām and sayyid of his era, Abū 'Abdillāh Usāmah Ibn Lādin, the pride of the Ummah and the crown of its new era [Wa Ya'ballāhu illā An Yutimma Nūrah – And Allah Refuses but to Perfect His Light]."

[49]   Sujata Ashwarya Cheema, "Sayyid Qutb's Concept of Jahiliyya as Metaphor for Modern Society." *Academia*. n.d., https://www.academia.edu/3222569/Sayyid Qutbs C oncept of Jahiliyya as Metaphor for Modern Society.

[50]   Johannes J.G. Jansen, "Faraj and The Neglected Duty; Interview with Professor Johannes J.G. Jansen," *Religioscope*. n.d., http://www. religioscope.com/info/dossiers/textislamism/faraj jansen.htm.

[51]   Bruce Lincoln, *Holy Terrors: Thinking about Religion after September 11.* Chicago: The University of Chicago Press, 2006.

[52]   Azzam drove the popularity of Jihad to an international scale while espousing a militant approach to Islam. His long-term goal to re-establish the Islamic Caliphate was a far more ambitious plan than those conceived earlier by Qutb or the Muslim Brothers. See Andrew McGregor, "'Jihad and the Rifle Alone:' 'Abdullah 'Azzam and the Islamist Revolution."

[53]   Assaf Moghadam, "Motives for Martyrdom." *Project Muse*. Winter 2008, http://muse.jhu.edu/journals/ins/summary/v033/33.3.moghadam. html.

[54]   Imam Abdullah Azzam, "Join the Caravan," *Religioscope*. n.d., http://www. religioscope.com/info/doc/jihad/azzam caravan 6 conclusion.htm.

[55] Quote by Azzam in Andrew McGregor, "'Jihad and the Rifle Alone:' 'Abdullah 'Azzam and the Islamist Revolution."

[56] Johannes J.G. Jansen, "Faraj and The Neglected Duty; Interview with Professor Johannes J.G. Jansen."

[57] Muhammad Abd al-Salam Faraj's manifesto, "The Neglected Duty." 1979: 195. Note—Islamists seem to use of the term "polytheists" to encompass a broad range of infidel people and at times use it interchangeably when describing Christians and Jews.

[58] Uriya Shavit, "Al-Qaeda's Saudi Origins." *The Middle East Quarterly.* Fall 2006, http://www.meforum.org/999/al-qaedas-saudi-origins.

[59] Karen Armstrong, "The deep roots of Islamic State." *New Statesman.* November 2014, http://www.newstatesman.com/staggers/2014/11/week-s-new-statesman-deep-roots-isis.

[60] While similar in nature to Wahhabism, the Salafi approach accepts certain scientific and technological aspects of modernity, where Wahhabism does not. Wahhabism idealizes the time of Mohammad.

[61] Both Osama bin Laden and Ayman al-Zawahiri rigidly applied Azzam's principle that jihad is a collective act of worship and that every group must have a leader, and that obedience to that leader is a necessity in jihad. Followers of Abu Musab al-Zarqawi, the eventual head of al Qaeda in Iraq were compelled to obey him under this principle.

[62] Bruce Lincoln, *Holy Terrors: Thinking about Religion after September 11.*

[63] Ibid.

[64] Shaykh Muhammad Saalih al-Munajjid, "843: Al-Malaa'ikah (Angels)." *Islam Question and Answer.* 2015, http://islamqa.info/en/843.

[65] Bruce Lincoln, *Holy Terrors: Thinking about Religion after September 11.*

[66] Karen Armstrong, *Fields of Blood.* New York: Alfred A. Knopf, 2014.

[67] Dawn Perlmutter, "Mujahideen Blood Rituals: The Religion and Forensic Symbolism of Al Qaeda Beheading." *Anthropoetics* 11. Winter 2006, http://anthropoetics.ucla.edu/ap1102/muja.htm.

[68] Sheikh Anwar Al-Awlaki, "Q & A with Sheikh Anwar Al-'Awlaki": 17-18.

[69] Bruce Lincoln, *Holy Terrors: Thinking about Religion after September 11.*

[70] Ibid.

[71] Ibid.

[72] From paragraph 31 of *Final Instructions to the Hijackers of September 11, Found in the Luggage of Mohamed Atta and Two Other Copies,*

Appendix A of Bruce Lincoln, *Holy Terrors: Thinking about Religion after September 11.*

[73]   See book review written by Mark Safranski, this publication, on: Moshe Halbertal, *On Sacrifice.* Princeton: Princeton University Press, 2012.

[74]   Dr. Sebastian Gorka, "Jihadist Ideology: The Core Texts."

[75]   Dawn Perlmutter, "Mujahideen Blood Rituals: The Religion and Forensic Symbolism of Al Qaeda Beheading."

[76]   Timothy R. Furnish, "Beheading in the Name of Islam." *The Middle East Forum.* Spring 2005, http://www.meforum.org/713/beheading-in-the-name-of-islam.

[77]   To get an idea of the numbers of beheadings by early al Qaeda, Dawn Perlmutter lists over 50 individual beheadings conducted by the Al Qaeda networked groups between 2000 and 2005, which included Saddam Fedayeen. Post-modern massive-scale beheadings were also beginning to emerge around this same timeframe, as evidenced by reporting of 30 beheaded bodies found in a village north of Baghdad, Iraq in March 2006. See also Lisa J. Campbell, "The Use of Beheadings by Fundamentalist Islam," *Global Crime* 7. August-November 2006: 597.

[78]   Assaf Moghadam, "Motives for Martyrdom: Al-Qaida, Salaa Jihad, and the Spread of Suicide Attacks." *International Security* 33. Winter 2008-2009: 46-78, http://insct.syr.edu/wp-content/uploads/2013/03/Moghadam-Assaf.2008.Motives-for-Martrydom.International-Security.pdf.

[79]   One of AQIM's leaders, Mokhtar Belmokhtar was nicknamed "le narco-Islamiste" related to the smuggling routes between Mali and Algeria.

[80]   Erin Banco, "As Sahel Trafficking Networks Grow, Al Qaeda Rebels Get Stronger in Mali." *International Business Times.* 2 July 2015, http://www.ibtimes.com/sahel-trafficking-networks-grow-al-qaeda-rebels-get-stronger-mali-1994724.

[81]   Colin Freeman, "Revealed: how Saharan caravans of cocaine help to fund al-Qaeda in terrorists' North African domain." *The Telegraph.* 26 January 2013, http://www.telegraph.co.uk/news/worldnews/africaandindianocean/mali/9829099/Revealed-how-Saharan-caravans-of-cocaine-help-to-fund-al-Qaeda-in-terrorists-North-African-domain.html.

[82]   Erin Banco, "As Sahel Trafficking Networks Grow, Al Qaeda Rebels Get Stronger in Mali."

[83]   Aaron Y. Zelin, "The War between ISIS and al-Qaeda for Supremacy of the Global Jihadist Movement." *The Washington Institute for Near East Policy.* June 2014, http://www.washingtoninstitute.org/policy-analysis/view/the-war-between-isis-and-al-qaeda-for-supremacy-of-the-global-jihadist.

[84]   Another precursor to IS, from 2006-2013.

[85]   Many of the Ba'athists under the initiative of Saddam Hussein had undergone some form of religious transformation (voluntary or forced) when Saddam transitioned the Ba'ath party from a secular to an Islamized state, See: Amatzia Baram, *Saddam Husayn and Islam, 1968-2003: Ba'thi Iraq from Secularism to Faith.* Washington, D.C.: Woodrow Wilson Center Press & Johns Hopkins University Press, 3 October 2014.

[86]   There were two forms of Wahhabism that emerged in its beginnings. One form was influenced by Muhammad Ibn Saud, who preferred to enforce Wahhabi Islam, and with the sword. Ibn Saud's son and successor later used another form, *takfir* (i.e., excommunication of an unbeliever) to justify the wholesale slaughter of resistant populations.

[87]   Ikhwan: (In Arabic: Brethren). in Arabia, Ikhwan are members of a religious and military brotherhood that figured prominently in the unification of the Arabian Peninsula under Ibn Sa'ūd (1912–30); in modern Saudi Arabia they constitute the National Guard. See: *Encyclopedia Britannica,* http://www.britannica.com/EBchecked/topic/282606/Ikhwan.

[88]   The word *hijra* was related to the term used to describe the Prophet's emigration from Mecca to Medina in 622, conveying the sense that one who settles in a *hijra* moves from a place of unbelief to a place of belief. By moving to the *hijra,* the Ikhwan intended to take up a new way of life and dedicate themselves to enforcing a rigid Islamic orthodoxy. See Helen Chapin Metz, Ed., "The Rise of Abd Al Aziz." *Saudi Arabia: A Country Study.* Washington, D.C.: GPO for the Library of Congress: 1992, http://countrystudies.us/saudi-arabia/9.htm.

[89]   Francis Martel, "ISIS Jihadist: Xanax makes us 'think tanks are birds' during warfare." *Breitbart.* 30 March 2015, http://www.breitbart.com/national-security/2015/03/30/captured-isis-jihadist-took-pills-that-make-you-think-tanks-are-birds-before-battle/.

[90]   Michael E. Miller, "Islamic State's 'war crimes' against Yazidi women documented." *The Washington Post.* 16 April 2015, http://

www.washingtonpost.com/news/morning-mix/wp/2015/04/16/
islamic-states-war-crimes-against-yazidi-women-documented/.

[91]   See "Impurity Requiring a Bath of Purification." *Laws of Religion: Laws
of Islam Concerning Ritual Purity and Cleanliness: from the Holy Quran,
major hadith collections and Islamic jurisprudence.* n.d., http://www.
religiousrules.com/Islampurity06bath.htm, and "Tahara (Cleanliness
or Purification)." *The Way to Truth: Discover Islam.* n.d., http://www.
thewaytotruth.org/pillars/tahara.html.

[92]   "Islamic State (ISIS) Releases Pamphlet On Female Slaves." *The Middle
East Media Research Institute.* 4 December 2014, http://www.memrijttm.
org/islamic-state-isis-releases-pamphlet-on-female-slaves.html.

[93]   See an account of a hadith and interpretation of the slaughter of
'Amr bin Hisham, pagan Arab chieftain and staunch opposition
of Islam in: Raymond Ibrahim, "Beheading Infidels: How
Allah 'Heals the Hearts of the Believers.'" *Frontpage Mag.* 11
September 2014, http://www.frontpagemag.com/fpm/240733/
beheading-infidels-how-allah-heals-hearts-raymond-ibrahim.

[94]   Quote from al-Bukhari and Muslim, "The Allies of Al-Qa'idah in
Sham." *Dabiq* 8 (1436 Jumada Al-Akhirah): 8.

[95]   Harbi are non-Muslims who do not enter the treaty of dhimmah
(protection) and they do not enjoy any safety or treaties from Muslims
[from being warred against], see https://iloveimamrabbani.wordpress.
com/tag/harbi/.

[96]   *The Middle East Media Research Institute*, "Jihadi Cleric Justifies IS
Beheadings: 'Islam is a Religion of Beheading.'" 25 August 2014, http://
www.memri.org/report/en/print8126.htm.

[97]   *Dabiq* 8 (1436 Jumada al-Akrhirah), "The Libyan Arena": 26.

[98]   *Dabiq* 2 (1435 Ramadan): 40.

[99]   *Dabiq* 7 (1436 Rabi' Al-Akhir/February 2015): 24

[100]   Ibid.

[101]   Ibid: 45. The greater signs of The Hour are the appearance of the Dajjal;
the appearance of Jesus; and the appearance of the Mahdi. For an in
depth explanation of the Hour, see David Cook, *Understanding Jihad.*
Berkeley: University of California Press, 2005: 158.

[102]   See M. Shemesh, "The Songs Of The Islamic State—A Major Tool
For Reinforcing Its Narrative, Spreading Its Message, Recruiting
Supporters." *The Middle East Media Research Institute.* 11 August 2015,
http://www.memri.org/report/en/0/0/0/0/0/0/8701.htm, and Aymenn

Jawad Al-Tamimi, "Aymenn Jawad Al-Tamimi's Blog." *Pundicity*, http://www.aymennjawad.org/blog/.

[103] Translated by Aymenn Jawad Al-Tamimi on "Aymenn Jawad Al-Tamimi's Blog."

[104] *Dabiq* 9 (1436 Sha'Ban/10 September 2014), "Slave-Girls": 45

[105] "Islamic State (ISIS) Publishes Penal Code, Says It Will Be Vigilantly Enforced." *MEMRI: Jihad & Terrorism Threat Monthly.* 17 December 2014, http://www.memrijttm.org/memri-jttm-islamic-state-isis-publishes-penal-code-says-it-will-be-vigilantly-enforced.html.

[106] Punishments by IS for homosexuality have thus far included beheading and being thrown from buildings.

[107] *The Middle East Media Research Institute*, "Jihadi Cleric Justifies IS Beheadings: 'Islam is a Religion of Beheading.'"

[108] Most often the victim is already dead when placed on the cross for display. For lesser crimes, the victim is crucified while alive, most often by being tied to a cross, displayed for several hours in a public place, then later released. It is not known at this time whether any victims have been intentionally crucified while alive with the intent by IS of a slow, painful death (i.e., no known similarity to the prolonged way Jesus died on the cross).

[109] *The Muslim Issue*, "Islamic State's Sharia Punishments." 8 April 2015, https://themuslimissue.wordpress.com/2015/04/08/islamic-states-sharia-punishments/.

[110] Adam Taylor, "How Saudi Arabia's harsh legal punishments compare to the Islamic State's." *The Washington Post.* 21 January 2015, http://www.washingtonpost.com/blogs/worldviews/wp/2015/01/21/how-saudi-arabias-harsh-legal-punishments-compare-to-the-islamic-states/.

[111] *The Middle East Media Research Institute*, "Jihadi Cleric Justifies IS Beheadings: 'Islam is a Religion of Beheading.'"

[112] Dawn Perlmutter, "ISIS Purifies Islam Through Fire." *The Counter Jihad Report.* 4 February 2015, http://counterjihadreport.com/2015/02/04/isis-purifies-islam-through-fire\.

[113] Christopher Holton, "Basis in Islamic Jurisprudence (Sharia) and Scripture for Execution of Jordanian Pilot." *The Counter Jihad Report.* 3 February 2015, http://counterjihadreport.com/2015/02/04/basis-in-islamic-jurisprudence-shariah-and-scripture-for-execution-of-jordanian-pilot/.

[114] Al-Baqarah: 194, *Dabiq* 7 (1436 Rabi Al-Akhir): 7.

[115] *Dabiq* 7: 7.

[116] *Dabiq* 9 (1436 Sha'Ban/10 September 2014).

[117] Ibid.

[118] Ibid.

[119] Walid and Theodore Shoebat, "Actual and Literal Islamic Human Slaughterhouses For Christians Discovered." *Shoebat.* 17 March 2014, http://shoebat.com/2014/03/17/actual-literal-islamic-human-slaughterhouses-christians-discovered/.

[120] Ibid.

[121] For an in depth analysis of the burning of Lt. al-Kasesbeah in terms of symbolism, see Dawn Perlmutter, "ISIS Purifies Islam Through Fire."

[122] *Live Leak,* "Two Christians, One a Priest, Beheaded" (Translated). 26 June 2013, http://www.liveleak.com/view?i=b57_1372272008.

[123] Ibid., Two men who were Catholic priests were beheaded in front of a large crowd after evidence was displayed that they had cooperated with the Syrian military. One form of evidence was a cell phone with phone numbers of Syrian military officers on it.

[124] A video of this event, revealed in March, 2015, took place in Syria and was reportedly leaked to an online source and translated.

[125] *Bare Naked Islam,* "Leaked video shows Muslim convert to Christianity being savagely beheaded by Muslims for his apostasy." 28 March 2015, http://www.barenakedislam.com/2015/03/28/leaked-video-shows-muslim-convert-to-christianity-being-savagely-beheaded-by-muslims-for-his-apostasy/.

[126] See Thomas D. Williams, Ph.D., "ISIS Crucifies Dozens for Breaking the Ramadan Fast." *Breitbart.* 8 July 2015, http://www.breitbart.com/national-security/2015/07/08/isis-crucifies-dozens-for-breaking-ramadan-fast/.

[127] Jacob Siegel, "Islamic Extremists Now Crucifying People in Syria—and Tweeting Out the Pictures." *The Daily Beast.* 30 April 2014, http://www.thedailybeast.com/articles/2014/04/30/islamic-extremists-now-crucifying-people-in-syria-and-tweeting-out-the-pictures.html.

[128] *Live Leak,* "Islamic Ritual Human Sacrifice Caught On Film." 16 March 2014, http://www.liveleak.com/view?i=6ad_1395015674.

[129] It is unknown who the victims were, but they were possibly Christians. It is also not confirmed that the killing was done by IS or another Sunni Islamic group. A blurry jihadist flag, black with white writing is displayed in the upper left corner of the video.

[130] *MEMRI TV*, "#4558 - Warning: Extremely Disturbing Images. Woman Stoned to Death by ISIS in Syria." 21 October 2014, http://www.memritv.org/clip/en/4558.htm.

[131] *Dabiq* 9: 29.

[132] Ibid: 30.

[133] Walid and Theodore Shoebat, "Actual And Literal Islamic Human Slaughterhouses For Christians Discovered."

[134] A photo of an IS member eating the heart of a Syrian soldier in 2013 is pictured online. See http://beforeitsnews.com/economy/2015/03/IS-cannibalism-is-defended-with-religious-edicts-by-the-highest-sunni-authorities-in-egypt-and-saudi-arabia-2713038.html.

[135] The edicts out of Al-Azhar University are of Sunni Salafi origin. Salafism, to which IS subscribes, as a movement began in Egypt. Its ideological forefathers are the same as those of the Muslim Brotherhood. See, http://www.clarionproject.org/factsheet/islamic-state-isis-isil.

[136] *Consortium of Defense Analysts*, "World-renowned Islamic university teaches it's okay for Muslims to cannibalize Jews and Christians." 14 April 2014, https://cofda.wordpress.com/2015/04/14/egypt-university-textbooks-teach-its-okay-for-muslims-to-cannibalize-jews-and-christians/.

[137] Ibid., see videos of interviews and text.

[138] Walid Shoebat, "Major ISIS Leader Recruits Eleven Muslm Men, And Sodomizes All of Them in Homosexual Islamic Ritual (Video)." *Shoebat*. 18 September 2014, http://shoebat.com/2014/09/18/major-isis-leader-recruits-eleven-muslim-men-sodomizes-homosexual-islamic-ritual-video/.

[139] A documentary broadcast on STERK TV entitled 'Gang of Degenerates' contained the horrific confessions of more than 20 members of IS regarding the inhuman methods of IS. The video may be viewed here: *Horrific Confessions of IS Members*, http://www.vidinfo.org/video/6909771/horrific-confessions-of-IS-members.

[140] Samuel Smith, "Cocaine Found in Slain ISIS Commander's Home Indicates Heavy Drug Use Among Jihadists, Despite Being Violation of Sharia Law." *CP World*. 17 January 2015, http://www.christianpost.com/news/cocaine-found-in-slain-isis-commanders-home-indicates-heavy-drug-use-among-jihadists-despite-being-violation-of-sharia-law-132234/. IS has published articles in its magazine along with photos of large-scale drug busts it has made against drug traffickers in the region, with implied harsh punishment issued on those caught.

[141] Sam Web, "Junkie Jihadi John? Expert claims slurred speech of ISIS executioner in beheading video of Brit hostage David Haines could have been down to drugs." *Daily Mail.* 18 September 2014, http://www. dailymail.co.uk/news/article-2760354/Junkie-Jihadi-John-Expert-claims-slurred-speech-ISIS-executioner-beheading-video-Brit-hostage-David-Haines-drugs.html.

[142] Francis Martel, "ISIS Jihadist: Xanax makes us 'think tanks are birds' during warfare."

[143] See Dawn Perlmutter, "ISIS Meth Heads: Tweaking in the Name of Islam," *Frontpage Mag.* 9 Mar 2015, http://www.frontpagemag.com/ fpm/252783/isis-meth-heads-tweeking-name-islam-dawn-perlmutter.

[144] David Cook, "Miracle Stories and Martyrologies," in *Understanding Jihad*: 153-157.

[145] Dr. Ahmad Murtada, "Boko Haram" in *Nigeria: Its Beginnings, Principles and Activities in Nigeria*. Kano, Nigeria: Online book publishing of www.SalafiManhaj.com, 2013.

[146] Ibid.

[147] *Journal of Religion in Africa*, "The Popular Discourses of Salafi Radicalism and Salafi Counter-radicalism in Nigeria: A Case Study of Boko Haram." 42, 2012: 118-144.

[148] Ibid.

[149] Other Islamic movements active in the 1980s that were similar in nature to Boko Haram but not linked to them included the Maitatsine group, the Kala Kato group and Darul Islam. Each of these groups espoused unorthodox beliefs and religious practices that became a part of the ethnic and religious violence in Nigeria.

[150] J.N.C. Hill, "Religious Extremism in Northern Nigeria Past and Present: Parallels between the Pseudo-Tijanis and Boko Haram." *The Round Table: The Commonwealth Journal of International Affairs* 102. 2013: 239.

[151] Zacharias Pieri, "Boko Haram's Islamic Caliphate is becoming a reality in Northeastern Nigeria." *ZP: Zacharias Pieri Blog.* 7 September 2014, http://blog.zachariaspieri.com/post/97761946322/boko-harams-islamic-caliphate-is-becoming-a-reality-in-northeastern-nigeria/.

[152] *Journal of Religion in Africa*, "The Popular Discourses of Salafi Radicalism and Salafi Counter-radicalism in Nigeria: A Case Study of Boko Haram": 118-144. See also Ninian Smart's phenomenological theory of religion, ways in which power animates the various dimensions

of religion. The will to appropriate the absolute power of God drives some religious leaders, such as preachers following the footsteps of prophets of monotheistic religions. Also from Smart: the preacher who carries on the mantle of the prophet to speak not only on his behalf, but for the powerful other as well. Charged with the sacred power, the preacher can 'catch the fear-making mode and take on what is supposedly divine anger'. Dr. Obaji Agbiji, "Engaging Christian faith communities in development in the context of violence," *Research Institute for Theology and Religion.* University of South Africa, n.d.

[153] J.N.C. Hill, "Religious Extremism in Northern Nigeria Past and Present: Parallels between the Pseudo-Tijanis and Boko Haram": 235-244.

[154] *Africa This Day,* "Full Text Of Boko Haram Leader's Latest Video Message". 7 May 2014, http://africathisday.com/tag/abubakar-shekau/.

[155] Robyn Dixon, "Leader of Boko Haram says God told him to carry out massacre," *Los Angeles Times.* 21 January 2015, http://www.latimes.com/world/africa/la-fg-nigeria-boko-haram-massacre-20150121-story.html.

[156] Emenike Ezedani, "Boko Haram Chibok Girls and All Things Nigeria Security," *bokowatch.com.* 2015, http://www.bokowatch.com/.

[157] *The Muslim Issue,* "Muslim Convert To Christianity Admit: In Boko Haram We Butchered Christians And Drank Their Blood." 25 August 2013, https://themuslimissue.wordpress.com/2013/08/25/muslim-convert-to-christianity-admit-in-boko-haram-we-butchered-christians-and-drank-their-blood/comment-page-1/.

[158] Ibid. See also Emenike Ezedani, "Boko Haram Chibok Girls and All Things Nigeria Security." According to Ezedani, Boko Haram has *Spirituality and Conversion* units, which are responsible for new recruits, indoctrination, conversion to Islam, the "charming up" of fighters and blessing martyrs bound for suicide missions.

[159] *Osun Defender,* "Stories of Three Former Boko Haram Members." 9 September 2014, http://www.naija.io/blogs/p/897087/stories-of-three-former-boko-haram-members.

[160] Emenike Ezedani, "Boko Haram Chibok Girls and All Things Nigeria Security"

[161] Blessed Usman, "Full length story of former Boko Haram member Balas Yusuf[f]." *Pray For Christians in Northern Nigeria.* 17 June 2013, https://www.facebook.com/PrayForChristiansInTheNorthOfNigeria/posts/393249187463084.

[162] *The Muslim Issue*, "Muslim Convert To Christianity Admit: In Boko Haram We Butchered Christians And Drank Their Blood."

[163] *Osun Defender*, "Stories of Three Former Boko Haram Members."

[164] Former Boko Haram member Bala Yusuf, in an on line interview said that he and other members were made to drink blood to take an oath and swear before Allah that they would do his will of fighting and killing of infidels, particularly the tithe collectors (i.e. Pastors). There was more reward from Allah for whoever kills a Pastor. Whether or not the blood was human cannot be confirmed. See Blessed Usman, "Full length story of former Boko Haram member Balas Yusuf[f]."

[165] *The Muslim Issue*, "Muslim Convert To Christianity Admit: In Boko Haram We Butchered Christians And Drank Their Blood."

[166] *TheReligionofPeace.com*, "In the Name of Allah." 2006-2016, http://www.thereligionofpeace.com/pages/in-the-name-of-allah.htm.

[167] *Journal of Religion in Africa*, "The Popular Discourses of Salafi Radicalism and Salafi Counter-radicalism in Nigeria: A Case Study of Boko Haram": 126.

[168] Aminu Abubakar, "Summary execution, beheading, amputation claims in Boko Haram fight." *Yahoo News*. 6 November 2014, http://news.yahoo.com/boko-haram-attack-ne-nigeria-kills-21-senator-202951099.html.

[169] *Nigeria Films.com*, "Multiple Bombing: Allah Has Given Us Victory Over Christians + Christians Must All Convert to Islam—Boko Haram." 19 June 2012, http://www.nigeriafilms.com/news/17843/53/multiple-bombing-allah-has-given-us-victory-over-c.html. Following a bombing of three Christian churches in northern Nigeria, Boko Haram thanked Allah for giving them the victory and stated, "today (Sunday) Almighty Allah has given us victory against Christian Churches in Kaduna and Zaria which led to the deaths of many Christians and security operatives."

[170] The Infinity Creations, "New Boko Haram video with English subtitle." *YouTube*. 15 May 2014, https://www.youtube.com/watch?v=SwB1DPA_agg.

[171] *TheReligionofPeace.com*, "In the Name of Allah."

[172] *The Muslim Issue*, "Muslim Convert To Christianity Admit: In Boko Haram We Butchered Christians And Drank Their Blood."

[173] *Osun Defender*, "Stories of Three Former Boko Haram Members."

[174] *The Muslim Issue*, "Muslim Convert To Christianity Admit: In Boko Haram We Butchered Christians And Drank Their Blood."

[175] For discussion on Boko Haram and suicide missions see Michael Nwankpa, "Boko Haram: Whose Islamic State?" James A. Baker III Institute for Public Policy, Rice University. 1 May 2015, https://bakerinstitute.org/media/files/files/e37325ec/CME-pub-BokoHaram-050115.pdf.

[176] *Scan News,* "Boko Haram resorts to blood sucking tactic: Slaughters 11 innocent Nigerians." 1 October 2013, http://scannewsnigeria.com/news/boko-haram-resorts-to-blood-sucking-tactic-slaughters-11-innocent-nigerians/.

[177] *The Clarion Project,* "Boko Haram Fighters Turn to Cannibalism in Nigerian Forest." 28 August 2013, http://www.clarionproject.org/print/news/boko-haram-turn-cannibalism-survive-nigerian-forest.

[178] Aislinn Laing, "Boko Haram leader taunts US over bounty." *The Telegraph.* 29 December 2013, http://www.telegraph.co.uk/news/worldnews/africaandindianocean/nigeria/10541793/Boko-Haram-leader-taunts-US-over-bounty.html. Shekau's statement post-battle: "Brothers pulverised 21 armoured tanks. People were killed in their multitudes, bodies scattered all over," [he said, adding that his forces] "blew out the brains" of soldiers who tried to hide under their blankets…"

[79] Al Qaeda has in 2014-15 publicly condemned the beheadings of ISIS. Its affiliates however, such as al Shabaab and al Nusra Front still conduct them.

[180] Videos cannot be verified. These are possible extermination centers in existence since 2011, possibly adopted by ISIS from Syrian rebel groups. Whalid A. Shoebat, "Actual and Literal Islamic Human Slaughterhouses For Christians Discovered," *Shoebat.com Awareness and Action.*17 March 2014, https://shoebat.com/2014/03/17/actual-literal-islamic-human-slaughterhouses-christians-discovered/

[181] From escaped Muslim captive's story of his conversation with his captor. Ibid.

[182] Istishhad is also defined as *deliberate martyrdom.*

[183] See ISIS *Dabiq* 9 (1436 Sha'Ban/10 September 2014): 28-32

[184] Ibid. "And Allah guides whom He wills to a straight path" (Al-Baqarah: 2013)

[185] WND, "ISIS Cites Quran to Justify Child Rape." 8 December 2014, http://www.wnd.com/2014/12/isis-cites-quran-to-justify-child-rape/#wEXcefiCoslrCd77.99.

[186] The pamphlet is titled "Questions and Answers on Taking Captives and Slaves;" a translated copy of it may be found at http://www.memrijttm. org/islamic-state-isis-releases-pamphlet-on-female-slaves.html.

[187] See *Dabiq* 4, "The Revival of Slavery Before the Hour," (1435 Dhul-Hijjah/October 2014): 14-17. An anonymous author speaks on the topic of slavery, as a firmly established aspect of the Sharia that "if one were to deny or mock he would be denying or mocking the verses of the Koran and the narrations of the Prophet…and thereby apostatizing from Islam." See also: Graeme Wood, "What ISIS Really Wants." *The Atlantic*, March 2015.

[188] See "New Boko Haram video with English subtitle[s]," *You Tube*. 15 May 2014, https://www.youtube.com/watch?v=SwB1DPA_agg.

[189] One of the abducted Chibok girls (a Muslim) speaking to Boko Haram member in a *You Tube* video shortly after being taken captive. Ibid.

[190] The information in this example was derived from *The New York Times*, "ISIS Enshrines a Theology of Rape." 13 August 2015, http://www. nytimes.com/2015/08/14/world/middleeast/isis-enshrines-a-theology-of-rape.html?_r=1.

[191] Shoebat Foundation, "LEAKED PHOTOS REVEAL Just How Horrific Life Is Under ISIS And The Obama And Hilary Clinton Backed Muslim Brotherhood, With Amputations, Beheadings Being Done On The Street In Public View And Cannibalism Being Promoted." *Shoebat.com Awareness and Action*. 6 March 2015, http:// shoebat.com/2015/03/06/leaked-photos-reveal-just-how-horrific-life-is-under-isis-and-the-obama-and-hilary-clinton-backed-muslim-brotherhood-with-amputations-beheadings-being-done-on-the-street-in-public-view-and-cannibali/

[192] See "Islamic State IS Releases Pamphlet on Female Slaves," *The Middle East Media Research Institute*. 4 December 2014, http://www.memrijttm. org/content/view_print/blog/8017.

[193] IS sometimes refers to Christians as polytheists as well, with possible reference to the Trinity.

[194] "ISIS Offers Female Slaves As Top Prizes For Koran Competition," *MEMRI: Jihad & Terrorism Threat Monitor*. 19 June 2015, http:// www.memrijttm.org/isis-offers-female-slaves-as-top-prizes-for-koran-competition.html.

Chapter 5

STEALING THE DEAD: CULTURAL APPROPRIATION OF LAS REGLAS DE KONGO AMONG NARCO TRAFFICKERS

Tony M. Kail

A number of violent non-state actors (VNSA) are appropriating various Afro-Caribbean based magico-religious cultures to meet social and psychological needs that arise as a result of involvement in the drug trafficking culture. Some criminal cases involving drug trafficking VNSAs have revealed the performance of rituals specifically used in the Afro-Caribbean religious traditions of 'Las Reglas de Kongo', a group of magico-religious practices from the BaKongo of Central Africa established in Cuba in the 16ᵗʰ to 19ᵗʰ century.[1]

Since their arrival in Cuba, the traditions of Las Reglas de Kongo have traditionally shared a reputation of being associated with sorcery and black magic. This reputation became established in early Cuban society where Kongolese slaves were viewed as 'pagan savages' that dealt in black magic. Additionally, the use of human remains in the practices of the slave religions like Las Reglas de Kongo became a controversial issue that brought on allegations of human sacrifice and child murder.[2] As Kongo traditions migrated into the United States and Mexico following the Cuban revolution and the later Mariel boatlift, they were met with skepticism and fear.

Following the 1980 Mariel boatlift in which mass numbers of refugees from Cuba were sent to the United States, Afro-Cuban religions became an issue of concern and fear in many American communities. Some law enforcement and public safety agencies began noticing unfamiliar tattoos, artifacts, and shrines associated with Afro-Cuban religions among the Marielettos. Evidence of ritualistic animal sacrifice began to appear in communities where religions of Las Reglas de Kongo and other African diaspora religions were practiced. As a result of criminal activity in the Cuban refugee communities, elements of Cuban culture including religion became associated with criminal and deviant behavior. As this history of fear and suspicion surrounding Afro-Cuban religions including Las Reglas de Kongo grew, incidents involving the religion came to be depicted in the news media as 'Voodoo' and 'devil worship' thus building on the nefarious reputation of Kongo traditions.

One of the most famous incidents involved a series of murders in 1989 in Matamoros Mexico. Several murders were committed by American drug dealer Adolfo de Jesus Constanzo and a group of narcotics traffickers. Constanzo's organization appropriated rituals and artifacts from Las Reglas de Kongo traditions and several other religions including Mexican Brujeria and Cuban Santeria. Constanzo exploited the religion's mythology, social structure, and rites of passage to create a 'narco cult.' A narco cult is "an individualistic, shamanistic, communal or ecclesiastical cult that functions as a source of spiritual or psychological empowerment for individuals or organizations connected to drug trafficking."[3] The members of Constanzo's narco-cult murdered several Mexican drug traffickers and an American college student that the group kidnapped. Constanzo instructed members of his organization to offer the remains of some of the victims to the deities of Las Reglas de Kongo by placing the victim's bones in shrines. The veracity of their crimes, combined with the pre-existing fears of Las Reglas de Kongo, served to only build the sinister reputation of the religions.[4]

The Matamoros incident would become one of many incidents where violent non-state actors involved in drug trafficking have appropriated elements of Las Reglas de Kongo into the trafficking culture. It is important to note that the majority of devotees of Las Reglas de Kongo are not involved in violent or drug trafficking activities. While the secretive nature of the religions makes it difficult to give any estimate of the total number of practitioners, there are considerable size populations of devotees in Miami, New York, Chicago, and Houston.[5] The religion is practiced in several communities throughout the U.S., Mexico, Cuba, and Venezuela.

What is the attraction of Las Reglas de Kongo traditions to violent non-state actors? What about this specific religion 'speaks' to the needs of those in the drug trafficking business? The motivation for using Kongo spirituality can be found in the religion's reputation, ritual behavior, and aesthetics.

Research Methods

The traditions of Las Reglas de Kongo are traditionally practiced in secret. As with many magico-religious traditions, the religions seek to protect the esoteric knowledge available only to those who have been initiated. Additionally, some of the practices in the Kongo religions are considered controversial to many westerners including the use of animal sacrifice and the use of human remains.

In order to gain information into the Kongo culture, ethnographic research is essential to gaining an understanding of cultural nuances and the emic perspective of the religion. It is important to note that some of the material used in this essay was gained through ethnographic fieldwork this author has performed among various magico-religious communities over the last 25 years. Fieldwork included the use of mapping, surveys, interviews, and participant-observation. In protecting the anonymity of my informants, I do not list specific names in this essay as some informants spoke to me under condition that I would not reveal their identity. Research was performed in accordance with the American Anthropological Association's Statement on Ethics which included gaining informed consent and permissions and, in utilizing anonymity, seeks to protect the identities of informants in doing no harm to members of the Palo culture. It is also important to note that the use of the term 'informant' in this essay is used to denote an anthropological research subject as an interlocutor not as a reference to the term in the context of a law enforcement 'informant.'

Historical Background

In order to understand the contemporary practices of Las Reglas de Kongo, it is helpful to understand the African traditional religion that forms the basis of these traditions. The traditions of Las Reglas de Kongo or 'Rules of the Kongo' find their roots in the magico-religious practices of the Bantu people of Central Africa. The spiritual practices of the Bantu Bakongo people centered around interacting with the spirits of nature (Kimpungulu Mpungo) and the dead (Nfumbe).

Bakongo religion recognizes the omnipotence of a creator deity known as 'Nzambi Mpungo'. Bakongo mythology teaches that Nzambi gave humanity the ability to heal using a sacred medicine known as 'minkisi'. In Kongo society, the power of Nzambi was believed to be manifested through the king (mfumu), the ritual expert (nganga), and the sorcerer (ndoki).[6]

The ritual expert (nganga) would create minkisi medicines that could be used in healing or harming individuals. Containers such as statues, cloth bundles and shells are used to house components representing medicine (bilongo) and a human soul (mooyo). Materials used in representing the spirit of the soul would include cemetery dirt, white clay (mpemba) and human remains. The visual appearance of nkisi figures were aesthetically stunning as they would commonly be found in the form of a wooden statue with sharp teeth and intense white colored eyes. Nkisi figurines could be buried, stabbed, and offered blood in order to manipulate the spirit residing inside the image into action. The nkisi could be used as means of alleviating social conflict. Sickness, disease, poverty, and war could be attacked utilizing the supernatural energies that resided in the nkisi object.

As many of the Bakongo were taken as slaves to Cuba, the role of the nganga and the use of nkisi became an important part of cultural and physical survival. The nganga would serve as a ritual specialist in Cuba for Africans, dispensing Kongo religious lore and practices in the New World. The nkisi spirit could be used to resolve conflicts as some were used to attack slave owners and provide a spiritual 'scout' for the slave community. The concepts of cosmology, ritual, and ritual specialists of the Bakongo were transplanted among slaves in Cuba where they were syncretized with elements of Spanish folk Catholicism and Cuban-Yoruba Regla de Ocha.[7]

The aesthetics of nkisi worship would change forms as overtly 'African' figurines that housed the traditional nkisi would be confiscated by colonialists. The nkisi in Cuba was placed in various mundane objects such as that of a three-legged cooking pot. This transition not only changed the ritual aesthetics of the religion but would also change the use of the term nganga to no longer refer to the ritual specialist but to that of the nkisi container. Several famous ngangas would be created and used by slave communities in the Cuban regions of Pinar del Rio, Havana, and Santa Clara.[8] The new hybrid of Bakongo religious traditions became known as 'Las Reglas de Kongo.'

A New Religion

The practices of Las Reglas de Kongo include spiritual traditions known as 'ramas' such as Palo Monte (also known as Palo Mayombe), Brillumba, and Kimbisa. Each tradition has its own specific mythologies, rituals, and artifacts. 'Palo' is the colloquial term used among various magico-religious communities to describe all three traditions. Palo is Spanish for 'stick' and refers to the religion's use of 21 sticks or branches in the creation of the nkisi container.[9] The addition of human bones, specifically the skull (kiyumba), 'infuse' the spirits of the dead with the materials in the cauldron.

The contemporary religion of Palo focuses on the control of the spirits of the dead and the spirits of nature that are placed inside the nganga. In order to create the New World version of the minkisi, human remains are placed inside of an iron or ceramic pot. Remains are traditionally obtained from a cemetery. The practitioner locates a grave and performs divination using various oracles. These oracles are used to ask the spirit of the dead to serve the devotee. Once this inquiry is satisfied, the cranium and several assorted bones such as the tibia and femur may be removed to be used in the creation of the minkisi.

A pact is forged between the owner of the nganga and the nfumbe that lives in the pot. The owner promises to provide a dwelling for the spirit of the dead in exchange for magical services provided by the spirit. The minkisi is constructed using soil from various geographic locations in order to obtain energy and domain over specific regions of land.[10] Soil is taken from the property of churches and houses of worship, jails, and various important locations of social gatherings. Along with the soil, the 21 tree branches (palos) are added with iron implements such as railroad spikes, animal bones, insects, and assorted materials. Many of the materials allude to the identification of the mpungo that is placed inside the vessel. Objects that reflect the element of iron may refer to the Mpungo Zarabanda while objects related to oceans and water may symbolize the spirit of the Mpungo Madre Agua.

A Palo priest then places material from a previously established nganga inside the vessel. The nganga is referred to as being 'born' from an established nganga. This builds a form of spiritual kinship between the priest and initiate. One the nganga is received, the initiate becomes known in the Kongo community as 'Tata Nganga.'

In order to operate the nganga, the tata nganga commands the mpungo spirit which, in turn, commands the nfumbe spirit to perform for the pot's owner. Adherents believe that the nganga contains a group of various spirits from nature that maintain a contractual relationship with the spirit of the dead.[11]

Ceremonial magic rituals are performed in which the spirits are commanded to carry out the bidding of the practitioner. Healing and sorcery are performed through the use of roots, herbs, and the creation of charms derived from African indigenous practices that anthropologist Victor Turner termed 'drums of affliction' or 'ngoma.'[12]

Reputation

Palo Mayombe is considered a very 'powerful' form of spirituality among various magical communities. Palo has been identified by members of magico-religious communities as being crude, powerful, fast, and effective.[13] Even in its earliest form, the use of Kongo minkisi was feared and respected in local communities. The minkisi in post-colonial society was believed to be able to cause and remove sickness, protect its owner from danger, and to inflict punishment.[14] This 'aura of power' that has remained with the religion is further boosted by various commentaries from magical communities that speak of the effectiveness and power of the religion.

As Monroe has observed, the fear and anxiety produced by this reputation only serves to promote the belief that Palo spells (bilongos) are very effective.[15] In some cases, the reputation of some Palo priests (Paleros) are increased by testimonies of clients and rivals. Some Palo priests have gained a reputation for performing harmful magic for paying clients. During my fieldwork, I interviewed a Palo priest who operated a spiritual supply store in Las Vegas, Nevada. He shared that one day a man entered his shop and asked to speak to him about a sensitive matter. The man shared that he had impregnated a woman and did not want to be a father. He offered to pay the Palero a large sum of money to magically murder the child. Then the Palero went on to share that it was Palo's powerful reputation that had sent the man into his store.[16]

Some Paleros have sought to advertise their ritual services for destructive magical operations. A key informant shared the story about a Palero in New York city that became known for sending photographs of his enemies to Haiti where rituals would be performed on the photographs. Rumors began to spread among the magical communities that the victims in the photographs would fall into a coma. Local folklore can serve to increase the reputation of power that surrounds many Paleros. Some Paleros boast of the aggressive nature of the religion in advertisements for magical services.

Ritual specialists who offer magical services to harm others have been equated with assassins. Obeyesekre states:

In both sorcery and premeditated murder, there is a real gap between stimulus and response. During the interim, there is a period the offender makes rational decisions regarding the type of sorcery he should practice, the sorcerer he should consult and the time, effort, expense and risk involved. The sorcerer is in effect the hired killer.[17]

Along with having a reputation of power, Palo shares a reputation of being a form of evil magic. Palo Mayombe has a long history of being labeled as 'witchcraft' or 'sorcery.' This has been the allegation since the early days of colonialism in Cuba. Cuban criminologist Fernando Ortiz shared stories of police confiscations of Palo artifacts and regional suspicions of Palo practitioners as sorcerers as far back as the early 1900s.[18] In the Eighties, New Age and esoteric authors began to publish books on Santeria and Afro-Cuban spirituality. As a result of books and horror films, Las Reglas de Kongo and the religion of Palo Mayombe specifically became known in American pop culture as the 'darkside of Santeria.' This description has been frequently used in mass produced books and movies depicting the religion as a sort of satanic inversion of the popular Afro-Cuban religion.[19] This description, while not culturally or historically accurate, does reflect the popular notion that Palo is a 'dark' or 'evil' religion. Many practitioners of Palo do not share this perspective and view the religion as an African traditional religion that practices healing and interacts with the environment that is simply misunderstood by the general public.

Among Palo practitioners, there is a distinction within the religion regarding positive or negative spiritual practices. Palo devotees who practice positive magico-religious rituals are known as 'Palo Christianos.' This position as a benevolent ritual specialist is indicated by the presence of a Christian crucifix within the nganga. This is said to indicate that the nganga has been 'baptized' with holy water. Those who work with adversarial powers such as that of the dark mpungo Kadiempembe are known as 'Palo Judios.' The name refers to the historical past in which Spanish Catholic colonialists spoke of those who did not accept Jesus Christ as the messiah as being 'of the devil.'

Gender Issues

The issue of sexuality and gender in Palo may serve as a lure for violent non-state actors in the drug trade. As in Mexican based narco culture[20], there appears to be a theme of machismo that permeates the Palo culture. Palo related literature, social networking sites, and decorations on spiritual supplies feature images of shirtless male priests holding ritual staffs (baston de muerto) standing in front of ngangas commanding spirits in herculean style poses. The style of magic that is being practiced in Palo speaks to a dominant male attitude as the nkisi is 'commanded' to perform for its owner. The implication is that the spirit is the slave to the owner of the nganga. Ritual implements such as bullwhips are used in ceremonies to deal with spirits as lesser beings and recall a cultural memory when Africans were slaves in Cuba.

Another issue in the Kongo traditions that may lend itself to the element of machismo ideology that draws violent non-state actors is the issue of sexuality. The topic of homosexuality in the religion is a hotly debated issue. Many traditional Palo and Kongo religious houses forbid gays and lesbians to be initiated into the religion.[21] Some researchers have criticized Palo taboos on gays in the religion as being homophobic.[22]

Rituals

Palo rituals utilize Sir James George Frazer's concepts of magic, including the use of homeopathic magic and contagious magic.[23] Evidence of homeopathic magic focusing on the law of similarity has been discovered in the sacred spaces and ritual artifacts of some violent non-state actors. Photographs of rivals, written names of rivals on paper and poppet images representing the target of magical workings have been found in ritual spaces.

The practice of contagious magic which uses the laws of contagion and similarity are evident in the ritualistic placement of materials in the nganga. A 2005 case in Orlando Florida involved members of a drug trafficking organization placing the shoes, watch, and cell phone of a rival inside the nganga. In Palo culture, the ultimate magical threat is to threaten to place someone's name or photograph into the nganga. This symbolizes the cauldron's owner having the ability to magically affect and manipulate the target of the spellwork through sympathetic magic. An example of this belief and practice could be seen in the example of former Los Zetas cartel leader Jesus Enrique Rejon Aguilar, aka 'El Mamito,' who was known to threaten his enemies by placing their names in his cauldron.

Key cultural informants in the religion as well as references in Palo literature have referred to Palo devotees waging 'magical warfare' against their enemies. Spirits sent by rivals or enraged spirits are viewed as the supernatural cause of problems in some cases. War is ritualistically waged against these spirits and their source. I have personally interviewed practitioners who have shared stories of performing rituals of protection and aggression toward rivals who have sent magical curses and workings to them. In some of the rituals, sacred drawings known as 'firmas' are constructed as a method of spirit evocation to bring forth a protective magical barrier for the devotee.

Many of the sacred shrines of Palo Mayombe tend to reflect the concept of war in their aesthetics. Items such as guns, knives, railroad spikes, spears, and machetes are all used to symbolically build domains for the spirits of the dead. While these items traditionally reflected the culture of slavery, revolt, and protection of the African people, the contemporary displays have become a part of the magico-religious narco culture among traffickers.

The fear that rivals can utilize a devotee's spirit is a common belief among the Palo community. During the initiation process, new initiates undergo a ritual scarring where a specific symbolic signature is given to them in order to call upon their personal spirit. Initiates are advised to never reveal this signature to anyone because ownership of this symbol gives the operator the ability to command that specific spirit. Interviews with key cultural informants in the religion have revealed that there are some unscrupulous practitioners who will steal and attempt to sell the signatures of others.

Narco-Magic

An advertisement for the magical services of a Palo ritual specialist was recently featured on a social networking site used by Mexican drug cartel members. The advertisement featured an image of the Palo divination oracle known as the 'Vitti Mensu,' an animal horn and mirror used to view messages from spirits and 'firmas,' and sacred symbols used in invoking spirits in Palo. The ad promised 'Supreme Black Magic without side effects or karma.'

There have been cases where traffickers have sought the spiritual assistance of Palo against their rivals only to discover that their rivals are also using spiritual practices. During the late 1990s, Florida law enforcement authorities conducted an investigation into a drug trafficking operation that used Palo Mayombe as a means of protection for their operation. Members of the group feared that a rival trafficking group were also using the religion to magically attack members of the organization. Members wrote the names of rivals on pieces of paper and wrapped them around the 21 branches inside their nganga. The spirit inside the cauldron was commanded to seek out any other ngangas that were being used by rivals. This demonstrates the power of belief and how this may affect the behavior of violent non-state actors.

Some devotees have given offerings of narcotics to the spirit in the nganga. Anthropologist Stephan Palmié shares the story of a drug trafficker:

One story about an nganga named 'avisa me con tiempo' (warn me in time) dealt with a drug dealer who fed his nganga lines of cocaine—not only to enhance the spirit's vigilance, but to bind him ever more closely into a relation of dependency.[24]

The belief that Palo is malevolent and powerful can be magically appealing to violent non-state actors who seek spiritual control over situations and circumstances. Traditional healing using witchcraft seeks to reduce stress and anxiety through the use of rituals and ceremonies. Fear of the unknown is combatted with powerful spiritual rituals. Witchcraft and sorcery may provide a means of therapeutically combatting police and rival traffickers. Some practitioners may specifically target enemies with a certain hardship. For example, there is a spell that is said to create insanity in an enemy. This spell is constructed using the human skull (kiyumba), vulture feathers, and mercury.[25]

Some popular literature related to Palo culture features spells and ritual techniques for calling upon spirits for protection from law enforcement. One such book available in many spiritual supply stores, written by now deceased Palo priest Baba Raul Canizares in 2002, describes the instructions for creating an amulet that will allow the owner to become invisible to police.[26] Artifacts used in the practice of Palo can be purchased through spiritual supply stores and include items such as candles and powders featuring names such as 'Law stay away.' These products help in creating the impression of a magico-religious narco culture where authorities are viewed as antagonists.

The violent non-state actor who finds themselves in trouble with the law can also find a number of Palo ritual specialists who offer magical workings for a fee. Palo priests who operate spiritual supply stores or advertise their services providing psychic consultations have been documented as advertising spiritual services for legal help. Palo literature includes instructions on winning court cases and escaping the law. Consider the following magical operation:

We take the judge's name, the lawyer, the district attorney and prosecutor. We get some soil from the courthouse, powder from the dead, powder from palos. We reward the nganga with a rooster and we take the rooster's tongue off. Then we look for several types of palos. Following this we write with chalk the name of the judge, the district attorney and the prosecutor with the sticks and seven types of threads. After this we ask the nganga how many days it is going to remain on the fundamneto. Finally we give this work to the interested person. We prepare a powder for him to throw at the courthouse door.[27]

To further the causes of violent non-state actors involved in drug trafficking, some Palo ritual specialists have become known for their ability to supernaturally protect traffickers. During my research in the Palo community, a member of the Santeria community explained to me that it is common knowledge among the Santeria and Palo communities on the East Coast which priests will perform protective rites to protect drug traffickers. Local and federal law enforcement agencies in Miami, Florida have reported that drug traffickers have hired Palo priests for protective rituals. Authorities in Georgia, Tennessee, and Texas have discovered Palo artifacts that were being used by drug traffickers for protective purposes. The following case studies, based on actual police investigations into VNSAs appropriating elements from Las Reglas de Kongo within their trafficking activities, will now be provided:

Case Study 1

A police department responds to a call involving shots being fired in a residential neighborhood. While investigating the scene, officers discover a shrine containing several iron cauldrons containing human skulls, boat oars, chains, railroad spikes, a goat's head, animal bones, knives, machetes, and 21 tree branches. There is a metal bucket containing a male skull. The skulls are covered in blood as are the surrounding walls of the building. A wooden statue of an unknown figure is adorned with a strand of multi-colored plastic beads and there is a green cloth tied around the figure's head. The figure clutches a spear in one hand and a photograph of an unknown black male in the other hand. There are several bowls of unidentifiable liquids, some filled with blood. There are several burnt candles in class containers. Officers discover drugs and weapons inside the shrine. The owner of this particular shrine admitted to firing a gun into the air in order to summon spirits that lived in the cauldrons. The owner was also part of an organized drug operation that was selling narcotics.

Analysis of the Scene

A detailed symbolic analysis of the scene reveals that the drugs and firearms were being kept in a sacred space of the shrine in order to protect them from police and rivals. According to Palo Mayombe beliefs, the various cauldrons contain a number of different spirits and the materials inside the vessels identify the spirit that resides in that particular pot. The yellow painted pot containing boat oars and items related to water is indicative of the spirit known as 'Mama Chola' or 'Chola Wengue,' the spirit of the river waters. Pots containing railroad spikes, machetes, knives, and various metal implements signify dedication to 'Zarabanda,' the spirit of iron and justice. The statue decorated in a green cloth and holding a metal spear is also indicative of Zarabanda worship. The iron pot containing a single skull with no other materials represent 'Nkuyu,' a wandering spirit.

Case Study 2

While executing a drug related search warrant on a residence, narcotics agents discovered a small wooden structure behind the residence. Inside the structure, the agents discovered an iron cauldron containing a human skull covered in a thick patina of blood, tree branches, railroad spikes, a wooden mask, cigars, feathers, a mousetrap, knives, and dirt. A rusting metal chain was stretched across the cauldron and secured with a lock. There was a bowl containing two white candles that had been burned. In front of the cauldron was a bottle of rum, an iron ball, and pieces of broken coconut shell.

Analysis of the Scene

The fact that the artifacts, particularly the nganga, were being housed in a separate structure behind the residence suggests this was being used as the 'nso nganga' or temple for the nganga. This is symbolic of the creation of sacred space and demonstrates the intense belief in the power of the nganga. Palo Mayombe beliefs ritually require that followers do not turn their back on the nganga or allow a menstruating female near the spirit.[28] This is consistent with rites of purity in many other spiritual traditions. The nkisi spirit is viewed as powerful and aggressive. While performing research in Orlando Florida with a Palo priestess (Palera), I was advised that the nkisi is similar to a rabid dog. Practitioners do not turn their backs to the pot when exiting the room as it can attack the person from behind.

The scene was a classic example of a shrine erected for the mpungo Zarabanda, the mpungo of iron and justice. The iron ball, iron cauldron, railroad spikes, and machetes are commonly used as symbols of Zarabanda. The blood on the skull indicates that the spirit has been given blood as an exchange for spiritual workings from the nkisi as the kiyumba represents the intelligence of the dead. The vulture feather inside the pot is used to represent the vulture known as 'mayimbe,' who is considered the messenger of the dead. The candles, rum, and cigars are offerings to it and are commonly offered to the nkisi as the devotee drinks and spews the rum on to the kiyumba and blows cigar smoke into the face of the skull. Coconut shells are divination tools known as 'chamalongos' and are used to interact with the spirit. The mousetrap is commonly used to trap or bind someone magically. Typically, a name written on paper or a photograph is placed within the mousetrap in order to magically hold the target of the spell.

Case Study 3

Federal agents posing as cartel members discover a 38 year old Hispanic male is manufacturing grenades and illegally possessing firearms. The man offers to sell the agents over 130 grenades to use in protecting drug related activities. During the man's arrest, agents discover a blood covered shrine including an iron cauldron filled with 21 tree branches, a human skull, horseshoes, railroad spikes, and dirt. The cauldron is covered with a metal chain fastened to a lock. The outside of the cauldron is decorated with various symbols.

Analysis of the Scene

The shrine is indicative of Palo Mayombe. The cauldron is wrapped with a chain that is used in keeping the spirit chained to the nganga. It also serves as a symbol of protection, keeping the spirit from leaving the pot. The cauldron is filled with materials indicative of the spirit Zarabanda. The symbols on the cauldron are the traditional firmas that are used in calling forth spirits and speaking a ritual language of intent to the spiritual realm. The skull was alleged to have been purchased from a medical supply store.

The trafficker who practices a magico-religious tradition such as Palo may hold the magical worldview that incidents do not simply occur by chance. The gaining of finances, an arrest by authorities, or even personal losses may be considered caused by the supernatural. In Palo Mayombe, supernatural occurrences may occur when a spirit is offended by the breaking of a specific taboo, sorcery, or ancestors have been offended. Blood sacrifices to the nkisi may be made in order to petition the spirit into action and to change the supernatural occurrence. Palo sacrifices include animals such as chickens, goats, rams, and doves but also includes a number of exotic animals including snakes, insects, and reptiles, as well as dogs. Some criminal cases involving Palo devotees have revealed the use of endangered species such as manatees, sea turtles, and condors.

Conclusions

In looking at the phenomena of the appropriation of Kongo religious traditions by violent non-state actors, there appears to be several factors relating to concepts of power, identity, gender, and symbolism that bring the violent non-state actor to use a religion in concert with criminal activities.

The appropriation of Las Reglas de Kongo appears to be part of the creation of a new 'magico-religious narco culture' that was ushered in with the recent popularity of folks saints such as Jesus Malverde and Santa Muerte in the U.S. and Mexico. This phenomenon appears to offer a new hybrid form of Kongo religions that embrace the deities and saints of other religions. During fieldwork with a Palo house in the Midwest, I noticed images of Santa Muerte being used in Palo Shrines while some popular literature includes spiritual personalities such as Santa Muerte and Brazilian based deities as forms of mpungo. Palo themed artifacts are being combined with an array of other magico-religious practices resulting in a self-styled form of spirituality. As many of the Mexican based translational criminal organizations grow, the cultural environment in which many members of these organizations have been raised is also influential. As opposed to strict cultural boundaries between religions such as Palo and Santeria, Mexican metaphysical religions are practiced interchangeably under the blank term 'esoterica.' It is here where we see artifacts, rituals, and sacred texts interchanged among religious traditions. Hedges uses the term 'esoteric nebula' to describe this culture that has "incorporated symbolic elements from esoteric traditions, parapsychology, divinations from various traditions, astrology, occult sciences, fortune telling and shamanism from the East and West."[29] An example of this conglomeration of spiritual traditions can be seen in one of the more public displays of Afro-Caribbean worship in Mexico. One of the first public Santeria temples in Mexico established in the Sixties, known as 'Templo Vudu Zambia Palo Monte,' in Mexico City combined a number of the African diaspora religions not only in name but in their practices as well.

In many cases, the practices and tools of Kongo traditions are utilized as opposed to the religious aspects of these faiths. This has not only been observed in VNSAs but among non-criminal devotees as well.[30] In the magico-religious worldview, this is translated as the practitioner utilizing 'thaumaturgy,' which is magic performed for mundane or secular purposes, as opposed to 'theurgy,' which is working with divine energy and implies a connection with worship.[31]

Law enforcement agencies will continue to see the growing hybrid of religions being appropriated by drug traffickers. This hybrid creates a number of challenges as it becomes difficult for investigative agencies to understand the cultural framework that a trafficker may be using as a means of protection or coping with stresses. This hybrid religion may manifest itself in the form of various religious artifacts discovered at crime scenes. This also creates a cultural environment which may be susceptible to charismatic leaders and prophets who wish to take advantage of the lack of accountability among hybrid religious communities.

The reputation of the Kongo religions, whether real or perceived as a religion of power and sorcery, lends to the spirit of contemporary narco-culture and its symbols of power and aggression. The symbols of cartel organizations such as Los Anthrax, which uses imagery of grinning skulls and biohazard symbols, project feelings of aggression and power. Likewise, the imagery of the Kongo religions with human skulls, witches cauldrons, and coiled serpents can project the same spirit of aggression and power which can be appropriated by VNSAs.

As the traditions of Las Reglas de Kongo continue to maintain a reputation as practices to be feared among Latin communities, these traditions will serve as psychological weapons that give traffickers a spiritual and mental 'edge' that could result in bolder acts of criminality and violence.

Notes

[1]   The spelling of Kongo with a 'K' instead of 'C' is traditionally used by Africanists to distinguish the difference between Kongo civilization of the Bakongo people from the Belgian Congo and the People's Republic of Congo-Brazzaville. See, Robert Farris Thompson, *Flash of the Spirit: African Afro-American Art & Philosophy*. New York: Vintage, 1984: 103.

[2]   Todd Ramón Ochoa, *Society of the Dead: Quite Manaquita and Palo Praise in Cuba*. Berkeley: University of California Press, 2010: 209.

[3]   Tony M. Kail, *Narco-Cults: Understanding the Use of Afro-Caribbean and Mexican Religious Cultures in the Drug Wars*. Boca Raton: CRC Press, 2015: 46.

[4]   Robert D. Hicks, *In Pursuit of Satan: The Police and the Occult*. Amherst: Prometheus Books, 1991: 72.

[5]   Stephen C. Finley and Anthony B. Pinn, *African American Religious Cultures*. Santa Barbara: ABC CLIO, 2009.

[6]   Robert Farris Thompson, *Flash of the Spirit: African Afro-American Art & Philosophy*: 107.

[7]   Lonn S. Monroe, *Corroboration and Contention in 'Congo' Consecrations: An Anthropological Analysis of Cuban Reglas Congas*. Dissertation. Gainesville: University of Florida, 2007: http://ufdcimages.uflib.ufl. edu/UF/E0/02/16/78/00001/monroe_l.pdf.

[8]   Natalia Bolívar Arostegui, Natalia y Carmén González. *Ta Makuende Yaya y las Reglas de Palo Monte*. La Habana: Unión, 1998: 32.

[9]   Todd Ochoa, "Aspects of the Dead in Cuban-Kongo Religion." In Mauricio A. Font, Ed., *Cuba Today: Continuity and Change since the 'Periodo Especial.'* New York: Bildner Center for Western Hemisphere Studies, CUNY Graduate Center, 2005: 248.

[10] Stephan Palmié, "Digging Up the Dead in Archeology and Afro-Cuban Palo Monte." *YouTube*. 22 October 2014, https://youtu.be/ PYvmF9DWc7w.

[11]   Robert A. Orsi, *Gods of the City: Religion and the American Urban Landscape*. Religion in North America Series. Bloomington: Indiana University Press, 1999: 182.

[12]   Todd Ochoa, "Aspects of the Dead in Cuban-Kongo Religion": 247.

[13]   Stephan Palmié, *Wizards & Scientists: Explorations in Afro-Cuban Modernity and Tradition*. Durham: Duke University Press, 2002: 164.

[14]   Wyatt Macgaffey and Michael D. Harris, *Astonishment and Power: The Eyes of Understanding Kongo Minkisi*: 21.

[15]   Lonn S. Monroe, *Corroboration and Contention in 'Congo' Consecrations: An Anthropological Analysis of Cuban Reglas Congas*: 53.

[16]   Personal interview with a Palo Priest in Las Vegas, NV.

[17]   Ganannath Obeyesekere, "Sorcery, Premeditated Murder, and the Canalization of Aggression in Sri Lanka." *Ethnology* 14. 1975: 1-23, http://isik.zrc-sazu.si/doc2009/rhch/007.pdf.

[18]   Fernando Ortiz, *Los Negros Brujos*. Miami: Ediciones Universal, 2005.

[19]   Carlos Galdiano Montenegro, *Palo Mayombe: Spirits, Rituals Spells: The Darkside of Santeria*. New York: Original Publications, 1994: 5.

[20]   Paul Rexton Kan, *Cartels at War: Mexico's Drug-Fueled Violence and the Threat to U.S. National Security*. Washington, DC: Potomac Books, 2012: 53.

[21]   Randy P. Lundschien Conner and David Sparks, *Queering Our Spiritual Traditions: Lesbian, Gay, Bisexual and Transgender Participation in African Inspired Traditions in the Americas*. New York: Routledge, 2004: 122.

[22]   Pierre Hurteau, *Male Homosexualities and World Religions*. New York: Palgrave-Macmillian, 2013.

[23]   Sir James George Frazer, *The Golden Bough: A Study in Magic and Religion* New York: Macmillan, 1922; Bartleby.com, 2000. See www.bartleby.com/196/.

[24]   Stephan Palmié, *Wizards & Scientists: Explorations in Afro-Cuban Modernity and Tradition*: 173.

[25]   Charles Wetli and Rafael Martinez, "Brujeria: Manifestations of Palo Mayombe in South Florida." *Journal of the Florida Medical Association* 70. August 1983: 629-634.

[26]   Baba Raul Canizares, *The Book on Palo: Deities, Initiatory Rituals and Ceremonies*. New York: Original Publications, 2002: 85.

[27]   Domingo B. Lage, *History Has Repeated Vol.1: Briyumba Con Mayombe*. Bell: Palibrio, 2001.

[28] Personal interviews with Palo clergy from 2000 to 2010.

[29] Paul Hedges, *Controversies in Contemporary Religion: Education, Law and Spirituality*. Santa Barbara: ABC-CLIO, 2014: 99.

[30] Eric Colon, "Sacrificing Blood in Palo Mayombe." *YouTube*. 24 April 2014, www.youtube.com/watch?v=dybG4iWG6mE.

[31] Phaedra Bonewits & Issac Bonewits, *Real Energy: Systems, Spirits and Substances to Heal, Change and Grow*. Franklin Lakes: New Page Books, 2007.

Chapter 6

THE LORD'S RESISTANCE ARMY: A RESEARCH NOTE

Pamela Ligouri Bunker

The Lord's Resistance Army (LRA) of Uganda is a group for whom the model of dark magico-religious violent non-state actor (VNSA) might seem to be tailor-made [see the editor's introduction in this work]. Having taken on the mantle of "defender" of the Acholi people of Northern Uganda after the defeat of Alice Lakwena's Holy Spirit Movement (HSM) in 1987, its leader Joseph Kony turned on the same, spreading his reign of terror over the civilian population of Acholiland to other cultural groups within Northern Uganda and, ultimately, crossing borders into Southern Sudan and the Democratic Republic of Congo (DRC).

Kony is a former alter boy and trained witch doctor who—like Alice before him—is said to channel a panoply of "spirits" inspiring his actions. While Alice Lakwena's spirits led her to direct her army to fight under the protection of little more than faith and charms, Kony's spirits, however, command him to direct his army to commit unspeakable atrocities in a quest to "purify" society in line with a syncretic spirituality combining aspects of Christianity alongside native animist beliefs. An article in *The Times*, UK, in 2006 made much of a purported statement by Kony that his aim was to "use the Ten Commandments to liberate Uganda," ostensibly from Musveni's government.[1]

Yet, early descriptions of the group by religious assistance organizations operating in the region sought to emphasize its darker nature, for example:

Whilst claiming to be the Lord's Army led by the Holy Spirit, the LRA is deeply occultic...As is common in occultism, LRA soldiers routinely collect their victim's genitals, livers, hearts, and the like for use as occult charms (juju) in cannibalistic blood rituals. According to testimonies from defectors and rescued children, Kony routinely enters a trance to be possessed by a spirit...The spirit reportedly alerts Kony to military movements, instructs him who to kill and is always hungry for more human blood.[2]

Likewise, tabloid newspapers picked up these sensational reports, with one describing the experience of a child soldier thus:

Children showing nervousness would be shot. Kony's commanders would force us to lick the blood of the people we shot. We had to cut their skulls open to remove some of the brain which we had to eat in front of them.[3]

Even more recently—when it has been recognized widely that the group is a shadow of its former size and strength—mainstream news sources have described the LRA's leader with a certain amount of awe:

Kony, 51, wields power over disgruntled members of the Acholi tribe of his native Uganda with a blood-curdling savagery and claims of being a spiritual medium protecting followers from witches and evil spirits. He has fostered a cult of personality, casting himself as a deity whom Africans confront at their own peril.[4]

The people of Amoko fear his return. He always claimed to be possessed by spirits and, to them, this makes simple logical sense. "That's why he does all the killings and all these weird things, "says Dorina [Adjero]. "A normal person who is acting in normal conscience wouldn't kill people in this way."[5]

Taken at face value, the picture painted above of the LRA by the media is one fitting squarely into the same slot occupied by other dark magico-religious VNSAs who practice ritual human sacrifice and/

or cannibalism—such as Adolfo Costanzo's group operating out of Matamoros, drug cartel members worshipping an extreme variant of Santa Muerte, or even extreme jihadists like those belonging to the Islamic State of Iraq and Syria (ISIS). How realistic these descriptions of the LRA were—even at the time they were made—has, however, been called into question. Whether Kony even made the statement regarding the Ten Commandments as presented is not without controversy, although certainly they are clearly incorporated into the group's rhetoric.[6] Further, if such reports did accurately describe Kony and the LRA at one point, we must ask whether these descriptions represent the LRA as it is today. Three recent books on the LRA paint a somewhat different and far more complex story of the Lord's Resistance Army and its formidable leader, leading the present discussion to be both a "review" with a mind to the potential "dark spirituality" of the LRA and a cautionary tale.

The most comprehensive and perhaps more academically oriented of the three works is that entitled *The Lord's Resistance Army: Myth and Reality*, published in 2010.[7] The work is edited by Tim Allen, professor of development anthropology at the London School of Economics and Political Science, and Koen Vlassenroot, professor of political science at the University of Ghent and director of the Central Africa Programme of Egmont, the Royal Institute for International Relations in Brussels— both of whom have carried out long-term research in the region. At 356 pages, it contains fourteen chapters plus an introduction and postscript as well as number of useful maps, tables, and figures along with several photographs.

As the title would indicate, beyond providing extensive and important background information about the conflict and the parties involved, it seeks to dispel certain assumptions regarding Northern Uganda as "barbaric periphery," especially in the nature of the ethnic politics and culture of the region, the seeming lack of a political agenda on the part of the LRA, and the strategic rationality of LRA "spirituality" and child abductions. Other chapters seek to point out the political "usefulness" of the conflict to the current government in terms of foreign aid and "control" of the population in the north and role of international involvement of other nations, NGOs, and the ICC in conflict resolution and the peace process.

Given the emphasis of this book project, focus here is placed on the role of spirituality in the ideology and operations of the Lord's Resistance Army as interpreted by these contributing authors and two are of particular note. Chapter Three focuses directly on "the spiritual order of the LRA." Written by Kristof Titeca, a postdoctoral fellow at the University of Antwerp, it decries the way in which the LRA and, in particular, its leader Kony have been sensationalized. As Titeca puts it:

> These often ethnocentric descriptions of religion and spirituality give exoticing and isolated reports which do not take into account the wider political, economic, and social context, representing the LRA's actions as radically irrational and as such neglecting, for example, how a spiritual discourse can act as a medium through which other grievances can be framed (p. 59).

He instead argues that, since culturally religion and spirituality are pervasive throughout African social life, to embody them is not a "retraditionalization" of society in the sense of other extreme fundamentalist VSNAs but rather a rational way of engaging politically since "in Africa, political practice is clearly situated within a religious universe"(p. 60). Furthermore, the LRA's own unique take on the spiritual order is a functional way of drawing on traditional belief systems in order to enact and enforce rules which are critical to "structuring life in the bush" (pp. 61-62). For example, the "spirit" is cited as demanding that everything be done quickly—for example, cooking must be done in thirty minutes—or else the enemy will be allowed to find the one who violates this rule (p. 63). Clearly, this is a pragmatic rule geared to avoiding detection of cooking fires by those tracking the LRA.

The associated rituals also both break down and re-create the social world for those inducted into its forces. It would certainly follow that by witnessing the killing of their families, children believe they have nowhere to go back to. Rituals involving abductees anointment with 'Moo ya' or shea nut oil is said to impart Kony with the ability to find them and read their minds should they want to escape (p. 62). This serves to impose internal control by imparting fear due to an uncertainty as to whether this is true. If a "singing" ritual gives a sense of "fearlessness," an individual is more likely to fight against the odds (p. 64). Titeca points out that for the LRA, following Diken and

Lausten 'it is rituals that create beliefs and not the other way around,' and it is in this way that Kony creates the "shared values" that hold the group together (p. 66). Because the rules are "pragmatic," however, they are subject to transformation over time and as the situation warrants and some may be abandoned altogether (p. 64). Rather than imply that one should ignore the spiritual aspects of the LRA, Titeca emphasizes that their real power lies in whether they "produce effects on the ground" both among followers and the general public alike (pp. 70-73).

Chapter Four reiterates Titeca's critique of popular reports of Kony. Sverker Finnstrom, associate professor of cultural anthropology at both Stockholm and Uppsala Universities, emphasizes that "Wars are partly what the media make of them" and that, in this case, focus has been skewed to that of the bizarre and extreme along with furthering colonial notions of the Acholi as "primordially violent." This occurs while also ignoring the fact that there is a real origin to the LRA in the opposition to Musveni and abuses of state power—stated in actual political manifestos by the group that the government denies exist and punishes those who argue contrary (p. 85). While acknowledging that the war has become "an end in itself" and that the cruelly violent tactics undertaken have alienated its audience, Finnstrom nonetheless challenges readers to ask whether "any claimed political rationale for fighting has resonance with issues to most people in Acholiland" (p. 75).

Finally, with pointed regard to our purposes here, Chapter 7 on the nature and causes of LRA abduction focuses on what the abductees themselves have had to say. Written by Christopher Blattmen, assistant professor of political science at Yale, and Jeannie Annan, a PhD in counseling psychology serving as director of research and evaluation at the International Rescue Committee, the emphasis is on what experiences are exceptional and which can be taken as the rule. As was seen above, those reports most emphatic in their emphasis on the spiritual "dark" side of Kony's LRA often note his forcing children to kill, often intimating that even aspects of forced "cannibalism" exist. Referring to a Survey of War Affected Youth (SWAY) Study, the authors maintain that the most sensational of reported practices occur rarely. They do not deny the widespread importance of spiritual practices, however, especially rituals. The authors maintain that:

Spiritual practices were central to motivating recruits—a clear attempt to create new social bonds and loyalty based on a shared cosmology (as well as fear). Kony created a cult of mystery and spiritual power which few abductees or civilians question even now (p. 141).

When referring to "spiritual practices," however, they divorce these from the religious nature of propaganda, citing abductee reports that no one they spoke to reported really believing in magical protection and claiming that the LRA offered them promises of political and material benefits as often as spiritual ones (p. 142).

The second recent work to be briefly discussed here is that entitled *Child to Soldier: Stories from Joseph Kony's Lord's Resistance Army*, published in 2013.[8] The work is authored by Opiyo Oloya, superintendent of education for school leadership with the York Catholic District School Board, who writes a weekly column of social issues for a Ugandan newspaper and left Uganda as a refugee in 1981. He conducts interviews with or—more accurately in Ugandan cultural terms—listens to storytelling by seven former child inductees in the LRA, with two of them more in-depth. These stories are supplemented with his own insights as one who grew up within the Acholi culture. The work is 217 pages consisting of an introduction, five chapters, and a conclusion along with eight pages of photographs.

For Oloya, the spiritual dimension to the LRA was, from the outset, a means by which to create a "moral dimension" to its war with Musveni's NRM/A and was thus undertaken as a "holy war mostly against the superstitious faith healers known as *ajwaka*, and those deemed unholy" (p. 58). Accordingly, religion became "a mask for the war Kony wanted to fight" (p. 60). It was only subsequently, the author argues, with the pervasive narratives of the Global War on Terror, that Kony's Lord's Resistance Army became in the eyes of the world a "transnational Christian fundamentalist rebel movement," a claim which is contradicted by Kony's own stated objectives such as the desire to transfer the Central Bank of Uganda to Gulu (pp. 67-68).

Oloya, in turn, characterizes the experiences of the child abductees interviewed as a "mix of physical violence, exploitation of Acholi cultural rituals such as wiiro moo yaa (anointing with shea-butter oil), and rigorous physical regimes" (p. 69). In Chapter Three, he adamantly states that for none of the interviewees was "religious indoctrination" a significant method of control and he goes to some length to reject the notion of apocalyptic spiritualism as a valid interpretation of the group's ideology (pp. 69-74). Rather, Oloya singles out a number of specific instances cited by the abductees as evidence that, more pertinently, it was the manipulation of Acholi cultural tradition that has allowed Kony to transform child abductees into combatants. Rather refreshing to this book is the fact that, through it all, Oloya never disallows the abductees own sense of agency. He insists that each of them come to their situation, not a blank slate, and that, for many, it is key to their survival (pp. 12-22).

The author outlines what he calls "eight phases in the liminal transformation of children into soldiers" and shows where Acholi (as well as other African) cultural perceptions are brought into play and are remade into a new LRA culture. These phases are: (1) Mak (abduction) which is often at night which is a time of 'evil' for the Acholi; (2) Wot ii Lum (going into the bush) which is a place of bad spirits which should not be brought home; (3) Lwoko wii Cibilan (washing the civilian mind) which tortures the individuals in order to emphasize they are no longer Acholi; (4) Neko Dano (killing a person or witnessing it) which exposes the individuals to *cen* or the evil spirit of the dead; (5) Wiiro Kom (anointing with shea butter) which in Acholi culture is used only on the most auspicious of occasions that bestow privileges; (6) Donyo ii Gang (entering a homestead) which serves to recreate Acholi village life; (7) Pwonyo Mony (military training) which fosters solidarity; and (8) Cito ii Tic (going to work) which instills a new identity within the LRA (pp. 78-95). His hopeful note is that, as it is based upon a twisting of existing culture, that the damage cannot be undone but the individuals and society can be healed through workings of that same culture (pp. 164-176).

The third book to be touched upon is that simply titled *The Lord's Resistance Army*, published in 2013 as part of the Praeger Security International (PSI) Guides to Terrorists, Insurgents, and Armed Groups Series.[9] Written by Lawrence Cline, a retired military intelligence officer and PhD and currently an adjunct instructor for the Counterterrorism Fellowship Program, Center for Civil Military Relations, Monterey, CA. Within its 226 pages, Cline has managed to include an introduction, eleven chapters, a 'lessons learned' section, photographs, as well as appendices including a number of useful maps, a timeline of events, and the text of the Juba Peace Accord and the ICC Indictment of Kony.

While this author somewhat divergently maintains that the LRA's early rhetoric and reliance on rituals may somewhat substantiate it as a group using *religion* as a "critical mobilizing and motivating tool," he also notes that this does not provide a full picture and to focus upon it emphasizes its differences over its commonalities with other VNSAs (p. x). He, like the earlier authors, recognizes that the religious environment in this region is complex. He cites the case of fighters in the Liberian civil war who widely used what he calls "spiritual tools," including the substantiated use of ritualistic cannibalism to gain strength for battle, often borrowing spiritual leaders from elsewhere in Africa to guide their course when suitable local experts were not available (p. 47). Uganda's own particular history has created a syncretic world wherein Christianity—particularly Catholicism—has been merged with Acholi traditional beliefs (pp. 3-5). Complicating this general picture is the belief in and practice of witchcraft which, Cline notes, is statutorily against the law in Uganda—in some sense legitimizing it—and part and parcel of this practice is the use of human body parts for witchcraft rituals, increasingly involving the killing of children (pp. 50-51). Notably, this is not linked to the LRA but to middle-class businessmen seeking certain advantages from these rituals.

Recognizing this general cultural mileau and citing Titeca (see the earlier work above) in recognizing the importance of the rituals effect on the group's members and the public, Cline believes that:

By tapping into a wellspring of preexisting spiritual sources of legitimacy, the LRA likely found a better mobilizational tool than it would have by using more "modern" systems such as nationalism or various purely political ideologies (p. 21).

Like the other authors above, Cline also finds that—because of its instrumental nature—the rituals and spiritual aspect of the LRA have decreased over time. While in the early days of the group Kony was regularly "possessed" by spirits telling him to "wage war against evil," these "possessions" along with many other rituals have shifted or been abandoned—to the end that many LRA members lack real understanding of the driving ideology (pp. 12, 15-16). At one point in the 1990s, he maintains, prayer rituals would "more resemble Islamic custom than Christian rites" as did the fact that they occurred five times a day and required a month long period of fasting—perhaps a nod to the group's support at that time from the Islamic government of Sudan (p. 16). The author attributes the decline in overt spirituality over time to a number of factors including the shifting of locales depriving it of bases within a fixed local population and that it now lacks any time or opportunity for the intricate rituals of its origin (p. 21). Ultimately, he contends that while "it is far from clear that LRA members remain as clearly religiously motivated as in the past" and that—beyond some residual belief in his power—they stay because "they simply have nowhere else to go" (p. 144).

Taken together, the picture of the Lord's Resistance Army of Uganda painted by these works differs greatly from the model of the dark magico-religious violent non-state actor presented in the media. With regard to the general "concentric circle" model of the VNSA exclusionary process presented in the editor's introduction, the LRA is certainly a violent non-state actor (VNSA) which seeks a sudden transformation of both governance and social organization within Ugandan society—however opaque in details this might be— and embraces a worldview which is overtly "spiritual" in nature. Arguably too, at its inception, its associated rituals could be classified as going beyond "normal prayer" into the realm of magico-religious activities—such as that wherein the application of shea-butter oil to the bodies of abductees was said to change them in a spiritually significant way. This review essay does not purport to have evaluated the multiple contributors to these works on the academic rigor of their case studies nor the unbiased nature of their reports. But across these most recent contributions to the literature on the LRA which come from authors from a diversity of backgrounds, there have been no reliable accounts presented indicating that the ideology of the group—despite the atrocities it clearly has perpetrated—embraced the dark magico-religious element wherein humans were killed or maimed for anything beyond the instrumental nature of the act (e.g. to create fear or silence opponents) such as in order to achieve spiritual benefits for particular individuals or groups or to placate a diety. In fact, Cline's work begs the question whether certain incidences of "dark" magico-religious activities undertaken by other groups or individuals in Uganda might be conflated with those of the LRA whether intentionally or unintentionally.

The chapters by Titeca and Finnstrom above indeed admonish us to be cognizant of the role of the media in framing the narratives of war. It is often part and parcel of the media's role in attracting readers/viewers/listeners to present information in a sensational manner. While the horrors of the LRA's terror over the civilian population of northern Uganda, Southern Sudan, and the Democratic Republic of the Congo would seem to require no embellishment, the nature of the group's syncretic spiritual mix—when viewed through the ethnocentrism of the reporter—lends itself to extreme explanations of what is being witnessed or heard secondhand, often with dark religious overtones. The same might be said of the various missionary and aid organizations active in the region who view the group through a particular institutional lens. The chapter by Blattman and Annan and the work by Opoyo indicate that in their experience of abductee accounts the extreme events often cited seem to in actuality have occurred rarely and are taken out of the wider cultural and historical context, not the least of which at the outset was Kony's need to recruit the remaining fighters of the newly dismantled Holy Spirit Movement.

It is here where the cautionary tale comes into play. While it is recognized that often the spiritual nature of a group is discounted prematurely as a valid element in its practices and motivations, the corollary is that initial impressions that 'dark magico-religious activities' are at play must also be seriously evaluated. First, if a VSNA appears for all intents and purposes to be engaging in dark magico-religious activities, consider the source. Is it credible or could this evidence be the product of ambitious reporting with an artistic flair? Similarly, one must consider the lens—for example, religious or institutional—through which events, while recognizably different, are seen as exceptional to the group in question, such as the LRA, rather than being a cultural difference at large. Granted, such evidence regarding spiritual aspects of VNSAs may be hard to come by except in second hand accounts and word of mouth but it should be viewed with a critical eye. Care needs to be taken to examine what is going on to see if there is an instrumental explanation underneath surface appearances. Titeca makes a good point as well about the nature of "fundamentalism" as neotraditionalism versus a VNSA attempting to create a new reality. Second, all the works above note that it should be recognized that activities take place in a slice of time and that a group is not static but somewhere on a trajectory in its development. Whether a group embraces certain dark magico-religious rituals at a certain point in time does not indicate whether these will increase or decrease in intensity or be disbanded altogether when circumstances change. If the LRA did indeed engage in dark magico-religious activities as some early media sources would suggest, it would appear that these do not play a wide part now and, rather, that the group is moving away from its embrace of magico-religious elements in the form of elaborate rituals entirely. Finally, many of the authors note that just because a group at large professes an embrace of certain religious/spiritual principles as a part of its ideology, this does not indicate that all or even most of its members embrace—or even understand—that ideology. All of these notes of caution have serious implications for those who are attempting to engage with, study, and mitigate the effects of these radical spiritual VNSAs on their greater societies.

Notes

[1]   Sam Farmer, "I will use the Ten Commandments to liberate Uganda," *The Times*. 28 June 2006, http://www.thetimes.co.uk/tto/news/world/article1982845.ece.

[2]   Elizabeth Kendal, "The Lord's Resistance Army (LRA) Terrorises— Southern Sudan, northern Congo, eastern Central African Republic (CAR), Uganda." *Religious Liberty Prayer Bulletin (RLPB) 025*. 7 October 2009, http://www.assistnews.net/Stories/2009/s09100045.htm.

[3]   Tom Parry, "Tragedy of kidnapped child soldiers forced to kill or be killed by Joseph Kony's savage Lord's Resistance Army," *Daily Mirror*. 16 September 2013, http://www.mirror.co.uk/news/world-news/joseph-konys-lords-resistance-army-2276555.

[4]   Carol J. Williams, "Savagery, witchcraft hold Africans in sway of warlord Kony," *Los Angeles Times*. 14 November 2012, http://articles.latimes.com/2012/nov/14/world/la-fg-wn-lords-resistance-army-201211135.

[5]   Will Storr, "Tragedy in Uganda: Joseph Kony massacre survivors tell their stories," *The Guardian*. 11 January 2014, http://www.theguardian.com/world/2014/jan/12/joseph-kony-uganda-massacres-survivors-stories.

[6]   Marieke Schomerus who was at that interview has written on those discrepancies, see for example, Chapter Three, Chasing the Kony Story, in Tim Allen and Koen Vlassenroot, Eds., *The Lord's Resistance Army: Myth and Reality*. London: Zed Books., Ltd, 2010: 93-112.

[7]   Tim Allen and Koen Vlassenroot, Eds., *The Lord's Resistance Army: Myth and Reality*.

[8]   Opiyo Oloya, *Child to Soldier: Stories from Joseph Kony's Lord's Resistance Army*. Toronto: University of Toronto Press, 2013.

[9]   Lawrence E. Cline, *The Lord's Resistance Army*. Praeger Security International (PSI) Guides to Terrorists, Insurgents, and Armed Groups Series. Santa Barbara: Praeger, 2013.

Chapter 7

THE DARK SACRED: THE SIGNIFICANCE OF SACRAMENTAL ANALYSIS

Charles Cameron

Introduction

A recent and widely cited article on the Islamic State by Christopher Reuter for *Spiegel Online*, titled "The Terror Strategist: Secret Files Reveal the Structure of Islamic State," reported on a trove of papers uncovered after the death of one Samir Abd Muhammad al-Khlifawi, better known as Haji Bakr, whom the writer termed "the architect of the Islamic State." The papers comprised "a folder full of handwritten organizational charts, lists and schedules, which describe how a country can be gradually subjugated"—the "blueprint" and "source code" of what Reuter termed "the most successful terrorist army in recent history":

> It was not a manifesto of faith, but a technically precise plan for an "Islamic Intelligence State"—a caliphate run by an organization that resembled East Germany's notorious Stasi domestic intelligence agency.[1]

It was "not a manifesto of faith"—but neither would an architect's blueprint for a mosque, temple, basilica or synagogue be, and for worshippers those structures are religious in nature, their architecture at the service of religion.

Since there is a lively polemic as to whether the Islamic State and many similar groups are best understood to be "political" in nature with an overlay of religion, or religious in nature, fed no doubt by political grievances yet fueled and focused by divine sanction, it seems important for us to "see through the eyes" of the religiously inspired as well as those of the pragmatically secular. The researcher Thomas Hegghammer[2] recently commented that after more than a decade studying terrorist groups, he had finally stumbled on the importance of their cultural activities—"bearded men with kalashnikovs reciting poetry, discussing dreams, and weeping on a regular basis"—in understanding them.

In this paper, I shall attempt to offer an analysis which draws on a variety of sacred teachings to understand "dark sacred" violence. In effect, this will be a "sacramental analysis"—operating on the assumption that "outward and visible signs" correspond in believers' hearts to "inward and spiritual graces."[3]

I shall draw on three texts in particular for this purpose:

• Joseba Zulaika's *Basque Violence: Metaphor and Sacrament*[4]

Supported by:

• Christopher Taylor's *Sacrifice as Terror: The Rwandan Genocide of 1994*[5]
• William Cavanaugh's *Torture and Eucharist: Theology, Politics, and the Body of Christ*[6]

The first, Zulaika's book, explores the theological and personal underpinnings of the Basque ETA, as viewed by a Basque native anthropologist, and details a hyper-local variant of Catholic understanding in the context of Basque separatism. Taylor's slim volume takes us into the magical world of the Hutu, where the body is an expression of flow and blockage, projected on the world at large, and seen as explanatory for the extermination of the "blocked" Tutsi. And Cavanaugh's volume renders the disappearances and tortures of Pinochet's Chile as an antithesis to the sacrament of the Eucharist—separating, isolating, and destroying persons the Mass would bring into unity, sacramental communion, and vibrant life.

Terminology

The terminology I am drawing upon here deserves further exploration and explanation, since the world we live in is a predominantly secular world, with secular biases and assumptions, while the world we are exploring here is a world in which spirits abound, in which it not improper to claim that, in the words of St. Paul in his Letter to the Ephesians:

We wrestle not against flesh and blood, but against principalities, against powers, against the rulers of the darkness of this world, against spiritual wickedness in high places.[7]

To clarify our terminology, then, we need to articulate a world view in which "spiritual" and "material" forces are mutually present. The word sacrament has its origins in Catholic practice and doctrine, and while there is a wider realm of "sacramental" significance, in Catholicism there are seven sacraments as such, listed in the Catechism thus:

Baptism, Confirmation (or Chrismation), the Eucharist, Penance, the Anointing of the Sick, Holy Orders and Matrimony.[8]

I quoted above the definition of a sacrament as the "outward and visible sign of an inward and spiritual grace"—but it is more than just the outward and visible sign, it is both that sign and the grace or spiritual reality to which the sign is an opening. The United States Conference of Catholic Bishops expresses this doubling of realities through a simple non-doctrinal metaphor:

We recognize that the Sacraments have a visible and invisible reality, a reality open to all the human senses but grasped in its God-given depths with the eyes of faith. When parents hug their children, for example, the visible reality we see is the hug. The invisible reality the hug conveys is love. We cannot "see" the love the hug expresses, though sometimes we can see its nurturing effect in the child.

The visible reality we see in the Sacraments is their outward expression, the form they take, and the way in which they are administered and received. The invisible reality we cannot "see" is God's grace…[9]

Catholic doctrine locates these sacraments within the teachings of Christ found in the canonical gospels; they are certainly ancient as human traditions go, and have been contemplated across the centuries by many minds—some orthodox, some heretical, some believing, some skeptical. It was his awareness of this centuries old tradition that brought the polymath Gregory Bateson, teaching psychiatric residents at the Palo Alto Veterans Administration Hospital, to formulate what he called "a sort of catechism" intended to get them thinking.[10] Among the questions he hoped they would be able to answer by the end of the course:

- What is a sacrament?
- What is entropy?
- What is play?

In his book, *Steps to an Ecology of Mind*, he writes:

The would-be behavioral scientist who knows nothing of the basic structure of science and nothing of the 3000 years of careful philosophic and humanistic thought about man—who cannot define either entropy or a sacrament—had better hold his peace rather than add to the existing jungle of half-baked hypotheses.[11]

But Bateson goes further, and takes the meaning of sacrament out beyond the specifics of its use within Catholicism, and it is his expanded use that I wish to avail myself of here. Bateson discusses with his daughter, Mary Catherine Bateson, whether the ballet *Swan Lake* is or can be a sacrament, coming to the conclusion that it can be either a metaphor—the ballerina can be a metaphor for a swan—or a sacrament—the ballerina can in some sense become a swan—the difference depending on the perception of the performer or audience member.

In sacramental perception, we perceive a reality within a reality, a point of intimate contact between two realms. The poet Coleridge, using the term symbol rather than sacrament, writes with similar intent:

> A symbol is characterized... above all by the translucence of the Eternal through and in the Temporal. It always partakes of the Reality which it Renders Intelligible; and while it enunciates the whole, abides itself as a living part in that Unity of which it is representative.[12]

We are speaking, then, of a simultaneous double perception, of an immaterial reality accessible via material means—bread and wine in the case of the Eucharist, the ballerina in the case of Swan Lake. To partake of a sacrament, then, is to partake of a reality beyond sign or symbol, a reality to which sign and symbol point and are in Coleridge's word, "translucent."

Coleridge's poetic predecessor, William Blake, is even more outspoken in describing his own experience of the translucence:

> "What," it will be Questioned, "When the Sun rises, do you not see a round Disk of fire somewhat like a Guinea?" O no no, I see an Innumerable company of the Heavenly host crying "Holy Holy Holy is the Lord God Almighty." I question not my Corporeal or Vegetative Eye any more than I would Question a Window concerning a Sight: I look thro it & not with it.[13]

No doubt Blake sees both, or he would not know that the "outward and visible sign" appears to be a round disc of fire—but he passes directly from sign to signified, from the outward and visible to the inward and spiritual, leaving the purely material disc of the sun aside in his joy at the spiritual reality it opens for him.

The Basque Case

The point of all this talk of sacraments and symbols is that those who live keenly in this kind of double world are nowhere so passionately engaged as when their symbols are activated.

Joseba Zulaika's book, *Basque Violence*, is subtitled *Metaphor and Sacrament*. In it, he writes:

Myth, war, heroism, and tragedy *may* seem pretentious themes for small-scale settings such as Itziar

—the village in Basque country Zulaika hails from and writes about—

yet it is the purpose of the narratives that follow to show the full force of such collective representations in the village...

The individual subject of this narrative condenses these various dimensions of historical mythification — from the imagination of the prehistoric past to the anticipation of the unconquered future, from the memory of recent wars to the participation in the present fight, and from heroic consciousness to its tragic results. This is a history made by and for the ongoing violence; as such, it affords an essential form of intelligibility to that violence.[14]

Zulaika traces that history back to its "prehistoric" origins, noting that the horse-paintings in the cave of Elkain are millennia old, while the skulls found a mile from the village in the cave of Urtiaga date back to the Azilian and Upper Paleolithic. To the Basque, these traces in prehistory are closely associated with the uniqueness of their language, Euskara, the sole surviving non-Indo-European language in Western Europe.

Moving to more recent, "historical" times, Zulaika finds "the first historical account of Itziar is based on the legendary apparition of the Amabirjina (Mother Virgin) in the early Middle Ages." And this legend, too, lives on: "A sanctuary built for the image has made Itziar a center of pilgrimage and Marian devotion for the past seven centuries." It may be helpful to note that pilgrimage, too, is associated with the double universe of the sacramental—a long and often arduous sequence of physical footsteps leading not so much to a geographical as to a spiritual location, building to the state of devotion of which Zulaika writes.[15]

History as Myth, Legend, and Devotion is the title of Zulaika's first chapter, and indeed myth and legend can be considered by the contemporary secular mind as ahistorical "spiritual" substitutes for history, but Zulaika notes their deep resonance in the everyday life of his fellow-inhabitants of Itziar.

Mythical and legendary narratives "are relevant in that they form part of the thought and social life directly observable" in the village. He writes:

We are not concerned with the historicity of the stories but with their mythical quality, for "a story may be true yet mythical in character.[16]

Once again, the point is one that is made with clarity by the poets. Thus Kathleen Raine:

Myth, when a real event may be the enactment of a myth, is the truth of the fact and not the other way around.[17]

For the people of Itziar, for the Basque generally, and for those who live strongly in the dual world of the magical, the sacramental, this is no fanciful statement but vivid, experienced reality. It is this vivid reality of what we might otherwise call the mythic, the dreamlike, the poetic, the visionary, that Zulaika is at pains to tell us lies at the heart of Basque life, and thus too of the violence of the ETA:

This kind of prehistoric and legendary coding of history is a significant aspect of Basque identity *and it becomes part of political attitudes* (emphasis mine).[18]

For a comparison with a similar "coding" on the part of bin Laden, see Michael Vlahos' section, "History revealed and enjoined through mystic literary form" in *Terror's Mask: Insurgency Within Islam*, in which he describes the videotaped discussion of bin Laden with an un-named "sheikh" in Tora Bora:

Thus there is no "past" as we understand it, and no future. It is all one. The *Hikayat* of Usama bin Laden joins all other heroic action as part of the greater story. We are told that the struggle, the jihad, continues until the Last Judgement, so that there is no final earthly triumph of human spirit and of human arms.

And because the whole story is a single unified narrative—"ahistorical or even anti-historical"—in which all join and all experience, and where time and space are folded into one, the specific outcomes of "real" History are less important than the actions of believers.[19]

Myth and history meet and mingle, *with myth adding its passionate intensity to history*, both in Itziar and Tora Bora. Without forgetting Itziar or Zulaika, it's worth considering the implications Vlahos postulates for bin Laden and Tora Bora:

What does the symbolic framework of these two warrior subcultures tell us?

- They believe not only in the rightness of their cause but also in its pre-figured outcome.
- They are inspired in their commitment by an all-encompassing religious Mythos.
- They use the literary forms of this Mythos to reinforce kinship and conviction.
- They embrace hardship, adversity, and sacrifice as personal fulfillment.
- The act of struggle itself is a triumph, joining them to God and to the River of Islam, so there can be no defeat as we know it for them.[20]

Consider the last two items in Vlahos' list, minus only the "the River of Islam" reference, the only item inapplicable to the Basque case. Zulaika quotes an article in the Basque youth group Herri Gaztedi's magazine, *Gazte*, "The Present Situation and the Christian." The piece begins by quoting Jesus:

If any man would come after me, let him deny himself and take up his cross daily and follow me. For whoever would save his life will lose it; and whoever loses his life for my sake, he will save it.[21]

Zulaika then notes:

The text is a clear indication of the bridge between the appeal to resist institutional oppression and the Christian models of sacrifice and martyrdom.[22]

Paraphrasing Vlahos, we might say of the Basque fighters in the late '60s that Zulaika is discussing, that the "act of struggle itself is a triumph, joining them to God and to the River of Christ, so there can be no defeat as we know it for them."

Again, Zulaika speaks of "the bridge between the appeal to resist institutional oppression and the Christian models of sacrifice and martyrdom."[23] A similar bridge can be found between the suicide bombings of the (presumptively secular) Tamil Tigers and earlier notions of martyrdom, as reported by Michael Roberts in "Tamil Tiger 'Martyrs': Regenerating Divine Potency?":

Contrary to claim, the Liberation Tigers of Tamil Eelam (LTTE) are not overwhelmingly secular in their practices. While their successes as a liberation movement have been built on organizational skills and techno-military prowess, they mobilize both the Hindu majority and a significant Christian minority within the Sri Lankan Tamil population via modalities that are deeply rooted in the lifestyles and religious practices of Tamils in India and Lanka. To grasp these capacities a reading of the deep history of Tamil civilization writ-large as well as the anthropological literature on religious cross-fertilization in Sri Lanka is essential. The weight attached to propitiatory rituals in Tamil culture inform the LTTE's burial of the dead and the building up of a sacred topography centered on their fallen (the mavirar). Just as heroic humans were deified in southern India's past, regenerative divine power is conceivably invested in today's Tiger mavirar. These facets of Tamil Tiger practice suggests that "enchantment" can nestle amidst secularized rationality in the structures of a modern political movement.[24]

There is more cross-cultural patterning here that may be apparent to those familiar only with one particular tradition, be it Tamil, Jihadist, or Basque.

There is much more to the ethnography of Basque violence than we can discuss in these pages, and Zulaika's book—originally recommended to me by the Australian counter-terrorism scholar Leah Farrall—is the appropriate resource for fuller appreciation of the details. To sense the depth or height of what, with Zulaika, I am terming the sacramental quality of Basque violence, we can consider this stunning sentences from Zulaika's description of a legend his father told him about St. Michael and a sinner named Goñi:

> There are two kinds of killings in the story of Goñi. At the outset he is portrayed as a criminal murderer for killing his father and mother...Then Goñi is made a heroic killer with the help of St Michael...
>
> The second type of killing clearly surpasses human individuality—the killer levitates upward into an archangel and the victim descends downward into a monster...[25]

"For human killing to be a 'normal affair'," he notes, "it must be preceded by a redefinition of categorical distinction":

> It is all right for an archangel to murder a beast. It is all right for an army to destroy an enemy target, or for a community to extirpate an adverse member—the higher whole and the lower part are categorically distanced...For men to manipulate these categorical distinctions and act out this ordinary tale of beasts and archangels, all that is need is the power of ritual metaphor.[26]

It would be hard to find a more poetic description of the psychological impact of demonization of an enemy—so common across human history, and among religiously-driven terrorists in particular—than this. The degradation of the enemy as a prelude to slaughter, by means of some alchemical balancing act within the imagination, enemy to beast, self to archangel, also uplifts and vindicates the self-perceived spiritual righteousness of the killer.

Thus the dark spirituality of those who "love death as we love life."

The Rwandan Case

We might say that the example Zulaika offers for our consideration from Basque country is one in which the sacramentalism, the "magic", is "white" while the application, terrorism, is dark. In the case of the Rwandan case, both the "magic" and the application, "genocide," are dark.

Just how far from secular reality can a sacramental or magical double reality take us? There's an instructive story in Peter Geschiere's *The Modernity of Witchcraft* in which a woman in Cameroon asks a Christian pastor for prayers, saying:

I have been driving all night. I drive a plane. We use the plane to transport food, rain and such from places of plenty to the Buea area. Very recently, white people have been attempting to take the plane from us. If I hadn't been so skillful, having piloted the plane for 30 years, they would have long gone with it.

The pastor continues:

She went on to explain to me that she has never seen an aeroplane, but she knows how a plane can be built. All planes are in the world of witchcraft, and when the white man gets it from the black man, he then interprets it into real life. As it is with planes, so with televisions, radios, telephones etc.[27]

For Geschiere, this is exemplary of syncretism; here, I use it to suggest the immense conceptual distances that are possible between worldviews. To understand the worldview behind the Rwandan genocide we must go "outside the box" of our own worldview and enter at least conceptually into the "box" of the Rwandans.

This is not necessary, if we are to answer the questions Taylor poses at the outset of his book, *Sacrifice as Terror*:

How does one make sense of events that defy reason—events like those that occurred in Rwanda during 1994, costing the lives of one million people, one seventh of the country's population? How many ways are there to understand mass violence and murder? What constitutes sense under such circumstances? Is it singular? Is it plural? Or is it neither, nothing but a useless conceit driven more by the scholar's need to explain than a world's desire to understand?...Are there 'magic bullet' insights out there whose revelation might break the cycle of crime and counter-crime that have plagued the region for the past forty years?...

And where to begin? With the historical antecedents? The political divisions? The social tensions? External pressures? Class disparities? Gender disparities? Or, as some have suggested, internal cultural proclivities to violence? How does one speak dispassionately of the unspeakable, the horror of genocide...?[28]

The ability to discover and enter, at least conceptually, into the worldview of the genocidal is not guaranteed to be a simple matter, in which "they" are "rational actors"— "just like us."

Indeed, the exercise is one that tends to bring the notion of "rational actors" into question, not only with respect to "them" but also "us." It is only when we recognized that "rationality" follows from what may be widely divergent sets of postulates—world-interpreting myths, if you will—that we can see the logic behind "irrational" behaviors such as genocide.

Thus Taylor quotes Bruce Kapferer, *Legends of People, Myths of State*:

Broadly, the legitimating and emotional force of myth is not in the events as such but in the logic that conditions their significance. This is so when the logic is also vital in the way human actors are culturally given to constituting a self in the everyday routine world and move out toward others in that world. Mythic reality is mediated by human beings into the worlds in which they live. Where human beings recognize the argument of mythic reality as corresponding to their own personal constitutions—their orientation within and movement through reality—so myth gathers force and can come to be seen as embodying ultimate truth. Myth so enlivened, I suggest, can become imbued with commanding power, binding human actors to the logical movement of its scheme.[29]

Those who participated in the Rwandan genocide, then, were acting in accordance with their myth.

Sacrifice as Terror is the title of Christopher C. Taylor's book on *The Rwandan Genocide of 1994*—his subtitle—and while terror on the grand scale is the application, the notion of sacrifice in this case is dependent on a different system of metaphors and analogies. The "outward and visible signs" here are linked in with notions of kingship, the sacredness of the king's body, human physiology, and the combination of weather, rain in particular, and harvest:

Beneath the aspect of disorder there lay an eerie order to the violence of 1994 Rwanda. Many of the actions followed a cultural patterning, a structured and structuring logic, as individual Rwandans lashed out against a perceived internal other that threatened in their imaginations both their personal integrity and the cosmic order of the state.[30]

We who refer unthinkingly to "heads of state" are operating under a similar metaphor, as memorialized in Shakespeare's line, "Uneasy lies the head that wears a crown" and explored in detail in Kantorowicz' classic, *The King's Two Bodies*.[31]

Realized analogy is at the heart of magic, as realized metaphor was at the heart of sacrament. In each case, a mapping of likeness becomes culturally embedded, so that the mind's understanding conforms to the values implicit in the analogy. Thus the Christ-enhanced body of bread, understood within the sacramental frame by a believer, creates in that believer the "mind of Christ": thus also King's body as Body Politic, understood within the frame of Rwandan cosmology, requires the elimination of blockages to its natural flow—blockages which can be eliminated in the bodies and persons of the Tutsi:

It was overwhelmingly Tutsi who were the sacrificial victims in what in many respects was a massive ritual of purification, a ritual intended to purge the nation of "obstructing beings", as the threat of obstruction was imagined through a Rwandan ontology that situates the body politic in analogical relation to the individual human body.[32]

It is this that explains the extensive practices of torture by the Hutu, which follow patterns Taylor had already understood as a medical anthropologist. Taylor describes the process:

In order to make these forms of violence comprehensible in terms of the local symbolism, It is first necessary to understand, as Pierre Clastres instructs us, that social systems inscribe 'law' onto the bodies of their subjects (1974). Occasionally physical torture is an integral part of the ritual process intended to inculcate society's norms and values. Using The Penal Colony by way of illustration Clastres states, 'Here Kafka designates the body as a writing surface, a surface able to receive the law's readable text.'[33]

Taylor bases his insight into Rwandan terrorist symbolism and metaphor on his previous fieldwork and observations on Rwandan folk medical practices, noting that these are based on conceptualizations "characterized by an opposition between orderly states of humoral and other flows to disorderly ones":

Analogies are constructed that take this opposition as their base and then relate bodily processes to those of social and natural life. In the unfolding of human and natural events, flow/blockage symbolism mediates between physiological, sociological, and cosmological levels of causality. Popular healing aims at restoring bodily flows that have been perturbed by human negligence and malevolence. Bodily fluids such as blood, semen, breast milk, and menstrual blood are a recurrent concern, as is the passage of aliments through the digestive tract. Pathological states are characterized by obstructed or excessive flows and perturbations of this sort may signify illness, diminished fertility, or death.[34]

That is the way Taylor's 1980s Rwandans "feel" and "understand" their bodies, and as Daniel Benveniste says, we too project our bodily metaphors onto the world around us. For us too:

Symptoms and the sense of reality are built out of the reified metaphors of the body.

From an open ear to an open mind; from a penetrating penis to a penetrating argument; from a receptive vagina to a receptive community; from a unified body and a unified culture to the construction of monotheism; from excretion to repudiation; from urination to getting pissed off; from the navel to the center of the world; from dismemberment to postmodernity, over and over again the metaphors of the body are projected onto and into the world.[35]

Translating the Rwandan understanding of bodily flows and blockage into the brutalities of terror, we find "the emasculation of Tutsi males, even those too young to reproduce," and the slashing off of female breasts. Taylor then points out the implications:

Both emasculation and breast oblation manifest a preoccupation with the reproductive system, and specifically with parts of the body that produce fertility fluids. In both cases, the symbolic function interdigitates with and reinforces the pragmatic function, but the symbolic function cannot simply be reduced to the pragmatic one of destroying the future capacity of a group to reproduce.[36]

It is no accident, then, but a continuation of the same bodily metaphor into the realm of terror, that many of the killings occurred, as Taylor notes, "at roadblocks erected on highways, roads, streets, or even small footpaths."[37]

The Chilean Case

The Basque example presented by Zulaika showed us a positive sacramental view of violence and martyrdom in the service of a group who perceive themselves as freedom fighters—albeit they are also terrorists both in their use of the tactics of terrorism and in the punitive eyes of the state—and the Rwandan case presented by Taylor portrayed a negative sacramentalism in the sense that the metaphor ruling the genocide was from a western perspective brutal and atavistic. In turn, Cavanaugh in *Torture and Eucharist* presents a case wherein the high sacramental value of the human individual in rich social context is pitted against torture and disappearance as the Chilean state's attempt to erase personhood and thus break the bonds of kinship, friendship and community—communion—by means of which humans achieve their fullness both as individuals and as members of a transcendent body, the Body of Christ. He argues that:

> [A] Christian practice of the political is embodied in the Eucharist, the remembering of Jesus' own torture at the hands of the powers of this world. The Eucharist is the church's response to torture, and the hope for Christian resistance to the violent disciplines of this world.[38]

For what it's worth, my own mentor Fr. Trevor Huddleston CR perceived a similar movement from the realm of high sacrament to that of human humane necessity. A close friend of Mandela, holder of the Isitwalandwe award and long-time chair of the Anti-Apartheid Movement, Fr. Trevor wrote in his book *Naught for Your Comfort*:

> On Maundy Thursday, in the Liturgy of the Catholic Church, when the Mass of the day is ended, the priest takes a towel and girds himself with it; he takes a basin in his hands, and kneeling in front of those who have been chosen, he washes their feet and wipes them, kissing them also one by one. So he takes, momentarily, the place of his Master. The centuries are swept away, the Upper Room in the stillness of the night is all around him: "If I, your Lord and Master, have washed your feet, ye ought also to wash one another's feet." I have knelt in the sanctuary of our lovely church in Rosettenville and washed the feet of African students, stooping to kiss them. In this also I have known the meaning of identification. The difficulty is to carry the truth out into Johannesburg, into South Africa, into the world.[39]

The recognition of Christ in the person and the imperative to oppose apartheid is as real for Fr. Trevor as the recognition of blockage in the person is for the Hutu who then massacres Tutsi (and moderate Hutu) with ease. For Cavanaugh, it is specifically the Eucharist or Mass.

Here the perpetrator of atrocity is neither pagan/indigenous, syncretistic or Christian, but secular in worldview, whether or not religious at some nominal level—and thus effectively nihilistic from a sacramental viewpoint. By contrast the Eucharist or Mass, as Cavanaugh sees it, elevates the recipient of the Body and Blood of Christ to a culmination outside of time, to participation in the Church as Bride of Christ in the celestial Marriage Supper of the Lamb—of which every Mass offers a foretaste.[40]

The particulars of the tortures and disappearances administered are not a symbolic or sacramental issue in this case. It is the denial by erasure of human personhood—in effect the erasure of the "image and likeness of God" in the singular cases of each and every individual tortured or disappeared, which counts. Here, if you will, it is the erasure of the sacramental vision itself which is at stake, and to which the fullest corporate expression of that vision—the practice and reception of the Eucharist—is and must be, in Cavanaugh's view, the Church's response.

It may be hard for the secular mind to grasp the conceptual and emotional profundity of the Eucharist for the devoted believer, but Dom Gregory Dix may give us a hint when, after 700 or so pages of detailed "dry" scholarship in his magisterial book, *The Shape of the Liturgy*, he lets fly with this paragraph, commenting on Christ's Eucharistic command, *Do this in remembrance of me*:

Was ever another command so obeyed? For century after century, spreading slowly to every continent and country and among every race on earth, this action has been done, in every conceivable circumstance, for every conceivable human need from infancy and before it to extreme old age and after it, from the pinnacles of human greatness to the refuge of fugitives in the caves and dens of the earth. Men have found no better thing than this to do for kings at their crowning and for criminals going to the scaffold; for armies in triumph or for a bride and bridegroom in a little country church; for the proclamation of a dogma or for a good crop of wheat; for the wisdom of the

Parliament of a mighty nation or for a sick old woman afraid to die; for a schoolboy sitting an examination or for Columbus setting out to discover America; for the famine of whole provinces or for the soul of a dead lover; in thankfulness because my father did not die of pneumonia; for a village headman much tempted to return to fetich because the yams had failed; because the Turk was at the gates of Vienna; for the repentance of Margaret; for the settlement of a strike; for a son for a barren woman; for Captain so-and-so, wounded and prisoner-of-war; while the lions roared in the nearby amphitheatre; on the beach at Dunkirk; while the hiss of scythes in the thick June grass came faintly through the windows of the church; tremulously, by an old monk on the fiftieth anniversary of his vows; furtively, by an exiled bishop who had hewn timber all day in a prison camp near Murmansk; gorgeously, for the canonisation of S. Joan of Arc—one could fill many pages with the reasons why men have done this, and not tell a hundredth part of them. And best of all, week by week and month by month, on a hundred thousand successive Sundays, faithfully, unfailingly, across all the parishes of christendom, the pastors have done this just to make the plebs sancta Dei—the holy common people of God.[41]

It is that—holiness in the Body of Christ, holiness in the individual person, holiness in the human body, holiness in the body politic, holiness in the Church as Bride of Christ—that is at stake.

Symbolic or Sacramental Analysis

The starkest setting of what I'm calling the dark sacred may well be the one given by St. Paul in the Christian New Testament, Ephesians 6.12. I quoted it at the top of this chapter, but it bears repetition now that we have seen its implications in recent and current events:

For we wrestle not against flesh and blood, but against principalities, against powers, against the rulers of the darkness of this world, against spiritual wickedness in high places.[42]

The actors in the human drama may be sacramentalists or seculars in worldview, holding the one-eyed vision which William Blake derides or the double vision that sacramental insight provides: it matters little from the perspective of this paper.

What strikes me as crucial is that we as analysts, counter-terrorism practitioners, devisers of alternative narratives, or interested observers, should understand that behind every act of terror or resistance there may be a sacramental or purely symbolic motive, "dark" or "light", acknowledged or not.

As Gregory Bateson said, the concept of sacrament is one of which we should all be cognizant, whether or not we happen to be believers in such a system.

Symbolic or sacramental analysis has a significant contribution to make to our understanding of both brutal violence and the urgencies of making and maintaining peace.

Notes

[1]   Christoph Reuter, "The Terror Strategist: Secret Files Reveal the Structure of Islamic State." *Spiegel Online International*. 18 April 2015, http://www.spiegel.de/international/world/islamic-state-files-show-structure-of-islamist-terror-group-a-1029274.html.

[2]   Thomas Hegghammer. "Why Terrorists Weep: The Socio-Cultural Practices of Jihadi Militants." *Paul Wilkinson Memorial Lecture*. St. Andrews: University of St. Andrews, 16 April 2015, http://hegghammer.com/ files/Hegghammer - Wilkinson Memorial Lecture.pdf.

[3]   This definition of sacrament derives from Augustine's use of the contrasted yet complementary concepts of visible sign and invisible grace. Bradley Hanson in his *Introduction to Christian* Theology. Minneapolis: Augsburg Fortress, 1997, writes, "In Christian sacraments, Augustine says there is an outward, visible. figurative sign or symbol and an invisible spiritual reality to which the symbol points." Thus in his *On the Catechising of the Uninstructed*, Chapter 26, Augustine writes, "On the subject of the sacrament, indeed, which he receives, it is first to be well impressed upon his notice that the signs of divine things are, it is true, things visible, but that the invisible things themselves are also honored in them, and that that species, which is then sanctified by the blessing, is therefore not to be regarded merely in the way in

which it is regarded in any common use." See http://www.newadvent. org/fathers/1303.htm.

[4]   Joseba Zulaika, *Basque Violence: Metaphor and Sacrament*. Reno: University of Nevada Press, 1988.

[5]   Christopher Taylor, *Sacrifice as Terror: The Rwandan Genocide of 1994*. Oxford: Berg, 1999.

[6]   William Cavanaugh, *Torture and Eucharist: Theology, Politics, and the Body of Christ*. Malden: Blackwell, 1998.

[7]   Ephesians 6.12.

[8]   The Catechism of the Catholic Church, Part II, Sect. 2, #1210, http:// www.vatican.va/archive/ccc_css/archive/catechism/p2s2.htm.

[9]   United States Conference of Catholic Bishops, "Sacraments and Sacramentals." See http://www.usccb.org/prayer-and-worship/ sacraments-and-sacramentals/.

[10]   Gregory Bateson, *Steps to an Ecology of Mind: Collected Essays in Anthropology, Psychiatry, Evolution, and Epistemology*. Chicago: University of Chicago Press, 1971: xxiv.

[11]   Ibid: xxviii.

[12]   Samuel Taylor Coleridge, *The Statesman's Manual*, in Lay Sermons, 30.

[13]   William Blake, from "A Vision of the Last Judgment," as found on the *Norton Anthology of English Literature* website. See http:// www.wwnorton.com/college/english/nael/noa/pdf/blake_From_ A_Vision_of_The_Last_Judgment.pdf.

[14]   Zulaika: 1.

[15]   Ibid: 3.

[16]   Ibid: 3.

[17]   Kathleen Raine, quoted in James McCorkle, Ed., *Conversant Essays: Contemporary Poets on Poetry*. Detroit: Wayne State University Press, 1990: 60.

[18]   Zulaika: 3.

[19]   Michael Vlahos, *Terror's Mask: Insurgency Within Islam*. Laurel: Johns Hopkins University Applied Physics Lab, updated 2003: 9-10, http:// www.jhuapl.edu/ourwork/nsa/papers/Terror_Islamsm.pdf.

[20]   Ibid: 10.

[21]   Luke 9:23-24.

[22]   Zulaika: 55.

[23]   Ibid: 55.

[24] Michael Roberts, abstract, "Tamil Tiger 'Martyrs': Regenerating Divine Potency?" *Studies in Conflict and Terrorism* 28. November-December 2005: 493-514.
[25] Zulaika: 264.
[26] Ibid: 267.
[27] Peter Geschiere, *The Modernity of Witchcraft*. Charlotteville: University of Virginia Press, 1997: 3.
[28] Taylor: 1.
[29] Bruce Kapferer, *Legends of People, Myths of State: Violence, Intolerance, and Political Culture in Sri Lanka and Australia*. Washington, D.C.: Smithsonian, 1988: 46., quoted by Taylor: 110-12.
[30] Taylor: 101.
[31] Ernst H. Kantorowicz, *The King's Two Bodies: A Study in Mediaeval Political Theology*. Princeton: Princeton University Press, 1857.
[32] Taylor: 101.
[33] Ibid: 106.
[34] Ibid: 111.
[35] David Benveniste, "Play and the Metaphors of the Body." *The Psychoanalytic Study of the Child* 53. 1998: 8.
[36] Taylor: 140.
[37] Ibid: 105.
[38] Cavanaugh: 2.
[39] Trevor Huddleston CR, *Naught for Your Comfort*. Garden City: Doubleday, 1956: 73.
[40] Cavanaugh: 227, referencing Geoffrey Wainwright, *Eucharist and Eschatology*. Oxford: Oxford University Press, 1981: 74-78.
[41] Dom Gregory Dix, *The Shape of the Liturgy*. London: Dacre Press, 1945: 744.

Chapter 8

REVIEW OF *THE STRANGE WORLD OF HUMAN SACRIFICE*

Andrew Bringuel, II

Jan N. Bremmer, Ed., *The Strange World of Human Sacrifice*. Lueven, Belgium: Peeters Publishers, 2007; 268 pages. €40.00.

"It is by its promise of an occult sense of power that evil often attracts the weak."

—Eric Hoffer

Introduction

The *Strange World of Human Sacrifice*, Volume 1 of the Studies in the History and Anthropology of Religion series, is edited by Jan N. Bremmer, an Emeritus Professor of Science of Religion and Comparative Religious Studies, University of Groningen, the Netherlands. This important work, derived from an international conference on human sacrifice, is an anthropological exploration of origins and motives leading to the not so uncommon practice of human sacrifice and self-sacrifice dating back as far as 1750 BC and the Classic Kerma Period in Egypt.

The practice of human ritualistic violence and self-sacrifice likely pre-dates the biological evidence, as the practice has its roots in the primitive emotional and cognitive process that is man. If biology makes man human, psychology makes man humane; living in social groups teaches man norms for humanity. Perhaps the biological state of man provides the urge for violence and man is destined to choose either productive or destructive pathways. Man chooses either pro-social productive behaviors or anti-social destructive ones. It is how man rationalizes the necessity for his behavior that justifies the use of social controls, including violence or social trust in resolving conflict and managing relationships. The book examines group behavior involving violent state actors (VSAs) from the pharaohs to the Japanese army. This review will look at the examples in the book and compare them to criminally violent non-state actors (CVNSAs) and their use of ritualistic violence through human sacrifice and self-sacrifice.

The book attempts to look at the motives associated with sacrifice, from war sacrifice, appeasement sacrifice, construction sacrifice, burial sacrifice, or layered motives. The various authors postulate that the motives for human sacrifice are multi-faceted. This includes making the killing of prisoners more palatable by removing guilt from the executioner, using the prisoners' ritualistic deaths and occasionally cannibalism to increase power through dark magic and/or religiosity, appeasing angry malevolent Gods, thanking benevolent Gods, ensuring blessed construction, and/or ensuring a life hereafter. So what is the connection between ancient acts of human sacrifice and behaviors seen today from CVNSAs? Are there common factors in terms of dark magico-religious activities, use of narcotics, and/or the process of radicalization that might help us understand these behaviors better?

Comparisons between the book's examples of VSAs and CVNSAs will follow a four-prong typology of political, social, economic, and/or personal motives. These motives coupled with the socialization process of group formation can lead to the phenomenon known as radicalization. We will start with a definition of radicalization as the process by which one who believes in a truth so absolutely that one develops a static, dichotomous mindset rejecting any alternative truths which leads to cognitive closure regarding a particular object issue. Very often these static mindsets are shaped around personal, economic, political, or social motives. Many times these mindsets are contextual belief states which promote intolerance and the rationalization of the necessity of behaviors that seem illogical or irrational but are perfectly normative for the individual and/or group that has defined them in a narrative. This contextual belief state promotes an "us against them" mentality where expressive emotions like anger can lead to disgust, contempt, and justification for the necessity of unlawful violence. Interestingly, this process of rationalizing these behaviors begins with group formation that includes the same process that leads law abiding groups to rationalize their pro-social behaviors. This group process is all about relationship development and management and includes recruitment, indoctrination, initiation, and education. These processes lead to the rationalization for the necessity of behavior, mobilization, and then action.

After a suicide bomber attacks, a video of a decapitated victim is distributed on the Internet, a cult commits mass suicide, or an act of immolation by a zealot occurs, our governments, academics, and citizens attempt to understand the reasoning behind these violent acts. In part, this is an attempt to make sense out of the senseless, but also to gain a better understanding of the breakdown of society's relationships. Merriam-Webster defines relationship as "the way in which two or more people, groups, countries, etc., talk to, behave toward, and deal with each other."[1] All relationships seek a state of stability and balance that provides predictability of behavior (POB) against a baseline of expected norms for behavior. All relationships maintain this state through the application of trust and/or control mechanisms. Conflict with the baseline means a disruption of trust and control that can lead to imbalance, instability and a lack of predictability of behavior. Three disruption elements in a relationship are those who simply reject a relationship by showing an unwillingness to engage, those who are part of a relationship but perceive a breach of trust and feel betrayed, and those who enter a relationship using deception and for nefarious reasons.

Violence including ritualistic or ceremonial violence such as human sacrifice or self-sacrifice can, therefore, be used as an intimidation tool by the VSA for enforcing social control, for example capital punishment. Capital punishment is not human sacrifice in the sense of dark magico-religious sacrifice but there are undeniable religious overtones from offering last rites to the condemned to ritualistic aspects leading up to the execution. This is not new to man. Perhaps the most infamous execution involved a radical who dared challenge the state, who went willingly as a sacrifice for others, and whose execution had political as well as religious overtones. The condemned was Jesus Christ and his execution is remembered and embedded in ritualistic practice by millions of Christians around the world. Capital punishment by VSAs is a form of lawful violence and not considered human sacrifice or even radical behavior. It is normalized behavior in the United States even though it has many ritualistic and ceremonial aspects leading up to the execution. Capital punishment could be described as ritualistic violence in furtherance of social and political goals since its intent is to deter crime. In Herman Te Velde's chapter entitled "Human Sacrifice in Ancient Egypt," he describes an ancient pharaoh grasping a kneeling, handcuffed enemy by the hair with one hand and a club in the other as he delivers a certain death blow. The author points out the act allowed the pharaoh to triumph over rebellious people and restore order to the cosmos.

Human sacrifice can also be enforced by rejecting social control such as beheading a kidnapped victim. Human sacrifice can also be motived by the ultimate altruistic selfless gesture of human trust, for example the self-sacrifice of Navy SEAL Michael Monssor who died saving his comrades or the ultimate response of distrust and doubt exhibited by Tunisian Tarek al-Tayeb Mohaned Bouazizi whose act of immolation was a catalyst for the Arab spring.

Political

In the book, author Michel Graulich reviews Aztec sacrifice. While the motives of the Aztec state certainly included an element of religiosity, it also included the punishment of prisoners as a way to maintain a high level of political control against the baseline of expected norms for behavior. The message was clear that the state was all powerful and the "priest" ensured that your behavior was inside society's norms or you stood a good chance of suffering ritualistic sacrificial violence. The idea of making violence part of a ceremonial or ritualistic process makes it less expressive or emotional; by making it instrumental through goals or objectives, it gives the violence meaning and may make it seem more humane. Through the development of a homogenous mindset that promotes the rationalization for necessity of behavior, the group ends up using lawful violence or unlawful violence. To the Aztecs, the acts they engaged in were normalized within the context of time and space.

Death makes more sense if it takes on the purpose of advancing political and or social objectives. The Aztec's ritualistic killing of prisoners had as much to do with furthering their social and political goals and objectives as it did servicing their Gods. Can we then make comparisons to the killing of Nicholas Evan Berg, beheaded by Abu Musab al-Zarqawi in Iraq during 2004? Zarqawi led Jam'at al-Tawhid wal-Jihad (JTJ) and was responsible for several be-headings including Berg's murder. The grisly video which included religious prayer and music was distributed on May 11, 2004 and had deeper socio-political goals and objectives than the gruesome act of murder. The video served the purpose of rejecting high levels of social control being used by coalition forces in the areas JTJ was attempting to influence. The video demonstrated how far JTJ was willing to go to further their own goals. The video served the purpose of instilling fear in some and inspiring others as well as disrupting relationships and developing relationships in the community JTJ was attempting to influence. The video was surrounded with ritualistic messages and ceremony that made the killing of Berg simply a means to deliver a message of warning to the U.S. and Iraq governments. In this respect, the Berg murder was similar to the Aztec murders of prisoners.

Zarqawi was labeled a radical as he held absolute truths and was unwilling to accept the terms for normative behavior in Iraq and he rejected any civil relationship. Did he follow the path of recruitment, indoctrination, initiation, and education leading to a rationalized mindset that allowed for the necessity of behavior? Clearly his rhetoric was uncompromising; he appeared to be a static thinker, intolerant, and unwavering. His actions were intended to disrupt connection to governance in Iraq and destroy the trust that existed in the relationship between the community and government. If it is true that the role of the government is to develop relationships with members of its community and disrupt relationships among its adversaries, then it is also true that the government's enemy intends to develop relationships with its sympathizers and disrupt the relationship between the community and the government. This dissonance is done by provoking, defying, and resisting the baseline for normative behavior under the law. By doing so, society sees Zarqawi as a radical, a CVNSA, and he was targeted and killed as an enemy.

Social

In a chapter written by Kengo Harimoto, he refers to the Samurai's culture and when it is acceptable to commit self-sacrifice at the time of defeat and under other conditions. This warrior culture existed in Japan during World War II when many soldiers choose self-sacrifice over capture by the enemy. It included acts of mass suicide called Banzai charges. These soldiers often believed in the Shinto religion and that they were giving their lives up for their emperor, himself a God, and so their altruistic act of trust would be rewarded in the afterlife. While these acts certainly had a political or personal component, they also represented a quasi-religious act of faith. These behaviors were taught as part of the culture and conditioned into the humanity of Japanese society. These soldiers were taught their sacrifice was a selfless act that would inspire others to follow. It is conditioned in the culture through recruitment and education that led to the radicalized mindset. There may be personal reward, but it is secondary to the benefit of the group. The modern day equivalent might be a thirteen-year-old boy named Hossein Fahmideh, who, in 1981, ran with an explosive charge and threw himself under an Iraqi tank during the Iran-Iraq war.[2] His act of courage was used as propaganda by the Iranian regime, saying that Fahmideh was a martyr and his faith would be rewarded in paradise. His selfless act of courage was followed by many similar acts of self-sacrifice. The Iranian society became more important than the individual. Whether it is to save imperial Japan, or to save Iran, the victim is willing to give his life in order for the social group to survive.

Economic

While the book does not talk much about human sacrifice in terms of economic motives, it does include references in a number of chapters including the chapter written by Jacqueline Borsje, "Human Sacrifice in Medieval Irish Literature." The author discusses the practice of human sacrifice honoring pagan Gods through the use of animals and humans as a form of currency. An ancient Irish family would be expected to offer the blood of their first born child to their God in return for milk and corn. The act of sacrificing the child and sharing the blood resulted in God's protection. While the link is not direct, there are examples today of economically motivated human sacrifice. It was reported by CBS news on April 3, 2002 that Saddam Hussein paid Palestinian families $25,000 if their son committed a suicide bombing attack against Israeli targets.[3] In these cases an economic incentive might lead to human sacrifice without any form of ideological radicalization taking place. The son doesn't have to be part of a social group, he can act alone as an associate member of the group and further the group's goals in a transactional manner. There is evidence suggesting that some Mexican drug cartels have used ceremonial violence including ritualistic human sacrifice in their perverted interpretation of Christian theology. The use of this ritualistic violence, most often against rival gangs and police, supposedly protects their economic interests through their saints like Jesus Malverde, Juan Soldado, and Santa Muerte.[4] The purpose in this form of human sacrifice. which has dark magico-religious overtones could be similar to the ancient Irish who used human blood as currency for divine blessing.

Personal

There are few examples of voluntary personal human sacrifice in the book. Herman Te Velde describes one case where a mortally ill pharaoh elicits a volunteer among his court to replace him in death. The chosen courtier was offered a state funeral including mummification and, while not enthused by the idea, the unlucky volunteer accepted the offer of replacement sacrifice thinking he had no other choice. This idea that one might voluntarily sacrifice at least parts of oneself in order to have another person live still exists today. Humans are willing to sacrifice their kidneys for transplants and suffer a loss as a consequence that they must measure by their personal gain. The donor must calculate the cost of being down to one kidney against the benefit of having their loved one survive. In 2012, a young Italian mother, Chiara Corbella postponed cancer treatments in order to protect her unborn child. The 28 year old Catholic woman had lost two children to birth defects and she was a popular speaker at pro-life events. Clearly her sacrifice took on a religious meaning and she did so voluntarily.[5] In Lourens Van Den Bosch's chapter entitled "Human Sacrifice Among The Konds," the idea of self-sacrifice took on religious meaning with the purpose of the human sacrifice being to foundationally produce fertile lands. The victim was bound between wooden planks, killed and chopped up before being placed in the ground. In some cases these "victims" were purchased, but in other instances they were willing participants who often received copious amounts of alcohol and opium before having their arms and legs broken to reduce possible resistance. The ritual would occur over three days during which time the victim was treated very well with food, drink, baths, and oils before being killed and butchered. The Konds entered a deceptive and disingenuous relationship with their victims and manipulated their behavior. While there are scholarly disagreements as to what attitude the Konds held toward the sacrificed victim, it appears that they considered the victim as becoming part of their God Tari through the sacrificial rites. This might make volunteering for such a sacrifice more tolerable if one thought they would be rewarded in an afterlife. Similarly, religion has inspired many to sacrifice themselves for a cause, not necessarily for the cause itself, but for the personal rewards promised for the unselfish act. Cases like Wafa al-Biri, a 21-year-old Palestinian woman who seemed to be the most unlikely suicide bomber may be of similar parallel. Wafa, like the low caste victims used by the Konds, was manipulated by militants using religion. Unlike the Kond's victims, Wafa's sacrifice to God was not to appease a God, as much as it was to appease personal grievance. Wafa claimed that Israelis killed her people and she was seeking revenge when she failed to blow herself up at a border checkpoint. She did this after Israeli doctors saved her life months earlier when she was severely burned by a gas cooker explosion.[6] While her life was saved, it was also changed forever. The scars on her body created even deeper emotional scars and, when she went home, she was approached by al-Aqsa militants who used the emotionally vulnerable woman for their own political gain. Wafa became a willing victim like those victims manipulated by the Konds. She might have been motivated by personal grievances, but she was manipulated by disingenuous operators.

The book also talks about cannibalism, saying that human sacrifice was sometimes combined with the practice by the ancient Celtics, Chinese, and Greeks. Today, one only has to look at Abu Sakkar and the infamous video of him eating a dead man's heart to witness ritualistic cannibalism. Sakkar now claims that he did not eat the heart; he stated he only held it for show even though the video clearly shows him biting into the man's organ and saying, "We will eat your hearts and your livers you soldiers of Bashar the dog." When asked later in an interview why he did what he did, Sakkar stated, "We have to terrify the enemy, humiliate them, just as they do to us. Now they won't dare be wherever Abu Sakkar is."[7]

Conclusion

While the book refers to VSAs in the examples of human sacrifice and self-sacrifice, there are correlations to the acts of CVNSAs as it relates to the motives for the acts. They both require relationships that are managed along a baseline of expected norms for behavior that most modern day societies reject. Still, like all relationships, they seek stability and balance in order to achieve predictability of behavior from their followers. The difference often comes down to the definitions for normative behavior which in society is usually codified into law. The CVNSA uses human sacrifice and self-sacrifice as unlawful violence. Additionally, parallels can be seen between the book's examples and the motives used by CVNSA as they fall within personal, economic, political, and/or social expressive and/or instrumental motives. It is true that at times these associated motives may be overlapping, with a person or a group having both economic and social motives for example. It is also true that one may commit acts of violence as an associated member of a CVNSA without being a radicalized member of the group. A member does not have to a radicalized unwavering true believer who is ideologically motivated to commit horrific violent acts. A member may have a radical mindset but never commit an unlawful violent act. Finally, the last parallel is that the social process leading to a radicalized unwavering true believing mindset is indistinguishable between law abiding and law breaking groups. It is the rationalization leading to the necessity for unlawful behavior and leading to mobilization and action that separates the CVNSA from the law abiding society. These groups and individuals represent the greatest disruption element against the baseline of social norms defined as the law.

Notes

[1]   "Relationships," *Merriam-Webster Online: Dictionary and Thesaurus.* 2014, http://www.merriam-webster.com/dictionary/relationships.

[2]   "Children in the Service of Terror," Middle East Media Research Institute, *Special Dispatch No. 2455.* 21 July 2009, http://www.memri. org/report/en/0/0/0/0/0/0/841/3435.htm.

[3]   John Esterbrook, "Salaries For Suicide Bombers," *CBS News.* 3 April 2002, http://www.cbsnews.com/news/salaries-for-suicide-bombers/.

[4]   Robert J. Bunker, "Santa Muerte: Inspired and Ritualistic Killings," *FBI Law Enforcement Bulletin.* February 2013, http://www.fbi.gov/ stats-services/publications/law-enforcement-bulletin/2013/february/ santa-muerte-inspired-and-ritualistic-killings-part-1-of-3.

[5]   "Emotional goodbye for young Italian mother who died for unborn child," *Catholic News Agency.* 21 June 2012, http://www. catholicnewsagency.com/news/emotional-goodbye-for-young-italian-mother-who-died-for-unborn-child/.

[6]   Richard Hartley-Parkinson, "'I would be a suicide bomber three times over if I could': Palestinian woman freed in Gilad Shalit deal vows to sacrifice her life," *Mail Online.* 20 October 2011, http://www.dailymail. co.uk/news/article-2051382/Palestinian-Wafa-al-Biss-freed-Gilad-Shalit-deal-vows-sacrifice-life.html.

[7]   Paul Wood, "Face-to-face with Abu Sakkar, Syria's 'heart-eating Cannibal,'" *BBC News.* 5 July 2013, http://www.bbc.com/news/magazine-23190533.

Chapter 9

REVIEW OF *UNDERSTANDING RELIGIOUS SACRIFICE: A READER*

Jóse de Arimatéia da Cruz

Jeffrey Carter, Ed., *Understanding Religious Sacrifice: A Reader.* New York: Continuum, 2003; 480 pages; $65.00.

Whether discussing a primitive or developed society, religious sacrifice is an integral part of any such grouping providing traditions, taboos, norms, and forms of ritual. According to Richard D. Hecht, "sacrifice is perhaps the most universal and intense form of ritual." In *Understanding Religious Sacrifice* (2003), religion scholar Jeffrey Carter, a Professor of Religious Studies and Director of the Castle Rock Institute for the Humanities in Brevard, North Carolina, provides his audience a collection of twenty-five influential selections devoted to the topic of religious sacrifice.

Religious sacrifice has been not only an integral part of many societies in the past, but in the increasingly globalized and high tech world of the twenty-first century barbarism and human sacrifice are making a resurgence in many locales where there is a political vacuum due to the disintegration of the nation-state.[1] For example, the Abu Musab al-Zarqawi's group beheading of U.S. contractor Nicholas Berg in Iraq in 2004 and the beheadings of members of the Los Zetas and Cartel del Golfo (CDG) are both present-day examples of the violent and the sacred coming together to legitimize actions otherwise deemed repugnant. As argued by the cultural theorist and literary critic René Girard, "the violence associated with ritual killing is the key to the origin of sacred" (p. 240). In the *Blood Sacrifices* book focusing on the interconnection between some violent non-state actors (VNSAs) and dark magico-religious activities, the important message is: violence and the sacred are inseparable despite its irrationality.

Indeed, covert appropriation by sacrifice of certain "properties of violence—particularly the ability of violence to move from one object to another—is hidden from sight by the awesome machinery of ritual" (p. 257). Acts of violence worldwide which may initially be seen as irrational or cold blooded murder gain some proper perspectives when seem from the VNSAs and dark magico-religious framework developed here by the other contributors to this special issue. Again, as articulated by René Girard, "the role of sacrifice is to stem this rising tide of indiscriminate substitutions and redirect violence into proper channels" (p. 249).

Carter operationalizes religious sacrifice as "any sacrifice where one or more of the central parties involved is believed to be, or to represent, an agent of the superhuman realm. Understood as supernatural, spiritual, divine, or sacred, this agent is most commonly the recipient during a sacrifice; for example, a god or ancestor receives an offering made by a human being" (p. 4). Obviously, defining and understanding sacrifice depends "for many thinkers, on the nature of the participants of a sacrifice—their status (ontological, social, political, economic, and so forth) and prior relationship vis-à-vis each other and the broader world. Whether seen as an exchange or not, every cultural example we identify as sacrifice involves interaction between variously interested parties, some active and others passive, some willing and others averse, and does include, generally, a third sacrificed domain. There will always be an agent acting sacrificially, employing some "thing" to be sacrificed, and, often, sacrificing "to" some other being (p. 4). In other words, society "is seeking to deflect upon a relatively indifferent victim, a sacrificeable victim, the violence that would otherwise be vented on its own members, the people it most desires to protect" (p. 244).

Each selection within this anthology presents a different theoretical point of view and teaches a different understanding about the origin of sacrifice, its meaning, or its overall significance for religion (p. x). Carter writes a brief introduction to each selection in order to place its author within a broader intellectual and theoretical context and to provide the readers an account of how the authors understand religion or ritual more generally. There are sociological theories, psychological approaches, structuralist theories of sacrifice, as well as a number of phenomenological, symbolic, or hermeneutical theories.

The reader are also exposed to a variety of concepts/ideas commonly employed in religious studies such as the idea of the gift, the notion of commemoration, the issue of power, the political dimension of religion and sacrifice, and the dynamics of inequality, agency, and control (p. 9). Carter attempts to show the readers that religious sacrifice must be recognized as a matter "of seeing it as a particular form of ritual" (p. 9).

Understanding Religious Sacrifice is divided into three main sections. The first part of this anthology is a general introduction examining the terms and theories commonly employed in discussions of sacrifice (p. 10); the second part, which is the main section of the text, consists of the selected writings. Carter organizes the essays in a chronological order by their date of publication thus allowing the reader to see the evolution of the development of sacrifice theory in the field of Religious Studies (p. 10). A listing of these numerous works and the theories associated with them is as follows:

1. E.B. Tylor, excerpt from *Primitive Culture* (1871): gift theory;
2. H. Spencer, excerpt from *The Principles of Sociology* (1877): fear theory;
3. W.R. Smith, excerpt from *The Religion of the Semites* (1889): communion theory;
4. J.G. Frazer, excerpt from *The Golden Bough* (1890): magic theory;
5. H. Hubert & M. Mauss, excerpt from *Sacrifice*, its nature and function (1898/1964): sacrifice theory;
6. E.A. Westermark, excerpt from *The Origin and Development of the Moral Ideas* (1912): exchange theory;
7. E. Durkheim, excerpt from *The Elementary Forms of the Religious Life* (1912/1965): combination of communion and gift theory;
8. S. Freud, excerpt from *Totem and Taboo* (1913/1950): guilt theory;
9. G. van der Leeuw, excerpt from *Religion in Essence and Manifestation* (1933/1986): combines a form of gift-theory with communion-theory;
10. G. Bataille, excerpt from *The Accused Share* (1949/1991): consumption theory;
11. A.E. Jensen, excerpt from *Myth and Cult among Primitive Peoples* (1951/1969): commemoration theory;

12. E.E. Evans-Prichard, "The Meaning of Sacrifice among the Nuer" (1954): substitution theory;
13. W. Burkert, excerpt from *Homo Necans* (1972/1983): hunting theory;
14. R. Girard, excerpt from *Violence and the Sacred* (1972/1977): scapegoat theory;
15. J. van Baal, "Offering, Sacrifice and Gift" (1976): communication theory;
16. V. Turner, excerpt from "Sacrifice as Quintessential Process: Prophylaxis or Abandonment" (1977): transformation theory;
17. L. de Heusch, excerpt from *Sacrifice in Africa* (1985): structuralist or relations theory;
18. V. Valeri, excerpt from *Kingship and Sacrifice* (1985): representational theory;
19. J.Z. Smith, "The Domestication of Sacrifice" (1987): elaboration or domestication theory;
20. R. Daly, "The Power of Sacrifice in Ancient Judaism and Christianity" (1990): Christian theological understanding of sacrifice;
21. B. Lincoln, "Debreasting, Disarming, Beheading: Some Sacrificial Practices of the Scyths and Amazons" (1991): ideology theory;
22. N. Jay, excerpt from *Throughout Your Generations Forever: Sacrifice, Religion and Paternity* (1992): descent theory;
23. W. Beers, excerpt from *Women and Sacrifice: Male Narcissism and the Psychology of Religion* (1992): narcissism theory;
24. M. Bloch, excerpt from *Prey into Hunter: The Politics of Religious Experience* (1992): violence theory; and
25. J.D. Levenson, excerpt from *The Death and Resurrection of the Beloved Son* (1993): obligation theory.

In the third and final section of this anthology is a short postscript addressing the question of why understanding sacrifice is controversial and why there has been such little common understanding when it comes to sacrifice (pp. 11 and 449). According to the author, there are several answers to this inquiry. First, the sheer complexity of sacrifice and the associated cultures and eras in which it has taken place makes it very difficult to organize everything under a common theoretical rubric (p. 449). A second reason is the fact that different researchers begin with different assumptions about the nature of religion (p. 450). A third factor, according to the author, contributing to the diversity of sacrificial theories springs from a widespread notion that religious systems are comprised of symbolic elements; that phenomenological forms gain their force from their "meaning" (p. 450). Finally, according to Carter, understanding sacrifice is controversial because it is possible to select and emphasize a single aspect of sacrificial phenomena and build from it an interpretation or explanation of sacrifice in its entirety (p. 450).

As this anthology so well illustrates, different authors can focus on different aspects of religious sacrifice, and different understandings will result (p. 451). Several of the essays incorporated in this work address some of the topics in *Blood Sacrifices* such as violent non-state actors, dark magico-religious activities and the use of drugs/narcotics in rituals. For example, the Dutch anthropologist Jan Van Baal in his essay "Offering, Sacrifice and Gift," argues that "gift-giving in all its religious manifestations can be understood as a particularly effective means of communication with the universe. In this way, sacrifice is a way for human beings to communicate with the divine realm. Destroying the sacrificial victim, killing it, eliminating its material presence, provides an unshakable factuality to the ritual event. It marks the reality of the communication" (p. 277). In another essay, written by the French anthropologist Maurice Block from his book *Prey into Hunter: The Politics of Religious Experience* (1992), the author argues that sacrifice could be understood as an integral component of the "violence theory" of sacrifice. Block sees violence as an inevitable product of social life. It is an integral part of the human attempt to create and maintain the social order, in particular the sense of transcendence, permanence, and truth such order requires (p. 397). Gangs in Mexico, Brazil, and some African nations are well known for utilizing violence as a means to maintain social order in a chaotic environment where the rule of law is nonexistent or the State is no longer the viable enforcer of the rule of law. When gangs or organized crime elements use religious sacrifice as part of their effort to enforce their views or values through the sacrifice ceremony, it becomes part of "magic theory" of sacrifice (p. 79). In an excerpt from James George Frazer's *The Golden Bough: A Study in Magic and Religion,* the reader is exposed to this "magic theory" of sacrifice, a viable theoretical model that can explain a great deal of sacrificial phenomena (p. 79). This chapter by James George Frazer fits nicely with our discussion in this work regarding magico-religious activities where these are "offerings or actions that involve severe and grievous acts that are criminal in nature and directed at human beings to provide magico-religious benefit to the perpetrators" as well the community as a whole.[2]

I highly recommend *Understanding Religious Sacrifice*. This anthology provides students and researchers of religious sacrifice and violent non-state actors with important concepts such as the origin of religion, totemism, magic, symbolism, violence, structuralism, and ritual performance. Students and researchers of comparative religious studies, ritual studies, history of religions, sociology, anthropology, and radicalism studies will benefit from Carter's historical organization, chronology, and thematic analyses presented in this anthology. In the final analysis, Carter's *Understanding Religious Sacrifice* is a refutation to the securalization thesis. According to this thesis, religion would wilt before the juggernauts of modern world.[3] But instead, we are witnessing religion and its ramifications becoming even more important in the globalized world of the twenty-first century. As pointed out by Toft, Philpott and Shah, "religious terrorism is a global phenomenon in which global dynamics and local issues are interlinked. Whereas most religious terrorism was conducted locally, today there exists a vast network of local groups with global ties that share ideas, resources, and personnel to wage their terrorist campaigns."[4] In conclusion, the post-industrial world of the twenty-first century, God's presence is even more important than ever. In the words of Toft, Philpott and Shah, "God's partisans are back, they are setting the political agenda, and they are not going away. This is what makes the present century God's Century."[5]

Notes

[1]   Hans Magnus Enzensberger, "The Resurgence of Human Sacrifice," *Society* 39. March-April 2007: 75-77.

[2]   Robert J. Bunker, "Introduction: Blood Sacrifices" in this work.

[3]   Monica Duffy Toft, Daniel Philpott, and Timothy Samuel Shah, *God's Century: Resurgent Religion and Global Politics*. New York: W.W. Norton and Company, 2011: 1.

[4]   Ibid: 122.

[5]   Ibid: 207.

Chapter 10

REVIEW OF *ON SACRIFICE*

Mark Safranski

Moshe Halbertal, *On Sacrifice*. Princeton: Princeton University Press, 2012; 152 pages. $25.95.

> And God said "Take your son, your only son Isaac, whom you love, and go to the land of Moriah, and offer him there as a burnt offering on one of the mountains of which I shall tell you."
>
> Genesis 22:2

When Bronze age man gazed at the heavens and imagined he saw there the rulers of his fate, the mysterious and all-powerful gods, he sought communion and relationship with them through a gesture of propitiation: the sacrifice. This monumental act wielded such totemic cultural power that sacrifice remained central to monotheism when it emerged, first literally, later symbolically, and finally secularized for its own purposes by the State, modernity's jealous rival to ancient faith. In *On Sacrifice*, Moshe Halbertal, Professor of Jewish Thought and Philosophy at Hebrew University, cautions us that while sacrifice is "an essential phenomenon," if appropriated by the State as "the sole locus of self-transcendence," the state risks becoming "a false idol."

In *On Sacrifice*, Halbertal has crafted a concise but profound examination of the role of sacrifice in six thousand years of religious and temporal affairs, including an explanatory model of political violence that is rooted in an understanding of the *Torah* and classical works of Western political philosophy. In just 114 pages of text, Halbertal wrestles with such prodigiously diverse topics as the role of sacrificial blood in atonement rituals, the reversal of God's position in charity, the limits of just war theory, the appeal of suicide bombers, Saint Augustine's teleology, and the State as the supreme altar of Moloch. Though not without flaws, *On Sacrifice* is an intellectual delight.

Halbertal divides his text into two parts, that which encompasses "Sacrificing *to*" and that which entails "Sacrificing *for*"; a division that emphasizes the differences and continuity of sacrifice in the realms of the sacred and the secular. The elimination and replacement of thousands of years of ritual animal sacrifice in monotheist religion with substitutionary practices was, in Halbertal's judgement, "a cataclysmic moment" in Western civilization. This now distant theological moment continues to shape modern societal mediation of violence and the "self-transcendence" of constructing and adhering to a moral and political order.

It is in *Genesis* and not in the rich history of the preceding eon of pagan religions that Halbertal makes the starting point for the role of sacrifice in the Western mind. In the story of Cain and Abel, sacrifice's "foundational moment" is twice cemented in innocent blood; first, that of Abel's sheep offered up to God and then the blood of Abel himself, spilled by his brother Cain. In rejecting Cain's offering of fruits, God's preference for blood sacrifice established the tie between sacrifice and violence. Here we see God in His Old Testament incarnation as a jealous, enigmatic, wrathful, tribal deity, harshly laying down His expectation of worshippers. The cause of Cain's rejection is itself, as Halbertal tells us, a "mystery", but the humiliation and rage at his exclusion from a relationship with God inspired Cain to slaughter Abel and thereafter be forever accursed.

From this biblical story and other passages, Halbertal draws forth the many distinct nuances and purposes entailed in "Sacrificing *to*": gift, offering, rejection, ritual, atonement and substitution. These, in turn, are intertwined in layers of theological ambiguity, as Halbertal writes:

> The inherent potential for rejection in the sacrificial act is manifested in the Hebrew term for the offering: *minchah*. In later priestly literature, this word was used to denote a subset of offerings—that is, vegetative offerings. Animal offerings were

designated by the term *korban*. Yet Genesis doesn't distinguish between the two kinds of sacrifices. Abel's offering from his flock and Cain's offering from his fruits are both called *minchah*. The term *minchah* is related to the verb *lehaniach*, which means to lay down or put before. The term *korban* is related to the verb *lekarev*, meaning to bring forward, approach or move closer [p. 9].

Halbertal's linguistic inference here is that blood sacrifice (*korban*) moved primitive man closer to God by being pleasing to Him for that purpose in a manner that other offerings (*minchah*) were not. This is a very reasonable inference, but it does not tell us why this should be so. The biblical text is "silent" here, as Halbertal freely admits. Cain and Abel approached God with uncertainty, neither knew beforehand whether their offering would be acceptable.. After Cain's example, mankind would approach sacrifices with even greater anxiety. In any gift-exchange cycles, gifts may be, as Halbertal tells us, refused by the recipient, short-circuiting a relationship before it can begin. Rejection of the sacrificial gift by God is the most consequential refusal of all.

More directly, was God's utterly terrifying commandment to Abraham to sacrifice his son Isaac, testing Abraham's faith and fitness for upholding His covenant, Isaac only being spared at the last possible moment. Pleased with Abraham's faith, God provided Abraham a ram as a substitute sacrifice to take the place of Isaac and further bestowed upon Abraham a remarkable promise:

And the angel of the Lord called to Abraham a second time from heaven and said, "By myself I have sworn, declares the Lord, because you have done this and have not withheld your son, your only son, I will surely bless you, and I will surely multiply your offspring as the stars of heaven and as the sand that is on the seashore. And your offspring shall possess the gate of his enemies, and in your offspring shall all the nations of the earth be blessed, because you have obeyed my voice."[1]

Halbertal makes a number of important arguments regarding sacrifice from these biblical examples as well as those of Hannah and Jacob. The first is that a sacrifice is a gift within a specific hierarchical context where the supplicant (the worshipper) cannot possibly stand on an equal footing with the recipient (God) to whom the normal gift-cycle ethical obligations do not apply, which makes the gift really an "offering" at risk of being rejected. This risk is lowered, along with the anxiety of the giver, by making the offering only through a prescribed ritual, the formula for which acts as a legal "shield" for the believer to approach God. As Halbertal writes:

> *Ritual is thus a protocol that protects from the risk of rejection.* In that respect, ritual is analogous to legal systems as a whole insofar as they impose order while confronting the unreliability and capriciousness of emotional responses.... Any change in the protocol might be lethal, like walking in a minefield [p. 15].

[emphasis in original]

The ritualization of sacrifice takes on, in Halbertal's view, a "magical reading" that gives the act of sacrifice the causal power to ensure success and ward off disaster.

The role of substitutes, a ram in the case of Isaac, in sacrifice relate to the purpose of sacrifice—atonement for sin—as well as demonstrating the cultural evolutionary path "sacrificing *to*" undertaken in monotheism. This is particularly the case in the transition from Temple to rabbinical Judaism when the destruction of the second Temple rendered it impossible for Jews to perform the prescribed rites of animal sacrifice. This required a theological migration by Jewish communities to other religious actions than burnt offerings to fulfill the act of sacrifice and secure atonement. For Christians, the transformation away from animal sacrifice ritual was even more radical as Jesus Christ assumed in Himself the role of substitute and the position of Melchizedek high priest in an act of eternal sacrifice.[2]

Halbertal explores the substitutes for animal sacrifice, notably charity, afflictions, suffering, prayer and martyrdom—the last also a bridge to the modern "sacrificing *for*" of the secular nation-state and the state's intrinsic predisposition for warfare and political violence. In seeking substitution for animal sacrifice, Halbertal postulates these things were forms of "offering" and often had the power to reverse the hierarchy that mandated sacrifice in the first place, writing:

> Charity is preferred over sacrifice because it erases the abyss
> between giving and receiving without recourse to ritual, which
> minimizes individuation. What is more, this way of giving
> reverses the hierarchical order implied in offering the sacrifice;
> charity reverses God's position from lender to borrower [p. 41].

The act of martyrdom, self-sacrifice, however was generally not obligatory in Halbertal's reading of Talmudic sources, except in one instance that has grave implications for modernity, the worship of false idols. On that score, any attempt to coerce public idolatry must be met with determined resistance, even over the most minor manifestations, to the point of martyrdom. The idea of Jewish martyrdom, as a "sacrifice *to*" God was borrowed from the early Christians, who shared with the Jews the same persecutors, the Romans; but this opens the gates, Halbertal explains, to "sacrificing *for*"—meaning "sacrifice can thus be expanded from the religious realm….to the ethical and political realm".

To Halbertal, the core of "Sacrificing *for*" is "giving up for the sake of," a moral ideal that permits or makes possible self-transcendence. In the modern age, this typically (though not always) means the morality that supports the construction of the political order and the existence of the state. Inevitably, this involves justly mediating self-interest, political violence, and especially war. Here, sacrifice—removed from its religious context and entangled with the roots of the political order and the survival of the state—creates, in Halbertal's view, dangerous moral hazards and lethal outcomes.

The discussion of the relationship between sacrifice and violence begins initially in section one, where Halbertal explains and rejects the contention of Rene Girard that violence has an accelerating, uncontrolled nature with an escalatory dynamic driven by retaliation; a cycle that can only be broken by a correctly situated sacrifice to appease one of the belligerents. Girard's view of the escalatory logic of violence and its possible cessation are largely in sync with those articulated by Clausewitz.[3] Halbertal's alternate theory that rejection of a sacrificial offering or "exclusion from the possibility of giving is a deeper source of violence than the deprivation that results from not getting" is well worth considering as an aggravating factor or driver of violence. It would certainly be useful in relating sacrifice to the specific phenomena of civil war, which replicates the fratricidal conflict of Cain and Abel which inspired Halbertal, but not as a general replacement for Girard's Clausewitzian logic.

More problematic, though extremely intriguing, are Halbertal's contentions regarding sacrifice, war, morality, and international law. His most interesting argument, and one which can find ample empirical support in military history, is that sacrifice can augment the will to power to wage war. Halbertal writes:

> What I want to claim in establishing the connection between sacrifice and violence is that war is not embarked on despite the risk and sacrifice that it involves; it is strengthened and motivated by this aspect. There is, in other words, a deep internal (and not accidental) connection between killing and self-sacrifice [p. 68].

Halbertal argues that several psychological reversals of the sacrifice paradigm are involved in rationalizing the justification for violence or war provided by sacrifice. The first is that valorous self-sacrifice sanctifies the cause for which the war is fought. The second, more sinister, reversal has the aggressor adopting the mantle of self-sacrificing victim and projects their guilt on to the target of their violence, thus escalating and justifying future violence. Halbertal's theory is probably sound, as sacrificial rhetoric has been a staple of western warfare since at least Pericles' funeral oration and it neatly serves the purpose of sustaining the "moral distance" that soldiers require to kill more efficiently and with less psychological distress on the battlefield.[4]

The arguments Halbertal makes regarding morality and the laws of war are, in light of contemporary conflicts, even more important, but withstand strict scrutiny less well. Drawing very heavily from just war theory, Halbertal takes an absolutist moral and legal position on the exclusion of civilians from armed conflicts both as participants and as lawful military targets; or as he declared:

> Civilians may not be targeted even if they belong to the aggressor's state that initiated an unjust war, and they cannot participate in fighting even if they are fighting against an unjust aggressor [p. 80].

To the extent this has ever really been the case, it has not been so to this degree for a century, and then only briefly during the fighting on the Western Front where the Allies and the Central Powers generally held to the strictures of the Hague Convention.[5] Not before nor again afterward was this the case, certainly not in the past half century when irregular conflicts, insurgency, civil wars, and terrorism have become the most frequent tactical expressions of warfare. International law has followed suit, carving out exceptions for spontaneous rising or *levee en masse* of civilians, granting temporary protections for suspected unlawful combatants and for organized groups under the Third Geneva Convention. When this is coupled with the general reluctance of states to punish perfidy and acceptance of collateral damage to civilians under the principle of proportionality, the absolute prohibitions assumed by Halbertal are really more rules of thumb or legally blurred starting points from which many exceptions have been whittled.[6]

With admirable candor, Halbertal admits that he does not think it is possible for a symmetrical right of self-defense to exist, that soldiers fighting for an unjust cause, even if scrupulously correct personally in terms of *jus in bello*, remain "presumably criminals" with only a duty to disarm and stand down. While this is a provocative theory, it is ahistorical as well as unworkable and likely counterproductive in practice to the very moral ends Halbertal might consider good. The Laws of War draw on just war theory and Grotius, but only in part. Pragmatism, based upon customary reciprocity between belligerents, benevolent neutrals, historical precedents like the Lieber Code, and international covenants are the foundation of large parts of international humanitarian law and their interpretation. Given that most sovereign states can make a reasonable legal argument in most conflicts that their waging of war is "self-defense" under the UN Charter, for states to act on the assumption that enemy soldiers are "presumably criminals" would de facto unravel all of the protections for combatants accepted in international law. In turn, there would then be little practical incentive beyond individual conscience for combatants to eschew atrocities against enemy civilians because, if captured, the soldier would already be regarded as a condemned criminal. In such a legal situation, where the only assurance of safety would lie in complete victory, the escalatory logic of violence would default to a democidal doctrine of "in for a penny, in for a pound".

Finally, that modern secular states have been dangerous stewards of the intrinsic power of "sacrificing *for*" and can assess but poorly the value of past sacrifices in guiding future conduct is something that Halbertal is at pains to stress:

> Yet in its binding and destructive power, a past sacrifice might work in the opposite direction. In such a reversal, it is not the case that something of value deserves sacrifice; rather it is the sacrifice that constitutes its intrinsic value and sacredness, by endowing it with that sort of ultimate meaning [p. 99].

This kind of power is easily mobilized in an unworthy cause and arguably, unworthy causes need to rely on such circular logic most to legitimize themselves. One thinks of elderly Russians bedecked with glittering medals from "the Great Patriotic War" against the Nazis, yet they fought for a homicidal regime that up until the moment of Operation Barbarossa, was busily engaged in torturing and executing its own citizens on an industrial scale. In *On Sacrifice*, Halbertal explicitly references Heinrich Himmler earlier in the text, and could as easily have been writing of Himmler's Japanese allies, with their kamikazes, death marches, hari-kiri rituals, and banzai shouts of "ten thousand years" for the Emperor when he called the state an "altar of Moloch" and "a false idol". The centralized state has brazenly usurped the ancient prerogatives of Yahweh for sacrifice along with His jealousies and wrath.

Having identified so well the state's capacity to harness the resonant power of sacrifice—indeed, to require them in a river of blood—to erect political projects rooted in epochal violence, Halbertal's failure to entertain violent resistance to the state, except to dismiss its legitimacy, is the major flaw in an otherwise strong work. Most of the moral "reversals" of sacrificial logic that Halbertal details, where past sacrifices and honored martyrs justify or sacralize the state, apply in spades to violent non-state actors, especially religiously or ideologically motivated insurgencies. "Martyrology" and suicidal-sacrificial gestures have been used by insurgent groups as diverse as the IRA, Tamil Tigers, al Qaida, the radical Sikh Damdami Taksal, Lakshar-e Taiba, Tibetan Buddhists, Hezbollah, ISIS, HAMAS, FARC, and the Kurdish PKK. Lacking the tangible trappings of power that come with ruling a state, an honor roll of martyrs becomes a macabre psychological talisman to reinforce group solidarity and attract new followers.

Furthermore, by eschewing examination of how sacrifice applies to violent non-state actors, Halbertal missed an opportunity to examine the nexus point where "sacrificing to" becomes or coexists with "sacrificing for". The Nazis, in their rise to power, were consumed with mobilizing the ascetic power of blood sacrifice in mass politics:

> Not far removed from apocalypse and conflagration was another element in Hitler's imagery, blood. Blood meant, of course, race, but it also meant battle and killing. The National Socialist party itself was drenched in blood. Literally, it was spilled in the 1923 putsch attempt and the street battles of the early years, in the Rohm Purge and the slaughter of war. The concept fascinated him, and he referred to it again and again in *Mein Kampf* and his speeches with such expressions as 'aryan blood', 'the infection of impure blood', 'a nation's blood-worth', 'blood ownership', 'blood and soil', 'blood-guilt', 'heroes blood', 'blood-witness', 'the blood-martyrs of the movement'.[7]

Once in power, Hitler and the Nazis institutionalized their fetish for martyrdom and sacrifice with honor temples, cenotaphs, songs, oaths, and torchlit rituals that indicated that martyred Nazis were not merely sacrifices *for* but *to* Germany. This raises an interesting question for modern terrorist groups like HAMAS, which make a complex propaganda cult of "shahids" who have died in their suicide-bombing attacks and the context of the retention of animal sacrifice in Islam as a rite of thanksgiving and celebration; are these "shahids" sacrificing themselves *for* Islam and Allah or *to* Him in their action? Both? Neither? Are suicide-bombings as sacrifice politically or religiously attractive to their intended audience and therefore an effective tool for insurgency or are they regarded as abhorrent?

On Sacrifice challenges the reader to consider the power of the primordial ritual, the sacrifice—and how its power has been expressed throughout Western civilization. While literal animal sacrifice in blood has long been eclipsed by recourse to other symbolic substitutes, the necessity of sacrifice to society or its cultural potency have not. If anything, the power of sacrifice in "sacrificing for" in the hands of bureaucrats and politicians has rendered that "the modern state's appetite for human sacrifice is insatiable." Instead of staying the anger of a demanding deity as "sacrificing to" once did, "sacrificing for" in the modern state context delivers not atonement, but a "vengeful eruption of political violence."

Notes

[1]   Genesis, 22:15-18, https://www.biblegateway.com/passage/?search= Genesis+22%3A1-19&version=ESV.

[2]   James Swetnam, "The Sacrifice of Isaac in Genesis and Hebrews: A Study in the Hermeneutic of Faith," *Letter & Spirit* 1. 2005: 33.

[3]   Carl von Clausewitz, *On War*. Michael Howard and Peter Paret, Ed., and Trans. Princeton: Princeton University Press, 1976: 85-86, 700-703.

[4]   David Grossman, *On Killing: The Psychological Costs of Learning to Kill in War and Society*. New York: Back Bay Books, 2009: 36; http:// kropfpolisci.com/cognitive.grossman.pdf.

[5]   "Convention (III) relative to the Treatment of Prisoners of War. Geneva, 12 August 1949." International Committee of the Red Cross, https://www.icrc.org/applic/ihl/ihl.nsf/Article.xsp?action=openDocument &documentId=2F681B08868538C2C12563CD0051AA8D.

[6]   "Customary IHL." International Committee of the Red Cross, https:// www.icrc.org/customary-ihl/eng/docs/v2_rul_rule14.

[7]   Frederic Spotts. *Hitler and the Power of Aesthetics*. New York: The Overlook Press, 2002: 114.

Chapter 11

REVIEW OF *MAGIC AND WARFARE*

Alma Keshavarz

Nathalie Wlodarczyk, *Magic and Warfare: Appearance and Reality in Contemporary African Conflict and Beyond.* New York: Palgrave Macmillan, 2009; 208 pages. $89.46.

In *Magic and Warfare,* Nathalie Wlodarczyk explores the challenges of the post-Cold War era associated with the emerging crises in the developing world. Specifically, Africa in its entirety became a case study among academics who shifted their focus towards a new phenomenon occurring in the region: the use of magic in warfare. The shift began with the violent civil war in Sierra Leone in 1991 and ended in 2002. The violence and proxy wars that were erupting across the continent appeared to be a signal to a "return to primitive tribal wars."[1] The 'primitive' tactics employed were a kind of military technology by VNSAs in the region with the notion that bulletproof bodies were "an inventive tool."[2] For instance, fighters in Liberia and Sierra Leone believed they were immune to bullets, which was attributed to rituals done during an initiation period to prepare for battle. Wlodarczyk also references the Lord's Resistance Army (LRA) in Uganda and their leader, Joseph Kony, who offered protection and direction as a surrogate for the Holy Spirit. The events occurring across Africa were challenging the traditional understanding of strategy and decision-making in warfare. There was something else happening which could not be easily explained within the conventional academic framework.

The author explains that there were two prominent arguments used to analyze the warfare strategies employed by VNSAs in Africa.

The first claimed that the African states were returning to a "violent tribal past after the civilizing influence of both colonialism and super power domination had been removed."[3] This explanation coincides with global environmental deprivation, expanding population levels in Africa, and an increasing economic divide being felt. As a result of these degradations and resource scarcities people will resort to warfare. The second interpretation believed that there was a rational motivation to the violence. This attempt relied less on "deterministic explanations of economic marginalization, changing interstate power-relations, reemerging political grievances and entrepreneurial criminal activity" and more on the traditional realities of seizing power via the gun.[4] However, both arguments failed to explain the role of "magic" as such. This review will define the term magic in African warfare, according to Wlodarczyk, and explain the process in which it was utilized to devise a military strategy. The Kamajor society in Sierra Leone is the focal point of the book used to explain how supernatural rituals are put to use on the battlefield.

Structure and Use of 'Magic'

Wlodarczyk argues that the role of magic must be analyzed within the context of African warfare to interpret its origins and its use. Magic has a function during initiation in preparation for battle as well as having an influence on fighters' behavior on the battlefield. Wlodarczyk notes that this type of warfare has been examined in the genre of anthropology, but the realm of international relations and strategic studies have largely avoided it. Thus, this book aims to show the link between spiritual beliefs and military strategies. In studying the return of the supernatural as practiced in warfare, albeit outside the realm of current strategic studies, it helps guide the analysis of how some VNSAs are influenced.

The term magic has come to have a number of definitions. Therefore, language has a role in studying the ontology of African warfare. The terminology is important within the context in which it is used. In the African context, the author believes that magic is intertwined with traditional religion. It "denotes a *practice,* informed by beliefs in a supernatural world, which invokes power to achieve a desired end without constraints imposed by strict doctrine or the assumed moral imperative of the source of power itself."[5] Therefore, magic has three functions: the beliefs (1) offer an existential service; (2) explain misfortune; and (3) through practice, offer a means of redress for perceived ills and can act as a strain for societal tensions.[6] These functions denote that power and supernatural activities are connected to the social and political environment with the underlying assumption that this kind of belief system is associated with the domain of the supernatural world.

According to Wlodarczyk, in many parts of Africa VNSAs utilized magic to recruit and train men for battle. The Zimbabwe African National Liberation Army (ZANLA) used spirit mediums for warfare. There was what Wlodarczyk calls a "spiritual order" that followed with this understanding of the use of mediums. Mediums had replaced the traditional authority, representing the "spirits of deceased chiefs (mhondoro)."[7] In Mozambique, the Resistência Nacional Moçambicana (Renamo) used "spiritual rhetoric" to focus on the complaint of the rural population, which was primarily resentment of government. The Frelimo's (Frente de Libertaçáo de Moçambique), rejected traditional religion altogether, censuring mediums and healers, while the Renamo radically embraced them. Later, the Naprama emulated the Renamo practices but more heavily emphasized traditional religious institutions.

Each of these movements have a hierarchy and structure for recruitment. The LRA, for instance, sprayed holy water on recruits as well as coating their bodies with shea-butter oil and white ashes. The actual initiation transforms into something more radical, which occasionally included murdering one or more fellow recruits. It is a form of intimidation meant to show recruits life on the battlefield. In the Renamo, fighters would drink a combination of goat's blood and herbal medicine prepared by a "witchdoctor" for immunity. The National Patriotic Front of Liberia (NFPL) would tattoo fighters or would cut them to allow them to become invulnerable to bullets. Blanks would be fired at recruits to prove the ritual 'works.' These were all meant to convince fighters that the rituals were successful and that they were indeed immune.[8] Some practices, however, were also meant to serve as intimidation against opposing force fighters. In Liberia and the Democratic Republic of Congo, cannibalism was reported to have occurred. Fighters would typically ingest the heart or liver of an enemy, though other body parts were not exempt, or partake in ritual killings. The Kamajors from Sierra Leone, which is the primary focus of this book, were involved in the practice of cannibalism in that consuming the heart of a strong man would transfer their power while also intimidating witnesses of the act. The function of magic in warfare is more than just mysticism; groups inculcate principles of violence that are embedded within rituals and initiation practices.

The Kamajor Society

The author borrows French sociologist Pierre Bourdieu's theory of practice to explain how magic fits within the mold of warfare. His theory "revolves around the mutually constitutive relationship of what he calls *habitus, field, capital,* and *power* to form *interests* and *strategies* and to create particular practices."[9] As the author suggests, in order to understand the role of magic in strategy and behavior, we must first understand how "rationality and logic" fit within the traditional context of warfare and apply that reasoning to African warfare. Hoffman (2011) cites James Siegal, who wrote "the power of magic...is a performance power. It is the power to make something true by saying particular words, those at least sometimes are thought to create truths via their enunciation."[10] The Kamajors were motivated by this supernatural power and practiced rituals to prepare for battle and protect their territory. They believed in the words of those conducting the rituals and put those words into practice once on the battlefield.

Yet, this is outside the scope of traditional military and strategic studies. Strategy, as we know it, is the practice of a rational procedure to implement a course of action for a desired outcome. Therefore, according to the author, we must understand the "ideological" principles of those who utilize magic as a warfare strategy. For instance, the Kamajors in Sierra Leone, the Holy Spirit Movements in northern Uganda, or the Renamo in Mozambique held immunization practices that would protect fighters from bullets. Ultimately, the rituals were meant to convince the fighters that they were immune, that they may be more willing to enter into battle. Wlodarczyk infers that the immunization practice before battle is the interplay between Bourdieu's habitus of the Kamajors, which integrates belief in the supernatural, the capital of "spiritual knowledge" and power required to stimulate the ritual to produce the desired end, and finally, the field of armed conflict. All of these elements revolve around the principle of spiritual power and applied towards a strategy.

Origins

The Kamajors, a name which translates to "hunter" in Mende, originated around 1995. Originally, the Kamajors were in southeastern Sierra Leone, protecting their community from wild animals. The society's formation was based on traditional herbalists and Qu'ranic scholars from Bunthe District, who gathered to bolster the power of local defense through their crafts and rituals.[11] Most importantly, they relied considerably on supernatural beliefs. The Kamajors became the largest and most well known civil defense group in Sierra Leone. While the Kamajors were recognized as a secret society, the Civil Defense Forces (CDF) were a fighting force officially authorized by the government. What set them apart was the Kamajor's reliance on tradition from the Mende south and east of Sierra Leone and, through initiation practices, recruits formed a bond or a sense of loyalty.

The "multireligious society" of Sierra Leone is worthy of interest. The country consists of both Christians and Muslims, of which the majority of the population is the latter. Given the higher proportion of Muslims to Christians and traditional use of Qu'ranic verses in rituals, Islam in its purest form does not have a direct influence on the Kamajor society and its practices. However, some Islamic beliefs and practices are analogous to traditional Mende beliefs.[12] As Wlodarczyk explains, secret societies incorporate religion with traditional rituals. For instance, the Mende have what are called 'medicine-men,' which is similar to the Islamic 'mori-men.' The main difference between these two, according to Mbogani (2013) is while the medicine-men are herbalists in the Mende rituals, the mori-men of the Islamic tradition follow a strict interpretation of Qu'ranic verses.

Rituals

The traditional Kamajor were highly skilled and knowledgeable of their environment, which made them excellent hunters. The power of knowledge, associated with Mende cosmology is the basis of Kamajor society power. The Kamajor fighters were suited for defense and warcraft. Young men were particularly drawn to mythical supernatural powers afforded by the Kamajor society at the height of the Sierra Leone civil war as well as the grandeur of the Kamajor namesake. The rituals and practices of the Kamajor society were then applied to war. Though not all men sought to join the Kamajors, the majority did. The author offers four main reasons for enlistment: (1) pride in helping to provide community defense; (2) extension of Mende tradition of waging war through secret societies; (3) protection and receipt of powers of immunity; and (4) being a member became 'trendy' among young Mende men to get the attention and respect of women.[13] To become a Kamajor, prospects must be nominated by the community and be vetted by the local chief. This process is necessary to ensure that the recruit has never been affiliated with the Revolutionary United Front (RUF) or Sierra Leone Army (SLA), and must not have a criminal record. This custom later changed as the traditional system eroded and violence became more prevalent.

Additionally, the initiation process is kept secret, making it hard to verify, but it is known to merge some spiritual beliefs from the Poro and Bondo societies and mori-magic. Supernatural entities and powers are a staple of the Mende tradition and the rituals are very much necessary to the overall practice of initiation. Ultimately, the Mende people depend on the guidance and support of supernatural entities.[14] Recruits are meant to forge a bond with the society during initiation. Therefore, it will motivate the recruits as fighters, instilling a sense of fearlessness. The Kamajors used their own blood rituals to establish a strong bond and commitment between fighters, a stark contrast to the RUF in which fighters were coerced to join and involved in public killings of fellow prospects or even civilians. The initiation process is meant to imbue a strong sense of commitment among fighters, maintaining strength and the belief in immunity while on the battlefield.

The mixture of a powerful belief system and the use of herbal potions in rituals formulated the basis of the use of magic by the Kamajor in battle. As mentioned earlier, the Kamajor tradition was later altered. For instance, acts of cannibalism and ritual killings have been recorded. The Yamorto Squad, which was a part of the larger Kamajor group, killed their enemies, dismembered, and cooked them, all while others watched. This was not only a part of the belief that ingesting the body parts of a strong man will transfer some of his strength and power but it was also an intimidation tactic employed by this group.

Conclusion

The style of fighting in battle in Africa has left many perplexed. They appear unorganized and inept in the use of weaponry. However, there is a purpose. Firing weapons is not meant to kill enemies specifically but to show, through loud weapons and rapid firing of ammunition, the power of their arsenal and fighting unit which would result in the desired strategic outcome of enemy retreat rather than a pitched battle. The author offers the example of the Kamajor attack on Koribundu in February 1998. The Kamajors initiated an assault but were greeted with heavy resistance from the Armed Forces Revolutionary Council (AFRC) and RUF, ultimately retreating after a short ten minutes of fighting.[15] However, the AFRC and RUF abandoned their territory the next night, purportedly to tend to a crisis occurring in Freetown stemming from the threat of potentially losing the city to the Economic Community of West African States Monitoring Group, or "ECOMOG." As a result the Kamajor viewed their initial tactical defeat in battle as meaningless because the nighttime AFRC and RUF withdraw from Koribundu ultimately provided them with a strategic victory. Rationalization of victories such as this, counterintuitive to Western military logic, portray the Kamajor's strong belief in the supernatural and its underlying influence on their style and manner of battle tactics. But, as Wlodarczyk notes, it is not clear whether this influence was "positive or negative" with respect to what we understand as success in traditional warfare. The fighters approach to battle stems from their belief in the immunization during the initiation rituals. Fighters are convinced that they are protected and immune from enemy fire. The goal is to "out-perform" the enemy rather than kill as many of them as possible. The bond forged by fighters through the rituals essentially created a mystical environment on the battlefield where magic and ritual was believed to facilitate military success. Fighters were not only motivated, but also believed they were intimidating their enemies. In other words, the magic aids the military success of the group.

Certainly, this is outside of the scope of traditional strategic studies. Cosmology and ritual practices in African warfare were the force guiding strategy and tactical decisions. To the Kamajor, and other VNSAs in Africa, belief in the supernatural and the rituals associated with initiation in many ways were effective in combat. They believed they were immune to enemy fire and were bound by a strong affinity for each other. *Magic and Warfare* immediately captures the reader's interest by suggesting the term magic is multi-faceted. The Kamajor case study puts the concept of supernatural rituals within the wider context of strategic decision-making in warfare. Though not widely studied in traditional international relations, it could prove useful to gain knowledge of enemy tactics precisely due to the growing use of supernatural tactics.

Notes

[1]   Nathalie Wlodarczyk, *Magic and Warfare: Appearance and Reality in Contemporary African Conflict and Beyond.* New York: Palgrave Macmillan, 2009: 2.

[2]   Danny Hoffman, *The War Machines: Young Men and Violence in Sierra Leone and Liberia.* Durham: Duke University Press, 2011: 227.

[3]   Nathalie Wlodarczyk: 3.

[4]   Ibid.

[5]   Ibid: 18.

[6]   Ibid: 19.

[7]   Ibid: 31.

[8]   Logical inconsistencies exist concerning the leaders of paramilitary units who realize that 'bullet immunity' and other forms of magical protection is a sham and thus fire blanks at their fighters. Debates exist concerning whether the rituals and dark magic they draw upon is fully believed by the new recruits or if the recruits themselves are so terrified by these leaders that they simply play along with this spiritual charade in order not to be killed. In the specific case of former Lord's Resistance Army (LRA) members a number have later stated that they did not believe in the group's spirituality but if they had said anything they would be summarily executed.

[9]   Nathalie Wlodarczyk: 46.

[10]   Danny Hoffman: 228.

[11]   Ibid: 62.

[12]   Lawrence E.Y. Mbogoni. *Human Sacrifices and the Supernatural in African History.* Tanzania: Mkuki na Nyota Publishers, 2013: 47.

[13]   Nathalie Wlodarczyk: 98.

[14]   Lawrence E.Y. Mbogoni: 45.

[15]   Nathalie Wlodarczyk: 119.

Postscript

RELIGION, WAR, AND BLOOD SACRIFICE

Pauletta Otis

This book takes on the complex subjects of religion, blood, and sacrifice—not in an effort to "explain everything" but to identify, characterize, and analyze a form of violence that has been traditionally overlooked. The case studies and comparative work were delimited to groups that are contemporary violent non-state actors (VNSAs), which promote radical social change, have some emphasis on eschatology, tend to use chemical substances to change body/mind balance, and seem out of the realm of "rational actors." The authors cross traditional academic disciplines and represent scholars, academics, and practitioners who truly think "out of the box," i.e. are synthetic in that they can pull from many explanatory frameworks. The very nature of the groups, the seemingly irrational behaviors, and the increasing number of victims calls for creative interdisciplinary thinking, solid information and analysis, and suggestions as to appropriate and effective countermeasures. This is simply a case of where the world has given us a really tough and extremely sinister problem and we need solutions.

Basic Query and Assumptions

The basic query of the book is 'Why do some groups use blood sacrifices that are criminal in nature and morally reprehensible to somehow cause, propel, or elicit social change?' When does the related violence tend to implode (e.g. become internal to the group) and when does it tend to explode (e.g. violence towards others)? The relevance of either internal or externally focused violence is not solely academic: anyone involved in responding to these situations—police, first responders, firefighters, medical personnel, or local inhabitants—need answers. Furthermore, the seeming contemporary growth in size and scope of these groups clustered in Mexico and other parts of Latin America, Western Africa, Iraq and Syria, as well as Afghanistan and Pakistan and now into Libya mandates that international law enforcement and military services are able to predict, prevent, and prevail over the destructive force of these activities.

The authors of this book have relied on certain basic assumptions. The first is simple: there is a reason that human beings do what they do. The authors also assume that the behavior of human groups is patterned, making analysis and even some degree of prediction possible, however remote it may seem. Groups displaying the same or similar *aberrant* behaviors, those not generally considered in the realm of predictable and patterned, present a unique challenge. The best way to study these groups and social behavior is through case studies and comparative analysis and the authors herein have done just that. This approach eliminates the idea that these groups represent psychopaths or sociopaths, as explained in Dawn Perlmutter's prefacing remarks, and instead places them in their appropriate cultural context. The book explicitly focuses on group behavior, patterns of hitherto unexplained violence, and suggestions for further study and analysis.

Cases and Comparative Analysis

Although the set of possible case studies identifies many such groups from historical and global reporting, the authors in this initial volume limit the case studies to contemporary groups. What becomes immediately apparent, by just viewing a sampling of the chapters in this work, is that the choices available put into stark relief the global scope of the problem:

- Marc Tyrrell offers a treatise on Type Two criminal magic as it relates to the Left Hand Path that exists in Western cosmology.
- Robert Bunker highlights material from the Americas related to the Mexican cartels and drug gangs and analyzes the narco saints, Santa Muerte, and related entities such as Aztec war gods.
- Lisa Campbell provides in depth case studies related to al Qaeda, the Islamic State, and Boko Haram and their radical Islamist (e.g.

old school Jihadi) belief systems that have devolved—at least in the case of the Islamic State—into blood cultist type behaviors.

- Tony Kail focuses on Afro-Caribbean spirituality—specifically Las Reglas de Kongo—and its appropriation by drug traffickers operating in the United States and in Mexico.
- Charles Cameron's chapter discusses cases from the Basque area, Rwanda, and Chile.
- Pamela Ligouri Bunker and Alma Keshavarz provide insights in their chapters into the Lord's Resistance Army and the Kamajors in Central Africa and Sierra Leone, respectively.

These book chapters are merely representative of the entire spectrum of bloody actors—other known groups in India, Indonesia, China, Peru, and the Pacific islands immediately come to mind as well.

A caution, however, is that the cases chosen might be seen to represent "the rest of the world," inadvertently leading the reader to conclude that *it's not really our problem*. However, the U.S. has not been immune to the reality of VNSAs—who can forget the Sun Dance, Scalp Dance, and Ghost Dance utilized by the Great Plains Indians of the mid-to-late 19th century meant to cleanse the individual, the tribe, and the world of evil doers. Historically, there is thus a rich body of work that arguably suggests that American indigenous peoples, the Ku Klux Klan, the Sicilian Mafia, the ethnically defined Tongs, and even certain urban street gangs all at some point offered bloody sacrifices, engaged in symbolic religious rituals, and used forms of violence not commensurate with "norms" of violence in the United States at that time. Contemporarily, there are other groups operating in the United States, such as cartel operatives and drug traffickers engaging in more extreme forms of Santa Muerte and Palo Mayombe worship, that sporadically engage in ritual killings as described in this volume. This should confirm that *it is our problem*.

Basic Theoretical Connections Between Religion, War, and Blood Sacrifice

Religion and war are about life and death. It follows that we should not be surprised that blood, inherent in religious concepts of the *sacra,* and the bloody violence of warfare are intricately linked in the human condition. Yet both religion and war concern themselves with life's meaning and preservation. Reconciling the ideas inherent therein with the conditions under which it is acceptable to take a life has been the challenge of philosophers and leaders throughout the history of mankind.

As the book's editor Dr. Robert J. Bunker suggests, the phenomenon of blood sacrifice has not been adequately addressed by psychologists, theologians, law enforcement, or the general public. Many authors have skirted the issue, ascribing esoteric reasons or avoiding it through academic obscurantism. Yet, the reality is that blood sacrifice is, and always has been, unsettling, disturbing, and even shocking. Perhaps it is because we want to believe that life has value and to destroy life flies in the face of such a noble perception.

The concept of blood sacrifice is not so far removed from our own experience. Most of the world's 37,500 religions have an association with blood and sacrifice in some form or another. The ideas of penance, obedience, and the symbolism of blood is in the first story in the Bible (and acknowledged by both Judaism and Islam as a teaching point about God and symbolic sacrifice.) Yet to recognize *symbolic* sacrifice is one thing whereas to see the pictures of *actual* sacrifice included in this book is discomfiting. The modern, civilized, and increasingly secular Western citizen believes that he or she is quite far from that reality.

That is NOT to say that these groups differ only in degrees of differentiation. We use blood as symbol, they use blood as symbol— therefore we are all the same. This is clearly *reducto ad absurdum.* We go from the known to the unknown in order to better understand these groups but, clearly, understanding a group's use of blood sacrifice is not the same as justifying their cruelty and wanton destruction in its name. The groups presented in this volume are clearly aberrational and socially destructive. They use blood and sacrifice concepts in ways that are "off the charts." Perhaps more information and analysis will contribute to appropriate countermeasures—in society, law enforcement, and religious communities.

Explanations

The contributors have described a number of groups and provided information and analysis pertaining to theory and the uniqueness of the groups they present. Why we, as individual human beings, seem to require symbolic sacrifice is unclear. What is more disturbing is that we do not have a clear idea of when blood sacrifices move from symbolic and practiced by individuals or small groups and turn outward to destroy the very societies of which they were a part.

The importance of this book is not only that it presents the phenomenon of blood sacrifice but that it has asked the very real and immediate questions of "Why now?" and "Under what conditions can identifiable steps be observed wherein relatively benign, socially constrained, and generally symbolic practices become something darker, using those beliefs and practices to sacrifice those around them?" Previous attempts at analysis and explanation of the genesis of these groups seems to variously fall into the following categories:

(1) That they emerge at or near the end of *episodic social/political violence*, reacting in frustration by escalation of the violence in terms of new forms and intensity or severity.

(2) The *nativist* explanation that somehow these groups are throwbacks to earlier barbaric civilizations invoking the descriptive adjectives of 'savage,' 'cruel,' 'uncivilized,' and 'vicious.'

(3) Invoking *poverty* or concepts of the *underclass* with the idea that civilization has left some groups behind—and the activities of cruelty and criminality are indications of frustration-aggression.

(4) That people are deluded by powerful *leaders* often in the form of a unique individual that synthesizes the history of the group, its expectations and its pain, and presents solutions.

None of these categories offers a satisfying answer, in and of itself offering an identifiable cause-effect relationship. Others have suggested that there is *no explanation*—that individuals belonging to these deviant groups simply have to be identified, targeted, captured and/or killed; essentially eliminated from the earth. After reading some of the materials and seeing the mutilated bodies of victims, there is a temptation to be repulsed and respond with proportional violence appropriate to the actions of the perpetrators. Nevertheless, this would be a moral cop-out, intellectually vacuous, and ethically disingenuous.

The reality is that blood sacrifice—both *for* and *to* God—is a global phenomenon, appears throughout history, and seems to be related to all of the world's religious practices. In contemporary studies, the reality is that blood sacrifices may range from symbolic to self-destructive within relatively isolated groups to becoming a threat to states, societies, and international order. The reason for studying blood sacrifice is thus to (1) understand the concept of blood sacrifice, (2) find appropriate explanations or theories to connect the phenomenon to other human behaviors, (3) discern whether it is a threat—and if so, how, why, and when, and (4) finally, if it is a threat, provide effective countermeasures.

As this volume has shown, there seems to be some patterns in these case studies; the groups tend to start out relatively small, tend to believe themselves neglected by the larger society, and have traditions of sacrifice available to be brought into the current environment. The syncretism of tradition and modern tools of sacrifice, to include newer technologies such as Facebook, Tumblr, Twitter, and 'App based' forms of social media such as Snapchat for mass communicative purposes, represent the continuing adaptation of societies to their environment.

The pictures included in the virtual image gallery supporting this volume are both fascinating and repulsive quite like the mongoose and the cobra. We cannot turn easily from the photographs. We struggle not to look too long as to do so may be an indication of prurient interest or fear that to stare too long will damage the soul. Perhaps this provides a clue as to why many scholars and practitioners do not want to read, study or know about the dark magico-religious practices of these groups—or simply dismiss them from their mind. It is a hard subject to study and yet the authors of these chapters have had the courage to do so.

Selected References

Andrew Abbot, *The System of the Professions*. Chicago: University of Chicago Press, 1988.

Aminu Abubakar, "Summary execution, beheading, amputation claims in Boko Haram fight." *Yahoo News*. 6 November 2014, http://news.yahoo.com/boko-haram-attack-ne-nigeria-kills-21-senator-202951099.html.

"Full Text Of Boko Haram Leader's Latest Video Message." *Africa This Day*. 7 May 2014, http://africathisday.com/tag/abubakar-shekau/.

Obaji Agbiji, "Engaging Christian faith communities in development in the context of violence," *Research Institute for Theology and Religion*. University of South Africa, n.d.

Sheikh Anwar Al-Awlaki, "Q & A with Sheikh Anwar Al-'Awlaki." *Inspire* 12. Spring 2014 (1435): 17-18.

Sahih al-Bukhari, "Book of Fighting for the Cause of Allah (Jihad)," (2790), http://sunnah.com/bukhari/56.

al-Bukhari and Muslim, "The Allies of Al-Qa'idah in Sham." *Dabiq* 8 (1436 Jumada Al-Akhirah): 7-11.

Tim Allen and Koen Vlassenroot, Eds., *The Lord's Resistance Army: Myth and Reality*.

Shaykh Muhammad Saalih al-Munajjid, "843: Al-Malaa'ikah (Angels)." *Islam Question and Answer*. 2015, http://islamqa.info/en/843.

Aymenn Jawad Al-Tamimi, "Aymenn Jawad Al-Tamimi's Blog." *Pundicity*, http://www.aymennjawad.org/blog/.

Dudley Althaus, "Are the Knights Templar Mexico's Third Most Powerful Cartel?" *Insight Crime*. 23 August 2013, http://www.insightcrime.org/news-analysis/knights-templar.

Stanislav Andrevski, *Social Science as Sorcery*. New York: St. Martin's Press, 1972.

Sean Anthony, "Crucifixion and Death as Spectacle: Umayyad Crucifixion in its Late Antique Context." *American Oriental Series* 96. 2014, http://www.eisenbrauns.com/item/ANTCRUCIF.

Peter Applebome, "Drugs, Death and the Occult Meet In Grisly Inquiry at Mexico Border." *The New York Times.* 13 April 1989, http://www.nytimes.com/1989/04/13/us/drugs-death-and-the-occult-meet-in-grisly-inquiry-at-mexico-border.html.

Karen Armstrong, *Fields of Blood.* New York: Alfred A. Knopf, 2014.

Karen Armstrong, "Wahhabism to ISIS: how Saudi Arabia exported the main source of global terrorism." *New Statesman.* 21-27 November 2014, http://www.newstatesman.com/world-affairs/2014/11/wahhabism-isis-how-saudi-arabia-exported-main-source-global-terrorism.

"Mexico's Vigilantes." *The Atlantic.* 13 May 2014, http://www.theatlantic.com/infocus/2014/05/mexicos-vigilantes/100734/.

Imam Abdullah Azzam, "Join the Caravan," *Religioscope.* n.d., http://www.religioscope.com/info/doc/jihad/azzam_caravan_|6_conclusion.htm.

Erin Banco, "As Sahel Trafficking Networks Grow, Al Qaeda Rebels Get Stronger in Mali." *International Business Times.* 2 July 2015, http://www.ibtimes.com/sahel-trafficking-networks-grow-al-qaeda-rebels-get-stronger-mali-1994724.

Amatzia Baram, *Saddam Husayn and Islam, 1968-2003: Ba'thi Iraq from Secularism to Faith.* Washington, D.C.: Woodrow Wilson Center Press & Johns Hopkins University Press, 3 October 2014.

Franz Bardon, *Initiation Into Hermetics.* Wuppertal: Dieter Rüggerberg, 1987 [1956].

"Leaked video shows Muslim convert to Christianity being savagely beheaded by Muslims for his apostasy." *Bare Naked Islam.* 28 March 2015, http://www.barenakedislam.com/2015/03/28/leaked-video-shows-muslim-convert-to-christianity-being-savagely-beheaded-by-muslims-for-his-apostasy/.

Gregory Bateson, *Steps to an Ecology of Mind: Collected Essays in Anthropology, Psychiatry, Evolution, and Epistemology.* Chicago: University of Chicago Press, 1971.

Gregory Bateson and Mary Catherine Bateson, *Angel's Fear.* New York: Bantam, 1988.

"Hamza attacked 'sugar daddy West.'" *BBC News.* 6 January 2006, http://news.bbc.co.uk/2/hi/uk_news/4616968.stm.

"Mexico troops sent to fight drugs." *BBC News.* 12 December 2006, http://news.bbc.co.uk/2/hi/americas/6170981.stm.

"Mexico arrests over La Santa Muerte cult killings." *BBC Online.* 31 March 2012, http://www.bbc.co.uk/news/world-latin-america-17570199.

Malcolm Beith, *The Last Narco.* London: Penguin Group, 2010.

Robert N. Bellah and Phillip E. Hammond, *Varieties of Civil Religion.* New York: Harper and Row, 1980.

Peter L. Berger, *The Sacred Canopy.* New York: Doubleday, 1967.

Reginald Bibby, *Fragmented Gods: The Poverty and Potential of Religion in Canada.* Toronto: Stoddard Press, 1990.

Reginald Bibby, *Restless Gods: The Renaissance of Religion in Canada.* Ottawa: Novalis Press, 2004.

Ian Black and Martin Chulov, "Syria mutilation footage sparks doubts over wisdom of backing rebels." *The Guardian.* 14 May 2013, http://www.theguardian.com/world/2013/may/14/syria-mutilation-footage-rebels-eat.

Mia Bloom, *Dying to Kill: Allure of Suicide Terror.* New York: Columbia University Press, 2007.

Martin Boas and Anne Hatloy, *Alcohol and Drug Consumption in Post War Sierra Leone—An Exploration.* Norway: Institute for Applied International Studies, 2005.

"Narco Terms." *Borderland Beat.* 3 April 2009, http://www.borderlandbeat.com/2009/04/narco-terms.html.

"Terror in Tepic: Two Men Skinned Alive." *Borderland Beat.* 7 April 2011, http://www.borderlandbeat.com/2011/04/terror-in-tepic-two-men-skinned-alive.html.

Alan Boswell, "In Mali, Diabaly Residents Helped Repel Islamist Militants." *McClatchy.* 24 January 2013, http://www.mcclatchydc.com/2013/01/24/180985/in-mali-diabaly-residents-helped.htmlS.

Robert J. Botsch, "Focus on Officer Safety: Jesus Malverde's Significance to Mexican Drug Traffickers." *The FBI Law Enforcement Bulletin* 77. August 2008: 19-22.

Maurice Bouisson, *Magic: It's History and Practice.* Trans. G. Almayrac. New York: Dutton & Co, 1961 [1958].

Julian Bourg, "On Terrorism as Human Sacrifice." *Humanity* 1. Fall 2010: 137-154.

Jan N. Bremmer, Ed., *The Strange World of Human Sacrifice.* Lueven, Belgium: Peeters Publishers, 2007.

David G. Bromley and Elizabeth Phillips, "Saint Jude the Apostle," World Religions & Spirituality Project VCU (Virginia Commonwealth

University). 26 May 2013, http://www.has.vcu.edu/wrs/profiles/StJude.htm.

David G. Bromley, Joel Best and James R. Richardson, Eds., *The Satanism Scare*. New York: De Gruyter, 1991.

Brujo Negro, "San Simon: Folkloric Saint of Guatemala." Nd, http://www.brujonegrobrujeria.com/page/page/3100370.htm.

Pamela L. Bunker and Robert J. Bunker, "The Spiritual Significance of ¿Plata O Plomo?" *Small Wars Journal*. 27 May 2010, http://smallwarsjournal.com/jrnl/art/the-spiritual-significance-of-¿plata-o-plomo.

Pamela L. Bunker, Lisa J. Campbell, and Robert J. Bunker, "Torture, beheadings, and narcocultos." *Small Wars & Insurgencies* 21. 2010: 145-178.

Robert J. Bunker, "Epochal Change: War Over Social and Political Organization." *Parameters* 27. Summer 1997: 15-25.

Robert J. Bunker, "Santa Muerte: Inspired and Ritualistic Killings," *FBI Law Enforcement Bulletin*. February 2013, http://www.fbi.gov/stats-services/publications/law-enforcement-bulletin/2013/february/santa-muerte-inspired-and-ritualistic-killings-part-1-of-3.

Robert J. Bunker, Ed., *Criminal Insurgencies in Mexico and the Americas*. London: Routledge, 2013.

Robert J. Bunker and Pamela L. Bunker, "Recent Santa Muerte Spiritual Conflict Trends." *Small Wars Journal*. 16 January 2014, http://smallwarsjournal.com/jrnl/art/recent-santa-muerte-spiritual-conflict-trends.

Robert J. Bunker and John P. Sullivan, "Societal Warfare South of the Border?" *Small Wars Journal*. 22 May 2011, http://smallwarsjournal.com/jrnl/art/societal-warfare-south-of-the-border.

Robert J. Bunker and John P. Sullivan, *Studies in Gangs and Cartels*. London: Routledge, 2013.

Robert J. Bunker, *Old and New Insurgency Forms*. Carlisle: Strategic Studies Institute, U.S. Army War College, 2016 (*Forthcoming*).

Roberto Bustamante, "San Judas Tadeo ¿el santo preferido de los delincuentes?" *Univision*. 28 August 2013, http://noticias.univision.com/article/1651754/2013-08-28/mexico/noticias/san-judas-tadeo-santo-preferido-de-los-delincuentes.

William H. Calvin, "The Six Essentials? Minimal Requirements for the Darwinian Bootstrapping of Quality" *Journal of*

Memetics—Evolutionary Models of Information Transmission 1. 1997, http://www.williamcalvin.com/1990s/1997JMemetics.htm.

Lisa J. Campbell, "The Use of Beheadings by Fundamentalist Islam." *Global Crime* 7. August-November 2006: 583-614.

Jeffrey Carter, Ed., *Understanding Religious Sacrifice: A Reader.* New York: Continuum, 2003.

'St. Death,'" *Catholic News Agency.* 3 November 2008, http://www.catholicnewsagency.com/news/archdiocese of mexico city issues clarification about st. jude and the st. death/.

William Cavanaugh, *Torture and Eucharist: Theology, Politics, and the Body of Christ.* Malden: Blackwell, 1998.

"'Angel of the Poor' smiles on Mexico's deadly drug trade." *CBC News.* 22 March 2010, http://www.cbc.ca/news/world/angel-of-the-poor-smiles-on-mexico-s-deadly-drug-trade-1.884413.

Sujata Ashwarya Cheema, "Sayyid Qutb's Concept of Jahiliyya as Metaphor for Modern Society." *Academia.* n.d., https://www.academia.edu/3222569/Sayyid Qutbs Concept of Jahiliyya as Metaphor for Modern Society.

R. Andrew Chesnut, *Devoted to Death: Santa Muerte, the Skeleton Saint.* Oxford: Oxford University Press, 2012.

Irina Chindea, "Coordination Failures Among Mexican Security Forces." *Small Wars Journal.* 16 June 2014, http://smallwarsjournal.com/jrnl/art/coordination-failures-among-mexican-security-forces.

"Boko Haram Fighters Turn to Cannibalism in Nigerian Forest." *The Clarion Project,* 28 August 2013, http://www.clarionproject.org/news/boko-haram-turn-cannibalism-survive-nigerian-forest.

Carl von Clausewitz, *On War.* Michael Howard and Peter Paret, Ed., and Trans. Princeton: Princeton University Press, 1976.

Lawrence E. Cline, *The Lord's Resistance Army.* Praeger Security International (PSI) Guides to Terrorists, Insurgents, and Armed Groups Series. Santa Barbara: Praeger, 2013.

Susan Collins and Carl Levin, "Preface" in Executive Sessions of the Senate Permanent Subcommittee On Investigations. Washington, DC: U.S. Government Printing Office, 2003.

"World-renowned Islamic university teaches it's okay for Muslims to cannibalize Jews and Christians." *Consortium of Defense Analysts.* 14 April 2014, https://cofda.wordpress.com/2015/04/14/

egypt-university-textbooks-teach-its-okay-for-muslims-to-cannibalize-jews-and-christians/.

Russell Contreras, "Drug convictions overturned thanks to Death Saint." *The Santa Fe New Mexican.* 3 July 2014, http://www.santafenewmexican.com/news/local news/drug-convictions-overturned-thanks-to-death-saint/article 2677e7ed-973d-595f-bdb3-d85d96a91744.html.

David Cook, *Understanding Jihad.* Berkeley: University of California Press, 2005.

Alfredo Corchado, "The Migrant's Saint: Toribio Romo is a Favorite of Mexicans Crossing the Border." *Dallas Morning News.* 22 July 2006, http://www.banderasnews.com/0607/nr-migrantssaint.htm.

Zaira Cortés, "'Narco Fashion' Takes Hold in New York City." *Voices of New York.* 20 May 2014, http://www.voicesofny.org/2014/05/narco-fashion-takes-hold-new-york-city/. Translated by Carlos Rodríguez Martorell from *El Diario/La Presna.*

James H. Creechan and Jorge de la Herrán Garcia, "Without God or Law: Narcoculture and belief in Jesús Malverde," *Religious Studies and Theology* 24. 2005: 5-57.

Martin van Creveld, *The Transformation of War.* New York: The Free Press, 1991.

"The Libyan Arena." *Dabiq* 8 (1436 Jumada al-Akrhirah): 25-26.

Miranda Dahlin-Morfoot, "Socio-Economic Indicators and Patron Saints of the Underrepresented: An Analysis of Santa Muerte and Jesus Malverde in Mexico." *Manitoba Anthropology* 29. 2011: 1-7.

"Voodoo practicing JFK baggage handler gets three life sentences for international drug smuggling ring." *Daily Mail.* 17 October 2012, http://www.dailymail.co.uk/news/article-2218771/Voodoo-practicing-JFK-baggage-handler-gets-3-life-sentences-global-drug-smuggling-ring.html.

Lizbeth Diaz, "Mexico troops enter Tijuana in drug gang crackdown." *Washington Post.* 3 January 2007, http://www.washingtonpost.com/wp-dyn/content/article/2007/01/03/AR2007010301382.html.

Lizbeth Diaz, "Mexican police ask spirits to guard them in drug war." *Reuters.* 19 March 2010, http://www.reuters.com/article/2010/03/19/us-mexico-drugs-idUSTRE62I3Z220100319.

Dom Gregory Dix, *The Shape of the Liturgy.* London: Dacre Press, 1945.

Robyn Dixon, "Leader of Boko Haram says God told him to carry out massacre," *Los Angeles Times*. 21 January 2015, http://www.latimes.com/world/africa/la-fg-nigeria-boko-haram-massacre-20150121-story.html.

Mary Douglas, *How Institutions Think*. Syracuse: Syracuse University Press, 1986.

Charles Dunlap, Jr., "Preliminary Observations: Asymmetric Warfare and the Western Mindset," in *Challenging the US Symmetrically and Asymmetrically*. Carlisle Barracks: U.S. Army War College Strategic Studies Institute, July 1998.

Emile Durkheim, *The Division of Labor in Society*. W.D. Halls Trans., New York: The Free Press, 1984.

"Con ritos de iniciación justificaban canibalismo." *El Economista*. 23 Marcha 2014, http://eleconomista.com.mx/sociedad/2014/03/23/ritos-iniciacion-justificaban-canibalismo.

Mircea Eliade, *Shamanism: Archaic Techniques of Ecstasy*. Princeton: Princeton University Press, 1964 [1951].

Stephen Ellis, "The Okija Shrine: Death and Life in Nigerian Politics." *The Journal of African History* 49. 2008: 445-466.

Hans Magnus Enzensberger, "The Resurgence of Human Sacrifice," *Society* 39. March-April 2007: 75-77.

E.E. Evans-Pritchard *Witchcraft, Oracles and Magic among the Azande*, abridged version, Eva Giles. Ed., Oxford: Clarendon Press, 1976.

Emenike Ezedani, "Boko Haram Chibok Girls and All Things Nigeria Security," *bokowatch.com*. 2015, http://www.bokowatch.com/.

Muhammad Abd al-Salam Faraj's manifesto, "The Neglected Duty." 1979.

Sam Farmer, "I will use the Ten Commandments to liberate Uganda," *The Times*. 28 June 2006, http://www.thetimes.co.uk/tto/news/world/article1982845.ece.

Iftikhar Fidous, "What Goes Into the Making of Suicide Bomber." *The Express Tribune*. 20 July 2010, http://tribune.com.pk/story/28976/what-goes-into-the-making-of-a-suicide-bomber/.

Richard C. Foltz, *Animals in Islamic Tradition and Muslim Cultures*. Oxford: Oneworld Publications, 2006.

"Cannibalism and the Initiation Rites of Los Zetas and Los Caballeros Templarios." *OE Watch: Foreign News and Perspectives of the Operational Environment*. Fort Leavenworth: Foreign Military

Studies Office, July 2014: 29, http://fmso.leavenworth.army.mil/OEWatch/Current/LatAm_03.html.

Dion Fortune, *The Training and Work of an Initiate*. Wellingborough: The Aquarian Press, 1982 [1930].

James G. Fraser, *The Golden Bough*. Third Edition. Cambridge: Cambridge University Press, 2012 [1911-1915].

Colin Freeman, "Revealed: how Saharan caravans of cocaine help to fund al-Qaeda in terrorists' North African domain." *The Telegraph*. 26 January 2013, http://www.telegraph.co.uk/news/worldnews/africaandindianocean/mali/9829099/Revealed-how-Saharan-caravans-of-cocaine-help-to-fund-al-Qaeda-in-terrorists-North-African-domain.html.

Kevin Freese, *Death Cult of the Drug Lords*. Fort Leavenworth: Foreign Military Studies Office, 2006, http://fmso.leavenworth.army.mil/documents/Santa-Muerte/santa-muerte.htm.

Robert W. Fuller, *Stairways To Heaven: Drugs In American Religious History*. Boulder: Westview Press, 2000.

Timothy R. Furnish, "Beheading in the Name of Islam." *The Middle East Forum*. Spring 2005, http://www.meforum.org/713/beheading-in-the-name-of-islam.

Paul Galinger, *Illegal Drugs: A Complete Guide to their History, Chemistry, Use and Abuse*. New York: Plume Books, 2004.

Diego Gambetta, *Codes of the Underworld*. Princeton: Princeton University Press, 2009.

Randall Garrett, *Lord Darcy*. Wake Forest: Baen Books, 2002.

Clifford Geertz, *The Interpretation of Culture*. New York: Basic Books, 1973.

Peter Geschiere, *The Modernity of Witchcraft*. Charlotteville: University of Virginia Press, 1997.

Vo Nguyen Giap, *People's War People's Army: The Viet Cong Insurrection Manual for Underdeveloped Countries*. New York: Praeger, 1962.

Carlo Ginzburg, *The Night Battles* and *Ecstasies: Deciphering the Witch's Sabbath*. New York: Pantheon Books, 1991.

Carlo Ginzburg, *The Cheese and the Worms*. Trans. John Tedesci and Anne C. Tedesci, Baltimore: Johns Hopkins University Press, 1992.

H. Nelson Goodson, "Ten Lemon Picking Workers Dead, 17 Injured After Leaving Labor Rally In Michoacan." *Hispanic News Network*. 13 April 2013, http://hispanicnewsnetwork.blogspot.com/2013/04/ten-lemon-picking-workers-dead-17.html.

Sebastian Gorka, "Jihadist Ideology: The Core Texts" (transcript of a briefing given by Dr. Sebastian Gorka), *The Counter Jihad Report*. 5 October 2010, http://counterjihadreport.com/jihadist-ideology-the-core-texts/.

George W. Grayson, *La Familia: Another Deadly Mexican Syndicate*. Washington, DC: Foreign Policy Research Institute, February 2009, http://www.fpri.org/enotes/200901.grayson.lafamilia.html.

George W. Grayson, *La Familia Drug Cartel: Implications for U.S.-Mexico Security*. Carlisle: Strategic Studies Institute, U.S. Army War College, December 2010, http://www.strategicstudiesinstitute.army.mil/pubs/display.cfm?pubID=1033.

George W. Grayson, *Threat Posed by Mounting Vigilantism in Mexico*. Carlisle: Strategic Studies Institute, U.S. Army War College, 15 September 2011, http://www.strategicstudiesinstitute.army.mil/pubs/display.cfm?pubID=1082.

George W. Grayson and Sam Logan, *The Executioner's Men: Los Zetas, Rogue Soldiers, Criminal Entrepreneurs, and the Shadow State They Created*. New Brunswick: Transaction Publishers, 2012.

Charlotte Greig, *Evil Serial Killers: In the Minds of Monsters*. New York: Barnes & Noble, 2005.

James S. Griffith, *Folk Saints of the Borderlands*. Tucson: Rio Nuevo Publishers, 2003.

Ioan Grillo, *El Narco: Inside Mexico's Criminal Insurgency*. New York: Bloomsbury Press, 2011.

Ioan Grillo, "Crusaders of Meth: Mexico's Deadly Knights Templar." *Time*. 23 June 2011, http://content.time.com/time/world/article/0,8599,2079430,00.html.

David Grossman, *On Killing: The Psychological Costs of Learning to Kill in War and Society*. New York: Back Bay Books, 2009.

America Y. Guevara, "Propaganda in Mexico's Drug War." *Journal of Strategic Security* 6. Fall 2013: 131-151.

Alma Guillermoprieto, "Days of the Dead: The new narcocultura." *The New Yorker*. 10 November 2008, http://www.newyorker.com/magazine/2008/11/10/days-of-the-dead-2?currentPage=all.

Jeroen Gunning, "Social movement theory and the study of terrorism" in Richard English et.al., Eds., *Critical Terrorism Studies: A new research agenda*. New York: Routledge, 2009.

Moshe Halbertal, *On Sacrifice*. Princeton: Princeton University Press, 2012.

Bradley Hanson *Introduction to Christian Theology*. Minneapolis: Augsburg Fortress, 1997.

Chris Harmon, *Terrorism Today*. New York: Routledge, 2nd edition 2008.

Elizabeth Willmott Harrop, "Africa: A Bewitching Economy—Witchcraft and Human Trafficking." *ThinkAfricaPress*. 17 September 2012, http://thinkafricapress.com/society/african-witchcraft-contemporary-slavery-human-trafficking-nigeria.

Richard Hartley-Parkinson, "'I would be a suicide bomber three times over if I could': Palestinian woman freed in Gilad Shalit deal vows to sacrifice her life," *Mail Online*. 20 October 2011, http://www.dailymail.co.uk/news/article-2051382/Palestinian-Wafa-al-Biss-freed-Gilad-Shalit-deal-vows-sacrifice-life.html.

Deborah Hastings, "Exorcism rituals on the rise as way to battle evil of Mexican cartels." *New York Daily News*. 17 January 2014, http://www.nydailynews.com/news/world/exorcisms-battle-evil-mexican-drug-cartels-article-1.1581063.

Hakim Hazim and Robert J. Bunker, "Perpetual Jihad: Striving for a Caliphate." *Global Crime* 7. 2006: 428-445.

"Beslan School Attackers Were Drug Addicts." Healthcare Customwire. 17 October 2004.

Thomas Hegghammer. "Why Terrorists Weep: The Socio-Cultural Practices of Jihadi Militants." *Paul Wilkinson Memorial Lecture*. St. Andrews: University of St. Andrews, 16 April 2015, http://hegghammer.com/ files/Hegghammer - Wilkinson Memorial Lecture.pdf.

Gustav Henningsen, *The Witches' Advocate: Basque Witchcraft and the Spanish Inquisition (1609–1619)*. Reno: University of Nevada Press, 1980.

Vladimir Hernandez, "The country where exorcisms are on the rise." *BBC Mundo*. 25 November 2013, http://www.bbc.com/news/magazine-25032305.

Jennifer L. Hesterman, *The Terrorist-Criminal Nexus*. Boca Raton: CRC Press, 2013.

Sharon Kelly Heyob, *The Cult of Isis among the Women of the Greco-Roman World*. Leiden: Leiden Brill, 1975.

J.N.C. Hill, "Religious Extremism in Northern Nigeria Past and Present: Parallels between the Pseudo-Tijanis and Boko Haram." *The Round Table: The Commonwealth Journal of International Affairs* 102. 2013: 235-244.

Eric Hobsbawm, *Bandits*. New York Press: New Press, 2000.

Eric Hoffer, *The True Believer*. New York: Time, 1963.

Danny Hoffman, *The War Machines: Young Men and Violence in Sierra Leone and Liberia*. Durham: Duke University Press, 2011.

Frank Hoffman and Michael C. Davies, "Joint Force 2020 and the Human Domain: Time for a New Conceptual Framework?" *Small Wars Journal*. 10 June 2013, http://smallwarsjournal.com/jrnl/art/joint-force-2020-and-the-human-domain-time-for-a-new-conceptual-framework.

Donald Holbrook, "Using the Quran to Justify Terrorist Violence: Analysing Selective Application of the Quran in English-Language Militant Islamist Discourse." *Terrorism Research Initiative*. 2010, http://www.terrorismanalysis.com/pt/index.php/pot/article/view/104/html.

Christopher Holton, "Basis in Islamic Jurisprudence (Sharia) and Scripture for Execution of Jordanian Pilot." *The Counter Jihad Report*. 3 February 2015, http://counterjihadreport.com/2015/02/04/basis-in-islamic-jurisprudence-shariah-and-scripture-for-execution-of-jordanian-pilot/.

Trevor Huddleston CR, *Naught for Your Comfort*. Garden City: Doubleday, 1956.

Edward Humes, *Buried Secrets: A True Story of Drug Running, Black Magic, and Human Sacrifice*. New York: Dutton Books, 1991.

Joris-Karl Huysmans, *Là-Bas*. Trans. Terry Hale, New York: Penguin Classics, 2002.

David Iaconangelo, "Knights Templar Drug Cartel Takes Over Control Of Iron Exports To China." *Latin Times*. 3 January 2014, http://www.latintimes.com/knights-templar-drug-cartel-takes-over-control-iron-exports-china-142298.

Raymond Ibrahim, "Beheading Infidels: How Allah 'Heals the Hearts of the Believers.'" *Frontpage Mag*. 11 September 2014, http://www.frontpagemag.com/fpm/240733/beheading-infidels-how-allah-heals-hearts-raymond-ibrahim.

The Infinity Creations, "New Boko Haram video with English subtitle." *YouTube.* 15 May 2014, https://www.youtube.com/watch? v=SwB1DPA_agg.

Frederick P. Isaac, "Indigenous Peoples Under the Rule of Islam," *Part II: The Rise and Spread of the Message (Al-Da'awa).* Bloomington: Xlibris Corp, 2002.

Johannes J.G. Jansen, "Faraj and The Neglected Duty; Interview with Professor Johannes J.G. Jansen," *Religioscope.* n.d., http://www. religioscope.com/info/dossiers/textislamism/faraj_jansen.htm.

Ronald H. Jones, *Terrorist Beheadings: Cultural and Strategic Implications.* Carlisle: Strategic Studies Institute, U.S. Army War College, June 2005.

"The Popular Discourses of Salafi Radicalism and Salafi Counter-radicalism in Nigeria: A Case Study of Boko Haram." *Journal of Religion in Africa* 42. 2012: 118-144.

Tony M. Kail, *A Cop's Guide to Occult Investigations: Understanding Satanism, Santeria, Wicca, and Other Alternative Religions.* Boulder: Paladin Press, 2003.

Tony M. Kail, "Crime Scenes and Folk Saints." *Counter Cult Apologetics Journal* 1. 2006: 4.

Tony M. Kail, *Magico-Religious Groups and Ritualistic Activities: A Guide for First Responders.* Boca Raton: CRC Press, 2008.

Tony Kail, *Santa Muerte: Mexico's Mysterious Saint of Death.* La Vergne: Fringe Research Press, 2010.

Tony M. Kail, *Narco-Cults: Understanding the Use of Afro-Caribbean and Mexican Religious Cultures in the Drug Wars.* Boca Raton: CRC Press, 2014.

Paul Rexton Kan, *Drugs and Contemporary Warfare.* Dulles: Potomac Books, 2009.

Ernst H. Kantorowicz, *The King's Two Bodies: A Study in Mediaeval Political Theology.* Princeton: Princeton University Press, 1857.

Bruce Kapferer, *Legends of People, Myths of State: Violence, Intolerance, and Political Culture in Sri Lanka and Australia.* Washington, D.C.: Smithsonian, 1988.

Robert Kaplan, *The Coming Anarchy: Shattering the Dreams of the Post-Cold War World.* New York: Vintage, 2002.

Elizabeth Kendal, "The Lord's Resistance Army (LRA) Terrorises— Southern Sudan, northern Congo, eastern Central African Republic

(CAR), Uganda." *Religious Liberty Prayer Bulletin (RLPB) 025.* 7 October 2009, http://www.assistnews.net/Stories/2009/s091000 45.htm.

Farhad Khorsrokhavar, *Inside Jihadism.* Boulder: Paradigm Publishers, 2009.

Alfred Korzybski, "A Non-Aristotelian System and its Necessity for Rigour in Mathematics and Physics" in Alfred Zorzybski, *Science and Sanity*, 5th Edition. Englewood: Institute of General Semantics, 1933: 747–761.

"Santa Muerte Altars Demolished in Matamoros." *KRGV News.* 16 January 2014, http://www.krgv.com/news/santa-muerte-altars-demolished-in-matamoros.

Aislinn Laing, "Boko Haram leader taunts US over bounty." *The Telegraph.* 29 December 2013, http://www.telegraph.co.uk/news/worldnews/africaandindianocean/nigeria/10541793/Boko-Haram-leader-taunts-US-over-bounty.html.

Friedrich Spee von Langenfeld, *Cautio Criminalis, or a Book on Witch Trials.* Trans. Marcus Hellyer. Charlottesville: University of Virginia Press, 2003 [1631].

Matthew A. Lauder, *Religion and Resistance: Examining the Role of Religion in Irregular Warfare*, Technical Note 2009-049. Toronto: Defence R&D, March 2009.

Charles D. Laughlin, "The Cycle of Meaning" in Stephen Glazier, Ed, *Anthropology of Religion: Handbook of Theory and Method.* Westport: Greenwood Press, 1997: 471-488, http://www.biogenetic structuralism.com/articles.htm.

Ed Lavandera, "The secret world of teen cartel hit men." *CNN News.* 6 August 2013, http://www.cnn.com/2013/08/06/justice/teen-cartel-killers/.

Brian Levack, Ed., *Witchcraft, Magic, and Demonology.* New York: Garland, 1992.

Claude Levi-Strauss, *Structural Anthropology.* New York: Basic Books, 1974.

James R. Lewis. Ed., *The Order of the Solar Temple: The Temple of Death.* Burlington: Ashgate Publishing Company, 2006.

Bruce Lincoln, *Holy Terrors: Thinking about Religion after September 11.* Chicago: The University of Chicago Press, 2006.

"Two Christians, One a Priest, Beheaded" (Translated). *Live Leak*. 26 June 2013, http://www.liveleak.com/view?i=b57_1372272008.

"Islamic Ritual Human Sacrifice Caught On Film." *Live Leak*. 16 March 2014, http://www.liveleak.com/view?i=6ad_1395015674.

Michael Lohmuller, "Zetas Training US Gang Members in Mexico: Witness." *Insight Crime*. 5 February 2014, http://www.insightcrime.org/news-briefs/zetas-training-us-gang-members-in-mexico-witness.

Robert MacCoun and Peter Reuter, *Drug War Heresies: Learning from Other Vices, Times and Places*. New York: Cambridge University Press, 2001.

Denis MacEoin, "Suicide Bombing as Worship—Dimensions of Jihad." *The Middle East Quarterly*. Fall 2009, http://www.meforum.org/2478/suicide-bombing-as-worship.

Patrick Maka, "After They Shot Juan." *San Diego Weekly Reader*. 4 December 1997, http://www.sandiegoreader.com/news/1997/dec/04/after-they-shot-juan/#.

Bronislaw Malinowski, *Magic, Science and Religion*. New York: Anchor Books, 1954 [1916].

Bronislaw Malinowski, *A Scientific Theory of Culture*. New York: Oxford University Press, 1960 [1944].

Robert Mandel, *Global Security Upheaval: Armed Nonstate Groups Usurping State Stability Functions*. Stanford: Stanford University Press, 2013.

Francis Martel, "ISIS Jihadist: Xanax makes us 'think tanks are birds' during warfare." *Breitbart*. 30 March 2015, http://www.breitbart.com/national-security/2015/03/30/captured-isis-jihadist-took-pills-that-make-you-think-tanks-are-birds-before-battle/.

Lawrence E. Y. Mbogoni, *Human Sacrifice and the Supernatural in African History*. Dar es Salaam: Mkuki na Nyota Publishers Ltd., 2013.

James McCorkle, Ed., *Conversant Essays: Contemporary Poets on Poetry*. Detroit: Wayne State University Press, 1990.

Andrew McGregor, "'Jihad and the Rifle Alone:' 'Abdullah 'Azzam and the Islamist Revolution." *Journal of Conflict Studies* 23. Fall 2003: 1-14, https://journals.lib.unb.ca/index.php/jcs/article/view/219/377.

James C. McKinley, Jr. "Mexican Cartels Lure American Teens as Killers." *New York Times*. 22 June 2009, http://www.nytimes.com/2009/06/23/us/23killers.html?pagewanted=all&_r=0.

"Islamic State (ISIS) Publishes Penal Code, Says It Will Be Vigilantly Enforced." *MEMRI: Jihad & Terrorism Threat Monthly.* 17 December 2014, http://www.memrijttm.org/memri-jttm-islamic-state-isis-publishes-penal-code-says-it-will-be-vigilantly-enforced.html.

"#4558 - Warning: Extremely Disturbing Images. Woman Stoned to Death by ISIS in Syria." *MEMRI TV.* 21 October 2014, http://www.memritv.org/clip/en/4558.htm.

Beatriz Mesa, "Mali Jihadists Mix Religion and Drugs." *AL Monitor.* 7 May 2013, http://www.al-monitor.com/pulse/security/2013/05/drug-trade-fuels-jihad-in-mali.html.

Alfred Métraux, *Voodoo in Haiti.* Trans. Hugo Charteris, London: Andre Deutsch, 1959.

Helen Chapin Metz, Ed., "The Rise of Abd Al Aziz." *Saudi Arabia: A Country Study.* Washington, D.C.: GPO for the Library of Congress: 1992, http://countrystudies.us/saudi-arabia/9.htm.

Steven Metz, *The Future of Insurgency.* Carlisle: Strategic Studies Institute, U.S. Army War College, December 1993.

Piotr Gnegon Michalik, "Death with a Bonus Pack: New Age Spirituality, Folk Catholicism, and the Cult of Santa Muerte." *Archives De Sciences Socalies De Religions* 153. Janvier-Mars 2011: 159-182.

"Children in the Service of Terror," Middle East Media Research Institute, *Special Dispatch No. 2455.* 21 July 2009, http://www.memri.org/report/en/0/0/0/0/0/841/3435.htm.

"Jihadi Cleric Justifies IS Beheadings: 'Islam is a Religion of Beheading.'" *The Middle East Media Research Institute.* 25 August 2014, http://www.memri.org/report/en/print8126.htm.

"Islamic State (ISIS) Releases Pamphlet On Female Slaves." *The Middle East Media Research Institute.* 4 December 2014, http://www.memrijttm.org/islamic-state-isis-releases-pamphlet-on-female-slaves.html.

Lawrence E.Y. Mbogoni. *Human Sacrifices and the Supernatural in African History.* Tanzania: Mkuki na Nyota Publishers, 2013.

Mary Midgley, *Beast and Man: The Roots of Human Nature.* Ithaca: Cornell University Press, 1978.

Julian Miglierini, "Narcocinema: Mexico's alternative film industry." *BBC News.* 28 September 2010, http://www.bbc.com/news/world-latin-america-11425913.

Michael Miklaucic and Jacqueline Brewer, Eds., *Convergence: Illicit Networks and National Security in the Age of Globalization.* Washington, D.C.: National Defense University Press, 2013.

Michael E. Miller, "Islamic State's 'war crimes' against Yazidi women documented." *The Washington Post.* 16 April 2015, http://www. washingtonpost.com/news/morning-mix/wp/2015/04/16/ islamic-states-war-crimes-against-yazidi-women-documented/.

Assaf Moghadam, "Motives for Martyrdom: Al-Qaida, Salaa Jihad, and the Spread of Suicide Attacks." *International Security* 33. Winter 2008-2009: 46-78, http://insct.syr.edu/wp-content/ uploads/2013/03/Moghadam-Assaf.2008.Motives-for-Martrydom. International-Security.pdf.

Molly Molloy, "The Mexican Undead: Toward a New History of the "Drug War" Killing Fields." *Small Wars Journal.* 21 August 2013, http://smallwarsjournal.com/jrnl/art/the-mexican-undead-toward-a-new-history-of-the-"drug-war"-killing-fields.

Shaylih Muehlmann, *When I Wear My Alligator Boots: Narco-Culture in the U.S. Mexico Borderlands.* Berkeley: University of California Press, 2014.

John Mueller, *Remnants of War.* Ithaca: Cornell University Press, 2004.

Ahmad Murtada, *"Boko Haram" in Nigeria: Its Beginnings, Principles and Activities in Nigeria.* Kano, Nigeria: Online book publishing of www.SalafiManhaj.com, 2013.

"Muslim Convert To Christianity Admit: In Boko Haram We Butchered Christians And Drank Their Blood." *The Muslim Issue.* 25 August 2013, https://themuslimissue.wordpress. com/2013/08/25/muslim-convert-to-christianity-admit-in-boko-haram-we-butchered-christians-and-drank-their-blood/ comment-page-1/.

"Islamic State's Sharia Punishments." *The Muslim Issue.* 8 April 2015, https://themuslimissue.wordpress.com/2015/04/08/islamic-states-sharia-punishments/.

2010 Tattoo Handbook California Hispanic Gangs. Unclassified/LES. Washington, D.C.: National Gang Intelligence Center (NGIC), April 2010: 31-78. For an online copy see http://cryptocomb. org/2011%20tattoo%20handbook%20for%20police.pdf;

El Lujo De Los Narcos (Narco Bling). National Geographic. 50 Minutes— 2012, http://www.youtube.com/watch?v=i--12v_evuk.

Jacob Needleman and George Baker, Eds., *Understanding the New Religions.* New York: The Seabury Press, 1981.

News Staff, "Santa Muerte shrine destroyed by Mexican authorities." *Valley Central News.* 27 June 2013, http://www.valleycentral.com/news/story.aspx?id=915163#.U8gLmhaIxFI.

"Multiple Bombing: Allah Has Given Us Victory Over Christians + Christians Must All Convert to Islam—Boko Haram." *Nigeria Films. com.* 19 June 2012, http://www.nigeriafilms.com/news/17843/53/multiple-bombing-allah-has-given-us-victory-over-c.html.

Michael Nwankpa, "Boko Haram: Whose Islamic State?" James A. Baker III Institute for Public Policy, Rice University. 1 May 2015, https://bakerinstitute.org/media/files/files/e37325ec/CME-pub-BokoHaram-050115.pdf.

Michael Odenwald, Harald Hinkel, et. al., "The Consumption of Khat and Other Drugs in Somali Combatants: A Cross-Sectional Study." *PLOS Medicine.* 2007: 1960, http://www.plosmedicine.org/article/fetchObject.action?uri=info%3Adoi%2F10.1371%2Fjournal.pmed.0040341&representation=PDF.

"Pharmaceutical Drugs and the Syrian War." *OE Watch.* Fort Leavenworth: Foreign Military Studies Office, December 2015: 11-12.

Plinio Correa de Oliveira, "St. Raymond Nonnatus, August 31." *The Saint of the Day.* Nd, http://www.traditioninaction.org/SOD/j144sd_RaymondNonnatus_8-31.shtml.

Opiyo Oloya, *Child to Soldier: Stories from Joseph Kony's Lord's Resistance Army.* Toronto: University of Toronto Press, 2013.

Gisela Orozco, "Narcoliterature explores the realities of Mexico's drug culture," *Chicago Tribune.* 30 May 2014, http://articles.chicagotribune.com/2014-05-30/features/chi-narcoliteratura-20140530_1_drug-trade-printers-row-lit-fest-panel-discussion.

Alfredo Ortega-Trillo, "The Cult of Santa Muerte in Tijuana." *San Diego News Notes.* June 2006.

"Stories of Three Former Boko Haram Members." *Osun Defender.* 9 September 2014, http://www.naija.io/blogs/p/897087/stories-of-three-former-boko-haram-members.

Robert A. Pape, *Dying to Win: The Strategic Logic of Suicide Bombing.* New York: Random House, 2005.

Tom Parry, "Tragedy of kidnapped child soldiers forced to kill or be killed by Joseph Kony's savage Lord's Resistance Army," *Daily Mirror*. 16 September 2013, http://www.mirror.co.uk/news/world-news/joseph-konys-lords-resistance-army-2276555.

Joshua Partlow, "Mexican bishop takes on cultish cartel in drug war battleground state." *The Washington Post*. 1 December 2013, http://www.washingtonpost.com/world/the_americas/mexican-bishop-takes-on-cultish-cartel-in-drug-war-battleground-state/2013/12/01/62eea6d4-508f-11e3-9ee6-2580086d8254_story.htm.

Dawn Perlmutter, "Mujahideen Blood Rituals: The Religious and Forensic Symbolism of Al Qaeda Beheading." *Anthropoetics* 11. Fall 2005 / Winter 2006, http://www.anthropoetics.ucla.edu/ap1102/muja.htm.

Dawn Perlmutter, "ISIS Purifies Islam Through Fire." *The Counter Jihad Report*. 4 February 2015, http://counterjihadreport.com/2015/02/04/isis-purifies-islam-through-fire\.

Dawn Perlmutter, "ISIS Meth Heads: Tweaking in the Name of Islam," *Frontpage Mag*. 9 March 2015, http://www.frontpagemag.com/fpm/252783/isis-meth-heads-tweeking-name-islam-dawn-perlmutter.

Juan Javier Pescador, *Crossing Borders with the Santo Niño de Atocha*. Albuquerque: University of New Mexico Press, 2009.

Zacharias Pieri, "Boko Haram's Islamic Caliphate is becoming a reality in Northeastern Nigeria." *ZP: Zacharias Pieri Blog*. 7 September 2014, http://blog.zachariaspieri.com/post/97761946322/boko-harams-islamic-caliphate-is-becoming-a-reality-in-northeastern-nigeria/.

Terrence E. Poppa, *Drug Lord: A True Story: The Life and Death of a Mexican Kingpin*. El Paso: Cinco Puntos Press, 2010.

Tom Porter, "Rotting Corpses and Chained Kidnap Victims Found in Nigeria's 'House of Horrors.'" *International Business Times*. 23 March 2014, http://www.ibtimes.co.uk/rotting-corpses-chained-kidnap-victims-found-nigerias-house-horrors-1441494.

Gary Provost, *Across the Border: True Story of Satanic Cult Killings in Matamoros, Mexico*. New York: Pocket Books, 1989.

Lady Queensborough, *Occult Theocracy*. Hawethorne: The Christian Book Club of America, 1933.

Asad Raza, "Intercession: Meaning and Philosophy." *Islamic Insights.* 28 September 2010, http://www.islamicinsights.com/religion/intercession-meaning-and-philosophy.html.

Tim Reiterman and John Jacobs, *Raven: The Untold Story of Rev. Jim Jones and His People.* New York: Dutton, 1982.

"Impurity Requiring a Bath of Purification." *Laws of Religion: Laws of Islam Concerning Ritual Purity and Cleanliness: from the Holy Quran, major hadith collections and Islamic jurisprudence.* n.d., http://www.religiousrules.com/Islampurity06bath.htm.

"MEXICO: El ostentoso narco-cementerio de Culiacán," *Reportero 24.* 17 May 2012, http://www.reportero24.com/2012/05/mexico-el-ostentoso-narco-cementerio-de-culiacan/.

Christoph Reuter, "The Terror Strategist: Secret Files Reveal the Structure of Islamic State." *Spiegel Online International.* April 18, 2015, http://www.spiegel.de/international/world/islamic-state-files-show-structure-of-islamist-terror-group-a-1029274.html.

Scott P. Richert, "What Is a Saint?" *About.com Catholicism.* 2014, http://catholicism.about.com/od/thesaints/f/What_Is_A_Saint.htm.

Joel Roberts, "American Beheaded in Iraq." *CBS News.* 12 May 2004, http://www.cbsnews.com/news/american-beheaded-in-iraq/.

Michael Roberts, "Tamil Tiger 'Martyrs': Regenerating Divine Potency?" *Studies in Conflict and Terrorism* 28. November-December 2005: 493-514.

Soraya Roberts, "Mexico man's face skinned and stitched onto a soccer ball in Sinaloa in threat to Juarez drug cartel." *New York Daily News.* 9 January 2010, http://www.nydailynews.com/news/world/mexico-man-face-skinned-stitched-soccer-ball-sinaloa-threat-juarez-drug-cartel-article-1.181143.

Jeffrey Burton Russell, "Witchcraft and the Demonization of Heresy." with Mark Wyndham. *Medievalia* 2. 1976: 1-21.

Jeffrey Burton Russell, *Satan: The Early Christian Tradition.* Ithaca: Cornell, 1981.

Jeffrey Burton Russell, *Lucifer: The Devil in the Middle Ages.* Ithaca: Cornell, 1984.

Jeffrey Burton Russell, *Mephistopheles: The Devil in the Modern World.* Ithaca: Cornell, 1986.

"ISIS sanctions organ harvesting from living 'apostates'...even if it kills them." *Russia Today.* 25 December 2015, https://www.rt.com/news/327078-isis-captives-organs-harvesting/.

"Boko Haram resorts to blood sucking tactic: Slaughters 11 innocent Nigerians." *Scan News.* 1 October 2013, http://scannewsnigeria.com/news/boko-haram-resorts-to-blood-sucking-tactic-slaughters-11-innocent-nigerians/.

Bettina E. Schmidt, "Anthropological Reflections on Religion and Violence" in Andrew R. Murphy, Ed., *The Blackwell Companion to Religion and Violence.* Oxford: Wiley-Blackwell, 2011.

Robert Lionel Séguin, *La sorcellerie au Québec du XVIIe au XIXe siècle.* Montréal: Leméac, 1978.

Uriya Shavit, "Al-Qaeda's Saudi Origins." *The Middle East Quarterly.* Fall 2006, http://www.meforum.org/999/al-qaedas-saudi-origins.

M. Shemesh, "The Songs Of The Islamic State—A Major Tool For Reinforcing Its Narrative, Spreading Its Message, Recruiting Supporters." *The Middle East Media Research Institute.* 11 August 2015, http://www.memri.org/report/en/0/0/0/0/0/0/8701.htm.

Walid Shoebat, "Major ISIS Leader Recruits Eleven Muslm Men, And Sodomizes All of Them in Homosexual Islamic Ritual (Video)." *Shoebat.* 18 September 2014, http://shoebat.com/2014/09/18/major-isis-leader-recruits-eleven-muslim-men-sodomizes-homosexual-islamic-ritual-video/.

Walid and Theodore Shoebat, "Actual and Literal Islamic Human Slaughterhouses For Christians Discovered." *Shoebat.* 17 March 2014, http://shoebat.com/2014/03/17/actual-literal-islamic-human-slaughterhouses-christians-discovered/.

Catherine E. Shoichet, "Mexican forces struggle to rein in armed vigilantes battling drug cartel." *CNN News.* 17 January 2014, http://www.cnn.com/2014/01/17/world/americas/mexico-michoacan-vigilante-groups/.

Richard H. Shultz, Jr. and Andrea Dew, *Insurgents, Terrorists and Militias.* New York: Columbia University Press, 2006.

Jacob Siegel, "Islamic Extremists Now Crucifying People in Syria—and Tweeting Out the Pictures." *The Daily Beast.* 30 April 2014, http://www.thedailybeast.com/articles/2014/04/30/islamic-extremists-now-crucifying-people-in-syria-and-tweeting-out-the-pictures.html.

P.W. Singer, "Caution: Children at War." *Parameters* 31. Winter 2001-2002: 40-56.

Benjamin T. Smith, "The Rise and Fall of Narcopopulism." *Journal for the Study of Radicalism* 7. 2013: 125-166.

Samuel Smith, "Cocaine Found in Slain ISIS Commander's Home Indicates Heavy Drug Use Among Jihadists, Despite Being Violation of Sharia Law." *CP World*. 17 January 2015, http://www.christianpost.com/news/cocaine-found-in-slain-isis-commanders-home-indicates-heavy-drug-use-among-jihadists-despite-being-violation-of-sharia-law-132234/.

Jon Sorensen, "Islam and the Crucifixion," *Catholic Answers*. 9 June 2014, http://www.catholic.com/blog/jon-sorensen/islam-and-the-crucifixion.

Lewis Spence, *The Magic and Mysteries of Mexico: The Arcane Secrets and Occult Lore of the Ancient Mexicans and Maya*. London: Rider, 1930.

Frederic Spotts, *Hitler and the Power of Aesthetics*. New York: The Overlook Press, 2002.

"Afghan Soldiers Report Getting Hashish Rations," *St. Louis Dispatch*. 25 May 1989: 18A.

Will Storr, "Tragedy in Uganda: Joseph Kony massacre survivors tell their stories," *The Guardian*. 11 January 2014, http://www.theguardian.com/world/2014/jan/12/joseph-kony-uganda-massacres-survivors-stories.

John P. Sullivan and Adam Elkus, "State of Siege: Mexico's Criminal Insurgency," *Small Wars Journal*. 19 August 2008, http://smallwarsjournal.com/jrnl/art/state-of-siege-mexicos-criminal-insurgency.

John. P. Sullivan and Adam Elkus, "Mexican Gangs and Cartels: Evolving Criminal Insurgencies." *Mexidata*. 30 August 2010, http://mexidata.info/id2783.html.

John P. Sullivan and Robert J. Bunker, *Mexico's Criminal Insurgency: A Small Wars Journal—El Centro Anthology*. Bloomington: iUniverse, 2012.

John P. Sullivan and Robert J. Bunker, "Rethinking insurgency: criminality, spirituality, and societal warfare in the Americas" in Robert J. Bunker, Ed., *Criminal Insurgencies in Mexico and the Americas*. London: Routledge, 2013: 29-50.

John P. Sullivan et al., "Film Review: Narco Cultura—a Tale of Three Cities," *Small Wars Journal*. 20 December 2013, http://smallwars

journal.com/jrnl/art/film-review-narco-cultura---a-tale-of-three-cities.

Jules Suzdaltsev, "Narco-Saints Are Melding Catholicism with the Drug War in Latin America." *Vice News*. 6 April 2014, https://news.vice.com/article/narco-saints-are-melding-catholicism-with-the-drug-war-in-latin-america.

James Swetnam, "The Sacrifice of Isaac in Genesis and Hebrews: A Study in the Hermeneutic of Faith," *Letter & Spirit* 1. 2005: 23-40.

Thomas Stephen Szasz, *Ceremonial Chemistry*. New York: Anchor Press, 1974.

Adam Taylor, "How Saudi Arabia's harsh legal punishments compare to the Islamic State's." *The Washington Post*. 21 January 2015, http://www.washingtonpost.com/blogs/worldviews/wp/2015/01/21/how-saudi-arabias-harsh-legal-punishments-compare-to-the-islamic-states/.

Christopher Taylor, *Sacrifice as Terror: The Rwandan Genocide of 1994*. Oxford: Berg, 1999.

"Tahara (Cleanliness or Purification)." *The Way to Truth: Discover Islam*. n.d., http://www.thewaytotruth.org/pillars/tahara.html.

"Etiquette of Sacrifice." *2 Eids*. n.d., http://www.2eids.com/etiquettes_of_sacrifice.php.

"In the Name of Allah." *TheReligionofPeace.com*. 2006-2016, http://www.thereligionofpeace.com/pages/in-the-name-of-allah.htm.

Ginger Thompson, "Santa Ana de Guadalupe Journal; A Saint Who Guides Migrants to a Promised Land." *The New York Times*. 14 August 2002, http://www.nytimes.com/2002/08/14/world/santa-ana-de-guadalupe-journal-a-saint-who-guides-migrants-to-a-promised-land.html.

Monica Duffy Toft, Daniel Philpott, and Timothy Samuel Shah, *God's Century: Resurgent Religion and Global Politics*. New York: W.W. Norton and Company, 2011.

Mao Tse-Tung (Mao Zedong) *On Guerilla Warfare*. Samuel Griffith, Trans., New York: Praeger, 1961; 1937 original Chinese.

Jo Tuckman, "Mexican 'Saint Death' cult members protest at destruction of shrines." *The Guardian*. 10 April 2009, http://www.theguardian.com/world/2009/apr/10/santa-muerte-cult-mexico.

Marc Tyrrell, "The Use of Evolutionary Theory in Modeling Culture and Cultural Conflict" in Thomas H. Johnson and Barry Scott

Zellen, Eds., *Culture, Conflict and Counterinsurgency.* Redwood City: Stanford University Press, 2014.

Marc Tyrrell and Tom Quiggan, "Fear and (In)Security theatre," *Broken Mirrors* podcast. October 2013, http://www.brokenmirrors.ca/?p=339 and http://warontherocks.com/2013/10/broken-mirrors-episode-3-fear-insecurity-theatre/.

Addressing Organized Crime and Drug Trafficking in Iraq: Report of the UNODC Fact Finding Mission. New York: United Nations Office on Drugs and Crime, 2005.

"The Book of Sacrifices" (Kitab Al-Adahi); Translation of Sahih Muslim, Book 22: *University of Southern California, Center for Muslim-Jewish Engagement.* n.d., http://www.usc.edu/org/cmje/religious-texts/hadith/muslim/022-smt.php.

A Tradecraft Primer: Structured Analytic Techniques for Improving Intelligence Analysis. Washington, D.C.: U.S. Government, 2009, https://www.cia.gov/library/center-for-the-study-of-intelligence/csi-publications/books-and-monographs/Tradecraft%20Primer-apr09.pdf.

Blessed Usman, "Full length story of former Boko Haram member Balas Yusuf[f]." *Pray For Christians in Northern Nigeria.* 17 June 2013, https://www.facebook.com/PrayForChristiansInTheNorthOfNigeria/posts/393249187463084.

Richard Valdemar, "Do You Speak Nahuatl?" *Police Magazine.* 18 January 2011, http://www.policemag.com/blog/gangs/story/2011/01/do-you-speak-nahuatl.aspx.

Al Valdez and Rene Enriquez, *Urban Street Terrorism: The Mexican Mafia and the Sureños.* Santa Ana: Police and Fire Publishing, 2011.

Paul J. Vanderwood, *Juan Soldado: Rapist, Murderer, Martyr, Saint.* Durham: Duke University Press, 2004.

El Velador (The Night Watchman), 52 Minutes—HD—2011, http://www.altamurafilms.com/el_velador.html.

Jeffrey S. Victor, *Satanic Panic: The Creation of a Contemporary Legend.* Chicago: Open Court Publishing Company, 1993.

Michael Vlahos, *Terror's Mask: Insurgency Within Islam.* Laurel: Johns Hopkins University Applied Physics Lab, updated 2003, http://www.jhuapl.edu/ourwork/nsa/papers/Terror_Islamsm.pdf.

Geoffrey Wainwright, *Eucharist and Eschatology.* Oxford: Oxford University Press, 1981.

Elijah Wald, *Narcocorrido: A Journey into the Music of Drug, Guns, and Guerrillas*. New York: Rayo, 2001.

Anthony F. C. Wallace, "Revitalization Movements." *American Anthropologist* New Series 58. April 1956: 264-281.

James Waller, *Becoming Evil*. Oxford: Oxford University Press, Second Edition, 2007.

Max Weber, *The Protestant Ethic and the Spirit of Capitalism*. T. Parsons, Ed., New York: The Free Press, 1958 [1905].

Max Weber, *The Sociology of Religion*, Trans. Ephraim Fischoff. Boston: Beacon Press, 1963 [1922].

Sam Webb, "Junkie Jihadi John? "*Daily Mail*. 18 September 2014, http://www.dailymail.co.uk/news/article-2760354/Junkie-Jihadi-John-Expert-claims-slurred-speech-ISIS-executioner-beheading-video-Brit-hostage-David-Haines-drugs.html.

Andrew Weil, *The Natural Mind*. Boston: Houghton Miflin, 1972.

Brannon Wheeler, "Gift of the Body in Islam: The Prophet Muhammad's Camel Sacrifice and Distribution of Hair and Nails at his Farewell Pilgrimage." *Numen* 57. 2010: 341-388.

Brannon Wheeler, "Collecting the Dead Body of the Prophet Muhammad" in Christiane J. Gruber, and Avinoam Shalem, Eds. *The Image of the Prophet between Ideal and Ideology* Berlin: De Gruyter, 2014: 45-64.

Neil L. Whitehead and Sverker Finnström, Eds., *Virtual War and Magical Death: Technologies and Imaginaries for Terror and Killing*. Durham: Duke University Press, 2013.

Michaela Whitton, "Captagon: The Jihadist's Drug." *Antimedia*. 27 November 2015, http://theantimedia.org/captagon-the-jihadists-drug/.

Carol J. Williams, "Savagery, witchcraft hold Africans in sway of warlord Kony," *Los Angeles Times*. 14 November 2012, http://articles.latimes.com/2012/nov/14/world/la-fg-wn-lords-resistance-army-201211135.

Thomas D. Williams, "ISIS Crucifies Dozens for Breaking the Ramadan Fast." *Breitbart*. 8 July 2015, http://www.breitbart.com/national-security/2015/07/08/isis-crucifies-dozens-for-breaking-ramadan-fast/.

Richard Winton, "Car dealer gets 12 years in house fraud." *Los Angeles Times*. 3 June 2010: AA3.

Nathalie Wlodarczyk, *Magic and Warfare: Appearance and Reality in Contemporary African Conflict and Beyond*. New York: Palgrave Macmillan, 2009.

Kristin Wolff, "New Orientalism: Political Islam and Social Movement Theory" in Ahmad Moussalli, Ed., *Islamic Fundamentalism: Myths & Realities*. Reading: Ithaca, 1998: 41-73.

Paul Wood, "Face-to-face with Abu Sakkar, Syria's 'heart-eating Cannibal,'" *BBC News*. 5 July 2013, http://www.bbc.com/news/magazine-23190533.

Mimi Yagoub, "Mexico's 76,000 Ton Iron Seizure Fraction of Knights Templar Exports." *Insight Crime*. 2 May 2014, http://www.insightcrime.org/news-briefs/mexicos-76000-ton-iron-seizure-just-fraction-of-knights-templar-exports.

Aaron Y. Zelin, "The War between ISIS and al-Qaeda for Supremacy of the Global Jihadist Movement." *The Washington Institute for Near East Policy*. June 2014, http://www.washingtoninstitute.org/policy-analysis/view/the-war-between-isis-and-al-qaeda-for-supremacy-of-the-global-jihadist.

Norman Zinberg, *Drug, Set and Setting*. New Haven: Yale, 1984.

Joseba Zulaika, *Basque Violence: Metaphor and Sacrament*. Reno: University of Nevada Press, 1988.

Biographies

Editor

Dr. Robert J. Bunker was 2015 Futurist in Residence (FIR) at the FBI Academy, Quantico, VA and is presently an Adjunct Research Professor, Strategic Studies Institute, U.S. Army War College, Carlisle, PA and Adjunct Faculty, Division of Politics and Economics, Claremont Graduate University, Claremont, CA. He holds degrees in Political Science, Government, Behavioral Science, Social Science, Anthropology-Geography, and History and has undertaken hundreds of hours of specialized intelligence and counter-terrorism training. He is a past Office of the Secretary of Defense (OSD) Minerva Chair and has worked for U.S. counter-narcotics, counter-terrorism, and law enforcement support entities. He has hundreds of publications including numerous books and reports related to the Mexican cartels and gangs, counter-terrorism, and emerging forms of conflict and weaponry. His edited books include *Networks, Terrorism and Global Insurgency* (Routledge, 2006), *Criminal-States and Criminal-Soldiers* (Routledge, 2008), *Narcos Over the Border* (Routledge, 2010), and *Criminal Insurgencies in Mexico and the Americas* (Routledge, 2013).

Contributors

Andrew Bringuel, II is a FBI Special Agent with the Ithaca Resident Agency. Until recently he was a Supervisory Special Agent with the Behavioral Analysis Unit 5, Critical Incident Response Group, in Quantico, VA. He has over 25 years of law enforcement and academic research experience. He has investigated terrorism, public corruption, organized crime, and computer crime investigations and has extensive experience training police worldwide. SA Bringuel is the recipient of several awards for his investigative and research work, including

Attorney General's Award for an Environmental Crimes investigation and UVA's Jefferson Award for terrorism research. SA Bringuel has published multiple papers and three books on various topics including the *On-Scene Commanders Guide for Responding to Biological/Chemical Threats* (NDPO, 1999).

Pamela Ligouri Bunker is a researcher and analyst specializing in international security and terrorism and an Associate with *Small Wars Journal—El Centro*. She is a past senior officer of the Counter-OPFOR Corporation. She holds undergraduate degrees in Anthropology-Geography and Social Sciences from California State Polytechnic University Pomona, an M.A. in Public Policy from the Claremont Graduate University, and an M.Litt. in Terrorism Studies from the University of Saint Andrews, Scotland. She is co-editor of *Global Criminal and Sovereign Free Economies and the Demise of the Western Democracies: Dark Renaissance* (Routledge, 2015) and has published many other referred and professional works including those on narco cults and epochal transition.

Charles Cameron has a research specialization in religious violence. He is presently Managing Editor for *Zenpundit* (http://zenpundit.com), a highly regarded blog covering military and intelligence matters, a Contributing Editor to LapidoMedia (UK), a charity providing religious background on current events for journalists, and a occasional contributor to *Pragati: the Indian National Interest Review*. Charles is the designer of the HipBone Games and Analytics, a freelance writer and independent national security analyst. He has made 1,500+ blog posts on the impact of religious, and specifically apocalyptic, thought on both Shiite groups (Iran, Iraq) and Sunni (Al-Qaida & affiliates, ISIS), along with other subjects. He is a former Principal Researcher with the Center for Millennial Studies, Boston University, and former Senior Analyst at The Arlington Institute, Arlington VA, and has guest lectured at USC and elsewhere. He holds a degree in Theology from Christ Church, Oxford.

Lisa J. Campbell is a Lt. Col. with the California Air National Guard specializing in predictive threat analysis, antiterrorism, and wartime air base operability. She holds a B.S. in Geology from Cornell College and graduated from the USAF Air Command and Staff College, Squadron Officer School, and Intelligence Officer Course and is presently in a M.B.A. program with the University of La Verne. Lt. Col. Campbell served as a Red Team analyst supporting U.S. Africa Command in Stuttgart, Germany and Kampala, Uganda. She has given hundreds of classes and briefings and is a past member of the Los Angeles Terrorism Early Warning Group. She has independently researched and written a number of articles and book chapters on Islamic and cartel beheadings, an order-of-battle assessment of al Qaeda, an operational assessment of Los Zetas, as well as related essays on violent non-state actors (VNSAs).

Dr. Jóse de Arimatéia da Cruz is a Professor of International Relations/ Comparative Politics at Armstrong State University, Savannah, GA and an Adjunct Research Professor at the U.S. Army War College, Carlisle, PA. Dr. da Cruz also has a visiting teaching appointment at the School of Economics in Prague, Czech Republic. He has served as visiting professor at the University of Stavanger, Norway, La Serena Universidad in La Serena, Chile. Dr. da Cruz holds a B.A. in Philosophy from Wright State University, Dayton, OH; an M.A. in Professional Communications and Leadership from Armstrong State University, Savannah, GA; a M.A. in Political Science/Political Philosophy from Miami University, Oxford, OH; an M.S. in Criminal Justice with an emphasis in cyber affairs and security from Armstrong State University, and a Ph.D. in Political Science from Miami University, Oxford, OH.

Tony M. Kail serves as a trainer and subject matter expert in the area of esoteric religions and security threats for a number of agencies including the National Gang Academy in Orlando, Florida and as the Southern Regional Coordinator for the Symbol Intelligence Group. He holds a B.A. in Cultural Anthropology from Ashford University, San Diego, CA. Kail has spent 25 years researching and training on the subject of religious groups and criminality. He has conducted ethnographic fieldwork among a number of esoteric religious communities in the United States and Africa. As a former law enforcement officer, Kail has provided training for state and federal agencies, including the U.S. Army, U.S. Capitol Police, Federal Bureau of Investigation, and several state gang investigator associations. His works include *A Cop's Guide to Occult Investigations* (Paladin Press, 2003), *Magico-Religious Groups* *and Ritualistic Activities: A Guide for First-Responders* (CRC Press, 2008), and *Narco-Cults: Understanding the Use of Afro-Caribbean and Mexican Religious Cultures in the Drug Wars* (CRC Press, 2015).

Dr. Paul Rexton Kan is a Professor of National Security Studies at the U.S. Army War College. He is the author of the books, *Drugs and Contemporary Warfare* (Potomac Books, 2009) and *Cartels at War* (Potomac Books, 2012). He is also the author of numerous articles on the intersection of drug trafficking, crime and modern forms of armed conflict including: "Anonymous vs. Los Zetas: Cyberwar in the Underworld"; "Drugging Babylon: The Illegal Narcotics Trade and Nation-Building in Iraq"; "'Lawyers, Guns and Money': Transnational Threats and US National Security" and "Criminal Sovereignty: Understanding North Korea's Illicit International Activities." In February 2011, he served as the Senior Visiting Counternarcotics Adviser at NATO Headquarters in Kabul, Afghanistan and he has provided advice to the U.S. Office of National Drug Control Policy (also known as the Drug Czar's office). He also continues to brief the Pennsylvania Attorney-General's Office on drug cartel activity in the state. His forthcoming book is *Drug Trafficking and International Security* (Rowman & Littlefield, 2016).

Alma Keshavarz is a Ph.D. student in Political Science at Claremont Graduate University. She received her M.P.P. from Pepperdine's School of Public Policy with a master's thesis focused on United States interests and policy towards Russia. She also holds a B.A. in Political Science and English from University of California, Davis. She is presently an Intern with *Small Wars Journal—El Centro* and has held various research intern and associate positions as well as serving as a graduate assistant at Pepperdine University. Her research interests include non-state actors, specifically Hezbollah, cyber security and warfare, and national security strategy with a regional focus on Middle East politics, specifically Iran, Lebanon, Yemen, and Syria. She is fluent in Spanish and Farsi.

Dr. Pauletta Otis is a former Professor of Security Studies at the Marine Corps University Command and Staff College. She has both theoretical and operational experience and expertise in sub-national violence. Her current research focuses on issues concerning cultural factors that impact military strategy and operations, religious factors in violence, and irregular warfare/insurgency analysis. She previously served as the senior research fellow for Religion in International Affairs at Pew Forum and was a tenured professor in Political Science and International Studies at Colorado State University-Pueblo. She has also taught in the Joint Military Intelligence College and National Defense University's National Security Education Program. She received her Ph.D. and an M.A. from the University of Denver, as well as an M.A. from the University of Southern Colorado.

Dr. Dawn Perlmutter is the Director of the Symbol Intelligence Group and an adjunct Professor in the Forensic Medicine Program at Philadelphia College of Osteopathic Medicine. She is considered one of the leading subject matter experts (SME) in the areas of symbols, symbolic methodologies, unfamiliar customs and ritualistic crimes. She has advised police departments and prosecutors offices on numerous cases of ritual homicide and presented expert witness testimony on ritualistic crimes. She is the author of *Investigating Religious Terrorism and Ritualistic Crimes* (CRC Press, 2003) and *Symbols of Terrorism* (IRORV, 2007) as well as numerous publications on ritual violence. She holds a Ph.D. from New York University and a Masters degree from The American University, Washington, D.C. Dr. Perlmutter is an active member of The American Investigative Society of Cold Cases (AISOCC) and The Vidocq Society, an exclusive crime-solving organization that solves cold case homicides.

Mark Safranski is a Senior Analyst at Wikistrat, LLC. and is a contributor to *Pragati: The Indian National Interest*; his writing has appeared in *Small Wars Journal, War on the Rocks, New Atlanticist, The Chicago Progressive, HNN, PJ Media* and other sites.. Safranski was the editor of *The John Boyd Roundtable: Debating Science, Strategy and War* and has contributed chapters to several books, including *Threats in the Age of Obama* and most recently *Warlords, Inc.* published by North Atlantic Books. He holds an M.A. in Diplomatic History from Northern Illinois University and a M.Ed. in Curriculum and Leadership from Benedictine University. Safranski is the publisher of the well regarded group national security and strategy blog, *Zenpundit* (http://zenpundit.com).

Dr. Marc W.D. Tyrrell is a symbolic Anthropologist who focuses on how people make sense of their lives using symbol systems, communications media, and rituals. He concentrates on symbol systems that developed to meet specific "breaches" in consensual reality such as modern Witchcraft; corporate rituals of firing, restructuring and alliances; the use of radical religious symbols in insurgencies; the interplay between music and radical action, etc. He is currently involved with several high tech startups as well as consulting. Previously, he was a Senior Research Fellow at the Canadian Centre of Intelligence and Security Studies, and taught Interdisciplinary Studies at Carleton University in Ottawa, Canada.

Printed in the United States
By Bookmasters